SIBLING ACTION

SIBLING ACTION

THE GENEALOGICAL STRUCTURE OF MODERNITY

STEFANI ENGELSTEIN

Columbia University Press
New York

Columbia University Press
Publishers Since 1893
New York   Chichester, West Sussex
cup.columbia.edu
Copyright © 2017 Columbia University Press
Paperback edition, 2020
All rights reserved

Library of Congress Cataloging-in-Publication Data
Names: Engelstein, Stefani, 1970– author.
Title: Sibling action: the genealogical structure of modernity / Stefani Engelstein.
Description: New York: Columbia University Press, [2017] | Includes bibliographical references and index.
Identifiers: LCCN 2017031094 | ISBN 9780231180405 (cloth) | ISBN 9780231180412 (pbk.) | ISBN 9780231542715 (e-book)
Subjects: LCSH: Identity (Philosophical concept) | Brothers and sisters—Miscellanea. | Relation (Philosophy) | Knowledge, Theory of.
Classification: LCC BD236.E54 2017 | DDC 111—dc23
LC record available at https://lccn.loc.gov/2017031094

Cover design: Jordan Wannemacher
Cover image: Antigone from "Antigone" by Sophocles (oil on canvas), Stillman, Marie Spartali (1844–1927) / Simon Carter Gallery, Woodbridge, Suffolk, UK / Bridgeman Images

For Rich, with all my love

CONTENTS

List of Illustrations ix
Acknowledgments xi

INTRODUCTION: THE SIBLING AND MODERNITY 1

PART I. RECUPERATING THE SIBLING
1. SIBLING LOGIC 35

PART II. FRATERNITY AND REVOLUTION
2. THE SHADOWS OF FRATERNITY 61
3. ECONOMIZING DESIRE: THE SIBLING (IN) LAW 87

PART III. GENEALOGICAL SCIENCES
4. LIVING LANGUAGES: COMPARATIVE PHILOLOGY AND EVOLUTION 127
5. THE EAST COMES HOME: RACE AND RELIGION 174

EPILOGUE: SPAWNING DISCIPLINES 225

Notes 239
Works Cited 309
Index 341

ILLUSTRATIONS

4.1. Author's illustration of Johann Gottfried Herder's Tree of History
4.2. Angelica Kauffman, *Iphigenie, Orest und Pylades*, from Goethe's *Iphigenie auf Tauris*, 1787
4.3. Chrétien Frederic Guillaume Roth, frontispiece to Pierre Monchon's *Table analytique*, 1780
4.4. Hartmann Schedel, genealogy of Duke Henry II of Bavaria from *Liber Chronicarum*, 1493
4.5. Friedrich Ritschl, stemma of Thomas Magister, 1832
4.6. Friedrich Ritschl, stemma of Dionysius of Halicarnassus, 1838
4.7. August Schleicher, "Die ersten Spaltungen des indogermanischen Urvolkes," 1853
4.8. František Čelakovský, family tree of the Slavic languages, 1853
4.9. August Schleicher, Sprachsippe (Sprachstamm) from *Die deutsche Sprache*, 1860
4.10. August Schleicher, Indogermanischer Sprachstamm from *Compendium der vergleichenden Grammatik der indogermanischen Sprachen*, 1861
4.11. Jean-Baptiste de Lamarck, table showing the origin of the various animals, from *Philosophie Zoologique* (1809), 1830 edition
4.12. Charles Darwin, "I think" sketch from Notebook B (1837)

4.13.   Alfred Russel Wallace, diagram of the affinities of the Fissirostres, 1856
4.14.   Charles Darwin, diagram from *The Origin of Species* (1859), 1896 edition
4.15.   Charles Darwin, "Principle of divergence, transitional organs/instincts," probably from early 1850s
5.1.   Antislavery medallion, Wedgwood Manufactory, England, 1787
5.2.   Friedrich Max Müller, diagram of history of religions, from *Introduction to the Science of Religion*, 1873

ACKNOWLEDGMENTS

One of the claims of *Sibling Action* is that the individual does not exist, and so it is fitting that the book is deeply indebted to a wide community of colleagues, scholars, institutions, relatives, and friends. The scope of *Sibling Action*, which expanded as I wrote, reflects my good fortune in working with colleagues whose own transdisciplinary research repeatedly inspired me to look at my topic from yet another perspective. During the years that I researched and wrote this book, I was equally fortunate to be affiliated with institutions that valued and fostered such research. I would like to express my gratitude to my colleagues and students in the Department of German and Russian Studies and the Life Sciences & Society Program at the University of Missouri; at the Zentrum für Literatur-und Kulturforschung, Berlin; in the German Department at Duke University; the German Program at the University of North Carolina, Chapel Hill; and the Carolina-Duke Graduate Program in German; and at the Max-Planck-Institut für Wissenschaftsgeschichte in Berlin.

I am deeply grateful to numerous colleagues who read chapters of this book or listened to talks derived from them: Roger Cook, Adrian Daub, Sean Franzel, Katja Garloff, Sander Gilman, Lily Gurton-Wachter, Noah Herrigman, Michaela Hohkamp, Sean Ireton, Kristen Kopp, Françoise Meltzer, Juliet Mitchell, Brad Prager, Marc Redfield, Helmut Schneider, Carsten Strathausen, and the anonymous readers for Columbia University

Press. Their comments and insights have vastly improved the resulting volume. Many thanks in addition to Lorraine Daston, Eric Downing, Kata Gellen, Jonathan Hess, Ted Koditscheck, Irmela Krüger-Fürhoff, Rob Mitchell, Jakob Norbert, Thomas Pfau, Henry Pickford, Chris Pires, Jack Schultz, Stephan Steiner, Georg Toepfer, Gabe Trop, and Sigrid Weigel for their intellectual engagement, provocative conversations, and supportive energy.

I appreciate the generous financial support that provided the time necessary for me to research and write this book: an Alexander von Humboldt Research Fellowship for Experienced Researchers, two University of Missouri Summer Research Fellowships, and a University of Missouri Provost's Leave. Thank you to Heidi Madden and Amy Jones for their tremendous help preparing both the images and the text of the manuscript for publication. Thank you also to Jennifer Arnold, Karla Carter, Margy Swanson, and Dorothy Thorpe-Turner for their friendship and good humor, and for keeping my institutional life in working order. I am grateful for the expert assistance of extraordinary librarians at all the institutions where I have worked.

Siblings are the topic of this book, and mine have certainly been constant formative forces in my life. I thank Brad and Courtney for their ongoing friendship and love, for all that we share as well as for what makes us distinctive. Thank you to my parents, Allyn and Joel, for their unwavering love and support, and for the drive and love of learning they instilled in me. I am grateful to Sheri for engrossing conversations and a sympathetic ear, and to Delphi and Dillon, who are a joy to spend time with. My love to my grandmother Millie and in loving memory of Philip, Ruth, and Julius. My in-laws, Dick, Diane, and Robin, have been a gift of good fortune, and after many discussions about what in the world I was researching, I only wish Dick were still here to discuss the final product. Finally, I wish it were possible to express the depths of gratitude I owe my husband, Rich. His unflagging belief in this project sustained me. He is my most valued critic, my most trusted supporter, and my best friend.

Sections of this book have appeared in earlier versions elsewhere, and I appreciate the permission to draw on this material for the expanded argument of the present study.

A revised version of "Sibling Logic; or, Antigone Again" (*PMLA* 126, 1 [Jan. 2011]) is reprinted as chapter 1 by permission of the copyright owner, The Modern Language Association of America.

A portion of chapter 2 appeared in early form as "Civic Attachments & Sibling Attractions: The Shadows of Fraternity" (*The Goethe Yearbook* 18 [2011]).

Part of chapter 5 appeared in early form as "Coining a Discipline: Lessing, Reimarus, and a Science of Religion," in *Fact and Fiction: Literary and Scientific Cultures in Germany and Britain*, ed. Christine Lehleiter (University of Toronto Press, 2016).

Elements of the introduction appeared in revised form as "Geschwister und Geschwisterlichkeit in der Epistemologie der Moderne" (*L'Homme* 28, 2 [2017]), a special issue on Schwesternfiguren, edited by Almut Höfert, Michaela Hohkamp, and Claudia Ulbrich.

SIBLING ACTION

INTRODUCTION

The Sibling and Modernity

We regularly look back on the eighteenth and early nineteenth centuries as a repository of foundational concepts that continue to structure our world, including the modern subject, the modern state, and the modern methodologies of the life- and human sciences. We are aware that we peer at this history through an anachronistic lens, however. This book argues that we have, as a result, missed something crucial—namely, the foundational status of the concept of the *sibling* as a link between epistemology and affect, and hence a key to both contemporary knowledge-systems and identity politics. When I speak of the sibling, I refer not primarily to flesh-and-blood people who share the same parents, although such siblings will play some role in this book, nor exclusively to the figure of the sibling in literature, to which we will return more frequently. Rather, the *long nineteenth century*—the period from about 1770 to 1915—developed a set of theories and practices that placed the sibling—envisioned as relation, structure, and *action*—at the foundation of epistemological systems on which subjectivity, civic organization, economic networks, and scientific methodologies were grounded. In the late eighteenth century, Europeans embarked on a new way of classifying the cultural and natural human world, namely, through genealogies that determined the degree of relatedness between contemporaries by tracing heritage back to a common ancestor. This methodology transformed contemporary terms in historical systems of development—whether languages, religions, races, nations, species, or individuals—into siblings of varying degrees. The sibling thus served a similar function across a wide but interconnected swath of fields and discourses focused on personal identity and collective classifications. As a boundary object that enabled definition through differentiation and simultaneously called into question the discreteness of terms through shared traits, the sibling forms an inextirpable, active fault line embedded within the knowledge structures of modernity. While reconstructing the role of the sibling will have a broad impact on our understanding of the long nineteenth century, the significance of recapturing the sibling for theory exceeds its historical import. Unearthing the function of the sibling term provides a first step to understanding and hence reimagining both modern epistemology and modern identity politics.

In this introduction I am faced with a double task: first, demonstrating the significance of the sibling across discourses in the period under study, and second, illustrating the cohesive role played by the sibling in spite of the breadth of fields referred to. The ubiquity of a term is often a sign of diffuseness of meaning, and certainly a real familial relationship like the sister or brother takes on multiple and divergent personal associations and significances. While such particularities fall outside the concern of this book, it is sometimes possible to misperceive as particular circumstances that in actuality follow common sociological patterns. The general closeness of sibling relations in this period falls into such a category. Indeed, I will argue that disciplines cannot be considered in isolation from one another or from their cultural context, connected as they are through permeable boundaries, repeated exchanges of information and methodology, and common lived praxes. As I shift my focus between discourses in the move from chapter to chapter, I will carry with me accumulated valances and associations: figures, I claim, circulate and reciprocally influence one another not only in textual form but even in social practice. The evidence points to a crucial consistency played by the sibling in emerging modern formations across theoretical, scholarly, and everyday life, as a constituent principle in organizing knowledge and in forming subjectivity, in and through sets of relations.

As we have known since Ferdinand de Saussure at the latest, definitions are relational, and hence within various genealogical systems it is the differentiation of similars—of siblings—from each other that enables the definition of terms. The sibling is, however, an ambiguous entity—not self and yet not-quite-other. It therefore marks the contingency and permeability of boundaries, the doubtfulness of integrity, and the insecurity of uniqueness. The structure of outward-branching genealogical systems thus necessarily generates a concept of identity haunted at every level by the nebulousness of margins. It is because of the precarious epistemological position instigated by the sibling term in an era obsessed with human classification that the sibling emerged in the mid-eighteenth century and remained until the early twentieth, the privileged figure for negotiating the boundaries of identity. If the sibling figures the epistemological contingency of classifications, illuminating a permeability between objects, between subjects, and across both, such insecurity also elicited defensive attempts to reinstate natural kinds. One goal of this book, then, is to reconstruct an episteme, to use Michel Foucault's term, one that has not been superseded but still forms the unrecognized grounding for our own classifications, collective identities, and subjectivities.[1] Moreover, exploring both sides of this dynamic—namely, the recognition of permeable boundaries and their reactive policing—offers new understandings of the history of human sciences such as anthropology, race theory, and comparative religions, as well as of the history of evolutionary theory and its social derivatives, and of political and economic theories of civic fraternity.

The twenty-first century is only now beginning to look back at the sibling and to recognize in it a structurally determinant element of our own culture. Such investigations are proceeding one fragmentary discipline at a time. My second goal in this study, then, is to develop a theory of the sibling that illuminates the function of the term across discourses and disciplines, as a necessary grounding that is, however, inherently unstable, as the splinter within all systems imagined as genealogical that deconstructs them from the inside out. Reawakening the theoretical potential of the sibling provides a much-needed tool for current critical theory, gender studies, and science studies and augurs less confrontational formulations of belonging, identity, and agency.

THE PERVASIVE SIBLING

The sibling as a theoretical concern was so ubiquitous in the long nineteenth century that it faded into an invisible background, like wallpaper, for later scholars. Confronted, however, it crystallizes into startling prominence. We may be most familiar with the eighteenth-century sibling in the form of *fraternité*. Still the least well-theorized of the three watchwords of the French Revolution, *fraternity* involved an affective solicitation that would seem to exist in tension with the rational, civic demands for liberty and equality.[2] Fraternity serves a necessary role in maintaining the civic system, however. The primogeniture that governed inheritance of title, privilege, and wealth in the early modern period depended on a substitutive logic. Brothers in such a system existed in a state of existential competition for the only available role that enabled continuity: that of replacing the father. Both the French Revolution and the emergence of capitalism contributed to the destruction of this substitutive logic and the stability it had engendered, replacing it with a model in which all siblings were potentially equal. In this new economic regime, siblings offered one another a new kind of stability in the form of networks of partnerships. The line between equality and sameness was an indistinct one, however, so that brotherhood continued to constitute a slightly modified threat. Replacing the risk of social displacement was a challenge to the newly significant notions of individuality, agency, and subjectivity. Extended across society, this slippery brotherhood demanded a remedy, which was found in the renewed dedication to the disenfranchisement of women—of sisters.

Recent feminist political theorists from Carole Pateman and Juliet Flower MacCannell to Annette Timm and Joshua Sanborn have investigated the confluence of biological and political thinking that contributed to reconceptualizing female subordination in the revolutionary period without dismantling it. While men no doubt benefited materially from maintaining their privileged position, I will, in chapter 2, read the new fraternal regime through a different anxiety, namely, the threat posed to a new and fragile notion of individuality by the idea of equal brothers. The difficulty of dividing concepts of equality from concepts of sameness was intensified by the rhetoric of brotherhood. Positing sisters, that is, women, as radically distinct and sequestering them into a domestic sphere helped to stabilize the system. With sex differences reified as natural, the sister-brother relationship could serve as a model for sibling affect free from the threat of absolute amalgamation. Meanwhile, the particularities of male sexual desire in the choice of wives provided a public demonstration of individuality that did not affect civic commitment to equality as long as wives remained outside the civic sphere. Fraternity, as Jacques Derrida has shown in *The Politics of Friendship*, imported affect into the reason envisioned as grounding the participatory state. But men could be re-created as citizens, equals, and affectively joined brothers only because of the sequestration of sisters.

The generation of sibling affect through women in order to bind together male agents as brothers structured politics and economics simultaneously. For Adam Smith indeed, as I discuss in chapter 3, the accommodation of siblings within a household becomes the model for the capitalist society. Smith, however, moves decisively away from both social equality and sameness, embracing distinctions of persons and divisions of labors. Siblings are put into circulation as the grounding for an exchange society and yet remain bound by sympathy. As David Warren Sabean and Leonore Davidoff, among others, have recently demonstrated, kinship structures of vital economic import were indeed built around alliances of siblings and their spouses, enabling finance capital and the formation of a bourgeois class. Economic theory remained intertwined with kinship theory in writers from Smith to Lewis Henry Morgan, Friedrich Engels, and Claude Lévi-Strauss. Meanwhile, there is sociological evidence for the inculcation of sibling affect in the nursery, as brothers and sisters underwent an education directed toward both gender differentiation and familial allegiance that facilitated the formation of economic and affective clans.[3] This education left traces, however, that undermined both the posited innateness of gender and the very integrity of the subject it was intended to reinforce.

If my focus on the sibling here is new, there is nonetheless a great deal of precedence for traversing political, economic, and social theory and relating each or all to subject-formations. However, it was not only brothers and sisters—both real and metaphorical—in the nursery, the polis, and the marketplace who embodied boundaries as relational negotiations. As I discuss in chapters 4 and 5, in the eighteenth century and increasingly in the nineteenth, global human diversity, both cultural and physical, was imagined as a set of family relations, merging classification and genealogy, epistemology and kinship. Within these constellations, the sibling term played a determinate role. In comparative philology, the *sister language* emerged as the central kinship term for membership in newly significant language families. In the physical anthropologies developed in the late eighteenth and the nineteenth centuries, brotherhood—whether rejected or embraced—became the central term of race rhetoric. By the late nineteenth century, fields from comparative religion to evolution had adopted variants of the theory of descent with modification from a common ancestor as their own basis for classification. And in each case, not only the determination of lineage but also and equally the isolation of terms from their similars, that is, their siblings, was a contested process attended by debates over natural kinds.

While many theoretical inquiries of the period are governed by a kind of sibling logic, we should also note that these fields are themselves genealogically related to one another and can be viewed as so many siblings and cousins. In this book I therefore take a genealogical approach myself to develop a genealogy of genealogical methodologies. My variant of this approach owes a great debt to those outlined by Friedrich Nietzsche and Foucault with their emphasis on contingency and their insistence on confronting the entwinement of value systems with historical research.[4] While I will return to Nietzsche and Foucault in chapter 4, my method differs from theirs as well. Both were interested in the historical contingencies attendant on lineage, but they were nonetheless wedded to the excavation of history along a single linear trajectory. What is fascinating about a genealogy, however, as anyone knows who has ever attempted a family tree, is the speed with which it sprouts branches and twigs, endless varieties of great-aunts, stepbrothers-in-law, and third cousins twice removed. Nothing like a line—straight or crooked—a family tree merges complex systems at every reproductive node, and these mergers result in multiple descendants open to their own future mergers. Equally compelling, however, is what any reconstituted genealogy hides and excludes. My genealogy is then one that, ideally, refuses definitive definitions in favor of fuzzy lines, unexpected mergers, and the open possibility of different potential futures.

This approach will lead me to complicate several orthodoxies about the rise of modernity in the late eighteenth and the nineteenth centuries: first, the consolidation of the ideal of an individual, sovereign subject; second, the decreasing importance of kinship; and third, the obsession with a search for origins. These three claims are linked. Standard historical narratives recount the emergence in eighteenth-century Europe of a modern subject, an individual credited with agency both political and economic as well as with a narrative history of development. The concept of the subject has come under significant pressure for over a generation now, but the story of its emergence remains largely untouched. One outgrowth of the increasing self-sufficiency of the individual, standard histories continue, was the waning importance of extended kinship formations in favor of conjugal families grounded on personal sentiment. Moreover, the newly self-important individual was inspired to trace heritage backward from the self or from the collectives to which that self belonged—whether nation, language family, race, religion, or species.[5] These nested narratives of self-development have been depicted by twentieth- and twenty-first-century history and criticism as primarily linear, concerned on the one hand with lineage and on the other with teleological development toward an autonomous self or a more civilized culture.

This volume will challenge these orthodoxies, not by denying either the appearance of a discourse of the subject or a discourse of origins in the eighteenth century but by complicating the primacy of lineage and of autonomy assigned to these genealogies by later interpreters. There is no doubt that in the eighteenth and nineteenth centuries, people busied themselves with the creation of genealogies, but these genealogies neither simply counted generations backward on a chain of descent nor provided the individual with a trajectory for predestined development into a unique and integral subject. Rather, histories, from their first emergence as explanatory forces, *branched*, and the concept of relatedness between branches as descendants of a common ancestor, as *siblings*, laid the foundation not only for the phylogenetic epistemological networks of which modern Europeans became the subjects but also for the ontogenetic development of such subjects. *Sibling Action* will illustrate the way the figure of the sibling served as an epistemological tool for differentiating terms as well as an educational tool for directing affect and desire. These two purposes were intertwined: genealogical system building was suffused with affect, no less at the macro level of nation, race, religion, and species than at the micro level of the subject, where desire arose along the porous boundaries of a still-nascent subjectivity. By reimagining historical systems in familial terms, the new human sciences both signaled and intensified the affect bound up with the process of assuming an identity as a member of a collective.

Sibling Action is thus a book about subjectivity and kinship but also a book about classification, about epistemological order, and about the ways in which figures of thought circulate among fields, disciplines, and registers. Kinship, subjectivity, and the science of classification are all the mutual and reciprocal products of a mutable but linked set of figures, methods, and heuristic tools from the genealogical tree to the comparative method. The terms on a genealogical tree, the subjects of a comparative methodology, must function within a kind of *sibling logic*, a logic that insists on the recognition of differential degrees of likeness in place of stark dichotomies.[6] While this nuanced understanding of identity was not always in evidence in the nineteenth century, indeed was often sorely lacking, we would do well to read defensive attempts to control and master boundaries as reaction formations to the horror of epistemological instability. Each chapter in this volume will document both apogees of this pendulum motion, from an openness to the potential of pervious boundaries to a conservative policing of borders posited as absolute.

It is important to clarify as well what this book is *not* doing. It does not suggest an idealization of some utopian lost era of the sibling. The long nineteenth century was anything but a haven for peaceful and egalitarian identity politics. Nor would I recommend either the resurrection of an old, or the building of some new, form of universal *fraternity, sorority*, or *siblinghood*. Rather, I would argue that to recognize what the sibling term whispered to the nineteenth century might also allow us to conceptualize a move beyond and outside of the sibling. Donna Haraway's blunt condemnation of kinship politics demands recognition:

> It is time to theorize an "unfamiliar" unconscious, a different primal scene, where everything does not stem from the dramas of identity and reproduction. Ties through blood—including blood recast in the coin of genes and information—have been bloody enough already. I believe that there will be no racial or sexual peace, no livable nature, until we learn to produce humanity through something more and less than kinship.[7]

While the bloodiness of a politics of bloodline is manifest everywhere in the history I will reconstruct in this book, there are two issues that need to be teased out of Haraway's formulation. First, while here Haraway sets as an ethical goal the "produc[tion of] humanity," she herself has contributed heavily to theorizing the posthuman, not least in this very article. The production of a species as a unit of care reverts to a methodology substantially similar to the kinship politics Haraway has just deconstructed. Indeed, we will shortly turn to Charles Darwin's evolutionary theory as one variant of the widespread genealogical methodologies in the long nineteenth century from which also sprang the theories of race and nationality Haraway is disassembling. If we concur with Haraway's goals of racial peace, sexual peace, and livable nature, then perhaps we need to stop searching for legitimacy in the structure of our classifications. Yet we cannot stop classifying altogether. Rather, we could instead recognize and revalue the terms that illustrate the contingency of classifications and work to deconstruct them from within, accepting the continuous deterritorializing and reterritorializing they imply. Haraway here equates blood with bloodline and kinship with lineage, identifying a constellation that Alys Eve Weinbaum has recently defined as the "race/reproduction bind": race and sex are rendered inextricably codependent through the notion of genealogy, and hence questions of race are always also questions of sex and gender.[8] We will see in *Sibling Action* the way that genealogies grappled with the link between lineage and sex not only when they are bound up in sexuality like race theory but also in fields Weinbaum does not discuss, where genealogies are imagined to function parthenogenetically, as in the evolution of languages. While this book explores the stakes of the sexual mergers still generally necessary for human reproduction, my main focus here is a second major breach in the linearity of genealogy, namely, ramification, and still more potently, the unstable borders of such sibling offspring.

RELATING THE MODERN SUBJECT

The idea of a self or subject with a history of development toward an idiosyncratic or even unique personality arose at the confluence of religious, economic, and social change over the course of the long eighteenth century. A new interest in personal identity can be documented through philosophical explorations of the topic beginning in the late seventeenth century, with increasing presence throughout the eighteenth. Perhaps the most canonical history of this phenomenon is offered by Charles Taylor's *Sources of the Self*, which gives a sweeping overview of the emergence of notions of self through concepts of moral responsibility retained even outside speculations about the existence of a soul.[9] Standard philosophical histories locate the origins of the subject in René Descartes and John Locke and trace it through Immanuel Kant to its culmination in G.W.F. Hegel. Dror Wahrman has more recently extended this exploration by locating the new constructions of self within the intersecting alignments of collective identities such as race, gender, religion, and character types, in discourses more widely culturally accessible at the time than philosophy, and she notes the shift toward a concept of individual uniqueness as a development of the late eighteenth century.[10] Among the sources Wahrman considers is literature, particularly the novel, following a long-standing critical connection between the development of fictional characters and the burgeoning notion of personal development. In the 1950s Ian Watt saw the rise of the novel as a key barometer of the increasing importance of the individual, evident in the expanding potential for personal choices in labor and consumerism, in politics, in religion, and in the emotional commitment newly tied to the institution of marriage.[11] For Watt, the individual itself is an ontological given, however, while changing norms influence the degree of significance accorded individual experience and desire. More recent literary criticism, such as that of Felicity Nussbaum and Nancy Armstrong, works through genre developments to map the ideological construction of the self or the individual through discourse, while Anthony Cascardi defines modernism through its invention of the subject, which remains, however, an unstable as well as historically contingent category.[12]

The new conception of selfhood that arose in the eighteenth century is most traditionally understood as a subject, an individual agent, reciprocally suited to new political and economic systems that emphasized the individual as citizen, consumer, and wage laborer. Locke transferred the root of identity from soul to consciousness and grounded persistent identity over time in memory.[13] Humans thus became beings conditioned by their own histories and historical moment—a concept of the self, one might argue, that laid the groundwork for the increasing significance of history in knowledge-formation in the eighteenth century. Historicity is not the only distinguishing feature of the modern subject, however. Harvie Ferguson has argued that modernity might be defined by three relations: the separation of subject from object which attributes autonomy to the former, the differentiation of self and other, and the dialectic between ego and the world.[14] If Ferguson sees his first two criteria as entailing strict division, the last is a form of inclusion in which the ego constitutes a part of the world, with complicated reciprocal consequences. In this book I will argue, however, that the former two relations are equally contested forms of division, that indeed self and other, subject and object, also participate in each other in the discourse of the long nineteenth century. It is not the successful demarcation of subject from object or self from other that characterizes modernity but the fraught process of negotiating their relationships, a process that often admits of permeable boundaries, though this permeability generates anxiety. As we will see repeatedly in this volume, the rampant discourse on the fetish, the "made thing" to which powers of agency are attributed (particularly chapters 3 and 4), and the many variations of race theory and anthropology (chapter 5) both document the desire to erect solid boundaries between subject and object, between self and other, and illustrate the failure of such attempts.

In exploring the limits of the subject, Raymond Martin and John Barresi point to a preoccupation first seen in Locke with what they term *fission questions*.[15] If the self is no longer connected to the substance of either a body or a soul but instead depends, as Locke claimed, on consciousness and memory, why could not more than one person reside in a single human? Locke himself poses this question explicitly in reflections on madness, on sleeping and waking consciousness, and the possibility of a day-man and a night-man inhabiting one and the same body.[16] One can certainly follow the progress of such fission anxieties not only through philosophical debates of the eighteenth century noted by Martin and Barresi but beyond both discipline and century to such fiction as, most famously, Robert Louis Stevenson's *The Strange Case of Dr. Jekyll and Mr. Hyde* (1886). Barresi and Martin are much less interested in what they refer to as *fusion* cases, namely, the difficulty of assigning a single self or compound selves to multiple bodies. The line between fission and fusion is itself coherent, however, only if one already accepts the notion of a whole self in alignment with a whole body. Indeed, the terms *fission* and *fusion* that Martin and Barresi choose make sense only if one takes the body as the starting point for identity.[17] Locke himself raises fission and fission potentialities in the very same sentence (*Essay*, 344). As Hillel Schwarz indicates in his work on the copy,[18] there is continuity between split personalities and conjoined twins, who also exercised a firm hold on the cultural imagination in the eighteenth and nineteenth centuries.[19]

Cultural fascination with conjoined twins extends beyond the jointness of bodies: they are only the most extreme example of a siblinghood that challenges the boundaries of the self in all its forms. In her exploration of the rise of a concept of individuality, Wahrman notes a shift from the 1770s to the 1780s in considerations of the identical twin. While in the earlier decade a fraud case involving identical twin brothers led to an emphasis on their indistinguishability, a decade later a certain T. Row would assert a more absolute individuality, claiming in the *Gentleman's Magazine* in 1786 that "two brothers have been seen so alike as hardly to be distinguished, but have often been taken one for another, and yet, when they have appeared together, the differences, the variation, has been very visible."[20] Locke also mentions twins in his reflections on personal identity, to insist on the distinctness of persons where consciousness is distinct. The twins Castor and Pollux may share a soul, each using it in turn while the other sleeps, but so long as each has no memory of what the other does, they lead existences as separate as that of any other two men (*Essay*, 110–11).[21] I would note, however, that already in 1759, Adam Smith had opened his *Theory of Moral Sentiments* with the avowal that "though our brother is upon the rack, as long as we ourselves are at our ease, our senses will never inform us of what he suffers. They never did, and never can, carry us beyond our own person, and it is by the imagination only that we can form any conception of what are his sensations."[22] The claims of Locke, Row, and Smith are meant to stress the distinction between separate persons, even brothers, even identical twins. And yet the use of the brother as the example of choice clearly conveys the expectation that the brother is a borderline case that carries the potential to disrupt or undermine the proper boundaries between persons. If Wahrman is interested in identical twins as doubles who raise the specter of replacement in the seventeenth and early eighteenth centuries, I am here instead interested in the implication explored in the long nineteenth century that siblings might render the boundaries between persons permeable. Smith insists that our senses cannot carry us across interpersonal limits—but also that our imagination can. It is thus significant that the literature of the late eighteenth century through the early twentieth is replete with examples of siblings—usually brother-sister pairs—whose senses are molded through the imagination, both of which unfold in childhood within a sphere of reciprocal communication and mutual experience shared between siblings.

The subject has gone through several crises since the nineteenth century, beginning with Nietzsche's and Sigmund Freud's dismantlement of its unity, and culminating in its dissolution into institutional power relations regulated through discourse in thinkers such as Foucault and Gilles Deleuze and Félix Guattari. Feminist theorists from Julia Kristeva and Luce Irigaray to Judith Butler have struggled with the ways that women might inhabit the place of the subject. Such concerns with relationality in the form of familial and societal interaction haunted the subject from the very beginning, however. In the eighteenth and nineteenth centuries, this instability bore the names *sister* and *brother*. We see the interrogation of the subject through the sibling in literature and philosophy throughout the long nineteenth century. At the same time, siblings gained dramatically in importance within the sociological practices of family formation, sharing a childhood newly valued as the affective and experiential foundation of self, which established this relationship as a touchstone for all future bonds.

KINSHIP IN THE NINETEENTH CENTURY

For decades, histories of the family in the eighteenth century have revolved around two transformations: the new commitment to companionate, emotionally fulfilling marriages and the concept of the nuclear family. Lawrence Stone's foundational work *The Family, Sex, and Marriage in England, 1500–1800* (1977) established the contours of a now-familiar argument, in which increasing individualism correlated with economic agency, personal preference was expected to guide the choice of a marriage partner in whom companionate love and sexual fulfillment coincided, childhood emerged as an idealized period of innocence and affectionate attachment, and a private sphere was generated around the newly named affiliation called the *family*.[23] Stone did not perceive the increased investment of emotional energy within the nuclear family as continuous over a lifetime, however. Rather, he posited a cyclical pattern in which marriage initiated the foundation of a new conjugal family that supplanted the earlier ties to birth family. Kinship beyond the nuclear and conjugal family, Stone argued, diminished in importance as the individual and the nuclear family waxed. Historians and theorists from Niklas Luhmann to Stephanie Coontz have built on aspects of Stone's foundational research.

The foundations for Stone's narrative, I would suggest, were set far earlier by the invention of kinship studies as the center of modern anthropology in the late nineteenth century.[24] While ethnographic inquiries had been popular for far longer, twentieth-century cultural anthropology took shape in the wake of three studies published from 1861 to 1871, namely, Johann Jakob Bachofen's *Mother Right* (*Das Mutterrecht*), John Ferguson McLennan's *Primitive Marriage*, and Lewis Henry Morgan's *Systems of Consanguinity & Affinity*, which together consolidated the field of cultural anthropology around investigations of kinship.[25] The *Oxford English Dictionary* indeed credits McLennan with the coinage of *kinship* out of the old word *kin* to represent the system that organizes such relationships.[26] As kinship became the key element for understanding non-Western cultures viewed as primitive, its significance within the cultures of the anthropologists themselves was suppressed. The distinction between levels of civilization was expressed in the associative disparity between the words *kinship* and *family*.

In 1998 David Warren Sabean's meticulous documentation of the formation of modern European class structures through kinship networks began to challenge the hegemony of Stone's narrative.[27] At the core of Sabean's reformulated history of the family in the eighteenth and nineteenth centuries lie alliances built around sibling ties. As one's siblings marry and have children, the original bond extends to link siblings-in-law, cousins, nephews, nieces, aunts, and uncles into economic units. Since 2000 Sabean has been joined by historians and anthropologists such as Leonore Davidoff, Adam Kuper, Michaela Hohkamp, Christopher Johnson, and Margareth Lanzinger in revealing the ways that intricate sibling bonds were cultivated to accomplish a number of functions from the inculcation of gender norms to the cementing of partnerships through marriage and the maintenance of family ties over time and distance through letter writing.[28] New research has thus fundamentally altered the previous paradigm, setting the newly affectionate conjugal pair in the context of an extended kinship network whose maintenance formed a large and crucial aspect of the activity of women in the long nineteenth century, and which was foundational for the emergence of a bourgeoisie in the newly capitalist economy.[29] The implications of this new research have just begun to penetrate disciplines beyond history.

Among the largest changes in family dynamics in the long nineteenth century was the popularity of cousin marriages. New laws across German-speaking territories in the mid-eighteenth century radically reduced legal impediments to kin marriage, confining incest bans to unions between siblings or those who stood in a direct lineage.[30] The legal changes reflected social pressure to allow marriages within acknowledged family but beyond the nuclear family. The definition of incest, in other words, changed as a function of tabooed degrees of relatedness between spouses. While nowhere in modern Europe was marriage between siblings or half-siblings allowed, cousins often referred to each other in correspondence as "brother" or "sister," and it was common to promote marriages between one's sibling and one's friend or between one's sibling and the sibling of one's own spouse (Davidoff, *Thicker Than Water*, 60–61). Marriage choices thus revolved around maintaining and deepening sibling bonds. Brother-sister relationships in the nursery were often idealized and projected as models for later marital happiness. Both in England and on the Continent, a long and heated debate arose in the nineteenth century over the legality and ethics of marriage between a widower and his deceased wife's sister. In England, where classifications of incest had generally been governed by church bans and customs rather than the legal system, a legal exception in the prohibition of these marriages lasted from 1835 until 1907. A similar debate can be traced through the requests for dispensations from the Catholic Church in parts of Europe, which were generally granted in the nineteenth century only when concern existed that the petitioners might convert.[31] Younger sisters often joined the households of newly married older sisters to help raise children and run the household until and unless they themselves married (Davidoff, *Thicker Than Water*, 79–85; Lanzinger, *Verwaltete Verwandtschaft*,

254–64). In an era of companionate marriage, these in-laws were desirable marriage partners in the case of a wife's death because of their familiarity with the household and close relationship to the children.[32] Construing the sister-in-law as a potential marriage partner, however, would also have meant sexualizing a nonconjugal relationship between adults frequently living within the same household. While eighteenth-century writers had speculated that God had conferred the incest aversion in order to maintain chastity in households, we see here how designations of incest were manipulated to create categories of tabooed relationships in the hopes of effecting this same end.[33] Given the reciprocal influence between sibling and conjugal relationships, it is no wonder that sibling incest haunted the nineteenth-century imaginary in literature, philosophy, political science, and biology.

Lawrence Stone notes that in the early modern period relationships between brothers and sisters were often extremely warm and affectionate. Such attachments contrasted with those between brothers, as primogeniture ensured that brothers were rivals in an inheritance pattern with extremely high stakes (*The Family*, 115–16). While Stone mentions that the quality of the brother-sister relationship remained warm in the eighteenth century, he does not speculate about the way the end of primogeniture and the rise of capitalism changed the relationship between brothers. Such a consideration is crucial to our study, however. From an economic perspective, brothers were transformed over the course of the nineteenth century from rivals to potential partners. It is also noteworthy that Stone does not mention the relationship between sisters at all. While gender deeply influenced the way in which sibling bonds functioned, the modern political economy generated *brothers and sisters* as a set, envisioned as collaborators and partners. Within such groups, sisters were viewed as the facilitators of relationships. Sister-sister and sister-brother ties consolidated the affiliation of brother-brother and brother-brother-in-law constellations. In this context, it is easy to understand why fraternity arose as the figure of choice for the affinities of a nation. Women, functioning simultaneously as sisters and wives, were expected to generate the fund of altruistic affection that tied citizens to each other and allowed the state to function. The necessity of playing this doubled role, however, tinged the fraternal nation with incestuous overtones.

Over the course of the eighteenth century the term *Geschwister*, a collective term for siblings that exists only as a plural, gained importance in

German; Adelung included the word as an entry in his *Wörterbuch* of 1811, while Zedler had not in his *Universal-Lexikon* of 1740.[34] The English word *sibling* is far more recent, having been coined in the early twentieth century by anthropologists who, as noted earlier, had newly begun to work within the field of kinship studies.[35] This derivation explains why the word sibling has remained far more clinical in its usage than its German counterpart. Like *kinship*, it originally served to distance the relationships of peoples under study by Europeans from the observers themselves. The difference in valence has not fully disappeared. It is telling, for example, that in common usage all animals also have siblings, but only pets also have brothers and sisters. Meanwhile, the expression that predates that term, namely, "brothers and sisters," has never gone out of use in English. Warmth is still carried disproportionately by the older kinship terms, which therefore still lend themselves more readily to rhetorical purposes urging ethical or affective behavior from civil rights to nationalism. My own use of the word sibling in this book is not meant to elide sex difference, to which we will return frequently. Rather, like anthropologists who have recently engaged in *kinship* studies of Europe, I do mean to turn the tables on our presumptions about our own culture. Moreover, with the word sibling, I indicate the reach of the concept of brother- and sisterhood beyond the concrete persons of brothers and sisters and beyond persons altogether to include all genealogical structures. Finally, I choose the word sibling to reassociate rhetorical usages of *fraternité* and *brotherhood* with their genealogical significance.

THE GENEALOGICAL SCIENCES

If extended family trees had important economic and political correlates, the notion of genealogy was no less central to the human sciences that emerged throughout the long nineteenth century. Already in early modern Europe, human diversity had been organized within the framework of the biblical story of the dispersal of Noah's sons after the flood, an account that classified peoples and languages genealogically by tracing them back to a set of three brothers.[36] Human difference resulted from divine marking, and its continuation over generations was read as the indication of divine presence in the world rather than the workings of natural laws. Discussions of physical diversity, linguistic diversity, and cultural diversity were intertwined in this paradigm. The tripartite dispersal of Noah's sons strongly influenced Sir William Jones, also known as Oriental Jones, when in 1786 he famously sparked the development of modern linguistics by postulating a lost mother language as the progenitor of Greek, Latin, and Sanskrit, establishing Indo-European as one of three discrete language families. The impact of this tripartite schema resonated through the nineteenth century.

In the late eighteenth century, genealogy itself underwent a transformation in which inheritance came to be understood as the result of a physical process subject to natural laws. The early modern theory of reproduction called preformationism had explained local family resemblances through two mechanisms. Preformationists theorized that all generations of humans came into being in a single act of creation, serially encapsulated like Russian dolls, so that all future human generations were embedded in the ovaries of Eve.[37] Resemblance within a maternal lineage, while not necessitated by such a theory, seemed a reasonable outgrowth of a conservative principle in creation. Paternal resemblances were explained as the imprint of the mother's imagination during pregnancy or at the moment of conception. The new epigenetic theories of the late eighteenth century postulated instead that maternal and paternal traits merged at the moment of conception, sparking the development of a truly new organization, a new organism.[38] While epigenesists posited competing theories, the most popular of which was a "formative drive" put forward by Johann Friedrich Blumenbach in 1781, they introduced regularity into conceptions of relatedness long before Gregor Mendel's mid-nineteenth-century experiments on peas or the twentieth-century development of genetics.[39] These new theories of inheritance were simultaneously applied to individual families and to population groups. Indeed, the early epigenesists such as Blumenbach and Kant were uniformly also interested in race, and race theory was intertwined with research into reproduction. It was the observation of a significant number of mixed-race children among slave populations and in colonial settings that spurred both inquiries into maternal and paternal inheritance and the desire to insulate in theory population boundaries that proved impossible to police in practice. Race theory entailed a debate between a monogenetic model of single origin and a polygenetic model that envisioned separate origins for racial groups. When in 1787 Josiah Wedgwood designed what was to become the preeminent symbol of the abolition movement—a ceramic imprint of a kneeling black man in chains under the words "Am I Not a Man and a Brother?" (see fig. 5.1)—the question was therefore by no means rhetorical. In fact, polygenesis was soon accepted as the more scientific theory, and it retained its predominance until Darwin's theory shifted the biological discourse on race. In this debate, as in its comparative method, race theory mirrored the comparative philology of the period, which was also a method of cataloging human diversity. Both monogenesists and polygenesists of race and of language posited genealogical systems thought to operate through diversification and diffusion from the point—or points—of origin. Darwin developed his genealogical theory of evolution in full awareness of these precursors, acknowledging his debt to both genealogical linguistic models and familial models of genealogy in his *Origin of Species* (1859). All three fields used comparative analysis to construct genealogical trees.

A comparative method had become common in both the study of organisms and the study of languages already in the seventeenth and eighteenth centuries. Working with anatomy in the one case and vocabulary in the other, affinities and resemblances could be established. As early as the seventeenth century, language affiliations were mapped not only morphologically but genetically in the original usage of that word, that is, as the result of descent. Differentiation over time was recognized and relations delineated through the terms *mother language*, *sister language*, and *daughter language*. In the famous lecture of 1786 already mentioned, William Jones declared that philosophical or scientific precision depended on "separating and comparing . . . ideas by the laborious exertions of intellect."[40] Comparative anatomy originally grouped species morphologically but not genetically. Affinity was acknowledged as causally related to descent only with the growing acceptance of evolution after Darwin, by which time a *comparative method* came to entail the plotting of historical development through common ancestry. By late in the nineteenth century, Friedrich Max Müller could declare in his introductory *Lectures on a Science of Religion*, "Why, all higher knowledge is acquired by comparison, and rests on comparison . . . the character of scientific research in our age is pre-eminently comparative."[41]

Looking back in 1963, Henry Hoenigswald defined the comparative method that dominated nineteenth-century science as a form of "genealogical reconstruction" and specified, as Darwin had, that through comparison "original features can be separated from recent ones."[42] Relationships between existing terms, in other words, were triangulated by positing a usually extinct common ancestor. Hoenigswald, however, makes a mistake common to twentieth-century considerations of the nineteenth century, when he claims that in the comparative method, "the aim of classification is subordinated to the aim of reconstruction" (ibid.). Hoenigswald adheres to a traditional view of the Victorians as primarily interested in ancestry, in puzzling out lineage and origins. And yet it is hard to maintain this conviction when actually reading Darwin, who employs his comparisons in order to discover "how it is that all living and extinct forms can be grouped together in one great system; and how the several members of each class are connected together by the most complex and radiating lines of affinities."[43] These complex and radiating networks are great kinship maps that establish identity only within and through relatedness, present as much as past.

Genealogically speaking, then, linguistics and race theory, as well as all comparative cultural fields from comparative religion and cultural anthropology to comparative literature, in addition to the broader but structurally similar theory of evolution, share a heritage.[44] Moreover, they share concerns with the possibility and the impact of hybridity, and with the difficulty of defining an individual term. These two worries were related. In every genealogical system, terms were created through the differentiation of similars who then became siblings. The existence of the sibling put pressure on the boundaries of terms. Denying hybridity could serve as a partial remedy to these fuzzy origins by turning individuality into an emergent property—even if indistinct at its beginnings, a term in a parthenogenetic system would individuate and consolidate its identity over time, leaving ever more space between itself and its original similars. If parthenogenesis constituted a kind of ideal, however, it could be generated only through various methods for suppressing the recognition of merger, an endeavor that proved more difficult in some fields than in others.

As we will see in chapter 4, the field of linguistics adhered most strictly to a purely diversifying structure. At the turn of the nineteenth century, comparative philology began to privilege the tenacious inner structure of grammar above readily borrowed vocabulary, demonstrating an ideological commitment to descent over influence as an arbiter of relatedness. This move enabled languages to be portrayed as pure carriers of culture, free from an intermixture clearly envisioned as taint. Linguistics remained largely attached to a kind of parthenogenesis until the second half of the twentieth century, although pidgins, creoles, and other forms of linguistic influence garnered a small amount of scholarly attention in the late nineteenth century. While comparative philology was adamantly diffusionary in its historical trajectory, we will see in chapter 5 that both monogenist and polygenist race theorists recognized mergers.[45] Indeed race theory originated, I would argue, out of a voyeuristic obsession with the widespread phenomenon of sexual encounters between European men and the non-European women over whom they exercised power, accompanied by a fascination with the traits of their offspring. Placing European attitudes toward these encounters, which oscillated between attraction and repulsion, at the center of the construction of race explains the otherwise puzzling pervasiveness of an aesthetic element to racial discourse.[46] We must recognize the overwhelming significance of pervasive sexual mixing—on both the politics of sex and the politics of race—for a culture that organized the world through genealogy. The nebulous boundaries of race were made manifest as an ongoing provocation in the form of close kinships simultaneously recognized and unacknowledged. Incest and miscegenation were the twin fears of the nineteenth century not because they formed the inner and outer limits of a pool of acceptable sexual partners but because they so often coincided. In slaveholding and colonial settings, the racial line divided sibling from sibling and cousin from cousin while simultaneously rendering one set sexually available to the other along a boundary in need of constant buttressing.

If we turn to the genealogical form codified by evolutionary theory, we might expect it to follow the sexual contours of a family or race tree. Species hybrids were, after all, a matter of intense discussion in Darwin's time, and Darwin included an entire chapter on the question of hybridity in domesticated breeding in *The Origin of Species*.[47] While Darwin, unlike many other biologists, accepted the possibility of mating across species boundaries, he discounted the influence of such hybridity as a mechanism for adaptation, never suggesting that hybridization happens in the wild, so that at the macro scale of species development, his evolutionary tree looked like a linguistic tree—diffusionary without mergers. This structure requires explanation, which, I argue, we can find in the extreme anxiety caused by Darwin's rejection of natural kinds. Darwin declared the definition of species boundaries contingent, accepting the sibling logic we have been discussing here. To many contemporaries, this contingency seemed to undermine the very possibility of definitive knowledge, prompting, I argue in chapter 4, several defensive rhetorical strategies on Darwin's part to downplay the consequences of indistinct boundaries between species. In 1940 Ernst Mayr, one of the chief architects of the modern synthesis through which genetics was incorporated into evolutionary theory, would devise a label for those troublesome points of indeterminacy "where pairs or larger groups of related species are so similar that they are generally considered as one species, or at least have in the past for a long time been mistaken for one another"—namely, *sibling species*.[48]

Now is the right moment to explore the history of the evolutionary tree in particular because it is currently under extreme pressure. Citing growing evidence of the scope of lateral gene transfer and hybridization in prompting adaptation, an increasing number of biologists have declared the tree an inadequate and indeed inaccurate model. The problem is clearest for the evolution of prokaryotes, very simple organisms like bacteria, which lack a nucleus, and which regularly participate in "lateral gene transfer" not only from one "individual" to another but across species boundaries.[49] Their process of adaptation does not only, or even primarily, involve descent, in other words. Such problems are not restricted to simple organisms. There are groups of species, such as the finches of which Darwin was so fond, that regularly produce new species through hybridization. And then there is the lack of direct correspondence between the phylogenetic map of a species and that of all its genes.[50] It is not uncommon, in other words, to end up with two different trees when analyses of two different genes in the same species are used to construct genealogies. Finally, there is the complication caused by symbiotic associations, where two species with distinct genealogical histories become so codependent as to call the boundary between individuals into question.[51]

These issues of merging and of lateral transfer vastly complicate the way we have tended to think of the relatedness of life in terms of roots, when we need to acknowledge the frequent reentanglement of branches.

Rhetorical and visual figures crystallize the preoccupations of the cultures that create them. The genealogical trees of the nineteenth century attest to the desires of Europeans to place themselves within certain kinds of family histories and familial presents, in the service both of controlling the contours of kinship and of naturalizing—and hence legitimating—systems of classification and knowledge.[52]

SIBLINGS IN LITERATURE

The segregation of literature into its own category in this introduction is artificial because literature functions as an experimental realm for the interrogation of each of the issues already considered. On the other hand, literature seems to require its own discussion precisely because it provides a theoretical arena in which each of the major epistemological realms that partake in the sibling designation are addressed in relation to the others. Literature does not provide sociological evidence for what *happens* in a culture but functions as a set of experiments in the realm of the hypothetical, performed to work out the assumptions and relations that organize the social and psychological world. Literature occupies a unique place in this study because it engages not only with its own intellectual and historical context and its own methodology but also with the structure and implications of multiple other discourses. Literature therefore constitutes a form of critical analysis in its own right, albeit one whose narrative and imaginative method are essential to its functioning. Reading literature in reciprocal dialogue with other disciplines and with the cultural, social, scientific, and political registers that inform both provides insight into the logic of their relations that could not be gained through a historical analysis in its absence.

The theme of sibling incest—whether consummated or unconsummated, a threat or an ideal—saturated literature across Europe around 1800, with a lingering presence in the intense sibling relationships depicted throughout the nineteenth century. The most pervasive literary touchstone of the century was Sophocles's *Antigone*. The consummate sister who, for the sake of burying her brother Polyneices, would consummate nothing else, Antigone appeared in countless reiterations throughout the century—literary, artistic, philosophical, and political.[53] But Antigone was not alone. Mignon, child of sibling incest in Johann Wolfgang von Goethe's *Wilhelm Meister's Apprenticeship*, achieved an afterlife across Europe in artistic and literary echoes. Gotthold Ephraim Lessing's Recha and the Templar Curd, Goethe's Iphigenia and Orestes, Emily Brontë's Catherine and Heathcliff, Ludwig Tieck's Eckbert and Bertha, Françoise-René de Chauteaubriand's Rene and Amélie, Lord Byron's Manfred and Astarte, Mary Shelley's Frankenstein and Elizabeth, George Eliot's Tom and Maggie Tulliver, and Richard Wagner's Siegmund and Sieglinde are only a tiny sampling of the fictional (sometimes foster) brother-sister pairs whose intense relationships resonated across Europe.

Early analyses of sibling incest in literature tended toward a psychoanalytic approach. A contemporary follower of Freud, Otto Rank, published a compendious study on *The Incest Theme in Literature and Legend* in 1912, half of which was dedicated to what he termed "The Sibling Complex."[54] Rank's analysis follows two principles that became commonplace for psychoanalytic literary interpretations. First, he relegated the sibling relationship to a secondary manifestation of the primary, intergenerational, Oedipal Complex, and second, he moved immediately from the text to a diagnosis of the author. The tendency to move from text to author was facilitated by the intense relationships of many authors of the long nineteenth century to their siblings, including that of William Wordsworth and his sister Dorothy Wordsworth, Johann Wolfgang von Goethe and his sister Cornelia Friederike Christiana Goethe, and Jane Austen and her sister Cassandra Austen in particular, but also her other siblings. One might think here also of the allegations of incest linking Lord Byron and his half sister Augusta Leigh. We could move beyond literary authors to note that Wilhelm and Jakob Grimm had a close working collaboration, as did Friedrich and August von Schlegel, and, somewhat less intensely, Wilhelm and Alexander von Humboldt, while Ernest Renan attributed the idea for his most popular book, *The Life of Jesus*, to his sister Henrietta Renan, publishing their letters after her death. Other equally significant sibling relationships of the period were less harmonious, such as that between George Eliot and her brother Isaac Evans, or between Friedrich Nietzsche and his sister Elisabeth Förster-Nietzsche. While the biographies of any of these writers would illuminate their work, the sheer volume of examples invalidates approaching these accounts purely as individual cases in need of psychoanalytic diagnosis, pointing instead to an epochal phenomenon. More recent psychoanalytic approaches have been both more creative and more fruitful. Lynn Hunt, for example, recasts the French Revolution as a reenactment of the primordial patricide of *Totem and Taboo*, equating the father's waning authority with an uncertain paternity she claims, far too absolutely, is necessary for the occurrence of incest in literature.[55]

The plot of unwitting incest—an attraction between young adults unaware of their sibling relationship—constituted the norm in eighteenth-century literature in Germany, France, and England.[56] As Alan Richardson notes, these plots gave way during the British Romantic period to narratives centered on pairs raised together as siblings, whether siblings, foster-siblings, or cousins. French literature featured an early example of conscious sibling incest, as a subplot in Baron de Montesquieu's *Persian Letters* of 1721, and reverts to it with Vicomte Chateaubriand's *René* in 1802. In Germany, however, the unwitting incest plot remained dominant throughout the nineteenth century.[57] While my work engages with the natural law, political republicanism, and sympathy that animate Wilson's, Hunt's, and Richardson's interpretations, respectively, national discrepancies in plot structure complicate their strategies for explaining the prevalence of the trope in the eighteenth and early nineteenth centuries. In British studies, recent work by Ellen Pollak, Leila Silvana May, and Mary Jean Corbett has begun to productively analyze connections between the incest paradigm and the naturalization of gender and race, thus revealing the way such literature comments on both colonialism and the construction of a public/private divide.[58] Building on their insights, I will look in this study beyond the British realm and outside of literature, illustrating the way the sibling both organizes and disarranges such constructions and divides.[59]

THE ACTION OF SIBLINGS AND THE STRUCTURE OF *SIBLING ACTION*

Already in this introduction we have encountered forcefully the way that classification and identity became historical concepts in the eighteenth century, that is, concepts that organized systems perceived as in motion, but also concepts that were themselves in motion. Foucault powerfully illustrated the introduction of time into knowledge systems in *The Order of Things*—describing the shift from representation to inflection that produced linguistics, the shift from structure to function that produced biology, and the shift from wealth to production that produced economics. Practitioners themselves were in fact cognizant of the turn toward action, chronology, and mutability as a new development. Still more significantly, however, as we will see here, many thinkers acknowledged the active nature of the process of classification itself, that is, the contingency of the identity of objects and the structure of systems as a function of interpretation that might therefore vary over time. In his definition of the human, for example, Johann Gottfried Herder agrees with Aristotle's designation of the human as a social animal but finds it still more fundamental that "the human being is a freely thinking, active being, whose forces operate forth progressively."[60] Lessing goes further and provides a meta-argument for the role of transmission and trust in constituting truth as a process, as we will see in chapter 5. Goethe not only established metamorphosis in living systems as the hallmark of his natural history but also illustrated the way that varying the shape of scientific disciplines generated distinct knowledge. While he founded and named a discipline to include not only "the principles of structured form" but also "the formation and transformation of organic bodies," he deemed *morphology* a new science capable of generating new knowledge "not because of its subject matter, which is already well known, but because of its intention and method."[61] Darwin expanded on Goethe's insight, as we have seen, by declaring the contingency of the classificatory categories pertaining to life, from kingdoms all the way down to species. In his thorough historicization of classification, not only human interpretation but human intention in determining the goals of classification were acknowledged to guide the process.[62] Elizabeth Grosz has illuminated this *philosophy of becoming* in Darwin, both at the level of life as "the consequence of actions and passions" and at the level of knowledge construction.[63] Following Darwin, then, Grosz defines concepts themselves as "what we produce when we need to address the forces of the present and to transform them into new and different forces that act in the future" (*Becoming Undone*, 80). The benefits of rethinking form as action that Grosz suggests for feminist theory will emerge in this book as well.

Once classification has been recognized as a system in motion constructed through continuous value-laden process, rather than a passive structure determined by immutable facts, the place of the sibling in genealogical systems can be better understood. As a factor necessary for the creation of each term, and yet simultaneously a repository of alternatives to it, the sibling does more than introduce uncertainty. Rather, it serves as a disruptive action within the very system it underwrites. Among the knowledge systems disordered by sibling action are not only the genealogical sciences but also both the family and the subject. In a search for queer models of identification, Eve Sedgwick once turned to the avuncular. The position of the aunt and uncle was occluded by the Freudian triangle that continues to dominate narratives of both child development and the modern family at the expense of wider kinship networks that she, following Stone's history, associated with the early modern period. Because the aunt and uncle attain that position through their sibling relationship to the parent, Sedgwick's avuncular theory encapsulates a sibling theory:

> Having aunts and uncles, even the most conventional of aunts and uncles, means perceiving your parents as somebody's sibs—not, that is, as alternately abject and omnipotent links in a chain of compulsion and replication that leads inevitably to *you*; but rather as elements in a varied, contingent, recalcitrant but re-forming seriality, as people who demonstrably could have turned out very differently—indeed as people who, in the differing, refractive relations among their own generation, can be seen already to have done so.[64]

The sibling, then, is always a sign of alternate histories and potential alternative futures, a splinter in the line of descent that fractures the Oedipal narrative and reveals the openness of the subject to its own variants. It not only provides a kind of differential logic but embodies the historical action that has brought about such differentials and instigates ongoing action and interaction.

In its exploration of the sibling as enabler of classification and simultaneous splinter of instability, *Sibling Action* will embark on a trajectory from the subject, to the family and state, to the classification of human diversity through language, race, religion, and species. While one could think of this path as a widening spiral, each chapter will illustrate the ways these systems and definitions constitute each other so that inward and outward become misnomers.

The entry point for this study is a discussion of the stakes of recuperating the sibling for critical theory. The neglected sibling is a model that allows us to deconstruct self/other and gender dichotomies, and to move beyond the mother-child dyad that forms the primary grounds for intersubjectivity in contemporary debates. Sibling logic instead recognizes the subject as embedded in a transsubjective network of *partial others*, with whom we crucially also share. Beginning in the late eighteenth century, Sophocles's *Antigone* became a touchstone for theory and literature because it scrutinizes interconnections that had again become relevant—between subject, family, community, place, the kinship of a population, the definition of the foreign, and the effects of colonialization. Chapter 1, "Sibling Logic," works through the critical elision of Antigone's siblings and her relationship to them as emblematic of the problematic omission of the sibling from twentieth-century theoretical discourses in general. In particular, the incestuous passion of Ismene for Antigone, which echoes that of Antigone for Polyneices, has been obscured by presuppositions about gender and sexuality.

A recognition of the perviousness of the boundaries of subjectivity and agency also motivated social and political constructs in the late eighteenth and the nineteenth centuries, which I turn to in the two chapters of part 2, "Fraternity and Revolution." As evidenced by the Friedrich Schiller ode that has become the anthem of the European Union, fraternity structured thinking about the problematic overlap of politics and affect throughout Europe in the late eighteenth century. With the discrediting of traditional authorities, the tension between two alternative foundations for allegiance—rational consent and affective ties—came under increasing scrutiny. While reason demands universality, passion introduces selection and exclusivity, with brotherhood poised ambiguously between these two necessary elements of participatory nationhood. The sister introduced an egalitarian form of affect, but only as erotic object does she generate masculine agency in the political sphere. Political and aesthetic theory from Locke and Rousseau to Schiller and Moses

Mendelssohn attempts to establish a serene affective commonality through siblinghood, a construct whose precarious nature is evoked and explored in the Marquis de Sade's *Philosophy in the Bedroom*, Schiller's *The Bride of Messina*, and Percy Shelley's *Laon and Cythna*.

If aesthetic political models investigated in chapter 2, "Shadows of Fraternity," attempt to transcend the erotic, economic models explored in chapter 3, "Economizing Desire," venture to regulate it by putting siblings into circulation, but at a cost. Friedrich Engels and Claude Lévi-Strauss developed competing family histories of the sibling relation that aligned with different economic theories. While Engels, following Lewis Henry Morgan's foundational kinship studies, posited that at the origin of culture all siblings were also spouses in communal marriages, Lévi-Strauss, adapting Adam Smith's economics, grounded culture on the incest prohibition, which instituted equal competition between men for women: free access vs. free market. An education of desire centered on sibling relations encouraged de facto endogamy in the form of cousin marriages and double-sibling marriages in the nineteenth century. Scholars such as David Sabean and Leonore Davidoff have recently demonstrated how sibling allegiances in the 150 years between Smith and Lévi-Strauss facilitated the formation of the bourgeois class. Literature frequently interrogated the production of the economic agent in an age of fratriarchy. While Goethe's *Wilhelm Meister's Apprenticeship* struggles to stake the subject in a new fraternal order, George Eliot's *Mill on the Floss* relinquishes the demand for integral and discrete subjects with agency over passive objects.

The genealogies in ascendency in the nineteenth century structured thinking about classification across a remarkable swath of disciplines and discourses, from family relations to fields and disciplines that attended to the organization of human variety spanning what we would now think of as the sciences, social sciences, and humanities. It is these sciences, or knowledge-systems, that I will turn to in the final section of the book, "Genealogical Sciences." In chapter 4, "Living Languages," we will explore both comparative philology and evolution, two fields that still depend heavily on the building of genealogical trees, or tree thinking. In the late eighteenth century, language as a human capacity was envisioned as a gift of the mother; language praxis, however, belonged to siblings. The *mother tongue* acquired the double meaning of native language and protolanguage, so that two genealogies cohabited in speech: an ontogenetic life history and a phylogenetic history of a language. The genealogical tree as a form of classification causally determined by common ancestry developed simultaneously in comparative philology and in biology with reciprocal influence between the fields. The sibling term in such trees calls the discrete nature of languages and of species into question. Meanwhile, the same authors discussed in the previous chapter, Goethe and Eliot, demonstrate the intertwining of the political and economic concerns from part 2 with these epistemological issues. The figure of the speaking sibling in narratives of encounter negotiates both subjectivity and cultural identity. To shore up classificatory boundaries, these genealogical sciences repudiated merging in favor of unidirectional diversification, an ideological choice with ramifications for the flourishing and problematic field of race science.

Attempts to form genealogies of race and religion confronted merging in the forms of sexual and conceptual intermixture from their inception and were forced to ask whether brotherhood was inherited or actively formed. Chapter 5, "The East Comes Home," explores the confluence, overlaps, and conflicts between ethnology, philology, comparative religion, and race theory in their kinship constellations. Even as race theory began to focus on skin color and continental geographies, literature in both Germany and Britain converged with philology in its fixation on the Muslim populations on the margins of Europe as the primary objects of cultural encounter, as apparent in authors such as Lessing and Byron. Early in the nineteenth century, not only linguistics but the ethnography and comparative religion with which it was closely allied instituted a primary contrast between the Indo-European, or *Aryan*, and the *Semitic*. Christian Europe found itself faced with an identity crisis, split between its "Aryan" linguistic and "Semitic" religious heritages. Increasingly, scholars and the lay public attempted to harmonize this history by Aryanizing Christianity. Even while acknowledging that linguistic affinity did not necessarily correlate with biological descent, the cultural genealogies of ethnography and philology in Friedrich Max Müller, Ernest Renan, and others hewed to race theory in order to shore up privileged identities. While Britain remained preoccupied with Muslims, increasingly as colonial subjects rather than as "Aryan brethren,"[65] emphasis in Germany shifted from the Eastern Muslim as religious and geographical boundary object to the Eastern Jew as racial intruder, an inassimilable inbred brotherhood, a transformation visible in the leaps from Lessing to Wagner to Mann. In both cases, the genealogical imagination ensured that borders between groups were envisioned in sexual terms and anxieties about them manifest in sexual politics. This chapter will confront the most poisonous reactions to sibling logic.

The specter of incest that haunted the genealogical fields was apparent not only in the works of fiction explored throughout this volume. As we will see in the epilogue, incest is a constitutive component of classification schemes, a specter arising out of the desire for certain types of epistemological purity. The incest taboo has long been credited with producing horror, repugnance, and disgust. It also spawns disciplines; from race theory to linguistics to comparative religion, the turn of the nineteenth century saw an explosion of fields that drew boundaries around identity in familial terms. In the twentieth century, psychoanalysis, structural anthropology, and sociobiology all defined themselves through their understandings of the incest taboo. These fields attempt to *claim* incest in order to establish their jurisdiction and to delineate the scope of the mechanism of transmission they study, whether that mechanism inheres in natural laws or in human institutions. We find ourselves currently in the midst of a surge of academic and popular interest in evolutionary psychology, which repudiates Freud and takes Edward Westermarck as its patron saint. The plausibility of the claim that mental attitudes are innate and heritable adaptations rests on the soundness of evolutionary psychology's account of the incest aversion. Evolutionary psychology provides a kind of inverse sibling logic. It returns to the sibling as the central focus of the incest taboo and to kinship as a pivotal motivation for behavior, dissolving the subject along the way, but only by positing an underlying innate determinism that in the end reifies, rather than disrupts, gender and the self.

In *Sibling Action*, then, we will traverse the horizon of the family structure as a model for knowledge-systems, and knowledge-systems as the grounding for an understanding of kinship. Illuminating the sibling as the ambivalent generator of the subject in and as a set of relations, and of classification as a process, will require an engagement with the inherent fluidity of all structural sources of identity. Siblings demonstrate, instigate, and instantiate the activity of shared agency and provide tools for us to reimagine ourselves.

PART I

RECUPERATING THE SIBLING

The relationship in its unmixed form is found, however, in that between brother and sister. They are the same blood which has, however, in them reached a state of rest and equilibrium. Therefore they do not desire one another, nor have they given to, or received from, one another this independent being-for-self; on the contrary, they are free individualities in regard to each other.

—GEORG WILHELM FRIEDRICH HEGEL, *PHENOMENOLOGY*, 274

Eckermann: He [Hegel's student H. F. W. Hinrichs] also appears to have had before his eyes merely the character and mode of action of this heroine [Antigone], as he makes the assertion that family piety appears most pure in woman, and especially in a sister; and that a sister can love only a brother with perfect purity, and without sexual feeling.

Goethe: I should think that the love of sister for sister was still more pure and unsexual. As if we did not know that numerous cases have occurred in which the most sensual inclinations have existed between brother and sister, both knowingly and unknowingly!

—JOHANN WOLFGANG VON GOETHE, "CONVERSATIONS," 173

I will skip the details of her [Antigone's] dialogue with Ismene.

—JACQUES LACAN, *ETHICS*, 7:265

1

SIBLING LOGIC

The compass of the sibling in nineteenth-century European culture can hardly be overstated. Siblinghood, in the forms of both fraternity and sorority, was intricately bound up with the political. Siblinghood also stood at the center of understandings of kinship in the long nineteenth century, encapsulating the significance of blood-relatedness, structuring marriage choices, and yet unsettling the boundaries of group identity. Collectives such as race and nation, and the epistemological structures that supported them, emerged from the interplay of political theory and kinship. The formation of modern subjectivity itself cannot be understood without working through the figure of the sibling. One index of this obsession can be found in the scope of the era's reflections on Sophocles's *Antigone* and on its title character, which extended far beyond the already substantial corpus explicitly dedicated to them and merged with the omnipresent stagings of siblinghood that dominated literature, philosophy, and graphic art throughout the century (see the cover of this book, for example). We return in this chapter to an *Antigone* in dialogue with the modern world in order to fashion a theory of subjectivity in relation to the sibling that weaves among these registers and sutures them to each other. All the theoretical concerns that will surface throughout *Sibling Action* thus make an appearance in this critical intervention into modern readings of *Antigone*.

George Steiner noted the "momentous" shift at the beginning of the twentieth century in which "Oedipus replaces Antigone" as Freud initiated an era of vertical kinship models that supplanted a more complex mixture of horizontal and vertical affiliations.[1] There can be no doubt that psychoanalysis has continued to embrace vertical lineages at the expense of understanding sibling relations, and indeed that this elision has been carried into other branches of critical theory.[2]

But in another way Steiner was mistaken—*Antigone* and Antigone never lost their popularity, in twentieth-century adaptations Steiner himself documents and in theory, from Martin Heidegger and Jacques Lacan to Luce Irigaray and Jacques Derrida. If Paul Allen Miller has recently been able to locate the roots of poststructuralism in classical texts including Sophocles's *Antigone*,[3] it is because poststructuralism traces its heritage to Romantic and classicist theory, which was drenched in translations of and commentaries on *Antigone*—by Friedrich Hölderlin, G. W. F. Hegel, August Wilhelm Schlegel, and Johann Wolfgang von Goethe, to name but a few.[4] As the twentieth century waned, Jean Bethke Elshtain called on Antigone as a feminist heroine and identified the Mothers of the Disappeared in Argentina as bearers of her standard, carrying Antigone into gender debates in political theory.[5] Judith Butler's *Antigone's Claim* then heralded a new wave of intense engagement with *Antigone* in literary and critical theory in the new century. The ongoing compulsion to return to *Antigone* derives from the drama's gripping interrogation of subjectivity, desire, and collective political life. However, it is equally motivated by *Antigone*'s resistance to a common element in these otherwise diverse readings—namely, a reductive view of the drama that reinforces limits on the conditions of possibility for subjectivity. This reductive view begins with Hegel and culminates with Sigmund Freud and later Freudian readings. Freud's effacement of the drama in favor of *Oedipus Rex* could be read, however, as a tacit acknowledgment of the impossibility of molding *Antigone* to fit the oedipal project.

Butler discovered in Steiner a provocation to a productive thought experiment: "What would have happened if psychoanalysis had chosen Antigone rather than Oedipus?"[6] Even the question as Butler poses it, however, reenacts the process of excision that regularly reduces *Antigone* to Antigone.[7] Lacan's laconic "What does one find in *Antigone*? First of all, one finds Antigone" embodies this pervasive trend.[8] Some critics have widened their sights, but only to include the ruler Creon, following the dual logic of Hegel's foundational dialectical reading of the play as the staging of a conflict between masculine and feminine, public sphere and family.[9] The consequences of these blinders extend far beyond questions of literary interpretation since critics turn to *Antigone* to unveil the roots of the very theories of subjectivity that the play challenges. To truly understand the attraction and potential of Sophocles's drama, we must be careful not to erect an Antigone Complex but to recognize instead an *Antigone* Complex[10]—a complex modeled on the web of relationships in play around Antigone, beginning with her siblings Oedipus (who is both brother and father), Polyneices, Eteocles, and, particularly, Ismene.[11] This chapter will first of all acknowledge the impossibility of locating an *individual* in this text, and not only within the incestuous Labdacid family. The intricate tenor of relatedness, the inability of characters to pluck themselves out of each other's being, confronts us with the complex in this complex. Bracha Ettinger, moving in this direction, has referred to the transsubjectivity that incorporates Antigone and Polyneices, the brother she gives her life to bury.[12] Lacan, Steiner, and Simon Goldhill have all noted the intimate forms of address that connect Antigone and her sister, Ismene, at the play's opening.[13] And we should not forget that startling vision of plural subjectivity inherent in the tragic form of the chorus, in which voices speaking in unison represent the intricately intertwined polis. While the polis differed radically from the modern state, it nonetheless shares some crucial concerns with the budding notion of nationality in the late eighteenth century that evolved into our own; *Antigone* scrutinizes the interconnections among subject, family, community, place, the kinship of a population, the definition of the foreign, and the effects of colonialization on identity. *Antigone* urges us, as it did not need to urge the nineteenth century, to interweave any understanding of subjectivity with understandings of kinship and of political community. We will return to these ideas throughout this book.

It is no coincidence that leading theorists of the subject in its outward relationality have felt drawn to *Antigone*. In different veins, Lacan and, more recently, Butler have extended the intersubjective operations of the psyche introduced by Hegel's dyadic dialectic of recognition and expanded by Freud. While Lacan opened the subject to a shared, constitutive linguistic sphere, the psychoanalytic model of primary relationality remains figured by interaction with a parental pair that functions oppositionally in the imaginary. The psychoanalytic social field, first narrowed to a familial threesome, thus further resolves itself into one and its other. Butler's work attempts to situate the subject more firmly in an intersubjective dynamic by analyzing the interplay between the discursive sociopolitical sphere and inner psychic processes. Her work continues to grapple, however, with the collapse of the intersubjective into an imaginary dualism implicated in an oppositional gender divide, in which, Eve Kosofsky Sedgwick noted, "the paths of desire/identification for a given child are essentially reduced to two."[14] This binary logic forecloses potentials for theorizing differential relationships and collective identities not only in the imaginary but also within the symbolic order. Juliet Mitchell has recently argued that "one of the reasons why theories of group psychology have not advanced further than they have may be to do with the fact that, firstly, siblings have been omitted."[15] The sibling as a model, I argue, allows us to move beyond both self-other dualisms and the mother-child dyad as the only grounds for intersubjectivity and positions the subject as instead embedded in a network of *partial* others, whose subjectivities are nonetheless partially, though differentially, shared. Such a model responds to Barbara Stafford's recent plea that in this "age of otherness, of assertive identities," we find a "relational way" that enables a "double avoidance of self-sameness and total estrangement."[16] A logic of differential degrees of likeness provides the foundation for less confrontational formulations of belonging, identity, and agency. As we reexamine paradigmatic (mis)readings of Sophocles's play by Lacan and Hegel, and correctives by Butler, Ettinger, and others, we will return repeatedly to *Antigone* as a guide to the potential of sibling logic.

THE ELISION OF THE SIBLING

Antigone's crime is to transgress the law of her uncle, Creon, who has decreed that the body of her brother Polyneices be left unburied. Antigone thus knowingly forfeits her life and with it her future role of wife and mother.[17] Lacan, in *The Ethics of Psychoanalysis*, provides a problematic reading of Antigone in the context of the beauty inherent in uncompromising devotion to the law of one's own desire. In Antigone's choice of the dead brother as object of desire, he sees an exposure of the normally screened hole in the real, the void that resists discourse and initiates the metaphoric substitution that structures the symbolic order. Antigone's desire therefore manifests itself as a death drive; her desire is the desire for the pure signifier, the Other writ large. Polyneices comes to inhabit this space for Lacan because he remains outside any chain of substitutions; he is irreplaceable. As Antigone herself argues in a passage that has puzzled and disturbed commentators for centuries, it is only for a brother that she would break Creon's law and sacrifice her own life, and not for a husband or child:

> If my husband were dead, I might have had another,
> and child from another man, if I lost the first.
> But when father and mother both were hidden in death
> no brother's life would bloom again for me.[18]

Lacan uses this passage to legitimate a move through a point posited as irreplaceable; where Antigone names *brother*, Lacan reads *mother's desire*. He delves through the brother to the parents: to Oedipus as complex, and to Jocasta in her incestuous relationship to her son. In her elevation of the brother, then, Antigone enacts the mother's desire for the son, repeating the "criminal desire" of the mother at "the origin of everything" (*Ethics*, 283).

Ettinger takes issue with Lacan at the point of this return to Oedipus, both literally and as complex, through Jocasta, rejecting the "folding of the womb into the phallus/castration stratum." Ettinger proposes a feminine difference arising "physically, imaginatively and symbolically" from female bodily specificity.[19] Outside the symbolic logic of castration but foundational for a different symbolic order, the womb enables a matrixial transsubjective linking, between mother and child and between siblings who share this space, whether simultaneously or sequentially. The "separation-in-jointness" thus engendered is no new-age harmony; it entails first and foremost the inheritance of trauma from one generation to the next. The effect of the potential for linkage initiated by the matrixial, however, reaches beyond the mother-child unit and beyond the family; this "matrixial awareness engenders a disturbing desire for jointness *with* a foreign world."[20] Ettinger's matrixial intervenes in psychoanalysis to open a space for female specificity that is not otherness but hybridity—that is, joint transformation in relationality.

Ettinger's reading attends to Antigone's own emphasis on the womb she shares with her brother.[21] In insisting on the mother's body as a locus of relationship formation throughout *Antigone*, Sophocles departs radically from Aeschylus's *Oresteia*, written about fifteen years earlier and frequently invoked as a foundational moment for all future patrilineage. In Aeschylus's trilogy, the order of law and the polis is established and maintained through a dispossession of the mother's stake in her children when Apollo inaugurates a court system and rules that the mother merely houses a growing fetus, without being related to it. The child thus belongs to the father alone, to whom the child owes allegiance.[22] Sophocles's *Antigone* establishes a very different concept of relatedness within the family. It is not Antigone alone who returns to the mother: the chorus stresses that Eteocles and Polyneices were "born of one father and mother" (lines 144–45). Antigone goes out of her way to further emphasize the role of the mother, referring to Polyneices in her self-justifications as "my mother's son" (lines 466–67), and to both Eteocles and Polyneices as born "from the same innards" (line 511, trans. mine). When Creon challenges her by asking if Eteocles was not also "of the same blood" (line 512, trans. mine), Antigone weaves this emphatic affirmation, "Yes, indeed, of my own blood from father and mother" (line 513). In contrast to Aeschylus, Sophocles focuses on the womb as shared between siblings but, crucially, does not do so at the expense of the shared relationship with the father.

While Ettinger turns to the matrixial as the logic of relatedness that connects siblings and establishes a relationship with the world based on fusion rather than fission, she still erects a structure that, like Lacan's, relegates siblinghood to a position mediated primarily by a single parent. By insisting on both parents as the source of the sibling bond, however, Sophocles establishes the tie between siblings as always in excess of either the mother-child or the father-child relationship. The sibling relationship is multiply mediated through a set of nuanced differentials: resemblance between siblings, differential resemblance to each shared parent (biological or otherwise), and not-quite-duplicated positionality. The relationship with the sibling in turn mediates and refracts relations both within and beyond the family from a perspective not quite same and not quite other. This multiplicity of vectors erects siblinghood as a paradigm for the overdetermined embedment of the subject in the networked world, marking the insufficiency of theories of identification based on a linguistics of substitution.[23] Sibling logic resists the metaphoric economy of castration, instead following the model of synecdoche, a part-whole relationship that does not entirely relinquish the object it moves away from. Irigaray has provided a powerful critique of Lacan's phallic, metaphorical logic throughout her work and has argued for a feminine fluidity of metonymy, of two lips touching, of mother-infant proximity.[24] Naomi Schor has pushed on both Lacanian and Irigarayan readings to undermine an oppositional binary of metaphor and metonymy in favor of the detail, the part, the clitoris, and hence the synecdochal.[25] If we begin to interrogate the boundaries of the whole to which the part can refer, however, the synecdochal reveals a still greater potential. A detail, I argue here, is always a shared component, although a subject is unique in its combinatorics. Synecdoche thus works as a link. Since the detail is not only or always the sexual organ, we can use synecdoche to move beyond the impasse of Irigaray's sexuation, the "irreducible difference, that which separates human being itself without a possible overcoming of this division."[26] This synecdochal logic of the sibling initiates a limping, forward propulsion into a transsubjective world. Even more powerfully than the matrixial proposed by Ettinger, the logic of the sibling fosters "jointness *with* a foreign world," a paradoxical cleaving of union and difference.[27]

Sibling love thus both evokes and revokes the narcissism onto which it is so frequently read. In an early work, Lacan interprets the initial relationship with the sibling as the "confusion of two affective relationships in this object, love and identification."[28] Steiner similarly remarks, "It is here, and here only, that the soul steps into and through the mirror to find a perfectly concordant but autonomous counterpart. The torment of Narcissus is stilled: the image is substance, it is the integral self in the twin presence of another" (*Antigones*, 17). And yet, as this very formulation makes clear, the self-lover who moves from the position of Narcissus to that of the sibling lover has only exchanged one dilemma for another—the reflection in the water will never become embraceable, but the sibling will always defy all pressure to be a manifestation of the self. Indeed, far from re-presenting an integral self with which to identify, the sibling hinders the illusions of both autonomy and integrity. The structure of sibling relations in *Antigone* is much closer to Ettinger's transsubjectivity than to mirroring. As Lacan himself notes in one of his few references to Antigone's sister, "The Greek term that expresses the *joining* of oneself to a brother or sister recurs throughout the play, and it appears right away in the first line when Antigone is speaking to Ismene" (*Ethics*, 255, emphasis mine).

PLURAL SUBJECTIVITY AND INCESTUOUS DESIRE

Mark Griffith notes some of these joining expressions in his philological gloss to *Antigone*, line 523, "Ant. coins special terms to describe her own φύσις ['nature'] and its inextricable involvement in 'family': συνέχθω ['to join in hate; to hate together'] and συνφιλέω ['to join in love; to love together'] are found nowhere else in classical Greek."[29] In addition, variations on the word *philia* are used in abundance throughout *Antigone*. Mary Whitlock Blundell defines one axis of tension in the concept of *philia* as its broad trajectory from the narrowest point—the self-love from which Aristotle derives it – through parent-child and fraternal relations and finally to the widest extreme—"broad racial ties."[30] The other axis of tension is in its affective tenor. *Philia* can designate the tie of duty, the emotion of love, or even erotic passion. While some commentators have noted a certain coldness in Antigone's obsession, her declaration, "I shall lie by his side, / loving him as he loved me" ("φίλη μετ' αὐτοῦ κείσομαι, φίλου μέτα") (*Antigone*, line 73), introduces the unmistakable aura of the incest that haunts the family.[31] The declaration of desire, however, is also a statement of identification, as the sentence is a polyptoton, a trope in which different forms of the same word recur in a sentence. The sentence could be translated as "I will lie with him, a loved one with a loved one," so that the same word (*loved* or philos, here used as an adjectival noun) in different grammatical cases and genders refers to both Antigone and Polyneices.[32] Antigone thus occupies throughout her life the space where love and identification coincide, but which we can now reconceptualize as the shared space of transsubjectivity. Antigone's actions simultaneously express her desire and enact her membership in a family composed of the prematurely and tragically dead. To speak with Butler, "When she buries her brother, it is not simply that she acts from kinship, as if kinship furnishes a principle for action, but that her action is the action of kinship, the performative repetition that reinstates kinship as a public scandal" (*Antigone's Claim*, 58). And yet not only the ritual quality of familial care in her deed but the fact that it condemns her to an early death marks Antigone in her own eyes as a true member of her family. In other words, it is simultaneously in the illicit burial and also in her death itself that the public scandal of her incestuous belonging is revealed and performed.

Lacan goes so far as to read Antigone as the incarnation of "the pure and simple desire of death as such" (*Ethics*, 282). Following in the footsteps of Hegel, for whom the brother represents *"pure being"* (*Phenomenology*, 270, italics in original) and "an empty singular" (271), Lacan transforms Polyneices into the brother per se, a structural position stripped of all contingent traits (*Ethics*, 279). For Hegel, this structural understanding underlies ethical consciousness. While family is in general a natural relationship, it can attain to ethics by emptying itself of personal attachment: "the ethical connection between the members of the Family is not that of feeling, or the relationship of love" (*Phenomenology*, 269). Hegel's interpretation of Antigone as a defender of familial ethics thus precludes desire from Antigone's motivation. Such emotion—that is, the right to a "particularity of desire" (275)—is reserved for men, who can actualize their ethical consciousness in the political sphere and hence do not need to do so within the family. For Hegel, as seen in the epigraph to this chapter, the sibling relationship epitomizes *pure* and unerotic ethical commitments. Lacan adapts this *purity* into a designation for Antigone's unswerving adherence to the law of her own desire.[33] And yet this so-called desire has not migrated far from Hegel's understanding of ethical commitment. Lacan's Antigone also figures the ethical, and Polyneices is still a structural position rather than a beloved person in his particularity; he is stripped of all contingent traits, of all history. He is amalgamated into the pure signifier, the phallus itself.

This interpretation of Polyneices as an empty signifier is not justified, however, by Sophocles's text. Lacan and Hegel have crucially misread *Antigone* in order to distance desire, and especially female desire, from particularistic attachment. It is just such particularity that Antigone demonstrates and that Ismene not only demonstrates but also explicitly defends. Lacan describes Polyneices's importance to Antigone as "having been born in the same womb . . . and related to the same [criminal] father. . . . [T]his brother is something unique" (*Ethics*, 279). This claim to structural uniqueness is patently false. Antigone is one of four siblings born from the same womb and the same father—two brothers, both dead, and two sisters, both living as the drama opens—not to mention the half brother born from the same womb who *is* her father. As Butler illustrates, Antigone's care for Polyneices is already a repetition of her care for her father-brother Oedipus, whom in *Oedipus at Colonus* she also helps to his final resting place after serving as his guide while he ages (*Antigones Claim*, 58–61). Moreover, Polyneices and Eteocles are hardly irreplaceable in the Theban dramas taken as a whole.[34] Indeed, Oedipus describes them as replaced; having spurned their filial duty to their father, they have been replaced in caring for him by their sisters Antigone and Ismene, whom Oedipus thus calls "men" (*Colonus*, line 1368; see also lines 337–56). In a blatant transgression of gender norms, according to which women belonged exclusively within the household, Antigone has led her father around on the open roads of Greece, "a ready victim / to be seized and raped by anyone" (*Colonus*, line 752), as Creon makes explicit, while Ismene, traveling alone, has tracked the pair down on horseback to warn them of Creon's schemes.

That both women can serve as substitutes for both men reinforces the fact that Antigone's decision to sacrifice herself for Polyneices cannot be seen as an ecstatic attachment to the pure form of siblinghood but becomes in the course of the play the elevation of one sibling above another, of Polyneices over Ismene, and hence the expression of particular choice. The play opens with Antigone's invitation to her sister to join her in burying their brother. Their conversation makes liberal use of the dual, an antiquated Greek grammatical form uniting two objects, and is dominated by rhetoric that implies merging.[35] Once Ismene refuses to participate in her plan, however, Antigone reverses her rhetoric and labels Ismene a hated "enemy" (*Antigone*, line 94). When Ismene later attempts to join Antigone in blame and punishment for the burial, Antigone repulses her. Most dramatically, in her lament before dying Antigone calls herself "the last" of her line (line 895), effectively "annulling Ismene" (Steiner, *Antigones*, 278).[36] The results appear to have been lasting: Ismene not only disappears from the action of the play but also has remained hidden from the regard and notice of its readers and critics.[37] Antigone's disowning of Ismene as a consequence of Ismene's choices and actions speaks directly against Lacan's description of the emptying of "historical drama" (*Ethics*, 279)—of everything one might have done or lived through—from Antigone's consideration of family belonging.[38] The slippage in Lacan's theory between the symbolic function of the phallus as the empty signifier and its continued sexual reference has led him to discount Ismene. But this should not be a problem as long as the love of two sisters for each other is after all and obviously, as Goethe has laid out for us in his conversation with Eckermann quoted in the epigraph, unerotic, *geschlechtslos*. Except that here it is not.

Ismene's passion for Antigone in Sophocles's drama should make visible the particularity of feminine desire, both her own and that of Antigone for Polyneices. Ismene's attachment to her sister reaches the same transgressive heights as Antigone's passion for her brother Polyneices. This passion is expressed in words that mimic almost exactly Antigone's words to and about Polyneices in *Oedipus at Colonus* and *Antigone*. Although the action of *Antigone* occurs chronologically last among Sophocles's three Theban tragedies, this play was written first, followed by *Oedipus the King* about fifteen years later, and finally by *Oedipus at Colonus* after an additional twenty years and just before Sophocles's death.[39] Since Polyneices's death in the attack on Thebes is foretold in *Oedipus at Colonus*, Antigone's attempt to convince him to abandon the fight is thus simultaneously a repetition and a foreshadowing of Ismene's identical attempt to dissuade Antigone from her doomed actions. When Antigone cries out to Polyneices, "Then I am utterly / destroyed if I must lose you" (*Colonus*, lines 1442–43), she repeats and foretells Ismene's anguished question to her, "What life is there for me, once I have lost you?" (*Antigone*, line 548). Left behind by a beloved sibling determined to die, both Antigone in *Oedipus at Colonus* and Ismene in *Antigone* describe themselves as "sufferer[s]" (τάλαινα) (*Colonus*, lines 1427, 1438; *Antigone*, line 554). Ismene's distress at abandonment evolves into her jealous reproach to Antigone for choosing the dead brother over the living sister, "You have a warm heart for such chilly deeds" (*Antigone*, line 88). Even Antigone's declaration of love for Polyneices discussed earlier, "I shall lie by his side, / loving him as he loved me" (lines 73–74), is almost immediately echoed by Ismene's reassurance that, however irrational Antigone's actions, "to your loved ones you rightly remain a loved one" (τοῖς φίλοις δ' ὀρθῶς φίλη) (lines 98–99, translation mine).[40] We here have a second case of polyptoton that doubles the first, as both instances of "loved one(s)" are again indicated by different cases of *philos*, so that the designation becomes a chain binding together multiple signified persons. Ismene's use of the plural here for Antigone's loved ones conveys a wide sense of a living and loving community that contrasts with Antigone's singular forms. Finally, Antigone's "Brother, how can anyone / *not* mourn, seeing you set out / to death so clear before you?" (*Colonus*, lines 1439–40) paradoxically expresses a mourning that will apply equally to her in the earlier (later) play.

While Butler comments on the aptness of this last line as a prefiguration of Antigone's own eventual progress toward death, she ironically overlooks the reiterative structure of the relationship between Antigone and Polyneices, on the one hand, and that between Ismene and Antigone, on the other. Butler's failure to notice Ismene is an outgrowth of centuries of disregard.[41] Luce Irigaray sums up the consensus opinion of Ismene as stereotypically feminine in contrast to Antigone, recounting her "weakness, her fear, her submissive obedience, her tears, madness, hysteria."[42] Reflections on Ismene center on two actions that appear contradictory—her attempt to dissuade Antigone from the burial, which has long been misunderstood as cowardice, and her attempt to join Antigone in death, regularly labeled hysteria. The two moments, however, are entirely complementary consequences of her devotion to her sister, as she first tries to save Antigone from death and then attempts to share this death, reenacting Antigone's behavior toward Polyneices. Once we recognize the hysteria and submissiveness as misreadings, what remain are Ismene's articulations of the intense particularity of love and the acceptance of difference within love. Ismene not only assures Antigone that love rightly persists through disagreements (*Antigone*, lines 98–99), she also counters Creon's structural understanding of the family in her attempt to dissuade Creon from executing Antigone, the fiancée of his own son, Haemon. Creon, foreshadowing Hegel, articulates a strictly substitutive position, declaring, "There are other fields for [Haemon] to plow" (line 569). Ismene's response, "Not with the mutual love of him and her" (line 570), values the personal over the universal.[43] By repeatedly situating Antigone in a loving community, Ismene also challenges Lacan's tendency to see Antigone as isolated at the limit of the human, a tendency that Antigone herself embraces. Ultimately, however, Ismene is unable to perform this repositioning on herself. Just as Antigone will choose death with Polyneices over life with her fiancé Haemon and with Ismene, Ismene herself will volunteer to die, unable to envision any life without or beyond Antigone. "What life can be mine *alone* without her?" (line 566, emphasis mine), she cries to Creon, intensifying with the addition of the word *alone*, her earlier lament to Antigone (line 548).

Ismene's desire thus reiterates Antigone's as self-constitutive and all-consuming. It has not helped critics understand Antigone's desire, however, because it has been utterly invisible. Even Butler's mining of the implications of *Antigone* for queer readings is circumscribed in this peculiar omission by a received structural limit to desire that Butler herself has worked to destabilize. This limit is certainly heteronormative, but it also renders femininity contingent and masculinity normative while reinforcing an understanding of ethical feminine desire as impersonal and structural. At issue within this desire is the discreteness of the subject, the imaginary status of understanding "I" as wholly distinct from "you." Françoise Meltzer has read Antigone as encapsulating a foreignness in excess of all such boundary drawing, whether around the subject, between genders, or between life and death. Desire, then, "may be the flight from self-consciousness," the flight from bounded subjectivity.[44] The desire among Ismene, Antigone, and Polyneices, I argue, makes visible the construction of a joint subjectivity through multiple differentials. Their relationships reveal a splinter in the imaginary—a constant, pointed reminder of the necessary incompleteness of the mirror stage, and an ever-present link with others. The itch to remove the splinter and allow an isolating skin to grow can be seen motivating the theoretical move from Antigone to Oedipus, to which we will return in the epilogue. In a milder form, however, it already inhabited the analyses of *Antigone* and the multiple iterations of sibling attachment in the long nineteenth century that invoked exclusively brother-sister relationships, which we will explore throughout this volume. The theory of gender complementarity provided a means to recuperate wholeness by moving from a singularity to a dyad.[45]

Butler has worked to counter this isolation by linking the inner and outer relationality of the psyche. She has identified that part of the self for which one cannot account, that part that renders each self non-self-identical and non-coherent, as the trace of our origin in intersubjectivity, "the way we are implicated, beholden, derived, sustained by a social world that is beyond us and before us."[46] This early and formative relationality is the opaque kernel rendered inaccessible to self-accounting by entry into the symbolic. And yet we must not forget that the relational does not end with this entry; the symbolic itself is assumed, conveyed, and constituted by relationships and remains a jointly occupied relational web. The limits to self-knowledge diagnosed by Butler are thus effects not only of a past, primal relationality but of the ongoing openness of subjects.

Antigone herself has frequently been proclaimed a hero of self-knowledge, in contrast to Oedipus, whose story, Hegel tells us in his *Aesthetics*, is primarily concerned with fate and unconscious action.[47] It is, of course, precisely the specifics of his foundational relationality that remain hidden from Oedipus. But Oedipus is not entirely without knowledge; after all, he solves the riddle of the Sphinx. August Wilhelm Schlegel recognized the irony that "to the very Oedipus who solved the riddle of the Sphinx relating to human life, his own life should remain so long an inextricable riddle."[48] Schlegel misidentifies the source of this irony, which he locates in the frequent human failure to apply general principles to oneself. Oedipus's life, however, absolutely fails to conform to the general principle of the riddle. If the human being, to answer the riddle alongside Oedipus, is what walks on four legs in the morning, two legs at noon, and three legs in the evening, Oedipus's humanity is in doubt. Exposed on a mountaintop by his parents as an infant, Oedipus was pierced through the feet by a leather thong to keep him from crawling. He reacts to the discovery of his transgression, moreover, by blinding himself and resorting to a walking stick, a third leg, in the prime of his life. Oedipus's problem is not the inability to apply general knowledge to the specific case of himself but the failure to imagine the violation of the norm that he embodies, the failure to recognize that some part of the human might lie beyond the boundaries of repeating normative structures.

Does Antigone truly represent a self-knowledgeable contrast, or does she resemble Oedipus in this failure? Hegel cites Antigone as an example of a premeditated breach of ethics (*Phenomenology*, 284). Lacan goes further when he reminds us, "One cannot ignore the meaning of the kind of self-knowledge attributed to [Antigone]" by the chorus (*Ethics*, 273). Lacan and Hegel are quite possibly influenced by Hölderlin's idiosyncratic translation of *Antigone*, in which the chorus states, "Dich hat verderbt [d]as zornige Selbsterkennen";[49] this German line could be rendered in English, "Enraged self-knowledge has been your undoing."[50] Grene's more standard translation of the Greek here, supported by Griffith, reads, "It is your own self-willed temper that has destroyed you" (σὲ δ' αὐτόγνωτος ὤλεσ' ὀργά) (*Antigone*, line 875). Kathrin Rosenfield, while pointing out the philological legitimacy of Grene's formulation, nonetheless believes that Hölderlin (and by extension Hegel and Lacan) grasped a crucial element of Antigone's character through this rendition ("Getting Inside," 120). It is doubtless true that Antigone knows the law of Creon against which she has transgressed, but does she therefore know her crime? Should we judge her static, self-assured, and death-directed self-interpretation as self-knowledge? Thinking of Butler, we might ask whether Antigone, with her insistence on family belonging, occupies a unique position of access to her own constitutive relationality and hence surpasses the normal limits of self-knowledge. I would like to resist such a reading; Antigone's justification of her crime as a necessary defense of family and divine law is an interpretation of the demands of relationality, not a transparent reading of it. Moreover, like Oedipus, she fails to imagine a way to deviate from a received pattern, although in her case that pattern is itself deviant. Antigone's interpretation is contested not only by Creon but also by that figure so defamed by criticism—her sister, Ismene. And it is Ismene whose name in fact means "one who knows." But what does she know?

Ismene's response to Antigone's demand that they bury their brother is not a recourse to a normative female role held in common with their sex, as is frequently claimed, but instead follows from an alternative interpretation of their family's history, a history that separates the sisters from other women.

> O God!
> Consider, sister, how our father died,
> hated and infamous, how he brought to light
> his own offenses; how he himself struck out
> the sight of his two eyes;
> his own hand was their executioner.
> Then, mother and wife, two names in one, did shame

> violently on her life, with twisted cords.
> Third, our two brothers, on a single day,
> poor wretches, themselves worked out their mutual doom.
> Each killed the other, hand against brother's hand.
> Now there are only the two of us, left behind,
> and see how miserable our end shall be
> if in the teeth of law we shall transgress
> against the sovereign's decree and power.
> You ought to realize we are only women,
> not meant in nature to fight against men,
> and that we are ruled, by those who are stronger,
> to obedience in this and even more painful matters.
>
> (*Antigone*, lines 49–64)

While the passage concludes with a reference to their sex, the claim does not affirm the appropriateness of gender norming but rather foretells the violent consequences of resisting force. The more significant and less frequently cited portion of the argument precedes these lines. Antigone believes that she has been born into a cursed family whom she is fated to join in a tragic death that will enact and confirm her identity. Ismene introduces a different interpretation, stressing in every line the self-willed actions that initiated and implemented the catastrophes. It is with their own hands that the family members become their own executioners. Moreover, each destructive action annihilates a multiple rather than a singular existence. Goldhill notes of this passage, "Nouns, verbs, and adjectives are all in the dual form.... [I]t makes the brothers a natural pair, like hands or eyes" ("Antigone," 152). These dual units are themselves not closed to further linkage, however; Ismene reads the two brothers as a double unit and the two sisters as another, so that the units double each other. Ismene thus constructs a complicated denial of fatalism. Knowledge here is also acknowledgment and acceptance of the fact that narratives of self are always simultaneously narratives of many. There is agency, and yet no individual wields it or suffers its consequences alone.[51] Antigone acts in togetherness with a dead brother, and her actions will exert a similar pressure on her remaining sister.

And yet the sisters are by no means identical. While Antigone insists uncompromisingly on the universality of her principle of action, Ismene recognizes the differentials that create particularity, a recognition that pervades her emphasis on differing interpretations as well as her reassurance to Antigone of love even in the face of disagreement, and her insistence to Creon that Antigone cannot be replaced in Haemon's estimation. The sisters constitute two nonidentical but transsubjective links in an alinear, synecdochal network. Ismene's plea makes clear that no singleton can exist in this family, that no *one* can be left behind—with or without a condemnation from Creon, Ismene will not survive her sister.[52] Their jointness is by no means naively celebratory but instead stresses vulnerability. And so Antigone is not entirely wrong to pronounce herself the last survivor of the family of Oedipus—her death wraps up within itself Ismene's end as well.

KINSHIP, THE FOREIGN, AND THE COLLECTIVE

The synecdochal intertwining exemplified by these siblings extends subjectivity beyond the immediate family and into the polis and the political. Rosenfield diagnoses a taint of incest that pervades the entire Theban polis through the autochthonous and fatherless origins of its first generation ("Getting Inside," 114).[53] Thebes combined the two common Greek myths for the origin of cities: autochthony and colonization. Cadmus, of the royal family of Phoenicia, founded the city of Thebes with the help of the Spartoi, warriors who sprang from the ground as offspring of the teeth of a dragon Cadmus had slain (*Spartoi* means "sown"). While the familial elements of the Greek polis are therefore blatant, autochthony in Thebes is highly ambivalent. The first act of the Spartoi is to attack one another in a mass fratricide. After the battle, only five remain to found the city with Cadmus and his wife Harmonia. Instead of combining harmoniously the ruling passions of Harmonia's parents, Aphrodite and Ares, however, the city oscillates between forbidden extremes of love and strife.

The sibling bond, however fraught, is not only the foundation of the polis but also its justification. Cadmus originally left Phoenicia in search of his abducted sister, Europa. Unable to find her, he turned to the oracle at Delphi for a new purpose and founded Thebes on the oracle's instructions.[54] Thebes itself is therefore an ersatz for a sister, though no neatly metaphoric one; Thebes does not leave its antecedent—the sibling—behind but rather transforms and carries it within. In the shadow of Thebes, siblinghood must be read simultaneously as the bond to a home and the impetus to leave it. If, to paraphrase Hegel from the epigraph, the sibling is a mirror in which one becomes conscious of oneself through becoming conscious of an other to which one is not linked as cause or effect, as parent or as child, it is not, however, a mirror that reflects back an image as a unitary ego ideal; instead it casts a hybrid image forward into an uncertain, interpenetrating world. The sibling relationship as thus revealed becomes constitutive not only for subject formation but also for the human ability to explore territory, build cities, and come to terms with the foreign. This same constellation of theoretical anxieties elevated the sibling relationship, and Sophocles's *Antigone* with it, to a central position in the European imaginary during the nineteenth century, an age of cultural encounter, as we will see throughout this book. Juliet Mitchell locates the sibling experience at the heart of all group psychology (*Siblings*, 12), speculating, "Does not the early sibling experience of creating 'otherness' out of sameness underlie the instant 'otherness' of race, class and ethnicity, an otherness that renders invisible the sameness that then has to be rediscovered at a greatly sophisticated level?" (48). We can, however, also turn this formulation around to see in the sibling experience a recognition of the coexistence of degrees of sameness and otherness. In chapter 5 we will turn to the repercussions for race and ethnicity inherent in the construction of difference and recognition of differential difference in sibling terms.

"If psychoanalysis had taken Antigone rather than Oedipus as its point of departure," Miriam Leonard notes, sounding the theme that has become common in the last fifteen years, "it would have given rise to a more explicitly politicized understanding of the psychoanalytic sexual subject."[55] Within the word *politicized*, of course, we view the ripples of the ancient *polis*, and yet the connotations of this political form are lost if we think of the polity in which Antigone resides as merely a *city*, or a *state*, the two most common translations of *polis*. Hegel read Antigone into an ethical narrative that is bound up with the political, but he did so in such a way as to exclude her as a woman, and to exclude women as such from a public sphere envisioned as universal. For Hegel, the sister serves as the bridge that enables the brother to cross—as she cannot—from the sphere of divine law to that of human law, moving from nature to spirit, from family to the political.⁵⁶ In the *Phenomenology*, Hegel denotes the public sphere occasionally with the word *Regierung* (government) and more often with the word *Gemeinwesen*.⁵⁷ In his standard translation, A. V. Miller renders *Gemeinwesen* as "community," and yet a better approximation might be "commonality"; Hegel's term indicates the being that is shared in common, rather than the messy community of particular beings.⁵⁸ In his analysis, Hegel thus reenacts the failed attempts of Creon to segregate the political from the personal and to reinterpret the polis as the set of collectivized subjects of government. Hegel is askew, for the polis is not a realm of commonality—of a universal, common voice—but a community of members who are, among other things, related to one another as a family is, tied together by the same bonds of *philia*. This idea was hardly unknown to Hegel, who closely observed its resurrection in neighboring revolutionary and postrevolutionary France.

In a story that has become legendary, days before Napoleon's troops marched into Jena in 1806, Hegel sent most of his manuscript of *Phenomenology of Spirit* out of the city to his publisher, carrying the final pages with him in his pocket as he fled his apartment before the advancing troops.⁵⁹ Hegel's debt, but also his aversion, to the contract theories that influenced the revolution are apparent already here and crystalize in the later *Philosophy of Right*.⁶⁰ Hegel's *Gemeinwesen* develops certain elements of the civic sphere common in contract theory from Locke through Rousseau and even informing the work of fellow idealist Johann Gottlieb Fichte. And yet where these earlier theories erect conduits that channel familial sentiment into civic society, Hegel sets a boundary around the family that is manifested by the sibling, "the limit at which the self-contained life of the Family breaks up and goes beyond itself" (*Phenomenology*, 275), but which the sibling as sibling cannot cross. Rather, the sister provides an avenue for the brother to leave the family through her recognition and become something more than brother outside its realm, as well an avenue for him finally to return to the family, through her reclaiming of his no-longer-civic corpse. It is no accident that Hegel restages the conflict in Sophocles's play to pit family, in the person of Antigone, against state, in the person of Creon; *fraternité* must not leak into the *Gemeinwesen* but rather remain safely segregated in a discrete sphere. By positioning Creon against Antigone as state to family and male to female, Hegel erects a barricade of his own—against the legacy of the French Revolution. Reducing the polis to government pares away the ancient resonances of relatedness within community that had become increasingly germane in the burgeoning nationalist discourse of his own time.[61] As Stuart Elden has argued, the "*polis* functions both as a place, a site, and the embodiment of the humans within it, close to our modern notion of community" ("Place of the Polis," 2). Moreover, "The Greek *polis* was founded on kinship" (30) and united by an origin myth that depended equally on kinship whether grounded in autochthony or in colonization.

A dual origin in autochthony and colonization differentiates Thebes from Athens, the city of Sophocles and the location where his dramas were enacted. Froma Zeitlin has identified the Thebes of tragedy as an uncanny other of Athens, a site where the home polis of author and viewers "acts out questions crucial to the *polis*, the self, the family and society" ("Thebes," 144), "without any risk to its own self-image" (145). As Nicole Loraux notes, Athens, as opposed to Thebes, considered itself a fully autochthonous city and used the myth of fraternal autochthony to derive its democracy. Indeed, Athenians believed the resulting sameness of citizens in their polis "protected the Athenians from the great familial crimes which are represented in tragedy" ("Born of the Earth," 53), as from "oligarchies and tyrannies" (22). The equality of democratic citizens was not conceived in the abstract terms of rights before the law but in terms of the homogeneity of kinship (52). But while Thebes may present a dark contrast to Athens on this point, it is hard to agree with Zeitlin's premise that the contrast makes Thebes a *safe* locus for experimentation. Rather, Thebes exposes what lies latent and threatening in the fabric of the community: the fraught relationship of community to place, the fragility of belonging, and the excess of desire and of hate that inhabits and indeed necessitates the bonds of duty.

These issues become explicit in the famous choral ode in *Antigone* known as the "Hymn to Man." The chorus locates the essence of humanity in a dual origin—both journeying and working the soil.

> Many are the wonders, none
> is more wonderful that what is man.
> This it is that crosses the sea . . .

> He it is again who wears away
> the Earth, oldest of gods, immortal, unwearied,
> as the ploughs wind across her from year to year
> ...
> So he brings the horse with the shaggy neck
> to bend underneath the yoke;
> and also the untamed mountain bull;
> and speech and windswift thought
> and the tempers that go with city living
> he has taught himself.
>
> (*Antigone*, lines 332–41 and 350–56)

This ode performs a delicate feat, identifying a human essence while acknowledging as fundamental the human ability to learn, change, and exist both communally and politically, that is, within history. In his interpretation of *Antigone*, Heidegger focused on this ode to illuminate a critical constellation of identity and foreignness, of journeying and dwelling at the heart of the play.[62] His readings nonetheless, as both Cornelius Castoriadis and Stathis Gourgouris separately argue, perform a violent misreading of the tragedy by excising the political and historical concerns that structure these terms for Sophocles. Heidegger posits as universal the isolated human, alienated from self, home, and community, while the ode projects this specter as the nightmare limit of human experience, a limit catastrophically arrived at by Antigone and Creon both but countered by human self-creation as communicative and communal.[63] In their obsessive adherence to their own law, Creon and Antigone each violate what Gourgouris refers to as "a differential autonomous plurality" that "does not only constitute in itself a political subject, but ... also embodies the subject of a specific politics, a politics which demands a collective knowledge emerging out of a shared commitment to self-interrogation" ("Does Literature Think?," 141). What is required for an ethical and successful political community is thus a recognition of and respect for difference, combined with self-analysis. I am sympathetic to Gourgouris's argument, and yet I would counter that Antigone's flaw does not lie in her law's singularity because her law arises in fact out of a shared subjectivity. Her flaw consists instead in her failure to recognize her ultimate belonging to the living community, as a result of the lack of self-interrogation he diagnoses.

Heidegger goes on to expand his misreading of humans in Sophocles as essentially isolated individuals to the scale of whole peoples. Writing in 1942 in the midst of Nazi genocide, Heidegger reaches the false, as well as culpable, conclusion of a fundamental incommensurability of peoples present in Sophocles and in the world. In fact, with their emphasis on both journeying and dwelling, Sophocles's Theban dramas undermine not only the boundaries of the subject within the community but also the boundaries of the community itself, that is, they undermine the possibility of erecting belonging that evades foreignness. The stranger Oedipus who journeys to Thebes and wins the hand of its queen discovers only too late that he has returned to his most intimate point of origin; Polyneices, who attacks Thebes with an army he has become related to through marriage, is nonetheless a native son; and Creon, who casts out and condemns his niece and son's fiancé Antigone, finds that he has brought ruin and destruction to his own most immediate family. Perhaps one could claim that Thebes is cursed by its lack of purity—its mixing of the foreign Phoenician with the indigenous soil—but the chorus instead claims it belongs to all human being both to journey and to bring forth from the soil and thus locates Thebes at the core of the human.

A litany of lost siblings: Europa—lost to her brother Cadmus; Oedipus, Polyneices, and Eteocles—lost to Antigone and Ismene; Antigone and Ismene—lost to each other; Ismene—lost to the critical tradition; and the sibling per se—lost to psychoanalytic and critical theory. What we have lost with them is a notion of shared subjectivity, interconnectedness, similarity in difference, and group belonging outside the stark terms of otherness versus introjection. Embracing the logic of sibling action would make possible a politics that discards dichotomies in favor of differentials, one that recognizes the subject within networks and vice versa. In the chapters that follow, *Sibling Action* makes a case for valuing rather than suppressing the lack of integrity of terms in collective systems.

Antigone and Ismene are the last descendants of Cadmus and Harmonia through the male line the Greeks considered direct descent. Yet their eradication cannot be read as the purging of a catastrophic foreign element from an otherwise indigenous population. The sacred spring at which Cadmus arrived after his wanderings was the *Ismenos*, and the dragon he slew and whose teeth generated the Theban population was the *Ismenian* dragon (*Antigone*, lines 1123–25). In a Möbius movement characteristic of Thebes, *Ismene* oscillates from progenitor of the autochthonous Spartoi to childless terminus of the colonizing lineage, encapsulating the entire history of Theban tragedy.[64] Ismene may represent a certain failure to mark the world with one's own hands, but she alone in her family escapes using those hands as tools of murder or suicide. Instead, she leaves behind a disposition worth pondering. The hero of Greek tragedy, as Gourgouris eloquently states, "is hardly a model but a problem, an agent of ambiguity and uncertainty about himself and all others" ("Does Literature Think?," 129). In a world that acknowledges agency, but even more strongly in a world of shared agency and plural subjectivity, a problem well illustrated offers the potential for learning and changing, for breaking cycles of repetition without relinquishing particular passion. That at least is what Ismene knew, and what she attempted to convey to her sister. This book is an attempt to hear her.

PART II

FRATERNITY AND REVOLUTION

Though our brother is upon the rack, as long as we ourselves are at our ease, our senses will never inform us of what he suffers. They never did, and never can, carry us beyond our own person, and it is by the imagination only that we can form any conception of what are his sensations.
—ADAM SMITH, *THEORY OF MORAL SENTIMENTS*, 9

[Natalie:] My life is so intensely bound up [verbunden und verwurzelt] with that of my brother, that when he suffers pain, so do I, and the joys he experiences are what gives me happiness. I can truly say that only through him have I learnt that the heart can be moved and uplifted, that there is joy and love in the world, and feeling which brings contentment beyond all need.
—JOHANN WOLFGANG VON GOETHE, *WILHELM MEISTER*, 330

. . . 'twas her brother's face—
It might resemble her—it once had been
The mirror of her thoughts, and still the grace
Which her mind's shadow cast, left there a lingering trace
—LAON REFLECTING ON HIS OWN FACE; PERCY BYSSHE SHELLEY, *LAON AND CYTHNA*, LINES 1680-83

In one plight entwined, three loving
Siblings, we will sink united
—FRIEDRICH SCHILLER, *THE BRIDE OF MESSINA*, LINES 2529-30

[I]n a word ... incest ought to be every government's law—every government whose basis is fraternity.

—DONATIEN ALPHONSE FRANÇOIS, MARQUIS DE SADE, PHILOSOPHY IN THE BEDROOM, 324

The Consanguine Family: It was founded upon the intermarriage of brothers and sisters, own and collateral, in a group.

—LEWIS HENRY MORGAN, ANCIENT SOCIETY, 395

2

THE SHADOWS OF FRATERNITY

The official website for the European Union explains its choice of the final movement of Beethoven's Ninth Symphony as the EU anthem, which sets to music Friedrich Schiller's "Ode to Joy," in terms of universality: "The poem 'Ode to Joy' expresses Schiller's idealistic vision of the human race becoming brothers—a vision Beethoven shared.... **There are no words to the anthem.** ... In the universal language of music, **this anthem expresses the European ideals of freedom, peace and solidarity.**"[1] While this exegesis leans on the universality of a musical language, it also acknowledges the role of the lyrics of Schiller's ode in the choice of the anthem. The connection between brotherhood and freedom comes across as self-evident, enshrined as it is in the familiar slogan of the French Revolution, *Liberté, Egalité, Fraternité*. Like the ode and the French rallying cry, however, the EU web text manifests a series of paradoxes in the understanding of fraternity. Europe, it seems, in spite of its status a politically discrete unit, here becomes the symbol of the universal. In fact, the website calls the symphony the anthem "not only of the European Union but also of Europe in a wider sense." In addition, the language of *brotherhood* is gendered in Schiller's German just as it is in the English description presented earlier. As a reading of Schiller's ode, moreover, rather than a piece of political rhetoric, the passage leaves much to be desired. The actual text of the ode raises serious doubts about just how universal the celebrated "brotherhood" was intended to be. While toasted as universal in the first verse of the ode, brotherhood is also revealed to be a "Bund," a band, a privileged circle: "Seal the holy circle tighter [Schließt den heiligen Zirkel dichter],"[2] the ninth verse counsels. Among its first exclusions, unsurprisingly, are potential sisters; "Whoever has won [errungen] a lovely wife" (1:169) has completed one of the qualifying experiences for membership. The women themselves therefore lurk at the margins of the club and the political fellowship it represents, beyond its boundary and yet constitutive of belonging in their very subordination to a victorious suitor.[3]

The paradox we have arrived at may seem expected, familiar, not to say tiresome already: fraternity cannot serve as a symbol of inclusive politics when it blatantly excludes half the population. Such a problem may also look easy to solve—with a simple switch to the gender-neutral language of universal siblinghood. But, in fact, the fraught ideal of fraternity reveals a series of ideological struggles within the three terms of the revolutionary motto.[4] The concept of liberal democracy, a political organization governed by liberty and equality, was built on a foundation of newly conceived subjects. As *free* individuals, such self-interested subjects could be assumed to compete and create strife in the polis. The rhetoric of *equality*, on the other hand, draws subjects rather toward similitude, challenging the growing validation of the individual. The byword of universal brotherhood serves to balance these opposing forces. On the one hand, it tempers self-interest by evoking the affective investments of individuals and redirecting them toward the general good; on the other, fraternity alleviates the abstract similitude of equals through a dynamic that preserves particularistic desire safely by projecting it, and hence its objects, into a realm outside politics. Fraternity thus creates the domestic sphere and polices its boundaries, channeling the exclusive ties of passion and kinship toward the nation, a sublimation of eros noted by Sigmund Freud eighty years ago in *Civilization and Its Discontents*. And yet the very rhetorical force of national fraternity derives from the acknowledgment of the particularistic, familial passion it excludes from the civic sphere. The metaphorical structure that links men as similars through the experience of shared civic space and similar disposition of erotic energies on distinct objects maps onto another generator of fraternity, namely, genealogy. The creation of brothers-in-law related through marriage becomes over generations the projected familial relationship of a nation. The universal moment in the rhetoric of fraternity thus underwrites and is underwritten by the exclusivity both of family and of a nationhood that bleeds into race.

Annette Timm and Joshua Sanborn declared in 2007 that "fraternity... is the least studied of the great principles of the French Revolution."[5] This lacuna is still evident in spite of excellent work since the 1980s by Carole Pateman, Juliet Flower MacCannell, Lynn Hunt, Jacques Derrida, and Timm and Sanborn themselves.[6] The studies that do exist focus predominantly on France. As evidenced by the Schiller ode, however, it was not only in France that *fraternité, fraternity, brotherhood,* or *Brüderlichkeit* took hold as an ideal principle. Indeed, it structured thinking about the problematic relationship of politics and domestic ties throughout Europe. As I will argue in this chapter, the sister serves two crucial purposes in the fraternal nation: first, *as* sister, generating an egalitarian love that serves as a model for affective commitment without particularity, and second, as the erotic object of particular preference that confers individuality on the male subject. Such individual choice remains safe for the republic only insofar as its object is removed from the political sphere and sequestered. This structure precludes both subjective passion on the part of women and their civic participation. The exclusion of women, in other words, cannot be wished away as an inessential afterthought in the history of civil society, nor can it be corrected by an adjustment of language alone. As Derrida notes:

> The fratriarchy may *include* cousins and sisters but, as we will see, including may also come to mean neutralizing. Including may dictate forgetting, for example, with "the best of all intentions," that the sister will never provide a docile example for the concept of fraternity. This is why the concept must be rendered *docile*, and there we have the whole of political education. What happens when, in taking up the case of the sister, the woman is made a sister? And a sister a case of the brother? This could be one of our most insistent questions, even if, having done so too often elsewhere, we will here avoid convoking Antigone, here again the long line of history's Antigones, docile or not, to this history of brothers that has been told to us for thousands of years.
>
> <div align="right">(<i>Politics of Friendship</i>, viii–ix)</div>

I too will avoid more than a hint of Antigone in this chapter, though the concerns unearthed in the previous chapter will resurface here. What, then, is the political education that can render the concept of fraternity docile? The epoch offered two answers to this question, I argue: an aesthetic education, which I will discuss in this chapter, and an economic education, which will be the topic of the following chapter. The aesthetic education amounts to an education of desire, most explicitly in Jean-Jacques Rousseau and Schiller but also evident in Immanuel Kant's exclusion of the erotic from notions of beauty. In the aesthetic and the political cases, the brother-sister relationship constitutes the fraught boundary of the two-sphere system, marking both its porousness and its fragility.

This chapter outlines the segregation of spheres symptomatic of modernity from a new perspective, tracking the role of the sibling relationship as the fault line between them. If the sibling bond figures the end of primogeniture and patriarchy, however, its function in the fraternal nation is split between egalitarian and particularistic affect. Friedrich Schiller did not touch on this constellation only in his famous ode but also and at more depth in his little-read drama *The Bride of Messina* and in his treatise *The Aesthetic Education of Man*. The education that raises aesthetics above desire renders sister-love the paradigmatic affective relationship of the polis but always fails to dissolve the erotic fully. Universal siblinghood leads, as Marc Shell has noted, to only two sexual alternatives: celibacy or incest.[7] The Marquis de Sade ventures to suggest, via a prorepublican pamphlet embedded in *Philosophy in the Bedroom*, "in a word, that incest ought to be every government's law—every government whose basis is fraternity."[8] As we will see at the end of this chapter, a generation after Schiller's and Hegel's attempt to expunge the erotic from the civic, Percy Shelley would instead embrace passion as the foundation of democratic, fraternal politics in a radical reformulation of civic participation, of desire, and of the family.

POLITICAL AND CONJUGAL CONSENT

The integration of family models into state politics and vice versa is hardly surprising. As Lynn Hunt notes, "most Europeans in the eighteenth century thought of their rulers as fathers and of their nations as families writ large" (*Family Romance*, xiv). This correspondence was the result of centuries of political theorizing that established an analogous relation between the *pater familias* and the head of state, the "father of the people."[9] In his *Patriarcha* (1680), Sir Robert Filmer laid out the natural-law argument for sovereign monarchy as based on the natural authority of fathers over their children, authorized by the Bible. Using the Bible as support for monarchy is actually quite difficult—Filmer has recourse to only two divine commands, which he must creatively combine: first, God's punishment for the Fall subjugates Eve to the rule of Adam, which is less obviously paternal than conjugal,[10] and second, there is the "Decalogue . . . which enjoins obedience to kings . . . in the terms of 'honour thy father'" (*Patriarcha*, 11). It is not the modern reader alone who notices the curtailing of the commandment in question. Eighteen years after its publication, John Locke retorts, "I hope 'tis no injury to call an half Quotation an half Reason, for God says, *Honour thy Father and Mother*; but our Author contents himself with half, leaves out *thy Mother* quite, as little serviceable to his purpose."[11] Locke is interested in the omission not primarily because he feels mothers have been unduly slighted but because he wants to undermine the derivation of political power from the biblical stricture by pushing the argument ad absurdum. In disputing Filmer's natural law theory and insisting on consent as the foundation of governance, Locke thus finds himself also grappling with the status of women.[12]

Unlike Filmer, then, Locke adamantly divides political from domestic, or so-called conjugal, power. The nature of this divide is not as clear as he might like, however. While claiming a contractual basis for political life, Locke does not dismiss the importance of natural law entirely. Indeed, natural law lays the foundation on which the contract is built. Most famously, Locke begins with ownership of one's own body and the labor it performs, from which he derives the rights of property and of employment contracts. Applying labor to raw materials, such as farming the land, extends those rights to the products produced by it and, less intuitively, to the land itself, which is also "improved" by cultivation (*Two Treatises*, 287–91). One could easily imagine deploying Locke's property argument through a long-established analogy between land and women, produce and progeny, to arrive at the subjection of children as products and of wives as fertile ground. Sophocles's Creon was already repeating a commonplace, albeit crudely, when, in *Antigone*, he referred to women as "fields... to plow."[13] Locke firmly rejects such an analogy, however. Instead, he begins by applying natural law within the family only to the raising of children. The duty of children to parents, which applies equally to both mother and father, Locke argues, derives from the mutual obligations of parents to raise and protect their children until they reach adulthood, at which point the exception to the equality of individuals ends (303–6). More remarkably, Locke extends the logic of the argument to the marriage itself, which he suggests "might be varied and regulated by that Contract, which unites Man and Wife in that Society, as far as may consist with Procreation and the bringing up of Children" (322). In other words, he recognizes marriage law as cultural and open to a fair degree of flexibility. Like civil law, however, marriage law rests on a natural foundation, not only that of procreation, but also of male superiority—in cases of disagreement between spouses, the determination "naturally falls to the Man's share, as the abler and stronger" (321). While Locke argues heatedly against Filmer's conflation of conjugal and political power, then, he establishes analogous systems in the two spheres—the political enters into and governs marital relations to a large extent, just as the natural grounds politics. And consent is the lynchpin of both relationships.

Carole Pateman has argued that the inclusion of consent in marriage law among contractarians is both a sign of hypocrisy and a screen for the violation of their own doctrines in this case.[14] While the public sphere is called political and becomes subject to a political discourse, the domestic sphere, sequestered in a sleight-of-hand whose political nature is obscured, is defined as outside of politics and hence immune to political rights (esp. *Sexual Contract*, 10–11 and 93–94). Pateman diagnoses this division as a move necessary to reconcile equality among men with a retention of male sexual privilege. The imputation of the contractual form of consent to marriage thus disguises the violence of conjugal power relations. I would like to introduce another motivation for the division at the heart of liberal civil politics, however. If women are constructed as less rational, less morally guided, and unable to bear the obligations of citizenship in precisely the ways that Pateman illustrates (esp. *Disorder of Women*, 1–29), this construction is based neither on the structure of female bodies or female minds claimed by the contract theorists themselves nor solely on the wish to retain male privilege diagnosed by Pateman but is also a reaction to the double-edged challenge posed by the inequity of desire, on the one hand, and the assimilatory pressure of the social order, on the other.

The eighteenth-century emphasis on fraternity highlights the question of where affect fits into a contractual relationship at precisely the period when norms shifted the basis of conjugal matches to emotional inclination, bringing the same constellation of affect and will to bear in the family. Rousseau, infamously the least egalitarian of contract theorists in the realm of gender, nonetheless requires consent from both parties for a valid marriage. And yet marriage would seem to breach the parameters of a contract. Contracts are based on reason, while the demands of the passions amount to an internal slavery. Rousseau insists of slavery and of tyranny, "To say that a man gives himself gratuitously is to say something absurd and inconceivable. Such an act is illegitimate and null, if only for the fact that he who commits it does not have his wits about him."[15] Things get much more complicated, however, when it comes to love. Rousseau's fictions revolve around love because of its presumed risks to both the individual and the social order. In love, the frank, hearty, and independent Emile becomes what no tyrant could legitimately make him—a slave.[16] The only way to protect civic order from the caprices and tyrannies of slavery is to keep this slavish portion of life segregated from the civic order, Rousseau is convinced.[17] While both men and women succumb to a form of slavery in passion, their subjection is not to be considered equal.

> While giving man inclinations without limit, [God] gives him at the same time the law which regulates them, in order that he may be free and in command of himself. While abandoning man to immoderate passions, He joins reason to these passions in order to govern them. While abandoning woman to unlimited desires, He joins modesty to these desires in order to constrain them.
>
> (Rousseau, *Emile*, 359)

Men have law, reason, and self-government. They can therefore also be trusted with the communal government of the state. Women have only two natural and opposed inclinations—desire and modesty. The way women balance these drives can be influenced by education but does not amount to reasoned self-government. Unable to govern themselves, they can hardly be trusted to participate in the collective self-government of the state. Indeed, without reason, it is questionable whether they possess even the ability to consent validly to the social contract. It is precisely the ability of Emile to understand the precedence of his collective duties over his passion for Sophie that elicits her acquiescence to a marriage proposal that takes the form of an acknowledgment of subordination. Foreshadowing the division between universal (male) humanity and the particularity of women in Schiller's ode, Emile declares to Sophie, "You can make me die of pain, but do not hope to make me forget the rights of humanity. They are more sacred than yours. I will never give them up for you." To which Sophie responds, "Be my husband and master" (441).

The undermining of reason in women, however, has consequences not only in the civic realm, which is therefore denied to them, but also in the sexual realm. Rousseau explicitly recognizes the repercussions of depriving women of the capacity for consent, and hence for refusal. He declares rape a fiction, a function of male gullibility (360). "The freest and sweetest of all acts does not admit of real violence," Rousseau assures us.[18] Suspended between two urges, his ideal woman after all cannot consent to satisfy desire without a reprehensible breach of modesty and must therefore refuse in words and actions even when desiring, even when willing, to proceed. Rather than committing violence against a woman's modesty by pressing for explicit consent, men must read women's consent from the subtlest signs. Such consent is an enslavement acquiesced to—exactly what he claims is impossible politically.[19]

> To win this silent consent is to make use of all the violence permitted in love. To read it in the eyes, to see it in the ways in spite of the mouth's denial.... If he then completes his happiness, he is not brutal, he is decent. He does not insult chasteness; he respects it; he serves it. He leaves it the honor of still defending what it would have perhaps abandoned.[20]

As Pateman has noted, theorizing the woman as unable to consent in the sexual realm undermines any potential female political participation, while theorizing the woman as unable to consent to the political contract renders her sexually vulnerable and sexually passive (*Disorder*, 75–77). G. W. F. Hegel, although himself an opponent of contract theory, declares in a quite Rousseauian vein, "But because it is only as a citizen that he is actual and substantial, the individual, so far as he is not a citizen but belongs to the Family, is only an unreal impotent shadow."[21] This impotent shadow is paradigmatically the woman.

The inner contradictions of such a system within a rhetoric of equality were seized on even in Rousseau's own time, not only by feminists such as Mary Wollstonecraft but also by that mocking critic of the Enlightenment, the Marquis de Sade.[22] In *Philosophy in the Bedroom*, Sade delves explicitly (in all senses of the word) into the sexual mores that accord with a democracy. Sade's Dolmance agrees with Rousseau's depiction of love as enslavement (286) but offers a far different solution to the problem. The political treatise he reads in a brief respite between orgies equates "exclusive possession of a woman" with the "possession of slaves" (318). The pamphlet not only recommends the abolition of marriage and the establishment of public houses for orgies but advocates a law requiring universal submission to any solicitation of sex. "All men are born free, all have equal rights" (318), the treatise declares, and foremost among these rights is the right to sexual enjoyment of another. The treatise goes some way to making its argument equivalent for both sexes, condemning the control of wives by their husbands, and including houses to satisfy the lust of the female sex, "ardent like *ours* but in a quite different way" (318, emphasis mine). In the end, however, the idea of equality falls by the wayside.[23] Where Rousseau dismisses the possibility of rape by claiming that women are strong enough to prevent it, Sade's pamphlet-writer denies the criminality of rape by claiming that women's *inability* to prevent it demonstrates the natural legitimacy of men's use of violence in attaining sexual fulfillment (319).

Not surprisingly, Sade does not focus on consent in his vision of republicanism, and indeed in Deleuze's words he "heaps derision on the principle of the contract," but he does bring a manner of liberty, equality, and fraternity in line with his vision of sexual libertinism.[24] Reversing Rousseau's emphasis on ascertaining paternity, Sade's pamphlet declares uncertain paternity and an entirely public and communal upbringing ideal for "a republic where every individual must have no other dam than the nation, where everyone born is the motherland's child" (*Philosophy in the Bedroom*, 321). Even more important than obscuring the father is excising the mother, the target of Sade's most virulent reprisals.[25] Belonging to the mother country alone, children will truly be raised with the fraternal affection celebrated by the revolution.

> Do not suppose you are fashioning good republicans so long as children, who ought to belong solely to the republic, remain immured in their families. By extending to the family, to a restricted number of persons, the portion of affection they ought to distribute amongst their brothers, they inevitably adopt those persons' sometimes very harmful prejudices.[26]

The paradox of fraternity as a national ideal crystalizes here, as Sade's pamphleteer advocates the transference of affection from "family" to "brothers," employing the latter familial term as a universal while importing the valence of the particular.

Where then do sisters come in? Are they "family" to be discarded, or are they "brothers" to be embraced? If extending to (potential) sexual partners the power to consent to, and by extension to reject, either laws or lovers, is disruptive to the ideal republic, then the sister perhaps unexpectedly gains a paradigmatic status. Sisters, after all, are born rather than chosen. Although their emotional attachment occurs within the problematically exclusive grouping of the family, its lack of selectivity introduces a universalizing quality that would seem to reinforce the notion of a safe, egalitarian love. This is precisely how Hegel envisioned the sister, as we saw in the previous chapter. Erecting the brother-sister relationship as a model for love relations in a republic inevitably ricochets back on the sibling model itself, however, which must then absorb the core problem of the unwilled passion inherent in eros.

SISTER-LOVE AND THE END OF PRIMOGENITURE

Jacques Rancière is only among the most recent theorists to expose the pleonasm of claims that the aesthetic is political.[27] The regime of the aesthetic emerges at the moment when art becomes political and yet autonomous, when artistic objects are seen to create a space within and around which community participates, so that, as Marc Redfield notes, its "disinterestedness is . . . more or less coeval with that of the nation-state, uncoincidentally."[28] It is clear why Schiller's *Letters on Aesthetic Education of Man* constitutes a primary example for Rancière and Redfield, as for Paul de Man before them. We must take into account, however, that *taste* was implicated in matters of public disposition in British writers such as Bernard Mandeville, Anthony Ashley Cooper, first Earl of Shaftesbury, and Francis Hutcheson before *art* became aesthetic. To follow Rancière's terminology, we could say that taste was already aligned with policing, with distributing and institutionalizing roles in society. Rancière claims that aesthetics became truly political in the late eighteenth century when it was implicated in staging the constant reconfigurations of enfranchisement between public actors. We might reformulate this claim by recognizing the *aesthetic* as the politically sanitized form of taste, separated from its erotic components, its interest in the body. It is no coincidence that only with Schiller does art entirely replace nature as the appropriate object of judgments of taste in philosophical considerations of the topic.[29] What happens in the realm of taste therefore directly parallels what happens in liberal theory: the political is shaped and defined through a politically expedient exclusion of the erotic that then structures the relationship between men in the civic, aesthetic sphere, and between men and women in a newly invented sphere designated as neither. I would argue that the limen—of the political as of the aesthetic—is constituted by the sister, who holds out the tantalizing hope that love and beauty can coincide with universality and hence slip back into the public sphere in purified form. In other words, as taste splits into the aesthetic and the erotic, the woman divides into the sister and the wife. Neither division can hold; the sister, always also a wife in a fraternal nation, fails to escape the erotic; she instantiates the paradox of the aesthetic, which is generated by and for the constitutive political need for a subject that transcends it.[30]

While Rancière focuses here on a beauty that allows sensory pleasure to be reconciled with reason, Schiller is also interested in a sublimity that facilitates the overcoming of natural imperatives. In his essay "Concerning the Sublime" (1801), he locates an essential human dilemma in the conflict between the freedom of will that is our unique quality and the necessity of death: "There is a remedy for everything, so goes the proverb, everything, that is, but death."[31] Sublimity lies in the subsuming of this contradiction; it is not an accident that so many of Schiller's plays revolve around a title character's epiphanic embrace of death. The line Schiller quotes may have become a proverb, but it has a distinct source, the famous choral "Ode to Man" in Sophocles's *Antigone*: "He has a way against everything, / and he faces nothing that is to come / without contrivance. / Only against death / can he call on no means of escape" (lines 358–62). *Antigone* also revolves around a willed death. But choosing death is not Antigone's only sublime overcoming of nature. She also relinquishes her role as wife and mother to embrace a common death with a brother.

Just a year after "Concerning the Sublime" appeared, Schiller published the drama *The Bride of Messina*, in which both methods of arriving at sublimity exist in relation to each other, but not in the same individual: it is a brother who chooses death and a sister who overcomes erotic desire. Indeed, I would argue that the undervalued *Bride of Messina* reveals that aesthetics and erotics require subjection to a constant process of segregation, not just to educate but to discipline the latter into the former in order to create an acceptable politics. The play contrives a radical aesthetic education, which brings a monarchy to ruin through the force of will of two siblings. While critics such as Peter Uwe Hohendahl and Gerhard Kaiser have long recognized that Schiller is experimenting with the patrilineal order, I believe he is engaged in a much more serious attempt to envision a *Brüderordnung* than either is willing to credit, not least because the notion of a distinct law of the sibling has lacked credibility in psychoanalytic discourse.[32]

The Bride of Messina was Schiller's most explicit attempt to create for the modern stage a drama that reproduced the effect of ancient tragedy. Schiller wrote to Goethe as early as 1797 that he hoped to find a subject for a tragedy of the same type as *Oedipus Rex*, so critics have read Sophocles's *Oedipus Rex* as the most significant intertext for *The Bride of Messina*.[33] Such critics are right to point out that the future king's abduction of his father's bride Isabella approaches the mother-son incest of the Greek tragedy as closely as modern sentiments allow. What has not been remarked on, however, is the disparity between *Oedipus Rex*, which sets the mother-son marriage in the center of the plot, and *The Bride of Messina*, in which this marriage is the prehistory of the story, the crime of the previous generation. Indeed, the protagonists of Schiller's drama are the fratricidal and incestuous offspring of the (step-) mother-son union, a plot that links them far more strongly to Sophocles's *Antigone*, Aeschylus's *Seven Against Thebes*, and Euripides's *Phoenician Women* than to *Oedipus Rex*.[34]

In *Die Braut von Messina*, not merely one but two brothers fall in love with the sister they have just met as a stranger.[35] The brothers in Schiller's drama, Don Manuel and Don Cesar, are the sons of Isabella and the now late King of Messina, whose recent demise has allowed the simmering rivalry of the two to erupt into a civil war. After a brief reconciliation brought about by their mother, Don Cesar discovers Beatrice, the woman he loves, in the arms of Don Manuel and murders him. Only later do Beatrice and Cesar learn that all three are siblings. The attempt of Cesar and Beatrice to renegotiate their relationship to each other and to their mother, after the murder and discovery of their relationship, illuminates a structural significance that cannot be subsumed under the parental.

The connotations of fraternity that elevated it to a rallying cry of the French Revolution include not only the note of affect but also the introduction of a new kind of leveling logic fundamentally at odds with monarchy. The dispute between the two brothers in Schiller's drama is never explicitly connected to a desire to rule; rather, their rivalry is existential in nature and most frequently circles back to competition over maternal love, which is throughout the play implicated in an inherently unequal rhetoric of political genealogy and natural hierarchy. "With what kind of parental reflections can the father or mother contemplate their younger offspring?" Thomas Paine demands of an aristocracy, "By Nature they are children, and by Marriage they are heirs; but by Aristocracy they are bastards and orphans."[36] Isabella's pleas to her sons to stop fighting rest on her description of the family as possessing a hereditary superiority to the foreign population over which they rule and a natural affiliation with each other.[37] While an ideal of equal maternal love informs Isabella's claims about her attachment to her sons, this ideal conflicts with the political reality of inherited rule that Isabella represents and defends, and indeed, it is an ideal she fails to live up to. While the brothers' attraction to Beatrice, then, cannot be separated from her resemblance to their mother, sibling love is structurally differentiated from parental love in the drama.[38] Cesar realizes this distinction when he shifts his need for love and validation from his mother to Beatrice with the words, "Stay, sister! . . . Mother may curse me . . . and all the world damn me! But you—do not curse me! From you I cannot bear it" (lines 2509–13).

If equal love from the mother is the frustrated desire of the younger son, love equally apportioned from the sister is claimed as a right in this age of inalienable rights. The fulfillment of this expectation generates a fundamental shift in the political landscape. Speaking of Manuel, whom Beatrice loved as a fiancé and has only just learned was in fact her brother, Cesar cries:

> Weep for your brother, I will weep with you
> And more still—I will avenge him! But do not
> Weep for your beloved! This preference
> That you give to the dead I cannot bear.
> This single comfort, the last, let me draw
> From the boundless depths of our misery,
> That he did not belong to you more intimately than I—
> For our dreadfully fulfilled Fate
> Levels our rights, as it levels our misfortune.
> In one plight entwined, three loving
> Siblings, we will sink united,
> and share equally the sad right to tears.
> But if I must believe that your grief
> Counts more towards the beloved than the brother,
> Then rage and envy will mingle with my pain,
> and the last comfort will depart, abandoning me to melancholy.
>
> (lines 2520–35)

The expectation of equality forms a sharp contrast not only with hierarchical, genealogical affection but also with the recognized partiality of erotic passion. Cesar's demand for a return of his love and his insistence on a sign of it from her distinguishes his actions as a brother from his imperious actions as a lover. In keeping with his prerogatives as a prince, when speaking to Beatrice for the first time, Cesar neither asked for any sign of love nor appeared unduly disturbed that she gave none. Beatrice's identical silence as a sister drives him to plead desperately for an acknowledgment of her love. When Beatrice, with great difficulty, manages to employ the egalitarian principle in applying, or at least in expressing, sisterly affection in her only address to him during the entire play, the effect is a reorganization of the political. Cesar does not alter his determination to kill himself after Beatrice's embrace. However, his suicide as vengeance on himself, as blood-feud, is transformed into an execution by the head of state (himself). Cesar here institutes a "distributive justice," which Thomas Paine diagnosed as incompatible with primogeniture under which subjects "begin life by trampling on all their younger brothers and sisters, and relations of every kind, and are taught and educated to do so" (*Common Sense*, 164). Cesar's emergence from aristocracy into the distributive justice of fraternity demands his self-subjugation to the rule of law and demolishes the legitimacy of a politics of genealogical privilege and the patriarchal rule, even if nothing in the play suggests that the Sicilians, for all their griping about capricious foreign rule, are ready to establish another form in its stead.[39]

Sisterly love—envisioned as will-governed affection—is the catalyst for the emergence of a new symbolic order based on equality and consent. And yet as the catalyst, the sister herself remains outside the reaction. And here we reach the crux of the sister's structural importance and paradoxical exclusion: given the new regime, her *consent* is sought; and yet in order for the power structure to survive, her consent is *required* and hence *demanded*. The judgment of an object as beautiful already entails renunciation of demands for possession, both Kant and Schiller agree. The sublime, however, goes one step further, demanding transcendence over nature. Erotic love is described in almost identical terms by all three siblings as a force beyond control and choice: "not freely chosen [nicht frei gewält]" (Beatrice, line 1039), "I have lost freedom and choice [die Wahl]" (Cesar, line 1154), "There is no resistance and no choice [keine Wahl]" (Manuel, line 1545). The repeated use here of *Wahl*—which means both choice and vote—is not accidental: this involuntary erotic passion is posited as contrary to political will, to republican choice. It is enslaving, Schiller agrees with Rousseau. It breaches the maxim of Gotthold Ephraim Lessing's *Nathan the Wise*, cited by Schiller as the opening to his essay on the sublime: "No human being is obliged to be obliged."[40] And so this despotism must be overthrown; Beatrice and Cesar must follow Recha and Curd, the siblings in Lessing's play, as well as Rousseau's Emile, in prioritizing the public good and in self-overcoming. They turn instead to a sibling love they evidently can *choose* and *will*, and which becomes then a model for the freedom of spirit over nature and instinct.

What the siblings lose by the exchange is the right to a particular desire. Even this loss is not egalitarian, however. Cesar's love only tentatively escapes its original erotic valence, while Beatrice's is forced to undergo a complete reversal, her passion not merely moderated but entirely excised. It is after all, the so-called capriciousness of female passion, "the disorder of women" to use Rousseau's phrase (*d'Alembert*, 109), that is perceived as the greater threat to the civic order. Hegel spells out this distinction quite explicitly when he permits men particular desire in their erotic choices because they achieve an ethical universality in the political realm. Women, on the other hand, cannot leave the realm of the household and must realize the limited universality allowed them within it by relating to their relations in a purely relational functionality. "In the ethical household, it is not a question of this particular husband, this particular child, but simply of husband and children generally; the relationships of the woman are based, not on feeling, but on the universal" (*Phenomenology*, 274).

Just as Cesar's suicide both demonstrates Schiller's sublime and also problematizes it, the love between brother and sister and between brother and brother that seems to inaugurate a more egalitarian society also threatens it. The familial bleeds into the political and the sororal into the erotic. Schiller opens the door, provisionally, to the construction of a *fraternal* social framework. We need to look elsewhere to find a more daring, if also flawed, exploration, an exploration of an order based on a sibling logic that attempts to extend both the ability to consent and the right to desire to brothers and to sisters alike.

GENERALIZING DESIRE

Schiller invokes Rousseau's turn toward affect on the title page of *On the Aesthetic Education of Man* (1795): "If it is reason that makes man, it is sentiment that guides him."[41] Schiller's treatise grew out of his disillusionment after the French Revolution's descent into mass bloodshed and terror,[42] but Plato's *Symposium* already posed the question about love that dominated its political valence in the eighteenth century and into the nineteenth, namely, whether the object of love is the particular or the general, whether love individualizes and hence distracts from the common good, or whether it abstracts good qualities and hence educates toward ethics.[43] In the *Symposium*, the character Socrates narrates his own instruction by Diotima, who described an ascending ladder of love, leading from love of physical beauty to love of the beloved's good qualities and finally to the pure love of the Good and the Beautiful. A strong contrast to this pedagogy of increasing abstraction also figures in the dialogue, however. The drunken Alcibiades arrives late on the scene and achingly confesses his long-standing love of Socrates, in all his peculiarities of body and personality,[44] a love conceived against cultural norms that called for the young, beautiful man to be the recipient rather than the instigator of such desire. Socrates, Alcibiades openly admits, has spurned his affections, attempting to educate him without physical intercourse. While Socrates therefore acts in a way consistent with his own understanding of progress toward the good, the efficacy of his pedagogy could be doubted. As his original audience would have been all too aware, Alcibiades went on to become the most notorious traitor of the ancient world, rotating his allegiance between his native Athens, its enemy Sparta, and Persia, the common enemy of both, more than once. One might argue that Plato chose Alcibaides for this role in order to impugn his particularistic view of love, proving indeed that virtue requires abstracting from the particular to the good in itself. On the other hand, it is possible to see Alcibiades's potential for political loyalty as a casualty of Socrates's personal rejection, a rejection that in turn prevents Alcibiades from attaching his own affect to a particular object, a particular polis. The treason of Alcibiades would hence reveal the faults of Socrates's program of education.

Rousseau in his novels and essays proclaims, like Socrates, the merits of an abstracting attitude towards love. In *Julie*, love is attached to an individual only insofar as the individual is representative. Julie and Saint Proux are both lovable to everyone, indeed to everyone of both sexes.[45] The secret to their lovableness is their absolute lack of individuality, their own tendency toward the universal. As their friend Edward reports to Julie herself:

> It is not that either of you has a distinctive character whose particular traits can be categorized at first glance, and it may well be that it was this difficulty of defining you that led a superficial observer to consider you as common souls. But it is just that which distinguishes you: that it is impossible to distinguish you and that the traits of the common model, at least one of which is lacking in every individual, shine equally in yours.... In your case... that sentiment was so intense that I mistook

its nature. It was not so much the difference of sex that produced this impression, as an even more marked character of perfection which the heart detects, even independently of love.

(161)

Even Saint Proux himself recognizes this universalizing character of his emotion toward Julie, addressing her, "O my wife, my sister, my sweet friend!" (122). While the narrative condemns Julie's father for refusing to consent to the marriage of Julie and her tutor and social inferior Saint Proux, the novel's central ethical conflict is the self-overcoming demanded of Julie, through which she should transfer her love from one good man to another, equally good one, in the process also fulfilling Hegel's later edict concerning women's duties in familial love. Rousseau himself, on the other hand, had a biography that complicates his pedagogical project by revealing proclivities in love that are surely more reminiscent of those of Alcibiades. As Bruce Merrill points out, Rousseau's *Confessions* present a very different aesthetic education from that advocated in *Emile* and *Julie*. Left to experience his own hardships, attractions, and disappointments without a kindly guide or tutor, and indulging in emotional and sexual libertinism, Rousseau nonetheless turns out more robustly invested in the public good than his more shepherded and malleable characters.

Social theorists throughout the eighteenth century and into the nineteenth took their cue from Rousseau's theoretical concerns rather than his biography, and the danger desire posed to a civic order was a common theme in writers from Schiller and Hegel, to Sade, to the British Jacobin novelists.[46] Universalizing love holds potentials perceived at the time as risks, however, as the passage from *Julie* illustrates. If the lovable consists merely of virtuous traits, then sex threatens to drop out of the equation, inviting a polymorphous and bisexual perversity. Moreover, if the traits that attract love are the same ones toward which each individual strives, all alterity is threatened. Incest, queerness, and solipsism are the related specters perceived as haunting the margins of the aesthetic state. They invite different conceptual solutions, however. The increasing naturalization of sexual differentiation that characterized the eighteenth century, and that Rousseau championed, served to direct love toward the newly "opposite" sex. And as long as such sex was posited as irreducible, the threats of solipsism and queerness also receded—

proper loving required the recognition of otherness. Within these parameters, however, incest becomes a still more present danger, as the ideal man and the ideal woman would resemble each other in everything that was not sex-specific, evoking the biologically impossible but imaginatively prevalent identical twins of different sexes.

In Schiller and Sade we have seen how sibling incest emerges from the attempt to mediate between the individual selectivity of passion and social equality. While Sade embraces, and Schiller recoils from, incest, both address it by curtailing choice through either the universalization of eroticism (Sade) or its taming (Schiller). It is not until a generation later, in Percy Shelley, that we see an attempt to imagine a more radically egalitarian society in which both men and women have the right to desire and the right to refuse. Reversing Rousseau, Shelley will focus on rape as a political crime, will ground legitimate government on passion, and will explode the ideology of domesticity, instead illustrating the interpenetration and mutual reinforcement of familial and political injustice.[47] Abandoning paternal or parental authority in any form, Shelley's sibling-lovers in the long poem *Laon and Cythna* initiate a peaceful revolution in political and social structures. Ultimately, however, Shelley's project still falters, and not only because the peaceful army of his democrats has no defense against massacre by the resurgent tyrant. Shelley's version of love struggles to retain any commitment to alterity. The message of communal love thus becomes an invitation to a narcissistic or even solipsistic realm, dependent on a form of emotional persuasion that shades into mental despotism. While Shelley departs radically from Rousseau, Schiller, and Hegel by insisting on the legitimacy of preference—male and female—in desire, the distinction begins to lose meaning in a world without personal differences. Shelley's own worries about establishing love as a relationship between similars were presaged by Edward's comments in *Julie*, where sexual difference falls away. As he worked on *Laon and Cythna*, Shelley also translated Plato's *Symposium* and wrote a treatise, unpublished in his lifetime, on, or rather *against*, "Greek love." While he classes incest among "artificial vices" and "crimes of convention"[48] to be disregarded, Shelley associates erotic love between men with "violation," "pain and horror," and "disgust."[49] What Shelley perceives as threat is, however, also opportunity, as Denis Flannery has recently noted in describing how "siblinghood can operate as a metaphor for the queer subject and queer practices," just as "to be someone's brother or sister is, in many ways, to be their embodied metaphor."[50] Upholding the sister's right to agency, activity, and desire, while allowing the brother to require rescue and submit passively to care in his poem, Shelley finds he has accessed a queerness in the sibling from which he seeks retreat. While that retreat leads in Shelley to solipsism, it leaves us nonetheless with a glimpse of the sibling's queer potential.

SPREADING THE LOVE: SIBLING INCEST AS MODEL FOR A JUST SOCIETY

Shelley composed *Laon and Cythna* in 1817 after returning to England from his elopement with Mary Wollstonecraft Godwin.[51] His notes in Mary Shelley's journal and his letters show his preoccupation during the trip not only with the course of the French Revolution itself—"the master theme of the epoch in which we live,"[52] as he wrote to Byron—but also with the disaffection and despair liberals felt in its aftermath.[53] While the poem celebrates the overthrow of an authoritarian government and explicitly champions liberty, equality, and fraternity, its theme is the inability of a single cataclysmic political event to change society. The foundation of any lasting improvement in social equality lies instead in thoughts, beliefs, and the quality of interpersonal interactions over generations. The odd title of the poem in its published version is significant in this context; *The Revolt of Islam* may at first glance allude to the revolt of the subjects of Ottoman rule, but the poem contains no references to the particularity of any religion.[54] The title renders a more productive reading if one considers the meaning of *Islam*, frequently discussed in England at the time, as *submission*.[55] While the success of the bloodless revolution in the poem is short-lived, the siblings die with the hope that *submission*, which Shelley interprets as voluntary subjection and resignation in the face of injustice, has begun to recede. The parallel between the role of the poet Laon and Shelley's hopes for his own poetic influence as "unacknowledged legislator" is unsubtle. While Laon's poetry may lay the grounds for revolt, however, it is his beloved sister Cythna's activities among the oppressed that foment the political movement. Indeed, given the poem's dedicatory love poem to Mary Shelley, it is not a stretch to assume that Percy Shelley meant his own infamously unconventional love life to serve as an extratextual supplement to the characters' interventions in the cause of liberty. Liberty for Shelley is not an abstraction but an interpersonal, affective activity. And poetry is not an abstract lesson but the basis of an aesthetic education of quite a different order from Schiller's, one that restructures passionate, affective relationships while maintaining them as the foundation of politics.

Accordingly, Shelley's poem illustrates the illusory nature of separate spheres, such that *political* interaction exists on a multidimensional scale from the violent breach of both will and desire, on the one hand, to the loving interpersonal correspondence of will and desire, on the other. The first extreme is exemplified equally by the tyrant Othman's rape of Cythna, enslavement of his populace, and annihilatory response to nonviolent revolt against his rule. Under Othman, the family unit is implicated in a policy of violence and oppression that legitimates its structure and yet violates its perimeter at will. Cythna describes a patriarchal society reminiscent of Filmer's, while reversing its valence:

> But children near their parents tremble now,
> Because they must obey—one rules another,
> For it is said God rules both high and low,
> And man is made the captive of his brother,
> And Hate is throned on high with Fear her mother,
> Above the Highest—and those fountain-cells,
> Whence love yet flowed when faith had choked all other,
> Are darkened—Woman, as the bond-slave, dwells
> Of man, a slave; and life is poisoned in its well.
>
> (*Laon and Cythna*, lines 3307–15)

Such a hierarchy of God over all, husband over wife, and parents over children is portrayed as a perversion of human brotherhood within which marital sex becomes poisonous violence at the site of life's origin. If Laon and Cythna find a way to reimagine these relationships, it is because of their own idyllic childhood, in which siblinghood serves as their only familial relationship. No father is mentioned in the text, and the mother appears only briefly and synecdochally in the first lines of Laon's account to the poem's first narrator, as "the fair breast from which I fed" (line 668), along with (other) natural objects such as brooks, vines, shells, and flowers. The verse disfiliates the children without negative affect, providing a form of mothering that is impersonal and universal.[56] Indeed, the word "mother" occurs most frequently in the text as a description of Mother Nature, who, unlike the nation as mother, allows all humans to become siblings. Cythna replicates this antiparental stance when she gives birth to a daughter after her rape by Othman. She remembers her child's infancy as a time when "We, on the earth, like sister twins lay down / On one fair mother's bosom" (lines 3021–22).[57] This fluidity of the family is first exposed and then utilized for communal purposes. Among the fraternal rebels, family terms circulate in ways that disrupt their hierarchical structure. They do, however, still attempt to capitalize on their affective power as signals of a special intimacy.[58] In a fascinating turn, Shelley also allows for a "brotherhood of ill" (line 3839) among Othman's army. Startlingly, sympathy, joy, and fraternity are available to all groups united in purpose, whether for good or for evil. Shelley thus recognizes that family roles are not only adaptable but available to exploitation. The distinction between the parties lies elsewhere, not in mere sympathy but in passionate love and the selflessness that accompanies it. If passion must be added to siblinghood to ground a just society, then incest is for Shelley, in quite another mood than for Sade, the watchword of republicanism.[59]

Laon and Cythna would seem to demonstrate the joint subjectivity of sibling logic discussed in the previous chapter. Certainly, they coeducate each other, becoming self jointly, and remaining inextricably intertwined. Inspired to sympathy by Laon's poetry, Cythna reciprocates by opening his heart to this emotion. This "true" siblinghood is contrasted with the projected fraternity Laon imputes to his earlier poetic encounters with an audience, when

> oft I thought to clasp my own heart's brother,
> When I could feel the listener's senses swim,
> And hear his breath its own swift gasping smother
> Even as my words evoked them . . .
> And the cold truth such sad reverse did seem,
> As to awake in grief from some delightful dream.
>
> (lines 812–19)

If Laon's first attempts to found brotherhood are abortive, he does eventually achieve a poetry that, with Cythna's help, extends passion into a wider social realm. This sympathy remains anchored in familial attachment centered on a similitude in which the physical and the spiritual merge. Laon may originally experience himself as the active principal in the relationship, but he eventually recognizes a reciprocity so strong that he later sees himself as a reflection of Cythna, identifying his reflection in a pool as

> . . . her brother's face—
> It might resemble her—it once had been
> The mirror of her thoughts, and still the grace
> Which her mind's shadow cast, left there a lingering trace.
>
> (lines 1680–83)

Where she originally registered "As mine own shadow. . . . A second self, far dearer and more fair" (lines 874–75), his sense of himself as *her* shadow has now become so strong as to cast doubt upon his very identity in her absence: "What then was I? She slumbered with the dead" (line 1684). This reflexivity clearly tends toward narcissism, but it has the oddity of being reciprocal. Moreover, the two do move through each other toward a wider sympathy and engagement with the world. By positing their love as the model for reciprocal affective union in the polis, Shelley, rather than welcoming alterity as Ismene had in the previous chapter, suppresses it. In his essay "On Love," written a year after *Laon and Cythna*, Shelley theorizes love not as an exclusive tie between two people but as the "bond and the sanction which connects not only man with man, but with every thing which exists" (*Poetry and Prose*, 473). And yet the outward movement demands no real encounter with difference. Instead, love is primarily self-centered and colonizing, an attempt to "awaken in all things that are, a community with what we experience within ourselves" (473).

Because Shelley's theme is not the overthrow of a regime but the revolution of an attitude and an affect, he must grapple with the subtle shadings of what constitutes consent in mental transformation. At what point might the persuasion effected by Laon's poetry and Cythna's oratory take on the form of the tyranny it hopes to dissolve? Laon's early attempts to reach a community through his poetry are firmly situated within the power structure of tyranny itself. His method is to take the physical suffering of the people, communicated to him in "sneers," "groans," wail[s]," and "innocent blood" (*Laon and Cythna*, lines 741–44) and to translate it into "words through which my spirit sought / To weave a bondage of such sympathy" (lines 802–3). There is a disturbing domination inherent in Laon's poetic eloquence, through which "all things became Slaves to my holy and heroic verse" (lines 933–43). Given that *bondage* and *slavery* are precisely the forms of evil against which Laon and Cythna's rebellion is directed, these descriptions raise uneasy questions about the possibility of liberty.[60] Unlike Laon, who "drew / Words which were weapons" (lines 841–42), however, Cythna's voice kindles love.

> . . . but when they heard
> My voice, they became silent, and they stood
> And moved as men in whom new love had stirred
> Deep thoughts. . . .
>
> (lines 3195–98)

Love here is no self-absorbed emotion but in turn inspires thought and action. As an answer to the problem of consent, love remains problematic, however. To serve as a guarantor of societal agreement, even the love Cythna inspires must rest on a universality that is portrayed as melting into sameness. Cythna appeals to shared humanity in her orations, telling the mariners, "we have one human heart—All mortal thoughts confess a common home" (lines 3361–62). Love among such similar beings remains a kind of projection and reflection.

Even within the fabric of this communal passion, Laon and Cythna form a core. Such a core is necessary in order to uphold the ethics of erotic choice for women as well as men that Sade, Rousseau, and Schiller discarded. It does, however, complicate Shelley's project of dismantling the public/private divide. Each sibling becomes politically active in the poem only in the belief that the other is dead. This belief calls forth a kind of phantom of the lost beloved in every stranger. Given the absence of evidence for the death of the beloved, this delusion appears to arise from the necessity of the lack as a motive for their own activity. Their reunion is accompanied by the explicit anxiety that they will fail in their social duties as a result. Cythna enjoins:

> . . . may all comfort wither
> From both the hearts whose pulse in joy now beat together,
> If our own will as others' law we bind,
> If the foul worship trampled here we fear;
> If as ourselves we cease to love our kind!
>
> (lines 2150–54)

The joy they feel in the merging implied by the common heartbeat carries with it the threat of loving "ourselves" more than "our kind."[61] The use of "ourselves" rather than "each other," as well as the singular form of "our own will" and "our kind," is striking, creating of Laon and Cythna a composite being. The risk inherent in such a position is enunciated as the temptation to extend that single will into a law for others. Only once the political activity is over, once the peaceful rebel army has been slaughtered, are Laon and Cythna, as the sole survivors, free to withdraw, both literally into a mountain hiding place, and also into each other. The first explicit sexual consummation of their love occurs in the literal vacuum of a civic space, an "Oblivion . . . of public hope" (line 2598). The fact that their fusion represents an escape not to a domestic, but to a wild, space does not ameliorate the problematic dynamic that excludes the source of passion from the civic, while demanding that passion permeate the civic.

At the end of the poem, Laon and Cythna sacrifice their united lives to become martyrs to the cause of liberty, publicly exposing the brutality of the joint forces of monarchy and religion and inspiring, they hope, a following generation to seek liberty. Although the lovers are in the Ottoman Empire, not in India, their fiery martyrdom on a pyre mimics *sati*, a custom that appalled European commentators even while it was celebrated as a symbol of the oneness of true love.[62] Their death enacts a symbolic cannibalism as "each upon the other's countenance fed / Looks of insatiate love" (lines 4580–81).[63] The desire of Laon and Cythna returns them to Freud's oral stage, which assimilates and annihilates the object through ingestion. While generally for Freud, subject- and object-identification remain distinct, he grounds all group identification on slippage between the two kinds of attachment, leaving all collective identity haunted by the threat of assimilation, of cannibalism.[64] Shelley tries to imagine a form of erotic interest that merges intensity of passion and the differentiation of preference with nonexclusive interpersonal respect and identification but finds himself trapped in the dynamic of the undifferentiated mass. While Shelleyan love opens the boundaries of the self to an other perceived as identical or to a whole perceived as a universal macrocosm of the self, a differential sibling logic would instead recognize difference in degrees and partialities. Such a sibling logic might do more than explode primogeniture or create of society a homogenous mass; it might allow us to reimagine identities as networks in flux, in action.

Shelley may reveal with particular force the way that the place of women in the fraternity lays bare the problem of all alterity in the republic, but he was not the first. When in 1783 Moses Mendelssohn published a treatise on the compatibility of religious diversity with nationality, he adapted the recognized model for managing individual and collective variety that marriage offered. Mendelssohn described the Jewish community through a conjugal metaphor, as "obviously a case of 'what God has joined together man may not tear asunder.'"[65] Jewish laws that prohibit marrying or even eating with non-Jews create of the Jewish community a marriage, legitimating Jewish difference as belonging to the private sphere, where it cannot threaten the smooth fabric of civic fraternity. Such segregation imperils the second valence of fraternity, however: the genealogical integration of bloodlines. Aware of the problem, Mendelssohn concludes his argument with a passage that interpolates his Christian readers as "dear brothers" (135), using the word "brother" no fewer than nine times in five pages (135–39). The term oscillates between its associations with "brotherly love" (136) and its designation of a "fellow citizen" (135), while evading the exchange of sisters Claude Lévi-Strauss will set at the foundation of society and to which we will return in the next chapter. Rather, Mendelssohn calls on fraternity to support an affective ethical commitment by sequestering that which divides men—whether religious differences or erotic preferences—but without enfranchising women.[66] The paring of the genealogical from the universal element of fraternity met stiff resistance, to which we will return.

The model of abstract aesthetic fraternity discussed in this chapter rested on the generalizing and taming of desire, but aesthetics was not the only solution posited to particularity in the polis. In the next chapter we will turn to an economic education that embraced difference and set it in motion as exchange.

3

ECONOMIZING DESIRE

The Sibling (in) Law

The French Revolution failed to establish a lasting republic, but it did cement a new age of economic and political relationships across Europe. Not only political enfranchisement but also a newly capitalist economy demanded the construction of a unit of agency. As we saw in the previous chapter, thinkers from Jean-Jacques Rousseau to G. W. F. Hegel, Friedrich Schiller to Percy Shelley, explored enfranchisement and agency in the context of desire and aesthetics and confronted the concern that a participatory civic society might require a collapse of alterity and particularity. An aesthetic education abstracting from desire was not the only solution theorized for this problem, however. This chapter will explore subjectivity and desire in the context of economic models such as those of Adam Smith, Friedrich Engels, and Karl Marx, models with lasting impact on the economic structures interwoven with the political and social organization of modern societies. Economic theorists and literary authors such as Johann Wolfgang von Goethe and George Eliot chose to experiment with models of subjectivity that might accommodate difference better than aesthetic models, coming to very different conclusions, however, about the threats, costs, and promise of such paradigms.

In the previous chapter we encountered fraternity as a mechanism for generating the affective commitment necessary to regulate a social system of equals. We should not be surprised, then, to find that political economics also worked through the figure of the sibling. The sibling is a boundary figure whose status as *similar*—not quite self and not quite other—must be negotiated in the construction of the person as an agent of exchange. The manner in which this negotiation is managed correlates with different conceptions of subjectivity and of political economy: merging with the sibling as an other half threatens to create a closed dyad incapable of interaction with the world; engaging with the sibling as a thread into the wider social fabric initiates a complicated realm of shared space or negotiated exchange; producing the sibling as a commodity alienated from the subject evacuates a liminal space by which an individual may be constituted, but at a cost; and finally, embracing the sibling as partially self and partially other opens the door to models of shared subjectivity and shared agency beyond an economy of exchange. Such constructions of the sibling were central to theorizing the modern economic subject throughout the nineteenth century and into the twentieth and remain central to the contemporary economic structures we have inherited.

The malaise of modernity that Friedrich Schiller hoped to cure with his aesthetic education amounted to a fragmentation both social and psychological. In his *Letters on the Aesthetic Education of Man* (1794), in the wake of the Reign of Terror that followed the French Revolution, Schiller argued that modern humans live restricted lives, in which each can learn only a small quantity of accumulated knowledge and live out only a fragment of potential human experience.[1] The aesthetic encounter lifts the individual above this splintered existence and facilitates an imaginary rapport with the plenary state of humanity. The practical import of such a moment lies both in the education of desire and in the communion it establishes above desires, building a bridge to the general interests that motivate the state, and thus also providing an antidote to the threat of the mob.

Schiller was not the only thinker obsessed with divisions in human knowledge and activity at the turn of the nineteenth century. Adam Smith famously begins the first chapter of *The Wealth of Nations* not with a critique but with a paean to the division of labor. Such fragmentation, Smith claims, serves not only the state, but also the individuals in it, as "it is the great multiplication of the productions of all the different arts, in consequence of the division of labour, which occasions, in a well-governed society, that universal opulence which extends itself to the lowest ranks of the people."[2] For Smith, society becomes well governed not by overcoming individual interests or particularity but by integrating activities and persons into a large and complex fabric. Smith introduces two universal instruments for this integration of differences—sympathy and trade—which he discusses in his two best-known works, *The Theory of Moral Sentiments* (1759) and *The Wealth of Nations* (1776). Only together do the two works provide an understanding of human community.

TRADING IN SYMPATHY

In *The Theory of Moral Sentiments*, sympathy for Smith is subject to an education that is antithetical to Schiller's aesthetic education, focusing on personal particularities and arising from the challenges of cohabitation. While sympathy is innate, it is not spontaneous but develops in childhood primarily through interaction with brothers and sisters, whose "situation renders their mutual sympathy of the utmost importance to their common happiness; and, by the wisdom of nature, the same situation, by obliging them to *accommodate* to one another, renders that sympathy more habitual, and thereby more lively, more distinct, and more determinate."[3] Unlike an aesthetic education, then, an education in accommodation functions through the acknowledgment of difference and the need for adjustment to promote the happiness of others. While this passage does not contradict the famous early line in the treatise that declares, "Though our brother is upon the rack, as long as we ourselves are at our ease, our senses will never inform us of what he suffers," it does place a burden of emphasis on the subsequent claim that "it is by the imagination only that we can form any conception of what are his sensations" (9).[4] The brother in this passage is chosen as the closest possible relative to the narrator and reader, presumed to be male. This closeness, however, is revealed by the later passage to be a matter of education, which then serves as the basis for ethical interaction throughout life. The sibling bond is dependent on proximity, not blood, and will be weak between family members raised apart, and strong between nonrelatives raised together. Even later in life, similar bonds can arise, such that "colleagues in office, partners in trade, call one another brothers; and frequently feel towards one another as if they really were so" (224). This brotherhood of financial partnership, we will see, is not always discontinuous from the first sibling impulses.

The experience of interdependence that allows such imaginative embodiment wanes with distance. At the point when personal acquaintance becomes tenuous, however, Smith saw systems of trade binding societies together in a vast fabric of commerce and joint labor. Smith figures that fabric through a humble one, namely, the common woolen coat. Over several pages of *The Wealth of Nations*, he spells out the variety of workers and kinds of labor required to produce such a commodity, moving outward from those directly involved with the ware, to those tending to the instruments of production, and to the needs of the first-order workers, until "we shall be sensible that, without the assistance and co-operation of many thousands, the very meanest person in a civilized country could not be provided, even according to, what we very falsely imagine, the easy and simple manner in which he is commonly *accommodated*" (23). At the basis of beneficial coexistence of siblings in the same house, and interdependence of inhabitants of the same sphere of civilization, lie the joint notions of interdependence and accommodation.[5] As Mary Poovey notes, harmony in the system of exchange does at a societal level what imaginative harmony between friends does at an individual level, namely, provides the support necessary for humans as dependent creatures.[6]

Smith dwells in *The Theory of Moral Sentiments* on first families—children, parents, and, particularly, brothers and sisters. Hardly a husband or wife is to be found. In *The Wealth of Nations*, by contrast, brothers and sisters disappear altogether in favor of wives and children who must be maintained and raised. If first families form a school for the intensification of our innate moral sentiments, second families become the appropriate economic units of a commercial society. Smith, however, seems unable to imagine, or uninterested in imagining, the transition from one form to the other, from sympathy to desire, or from sibling to spouse. A century and a half later, Claude Lévi-Strauss dedicated his anthropological theory to elucidating precisely this transition. Lévi-Strauss argued that the exchange of women for conjugal purposes that comprises the incest taboo is the constitutive moment that inaugurates culture. For Lévi-Strauss, the exchange, however indirect, of a sister for a wife occupies a unique position as the regulation and conversion of a natural function, namely, descent, into a social function, namely, alliance. It is only through the exchange of women that a group can maintain its existence as a group. If men married their own sisters, families would become monads, disturbing the harmony of the community. Even the constant exchange of sisters between two families could form a disruptive kernel within a social fabric.[7] The most smoothly operating societies therefore have complex general systems of marriage exchange, which demand trust and credit to facilitate circulation of the human currency in question. In such a society, "the group adopting it is prepared, in the broadest meaning of the term, to speculate." It is the acceptance of a capitalist system of credit and exchange that "brings in a profit, in the sense that with generalized exchange the group can live as richly and as complexly as its size, structure and density allow" (265).

Smith and Lévi-Strauss occupy a certain conceptual proximity, in that Lévi-Strauss adapts for his understanding of the very foundation of culture those theories of capital, commodity, free trade, and competition developed by Smith. Similarities extend only so far, however, since for Smith, the theory of capitalism applied not to the origin of culture but only to a certain contemporary phase in economic history. There is distance between them in another matter as well, namely, in their understanding of sibling relations. While Smith sees the sibling interaction as the root of affect in which all interpersonal relations are grounded, Lévi-Strauss converts the sister into a commodity—a good defined by the fact that its value to its producer (i.e., the first family) lies only in its exchange. In other words, while Smith sees value in the presence of the sibling, Lévi-Strauss sees value only its eventual absence. These two theorists of exchange form the historical bookends of what we could call, adapting Juliet Flower MacCannell's phrase, the regime of the sibling.[8] The way in which the value of the sibling defines or has the potential to redefine both systems of exchange and the production of the individual, particularly in relation to objects and commodities, will occupy us throughout this chapter.

In positing the exchange of sister for wife at the origin of culture, Lévi-Strauss was quite consciously rewriting the anthropological theory at the foundation of the modern discipline, while simultaneously claiming the mantel of its architect, the American anthropologist Lewis Henry Morgan, to whom he dedicates *The Elementary Structures of Kinship*. Moreover, by naming himself Morgan's intellectual heir, he is reclaiming the title from a more faithful disciple of Morgan's history of the family, Frederick

Engels, whose *The Origin of the Family, Private Property and the State* (1884) translates Morgan's materialist history of kinship into a critique of the capitalist family structure in stark contrast to Lévi-Strauss's vision.[9] We will return to Morgan and kinship studies in the epilogue. Here, however, we need to dwell briefly on the gulf between Morgan's and Lévi-Strauss's views of the originary kinship structures of human society. Morgan, and Engels after him, speculated that the earliest societies were constituted by single large families in which every generation functioned as both a set of brothers and sisters and a set of husbands and wives. In these group marriages, "brothers and sisters, male and female cousins of the first, second and more remote degrees are all mutually brothers and sisters, and *precisely because of this* are all mutually husbands and wives" (Engels, *Family*, 147). This "original communistic common household" (149), or "Communism in living,"[10] functioned as a joint unit of production and consumption within which everything was shared.

Like Lévi-Strauss, Engels saw the relationship between the sexes as a potential for intragroup conflict that needed to be overcome in order to form societies large enough to defend and provide for themselves. Each insists on a different "primitive" solution to this problem. While Engels posits group marriage, and hence equal and simultaneous *access* of men to women and of women to men, Lévi-Strauss argues for a specific type of exchange, namely, free *trade*—the ability of men to compete equally for women. In a system of exclusive relationships (whether of one or both parties), the incest taboo constitutes the lifting of a monopoly that would infringe on free trade. The free competition between merchants and the freedom of laborers to move between locations and professions were central to the healthy capitalist economy in Adam Smith. Encouraging circulation requires the leveling of privilege (Smith, *Wealth*, 135–59). Whereas Lévi-Strauss projects these conditions backward into marriage relations that instantiate culture, Engels perceives them as characteristic of the transformation of marriage in the age of capitalism. "To create such 'free' and 'equal' people was precisely one of the main achievements of capitalist production," Engels argues (*Family*, 186). Engels thus discovers a paradox in capitalist family relations, which both designate women as private property and also grant women the ability to enter into a contract as a consumer. Engels himself and early Marxian feminism in general focused primarily on the former component of capitalist family relations for the purposes of critique,[11] but it is the paradox itself that will concern us here, and which, I believe, is more productive for offering feminist alternatives.

In an insightful critique of Engels on the family, Alys Eve Weinbaum has focused on the text's blindness to domesticity as a form of oppression, and to domestic labor and childbirth as forms of production (*Wayward*, 110). Engels also engages the series of questions we saw already in the Marquis de Sade and in Percy Shelley. While Engels perceives the move to private property and the expectation of female faithfulness that accompanied it as a form of female enslavement, he adamantly refuses to countenance a return to what Morgan had called a society of group marriage between siblings or "Communism in living" (Engels, *Family*, 454). Engels's fears that incest would lead to health detriments in the species reflected the eugenic science of the time. But his main objection seems to lie elsewhere, in his discomfort with the idea of multiple simultaneous partners; he prefers a form of serial monogamy that continues, in his surface rhetoric, to allow for the ideology of romantic love between pairs and also enables the securing of paternity. In other words, Engels embraces a notion of sexual choice and sexual preference in accord with a view of the individual and of paternal inheritance patterns otherwise relinquished by socialist theory. Like Shelley, he must confront the problem of retaining such selective particularity within a social fabric constructed around equality. It is not surprising that in the same decade in which *The Origins of the Family* appeared, Edward Aveling and Eleanor Marx published a joint article claiming Shelley for socialism. The article dwells at length on the revolutionary tendencies of *Laon and Cythna*, which they recognize as inextricable from its critique of gender and of family relations. The authors embrace evolution more explicitly than Engels had, viewing as central to Marxism "the two great principles affecting the development of the individual and of the race, those of heredity and adaptation." It is therefore all the more notable that they do not shy away from the brother-sister incest motif of Shelley's poem, celebrating the pair as "equal and united powers, brother and sister, husband and wife, friend and friend, man and woman."[12] Neither side of the incest-eugenics debate, however, solves the problem of desire and particularity, from which socialism suffers every bit as much as republicanism. If Rousseau's Julie must learn to educate her desire to accord with social utility—and if her failure to do so fully is a sign of the impossibility of the democratic project—then the attempts of Engels and of Eleanor Marx and Aveling to maintain the individual regardless of sex as an agent of desire in the sexual instance reveals the paradox within the notion of consent as the basis of society. Sibling marriage may offer one, *communist* solution to this problem but only by revoking the right to particularity of desire, in the interest of revoking all particularity. Capitalism devised a different approach to the problem.

Having acquired "the right freely to dispose of themselves" in contract marriage, Engels makes clear, young people also acquired "the duty of lovers to marry each other and nobody else" (*Family*, 187). By the early nineteenth century, it had become positively disreputable to marry without love, and "on paper, in moral theory as in poetic description, nothing was more unshakably established than that every marriage not based on mutual sex love and on the really free agreement of the spouses was immoral" (188), even, and perhaps paradigmatically, within the newly formed bourgeoisie.[13] If love was required to drive marriage, however, marriage had not ceased to serve economic functions. The education of desire that has dominated the age of liberalism has not been a Schillerian aesthetic sublation but an economic molding. As Sharon Marcus notes in her study of women's relationships in Victorian England, desire is "a deeply regulated and regulating hierarchical structure of longing."[14] Economically and socially appropriate desire is a foundational product of capitalism. To discover how it was produced, we must bring into focus a long-overlooked element of the formation of liberalism, namely, kinship and, in particular, the sibling.

In spite of the large role played by siblings in his history of marriage, Engels experiences an odd amnesia that can also be seen in Smith before him and Lévi-Strauss after him, and he forgets that the first family does not dissolve upon the formation of the second. Meanwhile Gilles Deleuze and Félix Guattari, for example, follow Freud in forgetting altogether that the first family consists of more than father, mother, and child, that, in other words, brothers and sisters are also primal elements of first families. Smith's domestic sentiments do not vanish upon the building of economic networks, however, nor do Lévi-Strauss's sisters stop being sisters when they become wives. Rather, within an economic politics, the sibling is a site in which sentiment is produced and directed in ways that can advance particular configurations of business, capital, and subjectivity—or can resist them. It is for this reason that the *affective labor* recently recognized by the economic theorists Michael Hardt and Antonio Negri is not a newly significant element of the current financial system they call *Empire* but was crucially important to the formation of the bourgeois class.[15] Many of the various forms of immaterial labor Hardt and Negri identify—affective labor, information gathering, control and communication of knowledge—were performed in the long nineteenth century collectively by women within kinship groups, who were networked through letter correspondence, one of the major occupations of bourgeois women of the period. Child-rearing provided an affective education directed at allowing family businesses to grow while limiting risk through surveillance and the imparting of a sense of family obligation. This biopolitics was an integral part of the rise and maintenance of commercial and finance capitalism. While Michel Foucault uses the terms *biopower* and *biopolitics* in *The History of Sexuality* and in his lectures on the *Birth of Biopolitics* (1978–1979) primarily in relation to economic and military policies, he also reveals in the former work the emerging nuclear family as a mechanism for generating sexuality as an anchor of alliance and he recognizes the obsessive concern with incest taboos as a way of asserting the presence of law even in forms of power that fall outside legal jurisdiction.[16] The crux of this biopolitics, I would argue, was the domestication of the spouse, that is, the re-creation of husband or wife as a form of brother or sister constituted in negotiation with the boundaries of the incest taboo, which accompanied the transformation of ancien régime patriarchy into bourgeois fratriarchy. What I argue here is that examining this new regime of the sibling, which lasted about 150 years, also makes visible an unsuspected aspect of the ongoing construction of the subject and provides a site for reimagining its current boundaries and agency.

SIBLING NETWORKS AND THE MODERN ECONOMY

What Karl Marx called the "French bourgeois revolution"[17] illustrated the fusion of the political, the economic, and the psychological in constructing the ideology of the individual, autonomous agent. This autonomous individual, however, exists by suppressing awareness of the kinship and social networks that sustain it. It is not a historical coincidence that the individual, the domestic family, and the civic realm developed simultaneously. The individual is an optical illusion that appears to spring forward in space like the stairs in an Escher painting because other figures with which it is intertwined recede to form a background. The individual emerges when the fabric of society is folded to provide recesses around *him*. The novel, frequently said to have participated in the creation of an interiority that grounds the modern subject, is not only a site of emergence but also one in which the processes of subject formation can be interrogated or critiqued. This tension has inflected, in particular, the contested genre theory surrounding the purported *Bildungsroman*. Indeed, the history of the theory of this genre largely correlates with dominant theories of the individual. As one might expect, therefore, the novel credited with initiating the genre, Goethe's *Wilhelm Meister's Apprenticeship*, provides a complex staging of the personal, social, familial, and economic in relation to notions of subjectivity.[18]

Friedrich Schlegel first connected Goethe's *Wilhelm Meister* with the French Revolution in the Athenaeum Fragments, naming them, along with Johann Gottlieb Fichte's *Wissenschaftslehre*, the three greatest tendencies of the age, and identifying the novel as a kind of revolution in its own right in *Athenaeum* Fragment 216.[19] In the 1930s Georg Lukács argued for a still stronger connection between the novel and the French Revolution, insisting that Goethe's rejection of the methods of the revolution did not indicate "rejection of the social and human content of the bourgeois revolution. On the contrary."[20] Lukács read *Wilhelm Meister* as an attempt to envision the unfolding of the individual within bourgeois, capitalist society, an attempt that recognized its own necessary failure but wore an optimistic hue lent by the exuberance of the French Revolution. For Lukács the way out of this impasse would have been to replace the capitalist with a socialist revolution. Perhaps surprisingly, Friedrich Kittler in the 1970s built on Lukács's analysis, jettisoning the stress on humanism but still reading the novel as a recoding that participated in inventing the modern bourgeois family, and so a "cultural appropriation of a foreign revolution."[21] Rather than simply taking over the goals of a foreign revolution while rejecting its means, however, Goethe, I argue, confronts the Great Experiment of the age with a narrative of experimentation that grapples with fraternal and paternal economic, social, and psychological organization and tries to find a third way, a way to link them. *Wilhelm Meister's Apprenticeship* performs a series of trials in combining fraternity with authority, lineage with affinity, and cosmopolitanism with physical situatedness.

Kittler's work on Goethe appeared in the wake of the extremely influential history of the British family by Lawrence Stone, who argued that a reduced and consolidated nuclear family emerged out of the more expansive early modern household.[22] Kittler restricts this construct still further, however, focusing on the triangular constellation of father-mother-child, within which the father, having lost his role as educator, is a peripheral pressure on the maternal socialization of the child. The marginalization of siblings in Kittler's vision is so complete that he mistakes the makeup of Wilhelm Meister's family in the novel, claiming he has only one, insignificant sister, while Wilhelm actually has an unspecified plural number of siblings and more than one sister.[23] In fact, siblings form the central familial structure of the text. As Wilhelm travels away from his own family, joins and then leaves a theater troupe, is inducted into a strange secret society that convinces him to accept paternal responsibilities for a child who may be his son, and, finally, becomes engaged to an aristocratic woman he idealizes, the title figure stumbles repeatedly into networks of sibling relations.[24] The family Wilhelm marries into consists of four siblings—Lothario, Natalie, Friedrich, and the Countess—who raised one another in the absence of parents but with the help of an aunt and an uncle—the siblings of those missing parents, respectively. The leaders of the theater troupe are a brother-sister pair—Serlo and Aurelia. The incestuous parents of Mignon—Augustin and Sperata—are also siblings who have two additional brothers. Even the Abbé has an identical twin.

In fact, Kittler has given us a description not of the late eighteenth- and early nineteenth-century nuclear family, but of the Freudian family, which came to eclipse the role of siblings in theory throughout the twentieth century, and up until recent groundbreaking work that has reintroduced siblings to a number of fields. If this vision of the family in *Wilhelm Meister*—or in the late eighteenth century more generally—is distorted, then we also need to rethink the modern subject in its relationality. The correlation between the nuclear family and *Wilhelm Meister* has been challenged before now.²⁵ But we find, following recent work conducted by historians such as David Sabean, Leonore Davidoff, Christopher Johnson, and Margareth Lanzinger, that it is not only in the novel that we need to look beyond the familial triad, and even beyond the nuclear family.²⁶

Sabean and Johnson recently characterized the shift from father-son lineage to sibling-based kinship networks as the basis of social coherence at precisely this time. "Bourgeois class formation," they insist, "was cemented everywhere by connections of kinship, and the more relatives the merrier."²⁷ As both Kittler and Robin Tobin point out, the Latinate word *Familie* first came into wide usage in Germany in the late eighteenth century, replacing terms such as *Haus*/household, *Geschlecht*/stock, and *Weib und Kind*/wife and child, none of which carries similar connotations.²⁸ In English, the definition of the existing word *family* narrowed, slowly losing its reference to members of a household not related to one another by blood or marriage. At the same time, across Europe the word *generation*, whose definitions included "the set of people born in the same period," took on stronger connotations as a social collective with shared experiences.²⁹ In German, the word *Geschwister*, for siblings, gained visibility.³⁰ In English, where *sibling* is related to Old High German *sippe*, the phrase *sib group* referred to *all kin* throughout the nineteenth century, and *sibling* didn't develop to take on its current meaning until the rise of social anthropology and of genetics in the twentieth century.³¹ Nonetheless, brothers and sisters took on a crucial role in the nineteenth century in Britain as well as across Europe.³² The new sibling-based networks detailed by Sabean and Johnson allowed "kin-grids" (*Sibling*, 10) of affinity to replace lines of alliance and structured associations from businesses to "professions, government service—including the military—and intellectual and artistic circles" (13). These kin-grids enabled the rise of the bourgeoisie as the foundation of the new commercial and finance capitalism.³³ As discussed in the previous chapter, and not only in France, *fraternity* at the same time came to govern the new form of imagined community that became the modern nation. Family, society, and subject are mutually constitutive and thus mutually vulnerable. Goethe's novel, I would argue, grapples with what is at stake when this constellation is disrupted, and in fact this *stake* makes its own concrete appearance in the novel, in the form of a *tower*. The Tower Society, which regulates the lives of initiates, is most fundamentally an attempt to anchor within a certain familial institution—to stake, with Goethe's wonderful ironic touch—an emergent rhizomatic social network that has come to threaten, in his view, a certain kind of desired subjectivity.

Wilhelm Meister's Apprenticeship sets up a paternal ideology and a fraternal ideology as two poles between which it attempts to negotiate. On the one pole, paternity is revealed to be an artificial construct both projected onto nature and teleologically invested in the mechanized production of copies. We see this constellation modeled most clearly by a master of a group of tightrope walkers with whom the child Mignon first identifies the notion of fatherhood. One of the most effective performances of this troupe involves the exhibition of the children in ascending order of age, which is shown to correspond with skill. This powerful demonstration of teleological development represents the actual abuse of the children by the master as if it were an organic unfolding of a talent. A dance Mignon has learned to perform, the egg dance, for example, unspools "like a wound-up mechanism" (*Apprenticeship*, 64). The word for wound-up, *aufgezogen*,[34] echoes the word for "raised," *auferzogen*, and demonstrates the easy conflation of the two. The methods used by the tightrope director are extreme but its tendencies are by no means unique. Serlo's father was "convinced that a child's concentration was best aroused and maintained by beatings" (*Apprenticeship*, 160), and even Wilhelm's father acts "according to the principle that one ought not to let children see how much one loves them, or they will run rampant. One should appear stern while they are enjoying themselves, and sometimes spoil their pleasures" (8, trans. mod). Paternal education in the novel thus focuses on preventing deviation by combating both *pleasure* (*Freude*)—the heart of fraternity in Schiller's *Ode to Joy*—and *play* (*Spiele*). Play is an important term not only in Kant's theory of aesthetics as the "free play of the faculties" but also in natural history, where a *Spielart*, literally a play-type, indicates variation within a species, proof that reproduction is not mere replication.

If, however, Goethe is proposing a shift away from this teleological mode of child-raising, it is not clear what such a shift should be toward, or at what cost. The most explicit experience of a true republic in the novel ends, like its French counterpart, in violence, loss, and a reimposition of authority. A break-away theater troupe adopts "a republican administration" (*Apprenticeship*, 127), elects Wilhelm as its first director, establishes a senate, and, going beyond its French model, extends suffrage universally to both sexes. Wilhelm then convinces his "wandering colony" to travel along a route rumored to be dangerous (*Lehrjahre*, 585, my trans.). Almost immediately the troupe encounters the logical consequences of its new republican ideology in the form of a band of thieves who divest the troupe members of their private property and shoot Wilhelm in the shoulder. Perhaps the most significant result of the attack, however, is that a member of the troupe goes into premature labor and gives birth to a stillborn child (*Apprenticeship*, 137). The chaotic breakdown of the new republican troupe is a failure of friendship, a failure of democracy, and a failure of colonization, which cannot succeed after all without offspring. As so often in *Wilhelm Meister*, the characters have mistaken "games" [*Spiele*] (*Lehrjahre*, 577, my trans.) for "something really useful" (*Apprenticeship*, 127).

The speculative nature of lineage, a recurring theme in the novel, repeatedly transforms an uncertain paternity into a metaphorical fraternity. This dynamic is clearest in the relationship of Wilhelm to Felix, who may or may not be his son. At the moment when Wilhelm, acting like a traditional father, attempts to make a toy "better, more orderly, more purposeful" (*Lehrjahre*, 950, my trans.), Felix throws it away. Abandoning his pedagogical pose, Wilhelm converts Felix from son to brother, sympathetically exclaiming, "Come, my son! Come, my brother, let's saunter about in the world without any particular goal, as well as we can" (*Apprenticeship*, 349, trans. mod.).[35] Such purposeless sauntering retains joy, but at a cost. The question remains how to reconcile elements of paternity and fraternity—to accommodate purpose within play and join joy with usefulness. A law of the father does not seem capable of accommodating this union. And so the novel posits an alternative, namely, networks of multiples, of siblings, to provide both guidance and a bar to incest.

The power of fraternity as a structural bond lies in a paradoxical ambivalence, as it symbolizes an equality that appears universalizable, and yet draws its affective strength from the exclusivity of family. If the thieves in the novel demonstrate the limits of *universal* enfranchisement, one pole of fraternity, *exclusivity* of affect within the family, namely, incest, is just as problematic. Incest looms large as a threat that comes out of the elevation of fraternity in *Wilhelm Meister*. In fact, sibling incest is a pervasive theme in eighteenth- and early nineteenth-century European literature, as Lynn Hunt, Daniel Wilson, and Alan Richardson have shown in

French, German, and British literature, respectively, and as we will continue to see throughout this volume.[36] Peter Uwe Hohendahl and Lynn Hunt have offered oedipal explanations for this prevalence based on the general collapse of symbolic paternal authority, both religious and secular, at the time.[37] Psychoanalytic theory posits incestuous attraction as first and foremost the son's attraction to the mother, of which attraction to the sister is a secondary form, and Law is by definition that of the Father. In these incest narratives, however, we can trace the attempt to envision a symbolic framework that is truly fraternal rather than paternal, that is, that sees the shift away from paternal political authority not only as rebellion but also as the opportunity for the establishment of a new, fraternal law. This law would theoretically enshrine the ideal of consent rather than obedience and originate desire, prohibition, and the symbolic differently.

Hohendahl's expectation of an "affirm[ation of] incestuous relationships" at the turn of the nineteenth century is met, at best, partially in some works ("German Classicism," 82). The incestuous pair of the Harper Augustin and his sister Sperata in Goethe's *Wilhelm Meister* manifests instead a concrete threat—an inassimilable, closed dyad, rejecting community, communication, and even the communion of their original Catholic faith. The "sibling union" of the lilies that Augustine calls on to justify his incestuous relationship is after all also described as self-pollination.[38] The relationship of Augustin and Sperata distorts time itself, and the inability of their child Mignon to live beyond adolescence means that this sibling-dyad, like the republican troupe, swallows up futurity. Mired in projections of fate and denials of agency, the strange classical tragedy of the Harper and Mignon embedded in this paradigmatic modern novel provides a negative example that is structurally only a small and hence important (mis)step away from the affiliations of fraternal contract theory. To inaugurate a kin lattice or network, rather than collapsing in on itself, the mirroring of siblings must be incomplete or distorted. As we have seen, Hegel envisions a dialectic model more productive than that of Augustine and Sperata in his discussion of *Antigone* in the *Phenomenology*. There, the free and nonerotic recognition between brother-sister pairs provides a bridge to the political sphere. The asymmetry that allows this mirroring to reinforce subjectivity rather than collapsing it for Hegel, however, is the asymmetry of gender, which then restricts the sister to the role of bridge and enables the crossing only of the brother. Goethe, unfortunately, also introduces a sexual asymmetry to solve the problem of incestuous collapse.[39]

Augustin and Sperata haunt modernity as a warning, particularly to the thoroughly modern siblings Lothario and Natalie. The intensity of their relationship raises the threat of incest. Natalie describes the relationship to Wilhelm thus:

> My life is so intensely bound up [verbunden und verwurzelt (*Lehrjahre*, 918)] with that of my brother, that when he suffers pain, so do I, and the joys he experiences are what gives me happiness. I can truly say that only through him have I learnt that the heart can be moved and uplifted, that there is joy and love in the world, and feeling which brings contentment beyond all need.
>
> (Apprenticeship, 330)

Even Therese, whose love for Lothario is reciprocated, tells Natalie that "someone like yourself would be more worthy of him than I. I could and would gladly step aside for you" (326, trans. mod). The language of exchange is worth paying attention to here—Therese sees herself as a substitute for the only proper partner for Lothario, namely, his sister Natalie. Natalie herself meanwhile experiences only through him a cessation of exchange, "a contentment beyond all need." Because this perfect complementarity is so seductive but leads to the disaster experienced by Augustin and Sperata, mechanisms must be put in place to avoid it. Such a mechanism is not, here, a paternal injunction nor a direct substitute for it. The families created under its auspices do not replicate the previous generation but reach out horizontally, both metonymically through the society of brothers bound together through the marriages and literally on the geographic landscape.

The arranged network of exchanges that preclude the incest of Natalie and Lothario follow a nearly comically anti-oedipal trajectory. In a sense, the story begins oedipally. Lothario discovers he has slept with the mother of his fiancé, Therese, and so, in accord with a taboo against intergenerational incest, withdraws from the engagement. In this novel, however, maternity is every bit as questionable as paternity.[40] When it turns out that Therese's mother was not her mother but rather a foster mother, that is, when the entire group of characters and the novel itself free themselves from a focus on intergenerational incest paradigms, they can turn their attention to the more pressing threat posed by the affective brother-sister pair. The decision to treat a foster mother differently from a bodily mother is, in other words, neither natural nor obvious but heavily motivated by shifting priorities. The oedipal structure so pervasive in the novel through the prominent painting of the king's son, lovesick for his father's bride, and in the choice of *Hamlet* as the epitome of drama does not disappear but is shown to be a partial image and a screen that must be augmented through acknowledgment of the significance of the sibling.[41] The novel itself thus illustrates and participates in the shift in familial norms and the accompanying education of desire that occurred in the late eighteenth century, just as Friedrich Kittler once argued. The familial shift in question, however, is not from the early modern household to a triangular nuclear family but from a logic of generational replication of the father in the son, to one of horizontal networking through marriages and friendships structured around siblings.

Lothario's reattachment to Therese unlocks a marital gridlock that has developed, initiating a game of musical partners, and allows the novel to end with a series of substitute attachments, including Wilhelm's own engagement to Lothario's sister Natalie. These exchanges match the men up with more highly valued partners, while the women, with the exception of Therese, find themselves with little choice but to settle. Wilhelm thereby joins not only a new conjugal family but also a brotherhood run by his new brother-in-law and known as the Tower Society. It is impossible to overlook the phallic connotations of the tower, so we should not be surprised that the Society abjures the universalist fraternity of the French Revolution—its members are carefully screened, and one of its main functions is to protect their private property. The Tower Society combines the roles of insurance company, investment company, mentoring organization, surveillance agency, and matchmaker. It functions, in other words, a lot like a global family business.[42] The Tower dispenses not only insurance but also assurances of paternity to ground reproductive families, which are thus shown to be dependent on discourse, as well as sibling exchange. Having established a substitute for the Law of the Father through this network, the Tower Society can now provide a second attempt at the kind of "wandering colony" (*Lehrjahre*, 585, my trans.) that failed in the actors' republic and spread successfully across the globe

(*Apprenticeship* 345–346). The Tower is not merely a substitute father, something the Law of the Father could of course accommodate, but rather works according to a different logic, which combines vertical guidance with a certain amount of horizontal slippage, and institutes desire through a sister-figure rather than a mother-figure. Nathalie is the only member of this group—male or female—who has not exchanged romantic partners among them (and then, only if we exclude her attachment to her brother). The Symbolic drifts into the Metonymic. Goethe is indeed reluctant to move too far from the stability of paternity, however, and works to keep the system from becoming schizophrenic.

As recent criticism has turned toward the economic in *Wilhelm Meister's Apprenticeship*, it has become a commonplace to see in the Tower Society a figuration of Adam Smith's "invisible hand," and indeed the Tower's goal of correlating individual self-interest with the interests of society mirrors the function of the invisible hand in Smith.[43] This conflation fundamentally misunderstands Smith's conceit, however, according to which human self-interest and free-market economics exist in a happy correlation that promotes the growth of prosperity for all classes simultaneously as the economy grows. This coincidence of interests in Smith can be interpreted as fortuitous or God-ordained but in either case is posited as an emergent property of the capitalist system given human propensities. In other words, Smith's hand not only is invisible but lacks metaphysical existence, serving instead as a metaphorical description of supervenient conditions that justify a call for government restraint from intervention in the market. The Tower, on the other hand, intervenes repeatedly in individual lives. It has far less in common with Smith's invisible hand than with the hidden hand of the puppet masters whom Wilhelm as a child discovers behind the curtain of his beloved marionette theater.[44] The very spatial architecture of the society invoked by the appellation *Tower* elicits comparison with the marionetteer. While Adam Smith denies the need for a top-down biopolitics, substituting a bottom-up biopolitics we will return to in the last section of this chapter, Goethe betrays an extreme lack of trust in the innate coherence of systems of individuals.[45] Goethe thus reaches very early a form of the interventionism Foucault identified with neoliberalism in his lectures of 1977–1979—and which he contrasts with the liberalism of Adam Smith.[46] The means Goethe deploys, however, are the means favored at the turn of the nineteenth century, namely, the family.[47]

Standard descriptions of the *Bildungsroman* see in it the emergence of an individual out of a family, followed by his integration into society, and crowned by his own willed choice of a partner to form a new family. *Wilhelm Meister's Apprenticeship*, however, stages the falsity of assuming such emergence from family networks at all. Wilhelm tries to extricate himself from his own family, and his own siblings accordingly fade into the background, but he cannot free himself from kinship and so stumbles repeatedly into the inner workings of other families. If *Wilhelm Meister* therefore thematizes the interdependent and networked nature of modern subjectivity, it nonetheless also handles this relationality with the delicacy of a wound. Siblings form the margins of subjectivity, and so only their disappearance can create the mirage of isolating boundaries around an integral subject. Wilhelm's vanishing siblings provide precisely this alibi, screening from him the fact that *Bildung*, from its earliest roots, is thoroughly transsubjective.

While the pairing of Wilhelm and Natalie with which the novel concludes may seem unbalanced, they do suffer from complementary inabilities in their relationship to abstraction and exchange. Natalie answers Wilhelm's question whether she has ever been in love with the phrase, "Never—or always!" (*Apprenticeship*, 330). Wilhelm could say the same while meaning something entirely different. For Wilhelm is also always in love, successively and occasionally simultaneously, with Marianne, Philine, Mignon, Natalie as the unknown Amazon, Therese, and then Natalie again. In the final words of the novel, Wilhelm brings his personal economy to a standstill: "I have found a treasure I never deserved [earned, i.e., *verdient*]. And I would not exchange it for anything in the world" (373).[48] Wilhelm, in other words, regularly exchanges the objects of his affections before his engagement to Natalie, while Natalie distributes her affections over a potentially infinite number of objects. As noted previously, she is unique among both men and women in the novel in never switching partners. This habit would seem to suggest a special access on her part to a kind of universal currency of love, and yet she has trouble precisely with universal equivalencies in the form of currency. In her charity work as a young girl, she comes to understand the value of money as a solution to neediness only belatedly and with difficulty, preferring to supply actual goods to alleviate want (254, 322–23). While Wilhelm constantly acquires his particular desires, then, Natalie constantly supplies the particular needs of others, in this case with herself. Wilhelm's decisive and irreplaceable desire for Natalie is met by her acceptance of him because, as her other brother Friedrich predicted, "I don't believe you will marry until some bride or other is missing, and you, with your customary generosity, will provide yourself as a supplement to someone's existence" (346). While Natalie's attachment to her brother echoes that of Antigone, Natalie becomes the inverse of Antigone as imagined by Lacan. Lacan's Antigone is said to desire a structural position; Natalie *is* a structural position and hence cannot desire. In *Wilhelm Meister*, then, it is Natalie who, according to Elisabeth Krimmer, "marks a void. It is her emptiness that upholds the symbolic system."[49] Indeed, Anneliese Dick goes so far as to call her a "female eunuch" (*Weiblichkeit*, 123).

A kind of *sibling logic* is thus envisioned here as a stable system only insofar as it is both nonuniversalizable (only within a secret society) and nonegalitarian (in that it norms gender roles to biological sex and punishes female desire). If this is an appropriation of the French Revolution, it is a cynical appropriation that highlights the limits of the latter on both enfranchisement and joy. The ending of *Wilhelm Meister's Lehrjahre* has been problematized many times before: its questionable success, the irony surrounding its mystical, secret-society procedures, and its female-borne cost in relinquishing particular desire, which was similarly calculated by Hegel. Yet the irony with which the Tower is handled does not amount to a strong critique for the simple reason that no viable alternatives to the biopolitics of the Tower are suggested for the series of dilemmas developed in the novel.[50] While there can be no doubt that an aura of dissatisfaction with the mechanisms of the Tower pervades the novel, we are left with the disappointing sense that the modern world does not provide for more appetizing possibilities.

MARRIAGE AND THE SIBLING IN THE LONG NINETEENTH CENTURY

Goethe was prescient in his sketch of financial groupings based on sibling bonds as in so much else that structures modernity. Historians, sociologists, and anthropologists have recently begun to pay attention to the significance of kinship in modern European cultures. Leonore Davidoff has discussed in detail the practice of forming business partnerships across brothers, brothers-in-law, and nephews. "Clan-like families" were extended most clearly through sibling marriage alliances that were not directly arranged but "avidly encouraged."[51] Family businesses were practical for a number of reasons, particularly in light of laws that did not clearly limit debt responsibility within extended families. If a family member's business already put one at risk, then it made sense to also share in the profits and the decision making. Trustworthy partnerships, as the Tower Society recognized, allowed the spread of risk internationally and enabled control over the vertical production of a product from raw material to product sale (ibid., 57–58). Families provided an institutional scaffolding for building and maintaining such trust. Cementing bonds of trust was facilitated by multiple marriages within a family, or by repeated intermarriages between families who then formed a clan. In what Davidoff calls a "lattice of kinship," two siblings often married another two siblings. Such marriages were still more potent when they occurred between cousins (49). As Adam Kuper demonstrates (22), while double-sibling marriages were common among the rising bourgeoisie, first-cousin marriages were also popular among the aristocracy in Britain. They also became popular in German-speaking territories after the passage of new laws starting in 1741 that lifted restrictions on close-kin marriages.[52] It is worth noting that under the new system, the subsequent marriage of a man to the daughter of his first wife by another marriage—the scenario which in attenuated form originally prevents Lothario and Therese from marrying—was no longer legally prohibited.

In the new paradigm that emerged beginning in the eighteenth century, women exercised significant financial power within families in their role fostering social relations and goodwill among financially interdependent family members, and between family groups and the community. One's standing in society was significantly affected by the standing of close kin such as siblings and their spouses (Davidoff, *Thicker than Water*, 52), and managing social standing was a primary function of wives in the middle class, who thus also cooperated in large family groups.[53] The combination of networking and a good name provided a clear advantage in business and banking, which depended on the trust of the community.[54] Such feminine power should not be mistaken for, or conflated with, financial independence. While women could improve the fortunes of the families in which they lived, their unequal direct control over money was significant in shaping the differences between male and females lives in the eighteenth through twentieth centuries.⁵⁵ As David Sabean and Simon Teuscher clearly state, "the story of modernization has included the rise of the nuclear family and the cutting off of extensive kinship ties. What we are suggesting, however, is just the opposite."⁵⁶

Of course, as illustrated in the discussion of Engels, the late eighteenth century also witnessed the increasing importance of love and emotional commitment as the foundation of marriage. Niklas Luhmann has most influentially reflected on the emergence of love as a code bound up with theories of individualization that enshrined inner emotional development as independent from political and economic concerns.⁵⁷ His account is extremely incomplete, however, for two reasons. First, the specific code he describes was always restricted to the male experience; the discourse of female love at the same time deployed individuality in the instant of forming a preference but then culminated in a merger with the beloved which was coded as self-abnegating. Second, even for men, the code of love was accompanied by the idea of marriage as entry into the adult world of work, responsibility, and civic duty. The political nature of the construction of private and public, which Carole Pateman so thoroughly analyzed a few years after Luhmann's book appeared, is replicated on the level of individual life experience in the linking of love through the social act of marriage to civic and professional engagement and to the social duty inherent in child-rearing.⁵⁸ Sabean and Teuscher claim that the new elevation of love to the predominant precondition of marriage "was by no means contrary to economic considerations: the flow of sentiment and the flow of money operated in the same channels" ("Kinship in Europe," 22). In his own contribution to the same collection, Sabean is more cautious, stating that the "*healthy* social body was one where the veins through which capital and blood flowed were the same."⁵⁹ Such a statement begs the question. It is only through systems of surveillance, control, expectation, and education—however bound up with emotional care—that blood, sentiment, and capital can be made to circulate together. An affective education was thus necessary to regulate the flow of desire into economically appropriate channels. This education began with the sibling.

Childhood education implicitly and explicitly established models not only for gender roles in general but also for the mutual, but sex-differentiated, obligations of male-female pairs. Such education was often experienced as interrupting an earlier nursery ideal of egalitarian companionship. The sibling relationship, in other words, made the process of gender construction visible. Both the emotion and the coeducation of the brother-sister relationship carried over into marriage relations and indeed were seen as a model for them.[60] This emphasis on the brother-sister relationship as the ideal leads to a particularly comical misunderstanding between lovers in George Eliot's *Mill on the Floss* (in general a novel short on comedy) where Philip anxiously pushes Maggie (with whom he's in love) to admit whether "you really only care for me as if I were your brother. Tell me the truth." To which she replies enthusiastically: "Indeed I do, Philip."[61] The source of her misunderstanding is clear; earlier in the same conversation, she assures Philip, "I think I could hardly love any one better: there is nothing but what I love you for" (294). Her mistake is to know of nothing inside of love but outside of siblinghood. And since Philip would have made a wonderful brother, she is sure at this moment that he is the perfect object of her love.

Prioritizing the sibling bond is economically productive because it ensures that the sibling's marriage will channel value back into the original sibling dynamic. However much value such a process generated, it came at a risk because it rendered visible an aspect of subject development that the era, like our own, attempted to suppress. Siblings highlight the investment necessary to create and maintain the illusion of individuals as autonomous, integral wholes. Leila Silvana May has called attention to this "frenetic internal defense system" necessary to create and maintain the domestic as a space of unity, in which, however, difference is generated, and a space of purity, in which, however, desire is generated (*Disorderly Sisters*, 16). The sister is the key to this dynamic (ibid., esp. 16–43). If the sister according to Lévi-Strauss is a commodity, she is a commodity whose value to both brother and husband lies in a failure to change hands completely, and in her own activity in the joint and ongoing roles of sister and wife. The anthropologist Annette Weiner has described the sibling relation as the kinship counterpart of a kind of interaction she calls "keeping-while-giving" because it demonstrates how value accrues through retention, as well as in exchange.[62]

TRAVERSING THE FETISH

The sister in Lévi-Strauss occupies an uncomfortable position as a designated object of exchange who, he acknowledges in only two sentences at the end of his monumental tome, is also "still a person" and hence herself "a generator of signs." What we might call the uncanny position of the woman as a speaking sign in Lévi-Strauss's system produces, he believes, the "affective richness, ardour and mystery" of the relations between the sexes (*Elemental Structures*, 496). She is, in other words, evidence of a conflation of subject and object, a reminder of the illusory nature of autonomous human agency which requires management to screen the vulnerability it reveals, and yet is precisely therefore attractively enigmatic. This mysterious commodity, the sister who upon exchange becomes the wife, is thus an emblematic subset of Marx's "mystical" commodity, which, in an industrial society, assumes the identity of the fetish (Marx, *Capital*, 1:164). Marx's much-discussed theory of the commodity fetish attributes a life of desires and attitudes to things.[63] They assume such value by instantiating the process of interpersonal labor relations through which they are created, which otherwise never coexist in time and place. The process that imbues the object with such lively characteristics simultaneously strips agency from the alienated workers, who, through the formation of a chiasmic relationship between person and ware, become objectified mechanisms in the production process. Not only the worker but also the commodity owner are subject to the agency of the commodity: "Objects in themselves are external to man, and consequently alienable by him. In order that this alienation may be reciprocal, it is only necessary for men, by a tacit understanding, to treat each other as private owners of those alienable objects, and by implication as independent individuals" (1:182). The fetish thus marks a projection both powerful and effective but a projection nonetheless, since there is a truth of the objects "in themselves" that consists in their separateness and passivity. Just as artificial as the activity of goods, according to Marx, is the isolation of individuals.

In his series of articles on the fetish from the 1990s, William Pietz attempts to extract four commonalities from fetish discourse, a discourse that now stretches across more than three centuries, from early ethnology and comparative religion, to economics and cultural studies, to sex theory and psychoanalysis.[64] The four properties of the fetish that he identifies are its

> untranscended materiality...; (2) the radical historicality of [its] origin...; (3) the dependence of the fetish for its meaning and value on a particular order of social relations, which it in turn reinforces; and (4) the active relation of the fetish object to the living body of an individual: a kind of external controlling organ directed by powers outside the affected person's will, the fetish represents a subversion of the ideal of the autonomously determined self.[65]

To call something a fetish, in other words, is to perform a critique—to claim a blindness on the part of the fetishist toward the illusory and self-willed nature of the value invested in the object. The fetish names a problem to which the solution would be demystification. The assumptions implicit in the passage are that objects do not, and should not, have agency and that "the autonomously determined self" represents an ideal. Moreover, the blindness of the fetishist is said to be responsible for reinforcing the social relations that create the fetish, social relations assumed to be in need of critique. Returning objects to their rightful place as distinct from, and powerless over, the individual would, one might therefore expect, restore the individual to its proper autonomy. This description of the fetish is not quite as universal as Pietz would have it, however. For Marx, disempowering objects seems to be a precursor to allowing humans to develop meaningful and nonexploitive social relations, to releasing the idea of autonomy, in other words.[66] I would suggest that we can find in the nineteenth-century cultural imaginary yet another way past or through the fetish that Pietz has missed, one that recognizes intricate interpersonal involvement without denying the agency of objects. Both Bruno Latour and W.J.T. Mitchell have recently discussed reciprocal transfer of agency between purported subjects and objects in just this way, though Latour speaks of *factishes* and Mitchell of *totems*.[67] I would like to retain the language available to the nineteenth century, the language of the fetish, while showing that there is a strain in the nineteenth century that understands what Latour calls *"the wisdom of the passage,"* namely, "that which allow[s] one to pass from fabrication to reality; ...

that which gives *an autonomy we do not possess to beings that do not possess it either*, but that by this very token give it to us."⁶⁸ The reason the fetish interests us in this study is precisely that it enables such passage between subjects and between subject and object. It is the object correlate of the sibling.⁶⁹

The best path to arriving at this correlation is to turn to a well-known British sibling tragedy of the nineteenth century, George Eliot's *Mill on the Floss*. In this novel, Eliot experiments with the possibility of different ways of moving among and between interpersonal relations that might allow for value-rich bonds without requiring the creation and hence the isolation of the free, autonomous individual. Such interactions also call into question the process of releasing or of possessing objects, instead recognizing merged subjectivities and the agency of objects as exemplified by the narrator's love of moistness (6). In such a watery environment, however, drowning is a distinct risk, and the one that claims the lives of the siblings Maggie and Tom Tulliver, clasped in a last embrace at the end of the novel.

George Eliot's commitment to the deep significance of objects has long been recognized. Eliot famously uses the word "Fetish" to describe the disfigured doll Maggie Tulliver tortures as a young girl when she herself has been chastised or punished (24). The doll takes on different characters, "represent[ing]" the tormenting relatives who surround her (25). Maggie's Fetish has thus advanced beyond the most primitive stage of religion posited by Comte as fetishism⁷⁰ and toward idolatry, which requires enough abstraction to allow for representation.⁷¹ While Eliot uses the word only for this doll, the novel presents us with far more powerful fetishes. These treasured objects include moveable property, such as the hard currency both Mr. Tulliver and his sister-in-law Mrs. Glegg sequester and reserve, unwilling to commit to the abstract operations of a bank. At least as laden with emotional value are both Mrs. Tulliver's self-woven, initialed trousseau linens and her daughter Maggie's books, which the two must give up to auction after Mr. Tulliver loses the mill.⁷² The objects that are dwelt on with the most powerful narrative investment, and which exercise as well the most affective and effective power over the characters, however, are Dorlcote Mill itself, the neighboring family home, the surrounding landscape, the River Floss, and Tom and Maggie themselves. The novel participates in a recounting of the physical setting and of the family, which reveals the constructed character of this ostensibly natural environment.

For Eliot, as for Marx, what is at stake in the fetish is "material relations between persons and social relations between things" (Marx, *Capital*, 1:166).[73] For both, these relations have come to be sedimented there as a result of material, social processes that occur over time. For Eliot, however, the primary site of such sedimentation is not the factory but the family. Marx believed that alienable wealth was "an idea [that] could only arise in a bourgeois society, and one which was already well developed . . . and the first attempt to implement the idea on a national scale was made . . . during the French bourgeois revolution" (1:183). We are witnesses as the characters discover, to their dismay, that every part of the landscape they thought inalienable can be commodified, when they lose the mill, the house, the land, and most of their possessions and become tenants on, rather than dwellers in and with, their surroundings. The fact that the family experiences their relationship to the land as natural is revealed to be an act of selective memory and forgetting, and one that is explicitly social, tied up with the both childhood experiences and the knowledge of a family history. In this way, the Tullivers are very much a part of their community, the fictional town of St. Ogg's. Joshua Esty has analyzed the way Eliot uses autochthonous language to describe the town and also the subtle undermining of this organicism in the novel ("Nationhood," 104). As he notes, the text thus reveals the history of an absence of historical consciousness that haunts the landscape. Like the relationship of human to land, Maggie and Tom's relationship to each other as brother and sister, boy and girl, older and younger, practical and artistic, may be naturalized by their society onto gender and age relations, but it is not naturalized by the narrative, which reads a history of nuanced social and educational pressures into the way they are taught to behave toward each other.[74] John Kucich has read Eliot's refusal to envision "purely natural objects" as the record of a loss.[75] Kucich sees a partial remedy for this loss in Maggie's appreciation of the multivalence of objects in the human world.[76] In his understanding of the "network of relations" in the novel (332), Kucich remains committed to nature as a set of passive signs available for human representative functions. The novel, however, illustrates a world of objects and subjects that have agency without full autonomy. While Maggie grasps these relationships better than Tom, we need to look beyond the individual characters with whom criticism has remained too preoccupied and turn to the structure of the novel to see how the interplay of subjects and of things create meaning.

The excessive attachment of Maggie and Tom to each other and to the material elements of their childhood lays the groundwork for the tragedy of *The Mill on the Floss* but also offers the potential for a more viable alternative for living meaningfully. The novel is a tragedy by its own reckoning—a tragedy of "insignificant people, whom you pass unnoticingly on the road every day . . . of that unwept, hidden sort" (*Mill*, 172). Indeed, we might recognize the outlines of the tragedy in which a sister chooses sacred duty to a brother, not only over a lover but also over life itself; a tragedy in which the father of this sister and brother has "a destiny as well as Oedipus" (114). And yet the novel is not quite the same kind of tragedy as Sophocles's *Antigone*. Antigone, after all, as discussed in chapter 1, recognizes no claims outside the one she fulfills. In other words, she acts in accordance with an imperative as if she could singularly incorporate it, with no remainder and no division of her agency. Antigone, it could be said, succeeds in a strange way; she fulfills her own self-stated purpose. Maggie Tulliver, on the other hand, can never manage to fulfill the sense of all-encompassing obligation she suffers under because her claims pull her in multiple directions. She is like Ismene, then, who, as we argued in the first chapter, experiences conflicting claims. But Maggie is not quite like Ismene either. Ismene, at least in her entreaties to Antigone, gestures toward a way of acknowledging conflicting obligations while still evaluating them and choosing the life-affirming. Maggie, on the other hand, feels paralyzed by choice and returns to her brother as to a "root deeper than all change" (399), a root that predates the formation of competing relationships. Maggie, like Antigone, then, acts out of an imperative born of joint subjectivity with her brother. But unlike Antigone, she recognizes that such sharing is not limited—neither to one brother nor to a group whose demands all coincide in something as simple as death. For Maggie, bonds and obligations can and do proliferate. She yearns for a way to incorporate *every* obligation, *every* shared subjectivity, fully and entirely, with no remainder. She wants to be an Antigone toward every person with a claim on her. Maggie is not speaking metaphorically when she explains to Stephen Guest that she cannot elope with him because "we owed ourselves to others, and must conquer every inclination which could make us false to that debt" (416). As Neil Hertz notes succinctly, "to be rooted, in these novels, is to be indebted."[77] Maggie's feelings on the subject of debt thus accord exactly with those of her father and Tom, for whom paying off the debts that have driven the family to ruin is the highest priority.[78] Maggie states clearly what the other two also enact, that what is owed extends to the self.

The irruption of tragedy into bourgeois life is something we have already encountered in *Wilhelm Meister's Apprenticeship*. There, the incestuous siblings Augustin and Sperata represent a threat toward which the necessity of living lives bound together tends. The siblings Lothario and Natalie edge toward this threat but are saved from it by a combination of the machinations of the Tower Society and Natalie's relinquishment of preference. George Eliot places the seductive danger of tragedy still closer to home by focusing on a single brother-sister pair—by combining into one set of siblings both the striving of Lothario/Natalie and the yearning of Augustin/Sperata. It would be easy to argue that a split still exists here—that Maggie herself incorporates fateful tragedy and Tom a modern bourgeois commercial spirit. Tom, after all, joins his uncle's trading company and experiences great success there. In fact, the few critics who read the novel alongside *Antigone* have seen in Tom a conflation of Polyneices and Creon. Like Creon, they argue, Tom is narrow-minded, authoritative, and attuned to the civic, in this case to political economy, while Maggie remains focused on kinship. Such reasoning, however, does not do justice to the complexity of the novel and its integration of tragedy into the modern economic world. Nor does it take account of Eliot's own repositioning of the gender elements in the tragedy.[79]

Eliot herself reviewed a translation of Sophocles's drama in the *Leader* in 1856. Critics who have analyzed Eliot's comments have focused on her endorsement of a Hegelian reading of the play (by way of August Böckh).[80] Indeed, like Hegel, Eliot insists that Creon and Antigone each follows a moral principle, and also each transgresses one. Eliot, however, contradicts a fundamental element of Hegel's analysis, namely, the gendering of the two principles in question. While Hegel depicts Antigone as representing the sacred rights of the female realm of the family and Creon as the voice of the masculine civic sphere, Eliot reads the conflict as "that struggle between elemental tendencies and established laws by which the outer life of man is gradually and painfully being brought into harmony with his inward needs.... Wherever the strength of a man's intellect, or moral sense, or affection brings him into opposition with the rules which society has sanctioned, *there* is renewed the conflict between Antigone and Creon."[81] Once the drama has been interpreted as a struggle between internal principles and external norms, both Tom and Maggie become candidates for the role of Antigone in *Mill on the Floss*, while the role of Creon dissolves into the fabric of society as a whole, perhaps most clearly represented by "not the world, but the world's wife" (*Mill*, 431).

Maggie and Tom both evince a loyalty to family that alienates them from society and situates them in the place of Antigone. While critics have dwelt on Maggie's renunciation of both her suitors, Philip and Stephen, under the threat of rejection from Tom, Tom's own adherence to family allegiance at the cost of social integration has been largely overlooked.[82] His feelings toward his sister oscillate from love to repulsion but always manifest intense attachment. Even when he repudiates Maggie, "the thought of it made his days bitter to him" (439).[83] It is Tom, moreover, who inscribes a vow to avenge his father in the flyleaf of the family Bible, diverting the generational family lineage of marriages, births, and deaths into a regressive quest for revenge. This act, still more strongly than Tom's and Maggie's continued bachelorhood, demonstrates the way in which their particular brand of allegiance to family swallows up futurity. It is Tom who pledges himself to reclaim the past by buying back Dorlcote Mill, which had been in the Tulliver family for four generations before their father lost it through his civil suits.[84] His engagement with the modern commercial economy is shown to be only a means to this end for him. While critics tend to see Maggie's obsession as the impetus for the deaths of both siblings, both bear equal responsibility for the decision to embark on their last journey into the flood in the small, unsuitable holiday boat.[85] They commit themselves to the water together.

In Maggie, whose psychology is more fully elaborated than Tom's, we see an oscillation between the desire for amalgamation with others and a strict renunciation of all new ties.[86] She cannot reconcile her enthusiasm for the roots she is forever equating with memory, with her enthusiasm for the branching out of her relationship with the world of things and people, an oscillation that Hertz calls Maggie's "pulsation" (*Pulse*, 74). It is no wonder that Philip paints her as a dryad, a spirit of the trees. Gillian Beer has noted this absorption with "relations" and "origins" in *Middle-*

march. Here in this earlier novel we see the potential for the two drives to spiral away from each other into twin excesses that tear Maggie apart.[87] Since Eliot establishes the value of both impulses, of both roots and branches, the question posed by the novel is how to integrate the two. This should sound familiar from our discussion of Goethe, but Eliot moves in a very different direction from Goethe. And this is where we need to return to the fetish and to the sibling, both of which stand as testaments to the nonintegral nature of the subject. For Eliot, the history through which objects assume value beyond their demonstrable exchange value has a presence in memory. Nina Auerbach claims that the "'memory' [Maggie] invokes is actually a myth-making faculty that makes of the past a sanctuary against the present rather than its seeding ground" ("Power of Hunger," 167). Auerbach here establishes a misleading dichotomy, however. To call Maggie's recollection of an idyllic brother-sister relationship in her childhood a "false memory," as May similarly does, positions affective memory in a realm of objectivity that is foreign to Eliot's conception (May, *Disorderly Sisters*, 82). It is also worth noting that memory does not arise only in connection with Maggie. Tom and, still more significantly, the narrator both dwell on memories. The narrator speaks of "our" attachment to objects as an echo of a time when such attachment was not felt to be metaphorical, "where the outer world seemed only an extension of our own personality: we accepted and loved it as we accepted our own sense of existence and our own limbs" (*Mill*, 133). It would be a small leap to perceive in the yearning for this landscape, then, an attempt to repair a traumatic breach in a pre-oedipal unity, or to alleviate through the imaginary projection of physical wholeness the castration anxiety that Sigmund Freud set at the basis of fetishism.[88] Such reasoning would make the childhood home spaces and the sibling both symbols of some still earlier loss, that of the primal unity with the mother, or of security in the invulnerability of one's own body. Indeed, a vast amount of critical energy has been poured into the attempt to determine what, exactly, Tom is a replacement for in Maggie's psyche. Yet for a younger child, at the least, an older sibling is every bit as much a given in the family dynamic as a mother or a father, and is not structurally or functionally reducible to either. What do we make, then, of a fetishism that selects as its object precisely that which was originally lost?[89] Such a fetish would have to be a symbol of itself. Looked at from another angle, however, the object becomes neither metaphor nor symbol but a synecdoche for the system of relations that tie people and objects together. The fetish is generally considered to be an object that has taken on value from a set of relationships that the fetishist has repressed. This is as true for Marx as for Freud and Lacan. For Eliot, however, the recognition of such relationships as the source of significance does not absolve the fetish of its power. It maintains its hold.

Noting the intensity of objects in Eliot's fiction, Peter Melville Logan goes so far as to argue that Eliot's understanding of realism turns the novel itself into a fetish object, which through its "use of particularity thus encourages the reader to attribute a kind of life to the narrative" (Logan, "Eliot," 39). In so doing, Eliot's fictions participate not in a simple fetishism but in something closer to Bruno Latour's *factishism*, by demonstrating the ability of objects to retain life and agency in excess of the human relations and by allowing agency to flow in both directions. The conflict Logan finds between Eliot's perceived critique of fetishism and her own praxis disappears when we realize that she is not attempting to demystify the fetish but rather to illuminate the way that objects and subjects productively dissolve into networks of joint agency. In her notebook essay from 1868, "Notes on Form in Art," Eliot reflects explicitly on the relationship of parts to wholes and on the composition of objects from disparate categories of being:

> Thus, the human organism comprises things as diverse as the fingernails & tooth-ache, as the nervous stimulus of muscle manifested in a shout, & the discernment of a red spot on a field of snow; but all its different elements or parts of experience are bound together in a more necessary wholeness or more inseparable group of common conditions than can be found in any other existence known to us. The highest Form then, is the highest organism, that is to say, the most varied group of relations bound together in a wholeness which again has the most varied relations with all other phenomena.[90]

The organism is equally composed of matter, perception, dynamic, and fragment, and while the human form is a necessary whole, its edges are unclear, and this necessary wholeness is just as quickly reintegrated as a part in a system of relations just as varied and various.

While Maggie is ultimately unable to reconcile the claims on her, there is a tantalizing suggestion in the novel of an alternative that reaches conceptually toward this later essay. This suggestion lies in the ambiguous status of the narrator. The narrator of *Mill on the Floss* emerges in appropriately misty ways, generally moving out of Maggie's or Tom's perspective into a generalized "we," and never settles definitively into an "I." This narrator shares her characters' love of the same childhood objects and landscapes but survives such attachment without outliving it. She adamantly refuses to approach her story through abstraction, speaking of the cold stone of the bridge railing within the *setting* of her story that she leans against in the *telling* (*Mill*, 8).[91] Her movement, then, is a kind of synecdoche, a way of swimming through merged objects that neither entirely leaves them behind nor subsumes them. Synecdoche is the representation of a whole through a part, as in "counting heads." But if a part can be shared by two wholes, each of which shares other parts with other wholes, synecdoche becomes a way to envision networked jointure that is not identity.[92] The sibling, who is neither self nor fully other, the companion to whom one must early accommodate oneself, from whom one learns the habits of sympathy, is the obvious starting point of such travel.

"It is not possible simply to deduce alliance from filiation," Deleuze and Guattari state; "there are two memories that correspond to them, the one biofiliative, the other a memory of alliance of words."[93] These are evidently two irreducible processes: origins and relations, roots and branches. But what, then, do we do with the sibling? The sibling to whom Maggie always returns as to a root, the sibling that she associates always with language and with economy. One must, of course, make such a pervious sibling disappear out of the focal point of theory, make her or him a psychoanalytic substitute for mother or father; a structuralist unit of exchange between brothers-in-law; a Hegelian bridge from the family to the state. There is an irony in the fact that even Deleuze and Guattari should fail to notice the point where root and branch merge to become rhizome. It is here that the jointure of subjectivity is most evident, the co-agency of subjects and of subject and object, the melting of the fetish into a form of synecdochal representation that retains meanings while generating new ones, that cannot be abstracted from its materiality even while it reaches beyond.

THE SEDUCTION OF SYSTEM

In his discussion of the commodity as fetish, Marx focuses on the relations among worker, capital, commodity, owner, and consumer. The fetish by definition, however, neither represents nor symbolizes these relations for the fetishist but manifests power and agency in its very material. Nearly a century before Marx wrote, however, Adam Smith had already identified and participated in another sort of projection of value onto the commodity, one that treads the line between mystical fetish and representational idol. We have already encountered this Smithean mystification of the commodity as a condensation of global interpersonal relations, encapsulated in his glowing description of the different kinds of labor that go into making a wool coat. It is present as well in the enthusiastic encomiums to trade provided by Wilhelm's childhood friend and eventual brother-in-law, Werner, in Goethe's *Wilhelm Meister*, among many other enthusiastic capitalists in nineteenth-century literature.[94] The ware, particularly if acquired through trade with societies understood as primitive, acquires an attractive aura through its travel from distant places. It is no coincidence that this very trade also produced the discourse of the fetish in the first place. William Pietz recounts that seventeenth-century Portuguese traders distinguished the culture-specific value of fetish from the value of the trade object, which was assumed to transcend culture. The way in which material was understood could thus serve to differentiate stages of culture—matter was objective and passive for the Europeans, subjective and active for the natives (Pietz "Fetish, II"). It is, however, the subjectively experienced superiority of the trading civilization, combined with the air of mystique surrounding the primitive, that invests objects of foreign exchange with their piquancy. In other words, trade converts into fetishes for Europeans precisely those objects contrasted with fetishes by the European traders. Even wares produced domestically have histories of production that provide a screen for fantasizing. While Marx argued that the commodity fetish absorbs into its material the unacknowledged value generated by a production process, there is in fact a wide tendency in the nineteenth century to recognize that processes of production and distribution exist, but then to romanticize these processes, to sanitize them of exploitative labor relations. In other words, the fetish quality of the commodity is knowingly bound up precisely in a story of its production and transport history, but a story that has become a fairy tale.

This sanitization of the process of commodity production follows from Smith's own claim that sympathy depends on personal interaction. The scope of sympathy is, on the one hand, therefore very narrow—limited to one's circle of acquaintances—but, on the other hand, very wide—as it depends on imagination facilitated by knowledge of circumstances rather than on any kind of similarity or identification. Smith exemplifies this imaginative process by asserting, "A man may sympathize with a woman in child-bed; though it is impossible that he should conceive himself as suffering her pains in his own proper person and character" (*Moral*, 4). The man cannot conceive, but he can imagine. The move from personal relationships to economic system of relations entails a corresponding shift of focus from sympathy with the pain of this laboring body, on the one hand, to the attractions of the product, and indifference to the pain of the laboring body that produced it, on the other. Where system takes over from acquaintance in Smith, the ethical motivating power of sympathy is replaced by the aesthetic seductions of smooth functioning: "We naturally confound [luxury] in our imagination with the order, the regular and harmonious movement of the system, the machine or oeconomy by means of which it is produced. The pleasure of wealth and greatness, when considered in this complex view, strike the imagination as something grand and beautiful and noble" (183). The attraction of luxury items is derived less from the material comfort they offer than from an admiration bound up with their evocation of the entire system of capital, production, and distribution that makes them available.

This beauty of system shades explicitly into a police state, but a paradoxical one that fulfills a desire generated within each individual. "The perfection of the police, the extension of trade and manufacture, are noble and magnificent objects.... We take pleasure in beholding the perfection of so beautiful and grand a system, and we are uneasy till we remove any obstruction that can in the least disturb or encumber the regularity of its motions" (185). Smith's aesthetic state here prefigures Schiller's, revealing a universal desire after all beneath the division of labor and classes. While, for Schiller, artwork enables access to a universal that smoothes away particular desires, supplementing the fragmentation of society, in Smith the political economy is itself beautiful.[95] Its beauty lies in the order imposed by integration of difference into smooth functioning, demonstrating, as in Marc Redfield's penetrating analysis of the implications of Schiller's aesthetics, that the "machine, which seems the opposite of the organic work of art, is in fact its double, and the elegant turns of this technopolis simultaneously reveal and ward off the inhumanity and incoherence of the process by which humanity is being affirmed. Aestheticized political models... conceal real political injustice."[96] Aesthetics takes over from sympathy as a motive for action—perceived here as action for the common good. Biopolitics thus works as much from the bottom up as from the top down. As Howard Caygill has noted, even the attenuated idea of policing presented in the *Moral Sentiments* melts away entirely in the later *Wealth of Nations*, which enshrines the idea of laissez faire.[97] The move from sympathy to systematicity is more shift than leap, as both depend on the tendency to view oneself as the object of desired approval, which is likely to follow from either the ethical or the aesthetic action.[98]

While the laboring class in industrial England was never the main focus of Eliot's work, the side glance she cast at it in *The Mill on the Floss* reveals a sharp divergence from Smith's depiction of the elegance of system or Gustav Freytag's image of the threads of commerce peacefully binding together humanity (see note 94):

> But good society, floated on gossamer wings of light irony, is of very expensive production; requiring nothing less than a wide and arduous national life condensed in unfragrant deafening factories, cramping itself in mines, sweating at furnaces, grinding, hammering, weaving under more or less oppression of carbonic acid—or else, spread over sheep-walks, and scattered in lonely houses and huts on the clayey or chalky cornlands, where the rainy days look dreary. This national life is based entirely on emphasis—the emphasis of want, which urges it into all the activities necessary for the maintenance of good society and light irony.
>
> (Eliot, Mill on the Floss, 524)

Rather than reading the attractions of luxury as a consequence of the purported elegance of the system which generates it, Eliot fleetingly reveals the fetid underbelly of luxury in a vivid portrayal of *national life* as an unceasing activity of unpleasant labor coerced by a state of want.

If aesthetics and ethics are to remain linked for Eliot, it cannot be through a systematicity that produces and hides suffering. There are, however, other aesthetic possibilities that extend sympathy beyond Smith's required proximity. Already in 1766, G. E. Lessing outlined an aesthetic theory in *Laocöon* that depended on sympathy produced through imaginative reconstruction and projection beyond the limits of acquaintance.[99] Such a theory depended primarily on narrative, while Schiller's aesthetic education focused instead on visual art.[100] Sympathy within aesthetic theory was not superseded by a Kantian aesthetics, but continued to exert influence alongside it. In 1855 Eliot published a review article in a weekly newspaper called the *Leader* defending *Wilhelm Meister's Apprenticeship*—which had been translated recently into English—from charges of immorality. The main complaint was that sexually incontinent characters such as the aptly named Philine and Lothario were not punished. Eliot disparages the type of reading that comes from an immature habit of "associating our passions with our moral prepossessions, by mistaking indignation for virtue," and instead outlines an aesthetic experience both derived from and eliciting sympathy. The habit of sympathy is a way of moving from one set of particulars through a mild abstraction to another set of particulars, so that our own "fall and . . . struggles" combined with knowledge of the mixture of "help and goodness in the 'publicans and sinners'" allows us to recognize "that the line between the virtuous and vicious, so far from being a necessary safeguard to morality, is itself an immoral fiction."[101] If Eliot considers Goethe's fiction and her own, then, *moral* fictions in contrast to the "immoral fiction" of assuming the virtuous are distinct from the vicious, it is because she grants Smith's sympathy still wider powers than he was willing to.[102] Eliot holds out the possibility of moving from experience to imagined experience across gulfs that preclude even the most fleeting personal acquaintance. Smithian sympathy is formed through an education that establishes boundaries between siblings that can then be imaginatively bridged, so that needs can be alleviated through exchange. Eliot's sympathy, on the other hand, challenges these boundaries without assimilating difference. She therefore provides an antidote to the aesthetic and the economic education of the subject by embracing particulars and finding a means of interaction that is not exchange.

The sibling as boundary object both defined and challenged notions of self and of other that were crucial to constructing the subject—desiring, political, and economic—which we have now discussed in the first three chapters of this book. Genealogies also came to structure explorations of human population diversity from the mid-eighteenth through the early twentieth centuries. Family trees of languages, religions, and races—first rhetorical and then visual—dominated cultural histories that mapped human relatedness. In the middle of the nineteenth century, the genealogical methodology was reclaimed by the life sciences in the form of Darwinian evolution. In the final section of this volume, we will turn to the way such genealogical histories were used to define and cement the boundaries around slippery objects from languages and species, to religions and races, while always haunted by the failure of the sibling language, species, race, and religion to form an entirely discrete other.

PART III

GENEALOGICAL SCIENCES

A sister relationship stepped into the place of a daughter relationship.
—JOHANNES SCHMIDT ON LATIN AND GREEK, *THE FAMILIAL RELATIONS OF THE INDOGERMANIC LANGUAGES*, 19

[W]here pairs or larger groups of related species are so similar that they are generally considered as one species, or at least have in the past for a long time been mistaken for one another.
—ERNST MAYR, *SIBLING SPECIES*, 258

My fate is one with yours, close-knit together.
— IPHIGENIA TO HER BROTHER ORESTES; JOHANN WOLFGANG VON GOETHE, *IPHIGENIA IN TAURIS*, 113, LINE 1122

Seeing her, and the feeling of being bound up with her, of being interwoven with her, were one and the same
— CURD ABOUT HIS SISTER RECHA; GOTTHOLD EPHRAIM LESSING, *NATHAN THE WISE*, 75

His sorrow was my sorrow, and his joy
Sent little leaps and laughs through all my frame ...
A Like unlike, a Self that self restrains
—GEORGE ELIOT, "BROTHER AND SISTER," 323

Am I Not a Man and a Brother?
—MOTTO FOR ABOLITIONIST CERAMIC DESIGNED BY JOSIAH WEDGEWOOD

[Jews] confront the tasks of, for example, German civic life, with the detachment with which a jackdaw would fly over a copy [Exemplar] of the Antigone and Iphigenia lying open in a garden.

—PAUL LAGARDE, *JEWS AND INDOGERMANS*, 344

4

LIVING LANGUAGES

Comparative Philology and Evolution

As we have seen in the previous three chapters, the concepts of fraternity and sorority, as well as a commitment to wide lateral kinship networks, restructured political and economic thinking in the eighteenth and nineteenth centuries. Not quite self and not quite other, the sibling established the limit of the subject in political and economic systems but revealed this limit to be a precarious one. This same sibling logic came to structure the methodologies that arose for exploring larger human relations—those between human population groups and between humans and the rest of the living world. Comparative philology,[1] evolutionary theory,[2] cultural history,[3] comparative religion,[4] and race theory[5] all developed in concert to map global human relations, and all called on the family as a structuring principle. By the end of the eighteenth century, such methods were firmly historical, interested in lineage as a tool for understanding degrees of difference and degrees of relatedness among contemporaries. In the process, contemporary languages, peoples, cultures, religions, races, and eventually species were reimagined as sets of siblings or cousins in vast kinship formations, although ones that often failed to correspond across such disciplines. While one challenge in such a system lay in verifying lines of descent, demarcating terms constituted an equally fraught process. In any genealogical system, definitions are relational. The sibling designation, I claim, became the central epistemological tool through which to delineate boundaries between similars and therefore to define individual terms. Simultaneously, however, the similarity of sister languages or of contiguous species revealed the ambiguous nature of such classifications, threatening the integrity of terms, whether languages, species, or subjects. Just as fraternal political and economic theories reciprocally structured the contours of the modern subjectivity that emerged at this moment, so did the new epistemics of large-scale kinship. The discourse of the sibling circulated among scholarly disciplines and between the academy and the social fabric, both inviting forms of affective kinship affiliation and challenging the concept of natural kinds. These two sibling effects stood in tension with each other, a tension that many fields sought to resolve defensively in a variety of ways, such as shoring up boundaries and disaffiliating human groups.[6] The anxiety caused by contingency in classification is manifest in the particular structure of linguistic and evolutionary genealogies in the nineteenth century, which insist programmatically on ongoing diversification without the potential for hybridization.

At its founding in 1866, the Linguistic Society of Paris famously proscribed all papers on the origin of language, declaring unanswerable a question that had fascinated and plagued Europe for well over a century. This prohibition, I would suggest, did not mark an end to the obsession with the origins of the human that had motivated comparative philology; rather, it constituted a tacit acknowledgment that the issue of origins had been usurped by biology seven years earlier, in the wake of Charles Darwin's *On the Origin of Species*. Indeed, the commonalities between evolutionary theory and linguistics ran deep, encompassing not only an interest in origins but also a comparative methodology and a particular understanding of diversification within a continuous line of descent over time.[7] As the philologist August Schleicher announced in a public letter to Ernst Haeckel in 1863: "To point out how the main features of Darwin's theory are applicable to the life of languages, or even, we might say, how the development of human speech has already been unconsciously illustrative of the same, such a labour cannot fail to captivate you, the energetic champion of Darwinism."[8] Stephen Alter has demonstrated that Darwin was quite conscious of the illustrative value of linguistics for evolutionary theory, although Alter omits Darwin's most blatant acknowledgment of this influence, namely, his title, *On the Origin of Species*, which evokes the myriad of Origin of Language essays that had been published over the previous 150 years.[9]

Darwin's debt to linguistics could be thought at first to complete a circle of influence begun with Friedrich Schlegel's 1808 foundational work of comparative linguistics, *On the Language and Wisdom of Indians*, in which Schlegel explains that "the decisive point, however, which will illuminate everything here, is the inner structure of the languages or comparative grammar, which will give us entirely new information about the genealogy of languages in a manner similar to the way comparative anatomy spread light over the higher natural history."[10] A common vocabulary to describe the nature of descent persists in linguistics and evolution to this day. A book from 2008 on linguistics explains the essential term "'genetic relationship' among languages [as] . . . a phylogenetic, genealogical relationship, that is, descent from a common ancestor."[11] Notice that all the terms used to clarify the meaning of *genetic* in linguistics are themselves equally current within biology. The direction of this derivation is not so simple, however, as the word *genetic* itself was borrowed by biology from philological cultural history, notably from the first cultural historians, Johann Gottfried Herder in his "Origin of Language" essay, which won the prize of the Prussian Royal Academy of Sciences in 1770,[12] and August Schlözer in *Vorstellung seiner Universal-Historie* (1772).[13] The influence we observe here is not a circle but a braid that is still being woven.

Darwin's title is somewhat misleading since he avoids discussions of origins in favor of development, picking up the process of evolution *in medias res*. Darwin thus extenuates a trend that was already noticeable in Origin of Language treatises from Etienne Bonnot de Condillac to Jean-Jacques Rousseau to Herder, Wilhelm von Humboldt, Jakob Grimm, and beyond. Implicit in the puzzle of origins was the question of diversity, which became the explicit target of many of these works. In Condillac's second chapter, the paradigmatic "origin of language" fades into the "origin of languages,"[14] while Rousseau's first sentence reads, "Speech differentiates man from the other animals; language differentiates one nation from another."[15] What stands at the center of the debate over the origin of language is thus the double-edged question of what unites and what divides humanity, and how therefore to categorize the relationships between groups. A decisive moment in modern classification was reached in the late eighteenth century when historical descent came to be understood as the causal mechanism for morphological similarities.[16] Michel Foucault visualized the new historicity of the epoch as a shift from horizontal schemas to vertical progressions, and in the very realms also examined in this book—linguistics, economics, and the biological and human sciences. In gaining a history, language, life, labor, and "man" also came into being as epistemological objects, Foucault argues. Foucault overlooks, however, the significance granted by the new genealogical structures to lateral relations, reimagined as a function of history. Lineage, in other words, served to plot complex branching kinship relations, within which epistemology was embroiled.

This chapter investigates the way that not only comparative philology but also, and in tandem, philosophy of language turned to genealogical transmission to understand the development of language structures and of signification. While these theories were dependent on historical models at the turn of the nineteenth century, they placed the sibling at the forefront of signification and cultural identity. On the one hand, a performative language theory emphasized praxis between contemporaries—between siblings—as the basis of subjectivity, and, on the other, linguistics turned to grammar to consolidate kindred cultures as sisters. These two registers of language theory coincide in Johann Wolfgang von Goethe's *Iphigenia in Tauris*, which also considers the threat of incest opened by such imbricated identities. The branching genealogical tree of language development and the analogous evolutionary tree became an icon for successful scientific practice. In both fields the differentiation of siblings functions as constitutive of selves while marking an inescapable epistemological slippage at the heart of classification, a slippage handled tenderly in George Eliot's poem "Brother and Sister."

MOTHER TONGUES

Our language reports its relationship to us as familial, as a *mother tongue* or *Muttersprache*. The Latin expression *lingua maternal* arose in the twelfth century as a way to distinguish domestic vernacular languages from Latin, the masculine language of scholarship. The term itself drifted into vernaculars by the fifteenth century. In the wake of the Reformation and then particularly with eighteenth-century reification of the maternal, it began to reflect the idea that only such a language learned affectively in childhood could express interiority.[17] Such an affective understanding of the mother tongue intensified along with the eighteenth-century reification of the maternal. While Johann Heinrich Zedler's *Universallexikon* of 1731–1754 identified *Muttersprache* as "that language spoken in the place where one is born and raised,"[18] Johann Christoph Adelung in 1811 identified it as "a language learned from one's mother."[19]

Beginning in the seventeenth century, as comparative philology began to organize languages into families, the term *mother tongue* gained a second genealogical resonance, as the protolanguage from which a particular language family developed. George Metcalf has documented the emergence of a kinship understanding of language development and relations as early as the seventeenth century, complete with the genetic terms "mother language," "daughter language," and "sister language."[20] So Adelung's second meaning for the term *Muttersprache* reads, "an original language, which from appearance, or in a marked way, has not arisen from another; a main language [*Hauptsprache*], a stem language [*Stammsprache*] is designated a mother language in consideration of the daughter languages or dialects that have descended [*abstammen*] from it" (Adelung, *Wörterbuch*, 349–50, my trans.). Ephraim Chambers's *Cyclopaedia* of 1728 already defined *Mother-tongue* as "properly an original language from which others are apparently formed,"[21] while only the supplement published in 1753 uses the term in the sense of native language.[22] This double-meaning of mother tongue gestures toward two genealogical trees that cohabit in expressed language: an ontogenetic and a phylogenetic. In both cases, the mother language becomes an inherited and unconscious element of the self, either as the medium of one's own thought or as a primitive vestige that animates one's native language through its roots. Language thus defines identity internally and collectively simultaneously. And in both cases, language implies history, chronology, and development. The mother language is the fundament on which praxis of expression is built. The praxis itself, as I will argue here, however, involves not mothers but siblings.

This double-genealogy of language stood at the inception of both cultural history and the romantic philosophy of language, united in the work of Johann Gottfried Herder.[23] Herder was perhaps the single most influential figure in the transition from the Enlightenment to the Romantic period in Germany, not only for the fields of literature and philosophy but equally for investigations of linguistic and cultural diversity and history.[24] The origin myth in Herder's essay "On the Origin of Language" grounds human language in an act of abstraction, of *Besonnenheit*. A collective object—Herder's example is sheep—is thus named after their common auditory trait, here bleating. What is less frequently remembered is the trajectory of Herder's essay from a consideration of the origin of language to the communal use and development of language, and finally to language differentiation between groups.

The stages of Herder's theory—from origin to diversification—are unified through their integration into a single, causally interlocked system that is historical not only because it proceeds progressively from the archetypal mother language but also because this symbolic system participates in the diachrony of incipient human thought. Human language is thus necessarily auditory. Herder speculates, for example, that a creature more dependent on touch might spin expressive webs, and one more dependent on vision might enact pantomimes ("Origin," 108–9). But these creatures would be inhuman in innumerable ways. For humans, chronology is crucial: the old Mother herself, the oldest language, possessed a directness and passion long since refined, subdued, and attenuated through the generations of transmission, although differently in each discrete language tributary. So concrete is the personification of language in Herder that Michael Forster feels the need to add clarification in his English translation, for example, where Herder states:

> In a refined, late-invented metaphysical language, which is a degeneration, perhaps at the fourth degree, from the original savage mother [tongue (*MF's addition*)] of the human species, and which after long millennia of degeneration has itself in turn for centuries of its life been refined, civilized, and humanized—such a language, the child of reason and society, can know little or nothing any more about the childhood of its first mother.
>
> (68)

This series is a progression, and the form or forms of progression are the true theme of the essay. It is as "a linguistic creature" (110) that "the human being is a freely thinking, active being, whose forces operate forth progressively" (127). It is also as a linguistic being that the human is, as for Aristotle, a social creature. Herder adds to Aristotle, however, that the communal nature of humanity leads to the ongoing development of language, and thus, as communities develop differently, that languages diversify (147). The ontogenetic and phylogenetic trajectories are linked.

Subsequent to the foundational moment of abstraction that grounds representation, human language continues to retreat from its object and the affect associated with it over the course of generations. Born into language at a given historical moment, the infant acquires "tongue and soul [*Zunge und Seele*]" (142) through the parental language—both father- and mother tongue for Herder. In other words, for Herder, signification does not form a closed circle between the signifier and the concept of the signified but partakes in a lineage backward from the current speaker to the emotions of his or her infancy, and backward again through the generations to the originator of language in his relationship with the object.

It is because parents and children are the dominating familial roles in Herder's work that his introduction of the logic of the sibling, as it were, in spite of himself, is so striking. If Enlightenment progressive histories of humanity often crystalized into linear forms such as ladders or chains, Herder's transitional role in the development of historiography manifests itself concretely in the figure he chooses to represent history in "This Too a Philosophy of History for the Formation of Humanity," namely, a tree, which begins as a single line—a trunk, but which cannot be contained and finally fragments outward into branches and twigs. (See fig. 4.1, my own illustration of Herder's figures of speech.) Herder oscillates between two historical figures of speech, layering biographical terms with genealogical ones. The progression from the Orient to Rome represents, on the one hand, a development from childhood to maturity, and yet on the other, a sequence of generations according to which Egypt and Phoenicia are twin siblings, the children of Mother Orient.[25] This first sibling split, a knot in the linear development of the trunk, heals, but Herder must abandon linearity altogether for true branches when he arrives at the modern world. For Herder as for many thinkers since, ancient and modern are not strictly temporal constructs; Herder's trunk is composed of ancient Egyptians and Greeks but also of primitive peoples

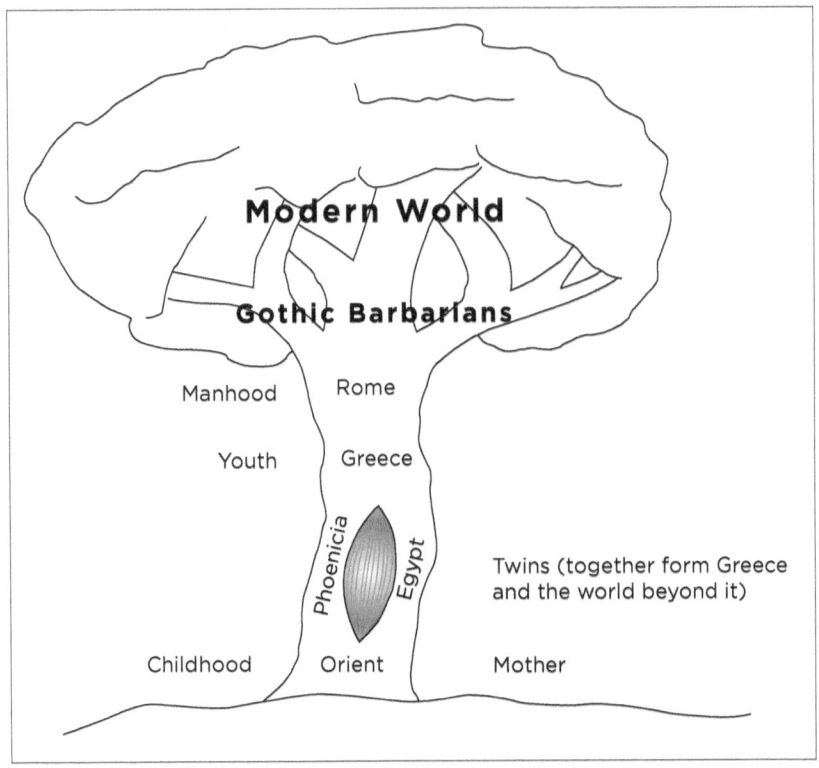

FIGURE 4.1 Author's illustration of Johann Gottfried Herder's Tree of History.

still living.[26] However, Herder elevates the primitive here in a way that is familiar from Rousseau through the Romantics. The European upper branches of the crown can reach their own source of nourishment only through exploitation of the more vital ancestral parts of the tree beneath. Faced with a world in which colonized people are becoming "God help us! ... *like us!*," a world in which "we are all becoming *brothers*" ("This Too a Philosophy," 325, 350, emph. orig.), Herder offers a biting critique of this rhetoric of brotherhood as a cover for imperial attempts at assimilation, and laments what would amount to the uprooting of human civilization if all humans, abandoning the trunk position, mounted into the branches as brothers. As we will see, by the time the genealogical tree becomes pictorial at the beginning of the nineteenth century, this prophecy has been fulfilled: the tree has lost its trunk.

SISTER VOICES

In 1786 Sir William Jones, also known as Oriental Jones, would classify Greek, Latin, and Sanskrit as descendants of an extinct common ancestor, spurring on what Raymond Schwab called the Oriental Renaissance in Europe. At the time that Herder wrote about languages a decade before Jones, however, the most widely accepted theory posited Scythian as an ancient and extinct mother tongue for European languages. Scythia was a Greek name for a region that included Crimea and the steppes north of the Black Sea, while Crimea itself was known as Tauris.[27] The Greeks identified Scythians as barbarians par excellence, a designation that conflated a spiritual with a linguistic inferiority.[28] The Scythian theory would undoubtedly have increased the appeal of the ancient tragic material that Goethe reworked into his *Iphigenia in Tauris*.[29] Begun in 1776 under the influence of his friendship with Herder, the *Iphigenia* was finally completed in 1787, when Goethe dedicated it to Herder with the address, "Here my dear brother, Iphigenia."[30] *Iphigenia in Tauris* encompasses the convergence of ontogenetic and phylogenetic accounts of language so central to Herder, and yet along the way it posits an entirely different philosophy of language. If Herder has illustrated the life of languages and of cultures through metaphors of biography, he has overlooked the way these metaphors critique his own commentary on the necessary aurality of language. It is not only sound that travels through time; most objects experience histories of metamorphosis and none so paradigmatically as living organisms, which is why methodologies could travel so easily between comparative philology and the life sciences. In his drama, Goethe embraces the materiality always present within systems of signification and thereby reconfigures language praxis as both presentist and performative. The adaptive potential of language does not occur merely at its point of transmission from one generation to the next as in Herder but conditions all subjectivity through the ongoing circulation of meaning and the transformation of material. The shift from a representative to a performative theory of language is visible in the move from a mother- to a sibling tongue.

Iphigenia in Tauris revolves around an injunction delivered by the oracle at Delphi to Orestes. Orestes has appealed to Apollo for release from the Furies who have pursued him since he killed his mother Clytemnestra to avenge her murder of his father Agamemnon. The oracle instructs him to bring home "the sister."[31] Orestes therefore sets out with his foster brother Pylades to retrieve the religious figure of Diana, Apollo's sister, from Tauris. In Tauris, he finds his own sister, Iphigenia, long believed dead by her family. The play manages to end well when Orestes reinterprets the oracle as a directive to bring home not the Taurians' sacred image of Diana but instead Iphigenia, his own sister.[32] *Iphigenia*, then, is a play about the relations—including kinship relations—between and among subjects and objects as mediated through language, representation, and *Bildlichkeit*.[33] The drama illustrates the ways symbolic practice both knits joint subjectivity and segregates cultural groups. Pushed to extremes, both of these operations made Goethe nervous, as we will see.

Iphigenia in Tauris opens with a number of figures who each experience their involuntary individual state as an unhealed wound, a tearing asunder from which each hopes to be healed (85, line 78). Only Pylades has an intact, coherent self-image, which rests on his lifelong intact relationship with Orestes. Indeed, he dates the beginning of his life to this attachment, insisting. "My life began when I began to love you" (100, line 654), and stating simply, "I have never lived nor wished to live / Other than with and for you" (100, line 640). Iphigenia proffers a similar understanding of her relationship to Orestes when she claims, "My fate is one with yours, close-knit together" (113, line 1122).

The necessary medium of such interweaving is language. And it is the voices of a friend and of a sister that heal Orestes.[34] Iphigenia cries:

> Oh if the voice of mother's blood once shed
> Can call in somber tones, far down to hell,
> Shall not an innocent sister's word of blessing
> Call, from Olympus, gods of help and rescue?
>
> (114, lines 1164–67)

It is not only significant here that the mother was herself a perpetrator of violence while the sister is innocent. Goethe's imagery conflates the blood-lineage with blood-guilt and distinguishes the role of the sibling as uniquely suited to healing. This scene thus prefigures the final scene of Schiller's *Bride of Messina*, discussed in chapter 2, when Don Cesar demands a sister's blessing to revoke a mother's curse. Here, however, the blessing is freely proffered.[35] What ultimately frees Orestes is a therapeutic language lesson directed by Pylades that combines voice with body and ties language to objects and people to one another.

> And do you feel the hand of friend and sister
> Holding you tight and still alive? Touch
> Us hard! We are not empty shades. Mark well
> What I say; hear my words.
>
> [... Faß'
> Uns kräftig an; wir sind nicht leere Schatten.
> Merk auf mein Wort! Vernimm es!]
>
> (119 and Werke 5:593, lines 1334–37)

The indexical of touch returns Orestes to the earliest stages of language learning, where words are brought into connection with objects as names. And yet the scene does not play out like Herder's originary moment of naming, nor is the assigning of classifications like "sheep," "friend," or "sister" the goal. While Herder pinpoints the emergence of reflection out of affect as the beginning of human language, Goethe demonstrates the necessity of both for signification to function. Pylades and Iphigenia use the coincidence of sound and touch to help Orestes reimbue the world with meaning. Neither the people nor the words are empty shadows. Rather, language re-calls Orestes to a presence marked by both materiality and temporality called *life*. Goethe admired Angelica Kauffman's sketch of this particular scene (see fig. 4.2), commenting, "She has brought into a simultaneous grouping what the three people speak one after the other, and transformed every word into gesture.... And it is truly the axis of the piece."[36] The axis here is not just the revolution in the plot but the transformation that Kauffmann performs, one of several metamorphoses from verbal *Bildlichkeit* to material *Bildlichkeit* to action, in a variety of directions.

Orestes's reinterpretation of the Oracle's command occurs at the conclusion of a long string of these metamorphoses, in which we can observe how agency shifts between humans and objects through the use of signs. In the prehistory of the play, Diana demands from Agamemnon his

FIGURE 4.2 Angelica Kauffman, *Iphigenie, Orest und Pylades*, from Goethe's *Iphigenie auf Tauris*. Goethe Nationalmuseum. By permission of Klassik Stiftung Weimar.

oldest daughter (*Iphigenia*, 94, line 423). Here we see the first fulfillment of an oracle in a manner contrary to the understanding of its recipient. Agamemnon assumes the command must entail Iphigenia's death, but Diana rescues Iphigenia from the knife and claims her alive, transporting her to Diana's own temple in Tauris. Iphigenia's family meanwhile believes she has been sacrificed. Iphigenia's own account of being wrapped away in a cloud hardly clarifies how such a misunderstanding could be possible. Is there a replacement body to bury? Euripides recounts the substitution of a bleeding deer for the daughter, suggesting to onlookers perhaps a miraculous transformation but maintaining at least a dying body as a placeholder for Iphigenia. Goethe gives us nothing in place of the deer; there is no token left behind, no substitution performed. Instead, the absence of any perceived absence, interpreted as Iphigenia's presence in the role of sacrifice, drives the cycle of violence. When Orestes and Pylades set out for Tauris in response to the later oracle, they have no pledge to redeem; they come to perform what looks like a theft, although it reproduces and reverses the original dynamic initiated by Diana.

The lack of a substitute for Iphigenia does not, however, mean that Diana's action has created no sign. On the contrary, her rescue of Iphigenia creates a *Bild* within Iphigenia, an image of the goddess as ethical actor who repudiates blood sacrifices. This image impels Iphigenia to abolish human sacrifice on the peninsula where she finds herself priestess. In a real sense she buys these lives—lives owed to her presence on Tauris—with those of her own parents, who die because of her absence and presumed sacrifice. In Tauris, Iphigenia ministers not to one but to two *Bilder* of Diana, the cult object over whose worship she presides,[37] and her own internal image of Diana as an ethical actor. When Orestes and Pylades appear with the intention of "rescuing" the idol, both of Iphigenia's divine images are threatened. In response, she offers up her most famous prayer to Diana, "Save me, and save your image [*Bild*] in my soul!" (130, lines 1716–17). When Orestes shifts the referent of the oracle, then, he does not substitute one sister for another but carries home both together—Iphigenia, whom he calls a "A sacred image [*heil'gen Bilde*]," and the image of Diana within her (142, line 2127, 5:618). Representation, substitution, and exchange turn out to be insufficient mechanisms for understanding the linguistic and the social processes in action here, as objects and images multiply and interweave, facilitating the entwinement also of subjects, most forcefully of Orestes and Iphigenia.

The image of Diana falls into the lively debates of the time about fetishes, discussed in the previous chapter. The word *fetish* or "made thing" originated in the fifteenth century with Portuguese traders, who used it to categorize religious objects in West Africa, and the term gained common currency through an ethnographic work by Charles de Brosses, *Du culte des dieux fétiches* (1760).[38] The concept of the fetish distinguished stages of civilization through distinct ways of relating to material: matter was objective and passive for the Europeans, subjective and active for the Africans.[39] The construction of this cultural discrepancy also solidified the modern subject-object divide in Western thought discussed in the introduction. Goethe's avoidance of the terms *fetish* or *idol* in favor of the word *Bild* grants the object fluidity in its relations with the various characters and their cultures, freely acknowledging slippage between internal and external, between object, idea, and representation, which in turn reveals the perviousness of any purported individual.[40] Like what Bruno Latour calls a *factish*, Goethe's *Bild* functions to suspend the theorized divide between truth and construct and enables a praxis in which the two are allowed to coincide. This play of representation also demonstrates the illusory quality of any individual subjectivity.

The siblings Iphigenia and Orestes accordingly demonstrate the formation of self through others without relinquishing those others, in a process that resembles the "keeping while giving" of Annette Weiner's anthropological work. After Orestes's arrival, Iphigenia turns not only to Diana but also to her brother Apollo for assistance, appealing to them as siblings to siblings, before asking Diana to "grant your blessed help to me through him [Orestes], / To him through me" (119, lines 1328–29). This formulation describes indeed how the two siblings together accomplish their release from Tauris. Their identity is so bound together that Iphigenia describes herself to Thoas in the form of a synecdoche, a part-whole relation that should lead him from his goodwill toward her to goodwill toward the pair she constitutes a portion of: "let your friendship grace / Brother and sister, as it did the sister" ["sei auch den Geschwistern wie der Schwester freundlich"] (137, lines 1963–64, 5:612). In German, the words themselves very nearly form a synecdoche, as *Schwester* [sister] lies nearly embedded within the word *Geschwister* [siblings].[41] The synecdochal relationship between siblings once again here speaks to their jointness, which each exceeds, and which leaves each open to other jointures.

In contrast to this consolidation dynamic, the divergence of languages disentangles Greeks from Scythians. Iphigenia classifies Thoas as part of a *Volk* through tone of voice or accent, while the drama distinguishes Greeks from Scythians by their stage in the progression of language history. Like Herder's barbarians, the Scythians are forceful and direct in their speech; it is said that Thoas "doesn't know / The art of bringing conversations 'round / From far off, slowly, subtly, to his purpose" (87, lines 167–68). At the other extreme of language sophistication, Pylades deploys language strategically, using, in his own estimation "cunning and wit" (103, line 766) or what Iphigenia less subtly calls "wretched lies" (121, 1405, 5:596) ["O weh der Lüge!"] to achieve his ends of stealing the religious figure. Pylades instantiates the hypocritical exploitation Herder saw lurking under the "enlightened" screen of universal brotherhood.

The speech of Iphigenia and Orestes would seem to represent an ideal middle ground, combining a heuristics of adaptive signification with honesty. I would argue, however, that the drama remains deeply uneasy not only with Pylades but also with Iphigenia and Orestes. The move away from directly representative language is part of the general disavowal of an anchoring authority most obvious in the French Revolution, that seismic shift from sovereign succession—from substitution—to fraternal thinking—or performativity. The Iphigenia myth depicts only murderous relations in both directions between the generations. This turn away from the parental generation is simultaneously a turn away from cosmopolitanism. Like Lessing's *Nathan the Wise*, *Iphigenia in Tauris* ends with the avoidance of a mixed marriage.[42] The younger generation represents instead *völkisch* and familial allegiance. Goethe's ambivalence toward this choice is manifest in its incestuous overtones. Iphigenia's insistence that "A shudder drives me from / A stranger, but my inmost being draws me / To a brother, irresistibly" (115, lines 1185–87) is matched by Orestes's cry, "Since my first youth there's nothing I have loved / As much as I could love you, Sister" (116, lines 1251–52). The dynamics of attraction that bind Iphigenia and Orestes show an exclusivity that threatens to bring an end to, or a new curse on, the family they hope to save. Here, in 1787, we can see Goethe working through a similar constellation of concerns about subjectivity in the face of sibling-resemblance, and erotic liaisons in the face of sibling-attachments, that he returns to when he picks up his work on *Wilhelm Meister's Apprenticeship*, completed in 1795. It is significant that part of Mignon's magnetic appeal in that novel lies in her voice lifted in song, but that the words of her songs are a confused mixture of languages over which she has no mastery. Her inability to work with and in language as Iphigenia and Orestes do reflects her parents' self-directed refusal of exchange.[43]

Language throughout the play thus constitutes a process of bringing into being and an interactive foundation of agency, but one that is already situated within a set of constraints relating to transmission through a community. As Ernst Cassirer has mused about language in an intersubjective world, "Instead of relating to the selfsame spatio-temporal cosmos of things, subjects find themselves and join together in a common action."[44] Cassirer approaches but stops short of Goethe here, assigning language creative powers over the object but not reciprocally over the subject; there is for him a discrete "individual" who enters into the "common world" of language (15). For Goethe, as we have seen, the subject is among the objects constituted in language, without, however, thereby losing its agency. In his intertwining of materiality, language, and agency, Goethe has granted language a life. Unlike later writers we will encounter in this chapter, Goethe does not envision this life as organic, that is, defined by an inner-directed and bounded cohesiveness that lifts it above human history. The life of language for Goethe is intricately woven into the lives of its speakers.

THE ICONIC TREE

A decade after Goethe began work on *Iphigenia*, William Jones delivered his "Third Discourse before the Asiatic Society" in Calcutta (1786), the date most frequently credited as the beginning of modern comparative philology. In this lecture, Jones posited the existence of an extinct language as a common source from which Sanskrit, Greek, Latin, and the Germanic languages were derived, thus delineating the Indo-European language family.[45] Although several other writers had suggested similar familial constellations of languages earlier, it was only with Jones and in light of the growing fascination with Sanskrit across Europe that the topic of an Indo-European, Indo-Germanic, or Aryan language family became a matter of widespread interest.[46] Within several years, Jones had adapted the early modern theory of language differentiation as a legacy of the three sons of Noah into a theory of three language families, each of which could trace "descent from a common ancestor" (*Discourses*, 2:63), namely, the Hindu, the Tartar, and the Arabian. Jones understood his task as an "inquiry into the genealogy of nations"—as peoples dispersed, so did the languages they spoke (1:146).

Goethe's decision to separate population groups in his play was representative of a general tendency to think of population groups in terms of divergence and diffusion. This branching pattern found iconic pictorial form in both linguistic and evolutionary trees, schemas with no room for merging, influence, or integration.[47] Now is a good moment to explore the emergence of the diversifying genealogical tree, because we are witnessing the end of its hegemony within the field of evolutionary biology, its longest-lasting derivative.[48] Most biologists date the idea of the evolutionary tree to Darwin's use of the expression "Tree of Life" in *On the Origin of Species*, but the image has a long and diverse history.[49] Sigrid Weigel has identified two types of early tree images: Trees of Knowledge, that is, static classification schemas (fig. 4.3), and Trees of Life (fig. 4.4), or family genealogies. Their merger in the evolutionary tree converted a history of descent into a causal explanation for classification, she notes.[50] The evolutionary tree is not the first or last instance in which common ancestry is acknowledged to cause morphological similarities, however. From biblical and Classical philological reconstructions of ancient texts, to comparative linguistics, to biology, each field that adopted descent with modification from a common ancestor as a causal mechanism for classification granted a kind of life to its object.

To create their model, these early genealogical fields choose carefully between the elements on offer in their precursors. From the family trees, they imported the ideas of descent and of transformation over time—lineage and progeny, and thus a wide set of kinship associations. From the schema, they adapted the branching structure, which had illustrated increasingly fine subfields and subcategories, into an image for diversification. By replicating this branching structure, the genealogical fields also rejected an element of family trees, namely, the merger of two equally complex family units in creating each new generation. Often pictorial familial lineages of the early modern period had similarly failed to take account of mothers. The ease with which the mixture of two lines to create children could be overlooked appears strikingly in the work of William Jones, who states that every human pair need only have *two* children for the population of the earth to explode because of the exponential nature of the proliferation (*Discourses*, 2.3). In context, it seems less likely that Jones has ignored daughters than that he has overlooked the numerical personhood of mothers. The genealogies of landed aristocracy and royalty often did take account of mothers, however, as marriages represented significant alliances, and some legal systems allowed for inheritance through the female line. The fifteenth-century genealogy depicted

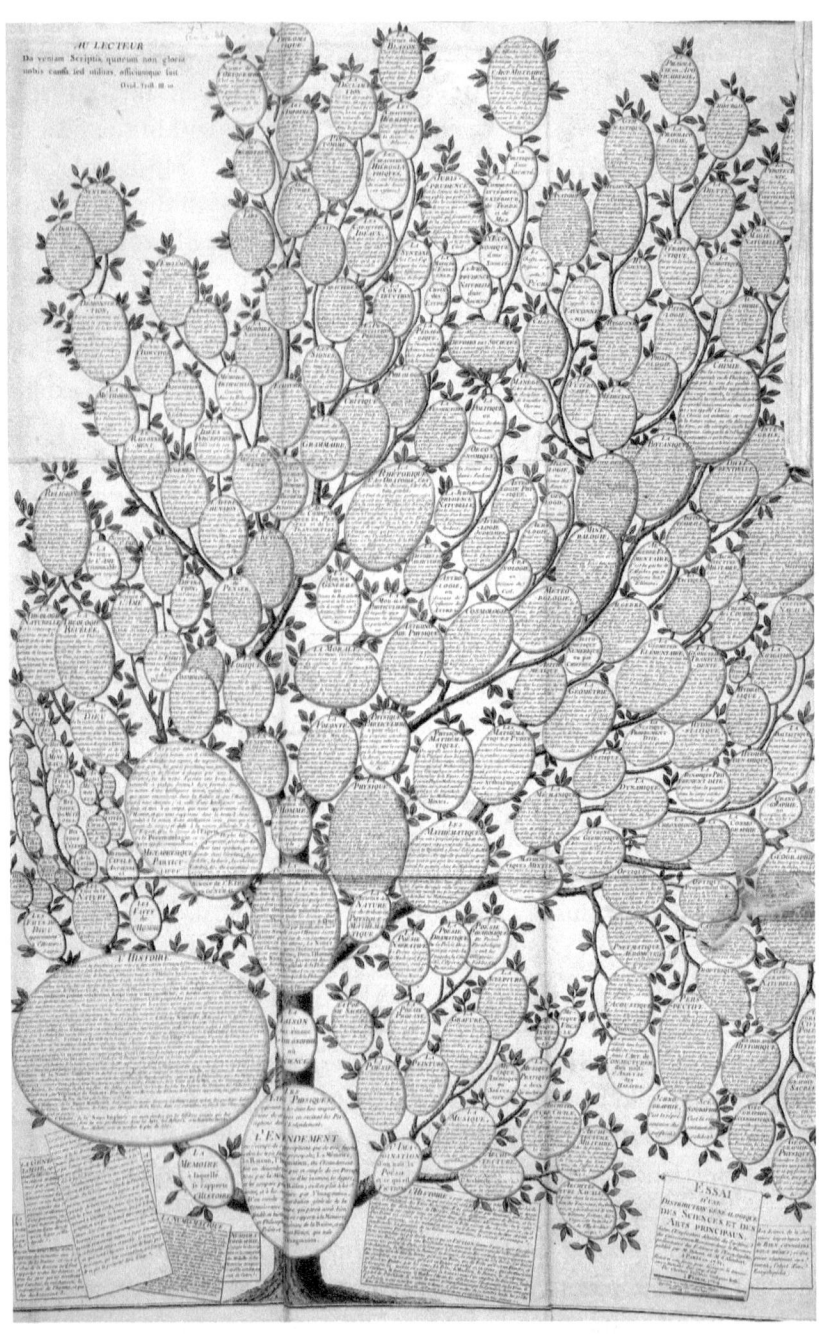

FIGURE 4.3 Chrétien Frederic Guillaume Roth, frontispiece to Pierre Monchon's *Table analytique*, 1780. Special Collections Research Center, University of Chicago Library.

FIGURE 4.4 Hartmann Schedel, genealogy of Duke Henry II of Bavaria from *Liber Chronicarum*, 1493. David M. Rubenstein Rare Book & Manuscript Library, Duke University.

FIGURE 4.5 Friedrich Ritschl, stemma of Thomas Magister, 1832. Duke University Library.

in figure 4.4, for example, does not represent daughters but does thread its genetic vine through the abdomens of wives. Marriages were often necessary to depicting and justifying inheritance in landed families.[51] As these family trees illustrate, complexity in the kinship relationships of a human being stretches backward as well as forward. Language and evolutionary trees are parthenogenetic, however, an ideological choice that requires explanation.

The earliest pictorial genealogical trees came from manuscript studies. By the mid-eighteenth century, biblical scholars had begun to think genealogically about manuscript transmission, followed in the late eighteenth century by Classical philologists.[52] Using the first instance of the introduction of a particular copying error to mark a node where lines of transmission diverge, such *stemmata* could trace manuscripts backward toward a lost original. The first images of the kinship of texts seem to have been published by Carl Johan Schlyter and Carl Gottlob Zumpt in 1827 and 1831, respectively, and Zumpt coined for them the term *stemma*, Latin for tree.[53] The first strict practitioner of the method was Friedrich Ritschl, who referred to such an image as "a formal genealogical tree [*förmlichen genealogischen Stammbaum*]"[54] before later adopting Zumpt's term *stemma*. Ritschl's first stemma, published in 1832 (fig. 4.5), deserves close attention. It represents a manuscript tradition in which copyists had had access to multiple editions simultaneously. Rather than reproduce a single example as faithfully as possible, the scribes intentionally imported emendations from various editions. The stemma thus includes a large amount of mixture, known in philology as "contamination." Commenting on this image in 1963, Sebastiano Timpanaro chides: "With all those intersecting lines, his stemma already resembles the ones that are found more and more often in recent critical editions and that aim to give some idea of the manuscript tradition in all its disarray, without convenient but arbitrary simplifications. But when the disarray is excessive, it is better to give up on the stemma!" (*Genesis*, 94). Rather than abandoning stemmata as a response to complexity, however, the genealogical fields instead suppressed disarray (see fig. 4.6.) Only much later did such disciplines attempt again to come to terms with the reality of crossings, influence, and mergers. The transmission between classical philology and comparative philology would seem to be fairly direct, as Ritschl was the doctoral advisor of August Schleicher, generally credited with devising the first language tree, which he published in 1853 (fig. 4.7).[55] However, complicating any genealogy of direct descent for the trees themselves from a unitary and verifiable original, we should note that František Čelakovský also published one the same year in Prague (fig. 4.8).[56] The idea of genealogy had after all been firmly connected with language development for several centuries, and the tree was a frequent rhetorical figure used to describe the relationships between languages long before it appeared as an actual image. Schleicher later experimented with the tree form, publishing increasingly diagrammatic trees, including an illustration of the concept in 1860 (fig. 4.9) and a depiction of the history of what he refers to as the Indogerman tree a year later (fig. 4.10), both before he encountered Darwin's tree diagram.

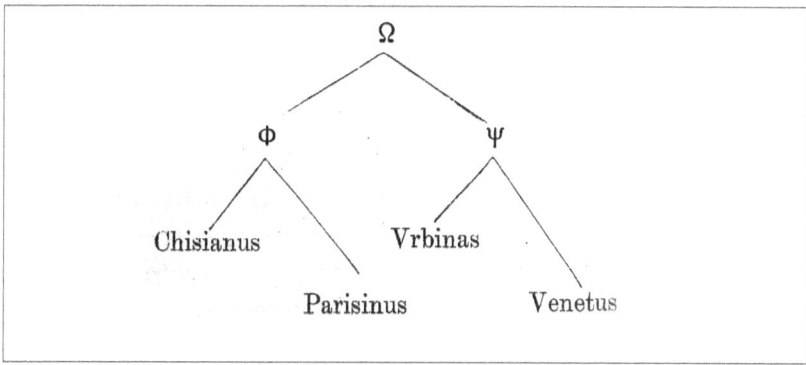

FIGURE 4.6 Friedrich Ritschl, stemma of Dionysius of Halicarnassus, 1866 reprint of 1838 original. University of North Carolina, Chapel Hill Library.

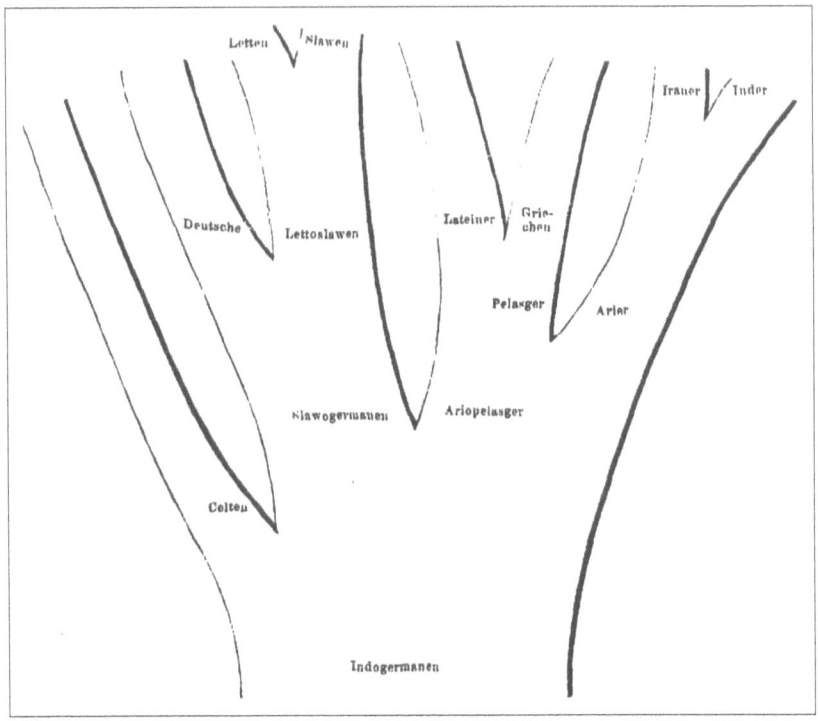

FIGURE 4.7 August Schleicher, "Die ersten Spaltungen des indogermanischen Urvolkes," 1853.

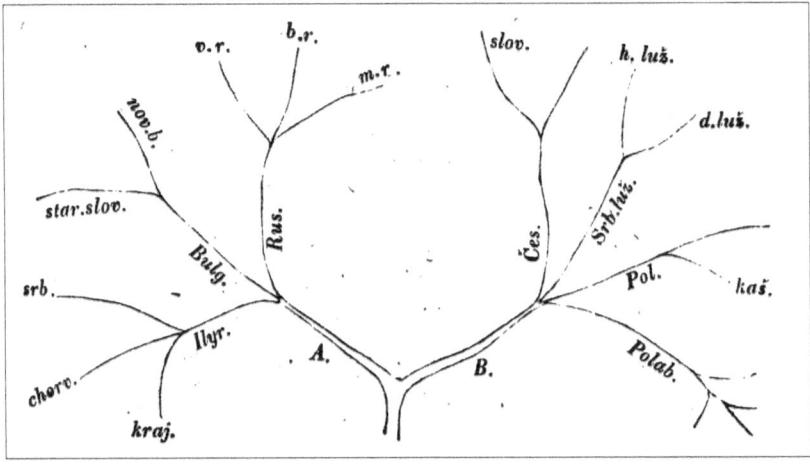

FIGURE 4.8 František Čelakovský, family tree of the Slavic languages, 1853. University of North Carolina, Chapel Hill Library.

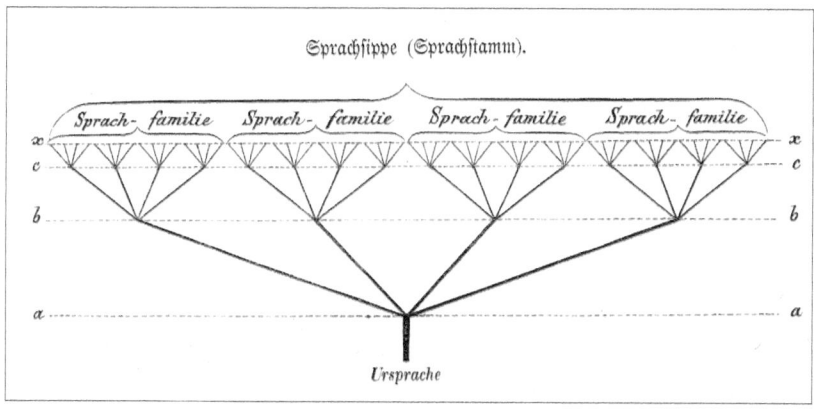

FIGURE 4.9 August Schleicher, Sprachsippe (Sprachstamm) from *Die deutsche Sprache*, 1860. Columbia University Library.

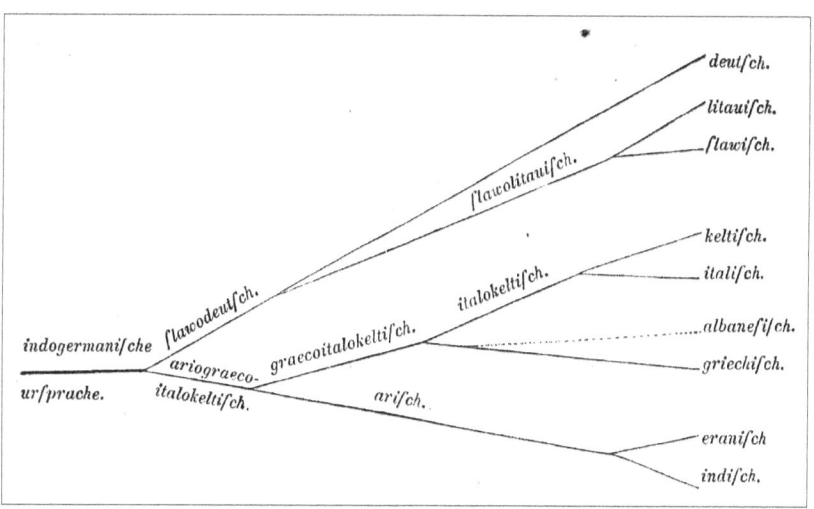

FIGURE 4.10 August Schleicher, Indogermanischer Sprachstamm from *Compendium der vergleichenden Grammatik der indogermanischen Sprachen*, 1866 reprint of 1861 original. Duke University Library.

The derivational tree form may have entered the life sciences with Jean-Baptiste de Lamarck's diagram from the *Philosophie Zoologique* (1899) (fig. 4.11). Lamarck became a transformationalist around the turn of the century and argued not only for ongoing adaptation within species but also for the development of one species from another. He did not, however, believe that all species had come from a single ancestor. Rather, for him all organisms progress toward complexity, and the differing stages of complexity observable around us are a result of repeated occurrences of spontaneous generation reintroducing simple organisms. The interpretation of the dotted lines on his diagram is thus ambiguous and may not indicate genealogy at all.[57] Darwin's famous "I think" sketch in his notebook of 1837 is the first to clearly illustrate the evolution, in the modern sense, of species and genera and also portrays extinct, in contrast to existing, species: the crosshatch rather counterintuitively indicates a still-surviving species that has reached the present (fig. 4.12). This image was published only posthumously, however. Alfred Russel Wallace published a tree diagram very similar to Lamarck's in 1856 (fig. 4.13). Wallace had published a paper attributing the introduction of new species to transmutation or evolution in 1855, but he makes no mention of this theory in the article on bird classification that accompanies the diagram. Wallace has therefore left the mechanism of relatedness ambiguous here, like Lamarck before him. In 1859 Darwin's *Origin of Species* appeared (fig. 4.14), accompanied by a single illustration, which firmly anchored the diagrammatic tree to evolutionary theory. The figure came to be known as the Tree of Life as a result of the following passage from the same chapter:

> The affinities of all the beings of the same class have sometimes been represented by a great tree. I believe this simile largely speaks the truth. . . . As buds give rise by growth to fresh buds, and these, if vigorous, branch out and overtop on all sides many a feebler branch, so by generation I believe it has been with the great Tree of Life, which fills with its dead and broken branches the crust of the earth, and covers the surface with its ever branching and beautiful ramifications.[58]

It is noteworthy, however, that this passage does not mention the diagram. Darwin had already spent seven pages elucidating this figure, in

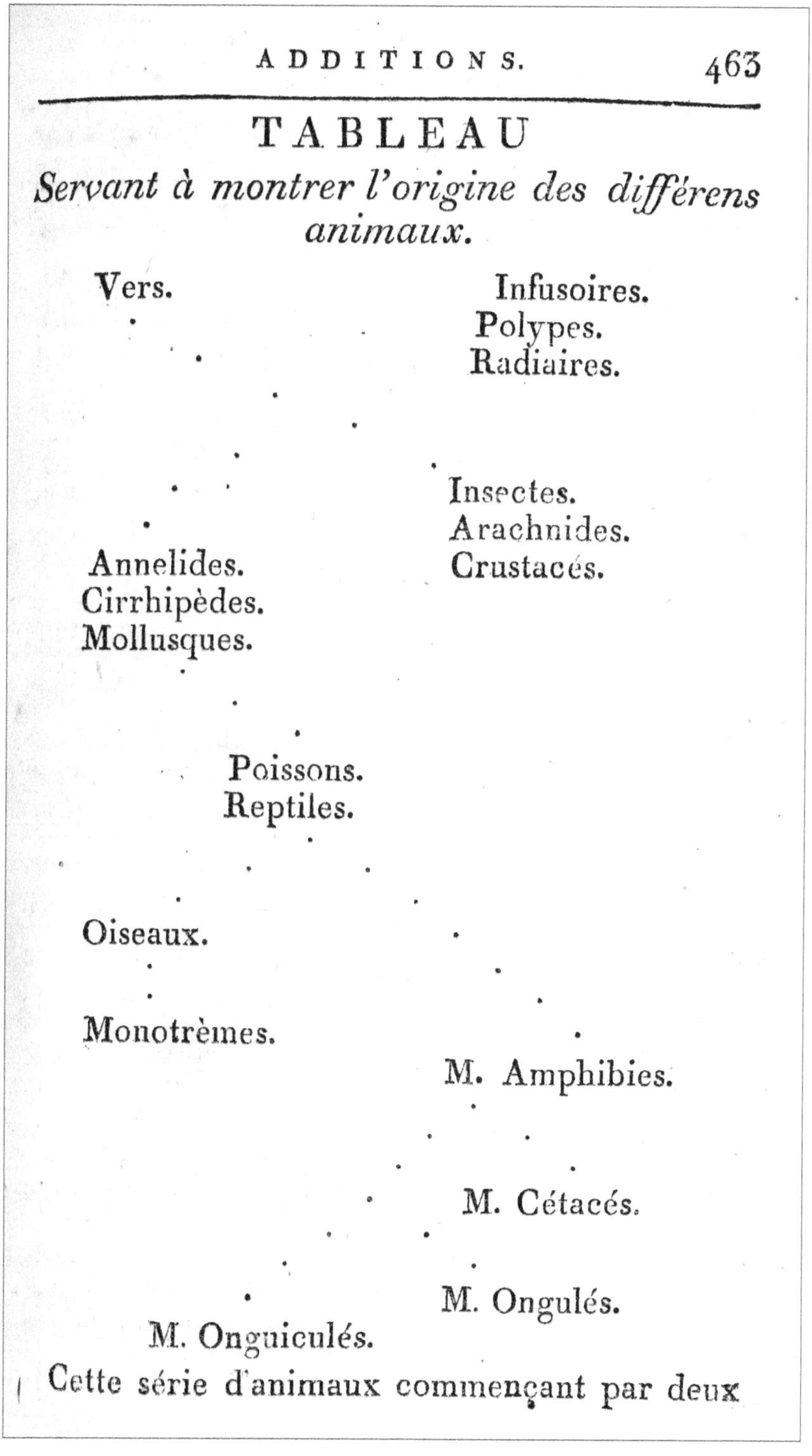

ADDITIONS. 463

TABLEAU
Servant à montrer l'origine des différens animaux.

    Vers.   Infusoires.
                           Polypes.
                           Radiaires.

                       Insectes.
                       Arachnides.
  Annelides.   Crustacés.
  Cirrhipèdes.
  Mollusques.

        Poissons.
        Reptiles.

Oiseaux.

Monotrèmes.
                    M. Amphibies.

                    M. Cétacés.

                    M. Ongulés.
    M. Onguiculés.

Cette série d'animaux commençant par deux

FIGURE 4.11 Jean-Baptiste de Lamarck, table showing the origin of the various animals, from *Philosophie Zoologique*, 1830 edition (original 1809). Harvard University Library.

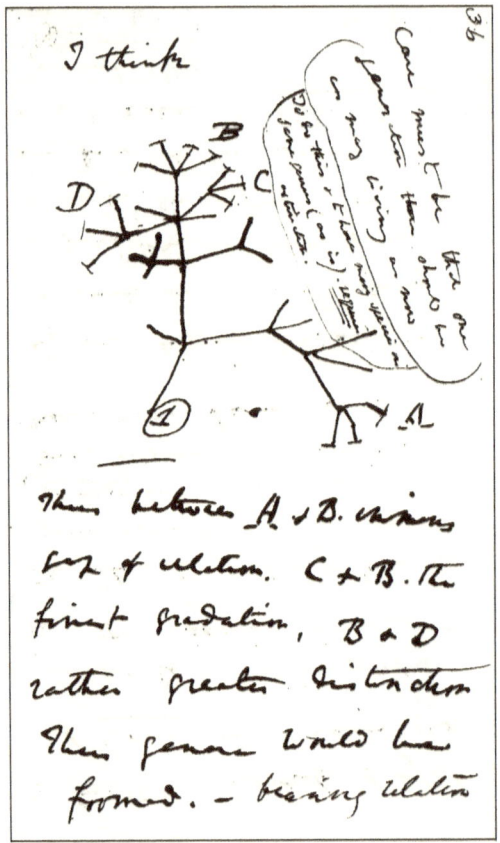

FIGURE 4.12 Charles Darwin, "I think" sketch from Notebook B (1837), reproduced by kind permission of the Syndics of Cambridge University Library. Classmark: CUL-DAR 121.

the course of which he never once uses the word "tree." In the past decade, several authors have pointed out the lack of illustrative correspondence between the figure and the discursive Tree of Life description, and one in particular, Horst Bredekamp (*Darwins Korallen*), has argued that Darwin was far more drawn to the image of coral—which grows in multiple directions—than to that of the tree as an appropriate figure for his thought but reverted to the tree to help bolster his claim to priority after seeing Wallace's tree diagram. In Darwin's earlier sketched depictions, the pictorial directionality of the diversification was far more varied,

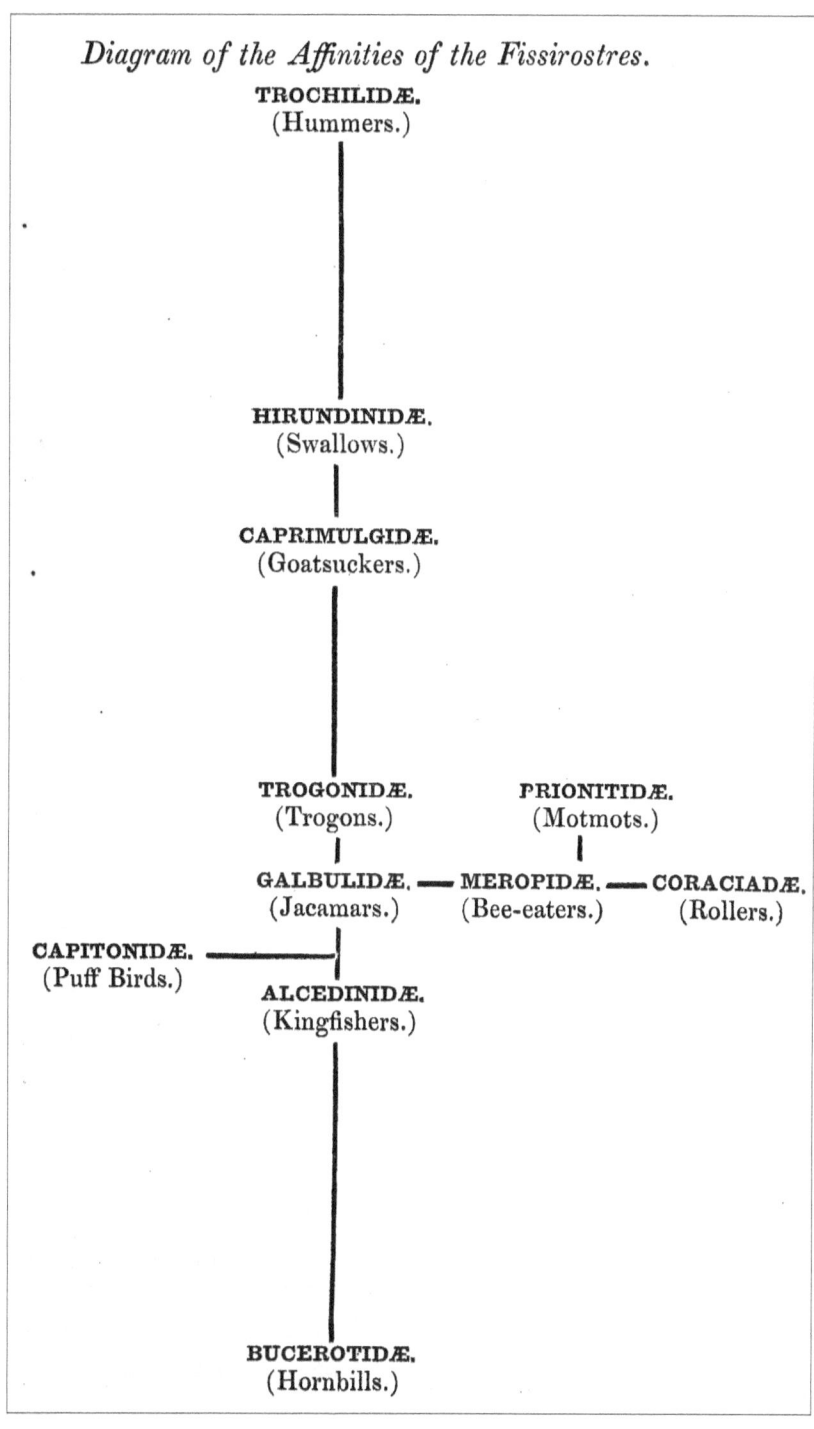

FIGURE 4.13 Alfred Russel Wallace, diagram of the affinities of the Fissirostres, 1856. Duke University Library.

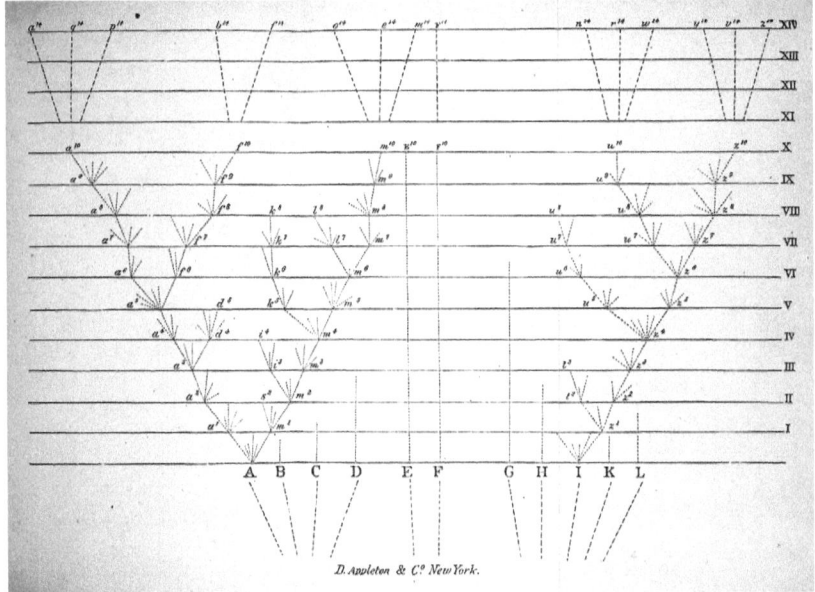

FIGURE 4.14 Charles Darwin, diagram from *The Origin of Species*, 1896 edition. Duke University Library.

even approaching the circular (fig. 4.15), and the natural phenomena represented appear more haphazard in their frequency and distribution.

It is worth noting three significant features of these diagrams. The first is something *not* visible in the images, namely, the mechanism for transformation. What remains hidden is whether the *evolution* in question results from the unfolding of natural law, the progress toward a teleological end (both of these first two involving regularity), or contingent history involving chance and/or human will. The issue of mechanism thus becomes an additional matter for argumentation in each field, and one that begins to separate the fields into different disciplinary categories. The second relevant commonality is one I have pointed to already, namely, the structural dependence on unidirectional divergence, without the possibility of merging, with the exception of the single Ritschl image discussed previously. This emphasis on ramification has three corollaries. First, by following the branches backward rather than forward in time, we move toward a single point of origin that unifies the entire system. While the

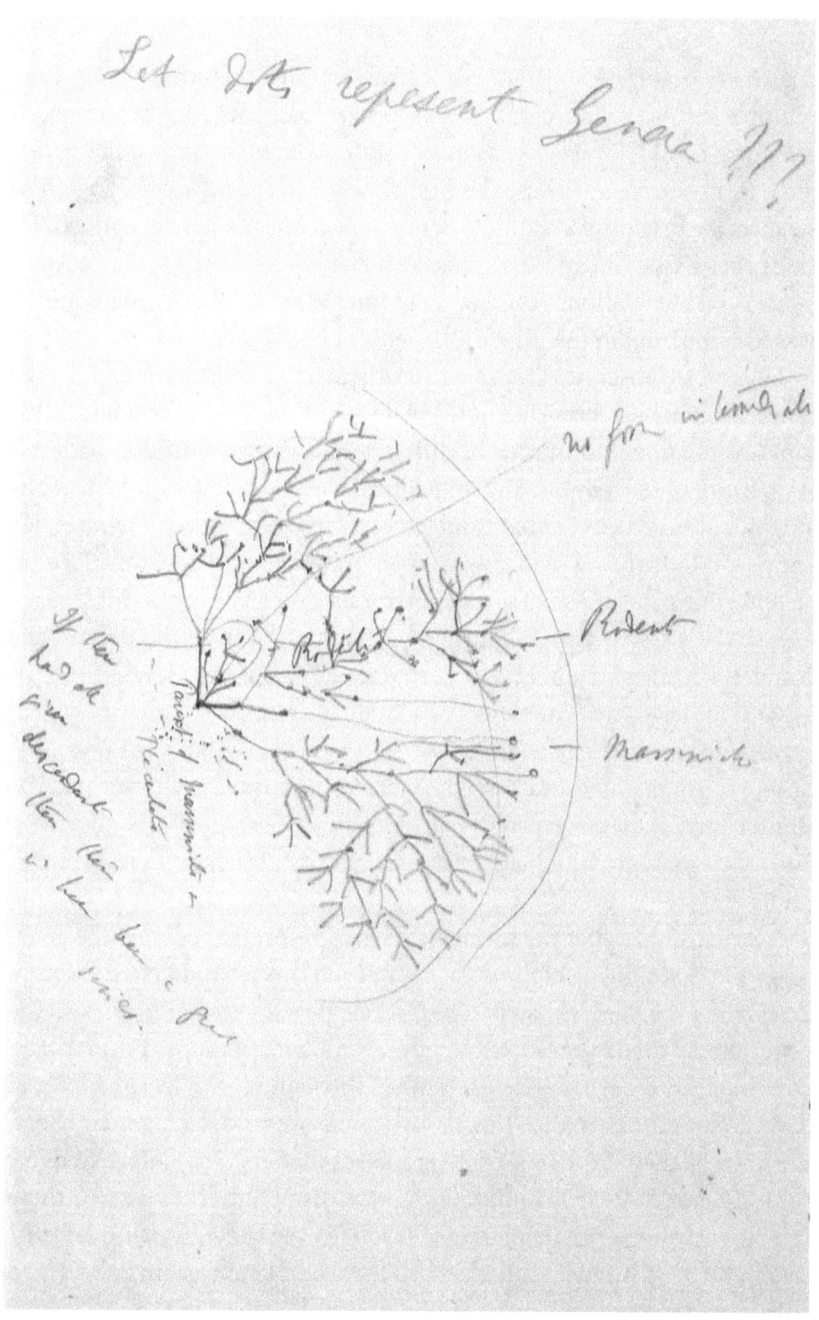

FIGURE 4.15 Charles Darwin, "Principle of divergence, transitional organs/instincts," probably from early 1850s. Reproduced by kind permission of the Syndics of Cambridge University Library. Classmark: Cul Dar 205.5.

degree is variable, the relatedness of terms is universal unless the trees are multiple.[59] It is this observation that historians focus on when they call attention to the nineteenth century's obsession with the search for origins. If, however, we follow the branches outward, we see that the new sciences or disciplines did not merely recognize the passage of generations in a single lineage but created an ever-widening system of distant lateral kinship relations. This contemporary kinship, I have been arguing, was as important to the nineteenth century as origins.

Finally, we observe in these figures that the identification and paring away of siblings creates each term. All definitions in a genealogical system are relational, a matter of differentiation from similars, within a framework of relatedness. The difficulties in explaining the close relationship of Latin and Greek that troubled early investigators of language, Johannes Schmidt noted in 1872, were ameliorated when a "sister relationship stepped into the place of a daughter relationship."[60] Schmidt's usage blends the sister with the cousin as generations cannot be definitively counted within a system in flux. Contemporary linguists retain the term "sister languages" for "members of a language family."[61] For every genealogical system, the existence of the sibling—not self and yet not quite other—both enables and puts pressure on the integrity of terms. The sibling thus achieves a privileged place in explorations of subjectivity and epistemology, which appears particularly clearly in literature and philosophy.

It is significant that the form of such diagrams, if applied to the genealogy of the sibling disciplines that employed them, would fail to capture adequately the complex structure of their developmental histories. The genealogical fields shared some, but not all, ancestors in common and continued to cross-fertilize each other throughout the nineteenth and early twentieth centuries. This failure turns out to reflect similar shortcomings in their depiction of their subject matters. The failure to allow for influence or hybridization has led the disciplines that created these trees eventually to call them into question. By the late nineteenth century, two students of August Schleicher had theorized language mixture. Hugo Schuchardt wrote specifically on Pidgins and Creoles in the 1880s. This area languished until the 1950s but has since become a rich branch of linguistic study, although the definition of "contact languages" as languages with mixed grammatical forms is still a fraught matter in linguistics, and books on the matter begin with obligatory legitimations of their field.[62] Significantly, Schuchardt and other linguists ignored the most prominent example of a mixed language in their near vicinity, Yiddish, to which we will return in the next chapter.[63] At the same time, in the 1880s Johannes Schmidt originated a wave theory of language influence that we will return to below, which slowly eroded the bedrock notion of unilateral descent. In evolutionary theory, the genealogical tree has only recently been the object of critique, but that critique has become increasingly intense, as discussed in the introduction. The tree is undermined not only by the frequency of hybridity, which calls the definition of species into question, but also by phenomena that challenge the definition of any individual organism, such as lateral gene transfer or symbiosis.

DIVERGING GENEALOGIES AND THE SCIENTIFIC METHOD IN LINGUISTICS

Herder's knot and Ritschl's contaminated stemma indicate that it was not inevitable that divergence would become a monolithic form for understanding genealogical development. As we will see, the establishment of a hegemony of splitting in linguistic and evolutionary genealogies served two important purposes: on the one hand, it stood as a bulwark against the epistemological uncertainty encapsulated by the sibling term, and on the other, it reinforced a disciplinary construction that in turn rendered the objects of the fields in question immune to the chaos generated by the failings and frailties of humanity . . . or the humanities. The tree itself grew into a prime example of a Latourian factish whose active agency is screened by practitioners. The construction of the visual genealogical tree facilitated the projection of genealogies as ontological objects, which quieted anxieties about the knowledge, control, and kinship affiliations of the inquiring subject.

Methodologically, the suppression of merging correlated with a shift in emphasis that we find already in William Jones, who moves away from lexical similarities—similar words—to grammatical similarities. Jones calls philology a historical science, but history for Jones is not a record of human will. He uses an older sense of history as an account of empirical facts. Not only philology but also anatomy, chemistry, and physic belong to this category (Jones, *Discourses*, 2:33–34). Reasoning on these facts is the work of *philosophy* (2:34), also known as *science* (2:37). Philology includes, then, a historical aspect manifest in collecting and a scientific aspect manifest in comparing. For Jones, however, *human* history plays no role in linguistic analysis.[64] Jones understood, of course, that human events such as conquest brought languages into contact, and he also speculated on the creation of peoples through admixture (2:2, 2:81). Languages, however, resisted such mixing: "Now the general effect of conquest is to leave the current language of the conquered people unchanged, or very little altered, in its groundwork, but to blend with it a considerable number of exotic names both for things and for actions" (1:28). Jones suggests that the "roots of verbs" and "the forms of grammar," that is, the aspects of language he thought most resistant to change, are the appropriate structures to examine to determine language affinities. Here we see the kernel of what was to become a guiding principle of linguistics throughout the nineteenth century: language as an anchor immune to the chaos of human history.

For Jones the difference between a *groundwork* and the more *exotic* elements of a language is still vague. Twenty years later, Friedrich Schlegel solidified this distinction into a hierarchy that attempted to expunge history from comparative philology in his *On the Language and Wisdom of Indians*. Here Jones's *groundwork* settles more deeply into an interior space, becoming the "inner structure of the languages or comparative grammar" (Schlegel, *Sprache und Weisheit*, 28) and explicitly excluding even roots. Looking at grammar alone insures correlation is "no accidental one, that could be explained through admixture; but rather an essential one, that points to a common descent" (1). The word Schlegel uses for admixture, *Einmischung*, means to mix in, with the connotation that what is mixed in is distinctly heterogeneous.[65] The linguistic division of lexicon from grammar had become a gulf between the surface and the depths of language, which manifested two different and unequally valued temporal operations: fusion and divergence. Put another way, the decision to privilege tenacious inner structure above readily borrowed vocabulary represented an ideological commitment to descent over influence as an arbiter of relatedness. This choice is also one of disciplinary self-definition, as Jones makes clear when he associates "the faculty of combining our ideas agreeably" with *fancy*, and that of "separating and comparing those ideas by the laborious exertions of intellect" with *philosophy*, which he elsewhere uses interchangeably with *science* (*Discourses*, 2:36–37). The idea of segregation lay at the root of science, and what was segregated included peoples.

The stakes of the concern with splitting and merging become clear at the latest in Wilhelm von Humboldt's foundational work in philology. Humboldt's major contribution to comparative philology was a massive work on the Kawi language—a forerunner of modern Javanese—and the identification of a far-flung Austronesian language family uniting languages of the Pacific spoken in the Philippines, New Guinea, Malaysia, and all the way across to Madagascar. Kawi was in a sense a language with a multiple personality disorder: its grammatical structure rendered it a Malay language, but the large majority of its vocabulary derived from Sanskrit. Humboldt encapsulated this tension, perhaps unintentionally, when he referred to Kawi as a manifestation of the "innigste Verzweigung Indischer und einheimischer Bildung."[66] While Peter Heath sensibly translates this phrase as the "most intimate intertwining of Indian and indigenous culture," the word *Verzweigung*, from the root *Zweig* or *branch*, almost always means ramification or branching.[67] Grimm's *Dictionary* identifies the beginning of the nineteenth century as the period when the metaphorical usage of the word as diversification came into vogue, a period we have just seen to be contemporary with the new methodological use of the genealogical tree as both temporal and causal.[68] Humboldt himself is cited for his use of the related meaning of *diffusion* or *dispersal*. The Grimms cite Humboldt's use of the word for its less common secondary meaning of *merging* or *interweaving* as the first known. Humboldt's turn toward merging was always already haunted by splitting.

Humboldt was fascinated by the Malay island because of both its ethnic diversity and the breadth of its cultural influences—including Indian, East Asian, Aboriginal, and Arabic. Or, to follow Humboldt's far more hierarchical explanation:

> We find then, the Malayan peoples squeezed, as it were, between such contrasting affinities and influences. On the same islands and island-groups which even to this day still harbour, in part, a population that

stands on the lowest human level . . . there has simultaneously taken root an age-old and most prosperously flourishing culture from India. The Malayan races have made it their own, in part, in all its fullness.

(19)

The sense of mixture here is complex, as the last sentences indicate with their vacillation between taking root and own-ness, between part and fullness. Humboldt sees the partial openness of the Malay peoples to the "ennobling" *Bildung* of the Sanskrit language and the customs of Sanskrit-speakers as a testament to their educability. And yet there is a limit to that adaptability. Even in this best case for intertwining, the Kawi language, "however many Sanscrit [sic] words it may have incorporated, does not cease on that account to be a Malayan tongue" (53). Language itself forms the national character and is its external expression. While national character is not inborn for Humboldt, it is nearly immutable once acquired. Joseph Errington has traced the repercussions of Humboldt's treatise on the politics of colonialism, which increasingly coalesced around the conviction that its eastern subjects, like the Javanese in the face of superior Sanskrit influence, were resistant to the European so-called civilizing mission (Errington, *Linguistics*, 65–69). The preference for grammar and reification of divergence thus solidified the role of linguistics as a science, committed to analytic rigor, and elevated its stature by reinforcing its political usefulness. Segregation, as method and result, served the new science well.[69]

In 1861 Friedrich Max Müller held his *Lectures on the Science of Language* at the Royal Institution in Great Britain. Max Müller[70] was the single most influential linguist of the nineteenth century—the century of linguistics. His public lectures were attended by tens of thousands (Arvidsson, *Aryan Idols*, 31), and Oxford created a Chair for Comparative Philology specifically for him (Masuzawa, *World Religions*, 212). In his lectures, Max Müller implies that differentiation is a necessary precondition of the scientific object, which grows naturally according to laws rather than developing according to historical contingencies.

[I]f strictly defined, the science of language can declare itself completely independent of history. If we speak of the language of England, we ought, no doubt, to know something of the political history of the British Isles, in order to understand the present state of that language.... The language of England may be said to have been in succession Celtic, Saxon, Norman, and English. But if we speak of the history of the English language, we enter on totally different ground. The English language was never Celtic, the Celtic never grew into Saxon, nor Saxon into Norman, nor Norman into English.... A language, as long as it is spoken by anybody, lives and has its substantive existence.... A Celt may become an Englishman, Celtic and English blood may be mixed.... But languages are never mixed ... not a single drop of foreign blood has entered into the organic system of the English speech. The grammar, the blood and soul of the language, is as pure and unmixed in English as spoken in the British Isles, as it was when spoken on the shores of the German ocean by the Angles, Saxons, and Juts of the continent.[71]

Max Müller is not innovating here. He repeats Friedrich Schlegel's embrace of comparative grammar to determine descent, and his exclusion of borrowed vocabulary as a criterion for classification. He also borrows from Humboldt's Kawi case.[72] Finally, he updates William Jones: humans can choose to join; nature divides.[73] The result is a second almost-human life superimposed on the first. Living language, an organism with blood and soul, has an advantage over people, namely, its parthenogenesis. Humans, with their messy histories of conquest and sexual desire, fail to conform to strict classification.

Even those who rejected organic descriptions of languages generally conformed to the interdiction on language mergers. The American William Dwight Whitney, who studied in Germany with Schleicher, disputed that languages were organisms and that they behaved according to laws indifferent to human history. In a groundbreaking intervention, Whitney assigned languages to a third category within human history, although beyond the control of individual speakers, a category shared by all multigenerational cultural *institutions*. The study of language, as a result, is not a natural science, Whitney concludes, but a social science like "the study of civilization at large, or any of its other constituents, of architecture, of jurisprudence, of history. Its many and striking analogies with the physical sciences cover a central diversity; its essential method is historical."[74] This institutionalization of language deeply influenced Ferdinand de Saussure and the development of structuralism, although structuralism departed from Whitney's interests by focusing on the ahistorical, synchronic in language.⁷⁵

In spite of his disagreements with Schleicher and Max Müller, however, Whitney accepted the unidirectionality of language splitting. Indeed, his pronouncements on the subject share the vehement abhorrence of the possibility of mixture:

> the grammatical system ... resists longest and most obstinately any trace of intermixture, the intrusion of foreign elements and foreign habits. However many French nouns and verbs were admitted to full citizenship in English speech, they all had to give up in this respect their former nationality.... Such a thing as a language with a mixed grammatical apparatus has never come under the cognizance of linguistic students: it would be to them a monstrosity; it seems an impossibility.⁷⁶

This *monstrosity* of mixing, characterized by such value-laden words as *resistance* and *intrusion*, is worth pondering. Whitney grants each language a national sovereignty, complete with citizenship requirements and borders. Much could be said about the construction of nationhood in Europe and the United States by comparing the organic understanding of language with the civic.⁷⁷ But for both Max Müller and Whitney, as for the linguistic discipline they represented, language played the role of guardian, policing boundaries by insulating sister from sister and language family from language family. In a world of impure races, insecure borders, and epistemological uncertainty, language, transcendent, serenely follows immutable laws, preserving the integrity of a classification that is also a human identity; it is the pure archetype of a *Volk*.

SPLITTING HEIRS: EPISTEMIC UNCERTAINTY IN EVOLUTION

Given its success, it is not surprising that Darwin turned to linguistics both to bolster and to clarify his claims in *On the Origin of Species*. Darwin illustrates his new genealogical structure for biology through two analogies, linguistics and family trees, which are worth citing at some length:

It may be worth while to illustrate this view of classification, by taking the case of languages. If we possessed a perfect pedigree of mankind, a genealogical arrangement of the races of man would afford the best classification of the various languages now spoken throughout the world; and if all extinct languages, and all intermediate and slowly changing dialects, had to be included, such an arrangement would, I think, be the only possible one. . . . The various degrees of difference in the languages from the same stock, would have to be expressed by groups subordinate to groups; but the proper or even only possible arrangement would still be genealogical; and this would be strictly natural, as it would connect together all languages, extinct and modern, by the closest affinities, and would give the filiation and origin of each tongue.

(406)

If evolutionary theory here leans on the prestige of linguistics, the development of languages is simultaneously naturalized to make it a firmer source of support. Darwin does not follow or prefigure August Schleicher here by turning languages into organisms but rather naturalizes language by mapping the history of languages onto the history of race, a practice we will return to in the next chapter. Darwin's second illustration of the "community of descent" (409) domesticates the idea:

> As it is difficult to show the blood-relationship between the numerous kindred of any ancient and noble family, even by the aid of a genealogical tree, and almost impossible to do this without this aid, we can understand the extraordinary difficulty which naturalists have experienced in describing, without the aid of a diagram, the various affinities which they perceive between the many living and extinct members of the same great natural class.

(412–13)

What is striking about these two passages from the same chapter is that, while Darwin uses both to cement the revolutionary idea that the classification of species must be understood as a familial history of descent, he does not point out the salient difference between language families and human families, to which this chapter keeps returning; any history that involves human offspring also necessitates merging. Joseph Errington notes that "Schleicher's parthenogenetic image of linguistic 'reproduction'" "blurs this basic conceptual difference" so that he can literalize metaphors of linguistic descent.[78] For Darwin, however, descent is no metaphor. Merging within sexual species would be visibly present on any evolutionary tree were the scale fine enough. And Darwin, unlike many of his contemporaries, believed that not only subspecies but even occasional separate species were capable of mating to produce fertile offspring. The absence of fuzz at evolutionary nodes, and of speculations about hybrids as an engine for speciation, is thus a matter of choice.

To understand why Darwin erases merging, conforming the evolutionary tree to the linguistic rather than the family model, we need to look past the most obvious anxiety raised by Darwin's theory for the century in which he wrote—the break with a biblical creation story—and locate another deep source of unease he introduced—namely, the unhinging of the species from ontology. Darwin decisively abandons natural kinds, making the shocking claim that species are nothing more than epistemological constructs, "merely artificial combinations made for convenience" (*Origin*, 456).[79] Elizabeth Grosz has written eloquently on Darwin's plunge into an epistemology of gradations and convention, "of differences without the central organizing principle of identity—not a difference between things, a comparison, but a difference which differentiates itself without having clear-cut or separable terms."[80] But Darwin knew his contemporaries and was aware that for his readers this complexity "may not be a cheering prospect" (*Origin*, 456). The order of nature was not only seen as evidence of an orderly intelligence, a divine hand, guiding human existence and that of the universe itself. It was also a testament to the possibility of knowledge and meaning, of classification and signification. As Max Müller explicitly warned, "the admission of this [Darwin's] insensible gradation through a series of organised beings would eliminate not only the difference between ape and man, but likewise the difference between peat and coal, between black and white, between high and low—in fact it would do away with the possibility of all definite knowledge."[81]

It is in this anxiety that we need to seek the evolutionary commitment to ongoing divergence, one of two ways Darwin combated the perceived threat to epistemology. His other strategy was to abandon the feminine familial designations used by linguistics. Darwin refers not to *mother*, *daughter*, and *sister* species but rather to *parent* species and their *offspring*. We may notice a term that is missing here—it is the central term of this book. The decision to neutralize gender eliminated any easy reference to the relationship between descendants of a common ancestor—as we saw in the introduction, the word *sibling* was not coined in English until the twentieth century. Of course, Darwin could have coined a new word, as anthropologists and geneticists did when they invented *sibling* and *sib*, respectively, in the early twentieth century. His decision not to coin such a word created a rhetorical distance between species so close that the boundaries between them were often open to debate. By leaving the relationship nameless and in need of mediation through the parental term, Darwin reinforced the illusion of an epistemologically comforting gap.[82]

The risk inherent in the term *sibling species* is borne out by its use in 1940 by Ernst Mayr, one of the chief architects of the modern synthesis through which genetics was incorporated into evolutionary theory. Mayr labeled as *sibling species* those points of indeterminacy "where pairs or larger groups of related species are so similar that they are generally considered as one species, or at least have in the past for a long time been mistaken for one another." His discussion goes on to refer to such situations as "species difficulties" or "'difficult' species."[83] Taken in combination with the fact that the word *species* itself is both a singular and a plural, the term sibling species here marks an obscurity in which classification is forced to recognize the indeterminacy of individuation.

Darwin had a theoretical as well as a rhetorical answer to the problem of definitive speciation. As a subset of a species developed an advantageous adaptation, it outcompeted its progenitors and tended to drive them to extinction. Parent species were likely to survive alongside their innovative offspring only if the offspring adapted to a different niche, preventing direct competition. In this case, however, both groups generally developed away from their joint starting point, becoming two descendants of a common ancestor rather than parent and offspring. Extinctions and niche specializations created gaps large enough for humans to perceive discrete species rather than a continuum. As in the literature of the revolutionary period and in Goethe's *Iphigenia,* the relation between generations was envisioned in terms of death and replacement.

Having been adopted by both linguistics and evolution, the iconic outward-branching tree structure had become a *fetish* of scientific legitimacy in general, or more aptly, to return to Bruno Latour's terminology, had become a *fact* that blocks productive practice by claiming for itself transcendence.

MERGING SYSTEMS

In the 1870s a student of Schleicher, Johannes Schmidt, dared to contest the impossibility of language mixture. Schmidt allowed for, indeed mustered evidence for the necessary recognition of, deep mixture. Schmidt documents not only lexical but also grammatical similarities that link together languages that have seemingly split off less proximally, while failing to link languages that have seemingly split more recently. Slavic languages, for example, share some similarities with Iranian-Indian languages (which Schleicher and Schmidt both call Aryan) that they do not share with Germanic languages, although Schleicher theorized that Slavo-Germanic split off from Iranian-Indian quite early. Meanwhile, Greek shares traits with Iranian-Indian that it does not share with Italo-Celtic, although Schleicher speculates that Greek-Italo-Celtic split off from Iranian-Indian quite early. How are such inconsistencies possible? A genealogical tree that allows only for forking, Schmidt argues, will never account for all language relationships because dialects continue to be influenced by neighboring relatives (Schmidt, *Verwandtschaftsverhältnisse*, 17); geographical proximity allows re-integration (15–16). Like Darwin's species, Schmidt's languages are epistemological constructs for convenience. And Schmidt's depiction of linguistic variety admits of still more gradations than Darwin's theory. "Everywhere we see continuous transitions from one language to another" (26, trans. mine). Even between dialects, one can detect finer varieties (28). The creation of sharper boundaries between spoken dialects is the result of a political version of Darwin's competition and extinction. Inequalities in political or economic power cause surrounding populations to shift to a dominant dialect, leaving behind a larger gap with neighboring populations. Schmidt substitutes a ripple theory of influence for the tree of descent (27–28). His examples, moreover, are not random. By demonstrating affinities between Greek and Iranian-Indian, on the one hand, and between Slavic and Iranian-Indian, on the other (19, 24), Schmidt blurs the borders between Europe and Asia in both north and south, borders we will return to in the next chapter. The reciprocal influence of languages across the continental divide undermines the hope that borders become impenetrable and kinds become definitive through a natural process. Language hybrids, moreover, illuminate the significance of the sister designation, not merely as a historical legacy but in the closest cases as indicative of entwined entities that continue to share in each other, engaging in *sibling action*.

As we have seen, both Darwin and Schmidt recognized as pervious the boundary between neighboring terms—between sister dialects, sister languages, and species that are the offspring of a common parent. Let us return for a moment to a figure familiar from the previous chapter, Goethe's Harpist from *Wilhelm Meister's Apprenticeship*, who fell in love and had a child with his sister Sperata. Like Latin and Greek or Slavic and Germanic, Goethe's Harpist Augustine and his beloved sister grow—in the language of the Harpist himself—as two (lily) blossoms "on one and the same stem."[84] Augustine and Sperata, however, do not see themselves as two twigs on a wide and bushy tree of kinship but as a self-completing pair, segregated from the world at large. Seventy-five years later, in 1869, George Eliot also wrote of a "Brother and Sister" in a poem by that name as "two lives [that] grew like two buds that kiss / At lightest thrill from the bee's swinging chime, / Because the one so near the other is."[85] Eliot's poem has almost uniformly attracted attention as an autobiographical reminiscence of her close childhood relationship with her brother Isaac Evans, from whom she was estranged as an adult.[86] The autobiographical analysis has unfortunately overshadowed a reading of the poem as an exploration of the formative nature of the sibling relationship in relation to language, emotion, and subjectivity.[87]

Rather than producing as offspring a child who, like Augustine and Sperata's child Mignon, cannot speak a coherent or cohesive language, Eliot's eponymous brother and sister teach each other to speak through love, and to love through speech, in a way that opens the world to them and enables both other loves and other linguistic pursuits. The sibling here becomes an affectively invested epistemological vehicle. As in Percy Shelley's *Laon and Cythna*, a mother makes a brief and benevolent appearance as a point of departure, but it is the siblings who serve mutually for each other as the origin of significance for the world's objects and words, for their own activities, and for all future relationships. Like Herder's primitive humans whose language combines passion and action, the brother and sister "Thus rambling . . . were schooled in deepest lore, / And learned the meanings that give words a soul, / The fear, the love, the primal passionate store, / Whose shaping impulses make manhood whole"

("Brother and Sister," 7). This primal prehistory could apply exactly to Herder's phylogenetic developmental trajectory of language. From this starting point, the children move in a world filled "with life unknown to me" (6). Their landscape is composed of plants and animals, topographical features, and human artifacts which have not achieved a differentiated existence, and are "but my growing self, are part of me" (8). Within this wide latitude of experienced self, the sibling position constitutes a unique reference, providing the foundation for "Widening its life with separate life discerned, / A Like unlike, a Self that self restrains" (10). How is it that the sibling is a "Self" that restrains "self" and also, as the rest of the world is not, a "separate life"? Eliot's narrator could be referring to the concrete ways, explicated in the poem, that difference demands accommodation, and accommodating another introduces solicitous restraints on one's own behavior. Such a reading would return us to Adam Smith's view of siblings and sympathy discussed in the previous chapter. I think the better reading, however, is that the recognition of "a Like unlike" restrains the concept of an isolated selfhood. Like Schmidt's languages and Darwin's species, as stressed by Eliot's companion Lewes, the self is not a closed ontological entity but a complex nexus that admits of sharing and blurred boundaries.[88] The sibling here both binds life to life and allows for the separation of life from life as a form of discernment, of perspective.

The trajectory of the poem is from nearness to distance in the sibling bond. Echoing Nathalie's description of her relationship to her brother Lothario in a quote from *Wilhelm Meister* explored in the previous chapter, the narrator here reminisces, "His sorrow was my sorrow, and his joy / Sent little leaps and laughs through all my frame" ("Brother and Sister," 10). Two lines earlier, however, she speculates about the present that "His years with others must the sweeter be / For those brief days he spent in loving me" (10). The brother whom the sister-narrator considers from this adult perspective is not only emotionally opaque but evidently inaccessible through space and to communication. And yet the interaction between brother and sister cannot be viewed as a transition from primal unity to individuation; rather, the two children come to be through and in their reciprocal experiences as similars, neither entirely separate nor entirely joined. In this way, they resemble Schmidt's related linguistic practices that continue to change each other as long as they remain proximate and communicable, and whose mutual influence is incorporated into the fabric of their linguistic being. Like Schmidt's entities, which resist ontological linguistic definition, they become selves only in a process of approximation. Retaining elements of each other within themselves, they are synecdochally intertwined.

Ironically, what parts the siblings in the poem is the masculine schooling that removed boys from their families to impart, paradigmatically, the philological fields of Latin and Greek.

> School parted us; we never found again
> That childish world where our two spirits mingled
> Like scents from varying roses that remain
> One sweetness, nor can evermore be singled.
> Yet the twin habit of that early time
> Lingered for long about the heart and tongue:
> We had been natives of one happy clime
> And its dear accent to our utterance clung.
>
> (11)

As noted at the beginning of the chapter, the original Latin meaning of *mother tongue* was disparaging, as it distinguished a female domestic language from a masculine language of learning. While the valence of *mother language* changed as the domestic vernacular came to be a celebrated national marker, we see that knowledge of Latin as a gendered privilege that divided the sexes never disappeared. The acquisition of scholarly languages by the brother alone ends their shared participation in a native language, which can here only be called a sibling- rather than a mother tongue.

SISTER DISCIPLINES

As Schleicher and Max Müller were reaching the apex of a comparative and genealogical methodology in linguistics as a hallmark for successful science in the 1860s and early 1870s, Friedrich Nietzsche was first studying classical philology at the Universities of Bonn and Leipzig and was then appointed to a position as a professor of classical philology in 1869 at the University of Basil at the extraordinary age of twenty-four.[89] By this time, *philology* in German-speaking lands had come to mean primarily the study of cultural, literary, and other textual history within a single language (a meaning still carried by the word *Philologie* in German), but it also included analysis of the linguistic development of that single language.[90] *Linguistics* or *Sprachwissenschaft*, on the other hand, was understood to be the study of language development in general, which unfolded temporally, but whose historical, that is, human, qualities were denied. Linguists tended to ally their field with the natural sciences. This division was recent and contested enough, however, for Nietzsche to comment in his unpublished "Untimely Meditation" from 1875, entitled *We Philologists*, that "Linguistics had itself generated the biggest diversion, desertion among philologists."[91] Nietzsche would have had firsthand evidence of this desertion through his doctoral advisor, Friedrich Ritschl, whom we have already encountered for his development of the comparative methodology and his building of stemmata for manuscripts, and who was also the doctoral advisor of August Schleicher.[92] The ongoing methodological links between philology and linguistics can be deduced from Nietzsche's inaugural lecture upon his appointment to the professorship in Basel, "Homer and Classical Philology," in which he notes the presence in philology of both "historians" and "natural scientists" (*Naturforscher*), who work comparatively on morphological rules of language development (KG, 2.1:252).

Michel Foucault famously described the way Nietzsche's "genealogy... opposes itself to the search for 'origins.'"[93] Foucault found in Nietzsche a rejection of a metaphysically absolute origin or *Ursprung* in favor of *Herkunft* (ancestry) or *Entstehung* (emergence). Such a genealogy is historical in precisely the way that Max Müller so adamantly rejects, embracing contingency, discontinuity, and reversal. But the field in which Nietzsche operated was not as uniform as Foucault's description of his rebellion would imply. There was certainly an obsession with the quest for origins in the nineteenth century, as seen in this chapter. By the time Nietzsche wrote, however, that obsession had been tempered by a sense of the goal as an illusion, a mere hypothetical background to more practical knowledge-creation. Recall that the Linguistic Society of Paris formally came into being with the interdiction on studies of the origin of language. Monogenesists and polygenesists alike had agreed that no available evidence enabled the reduction in the number of language families below a contested plural number. Even Darwin belied the title of his foundational work by refusing to draw definitive conclusions about the ultimate origin of species, claiming hesitantly—or perhaps only cautiously—that "I believe that animals have descended from at most only four or five progenitors, and plants from an equal or lesser number. Analogy would lead me one step further, namely, to the belief that all animals and plants have descended from some one prototype. But analogy may be a deceitful guide" (*Origin*, 484). Foucault is right, in other words, to point out Nietzsche's refusal to give final significance to a single originary form, but this is neither Nietzsche's most original nor his most significant contribution to the genealogical methodologies of his time. That achievement lies instead in his transformation of the philological method into a genealogical form of cultural critique. In *On the Genealogy of Morality*, Nietzsche clarifies the history of ideas on which he builds, providing a short genealogy of his own thinking in the preface. Nietzsche credits his "training in history and philology" not for the initial impulse to discover the origin of good and evil, but for the understanding of that inquiry as an issue of the human *invention* of values and for his shift towards a question he considers "much more important than the nature of hypotheses, mine or anybody else's, on the origin of morality (or, to be more exact: the latter concerned me only for one end, to which it is one of many means). For me it was a question of the value of morality."[94] Nietzsche develops his methodology under the influence, not surprisingly, of those he critiques most thoroughly in order to distinguish his innovations: the British psychologists such as Hume who initiated the search for the invention of morality, the philologists who introduced analysis of etymologies and shifts in meaning, and evolutionary theorists who connected behavior to the vitality of a species. All three groups are comparative genealogists. If Nietzsche bids philosophers look to linguists to learn productive methods, what he expects them to find is *evolution*: "What signposts does linguistics, especially the study of etymology, give to the history of the evolution [*Entwicklungsgeschichte*] of moral concepts?" (34). Not only organisms and languages, but also concepts undergo "a long history and metamorphosis" (37) / "eine lange Geschichte und Form-Verwandlung" (KG, 4.2:310). Nietzsche, however, also strongly critiques evolutionary theory and linguistics, castigating these branches of knowledge (*Wissenschaften* is often translated as *science* but includes all scholarship) for denying the perspectival, the subjective, and the historical.

> The democratic idiosyncrasy of being against everything that dominates and wants to dominate, . . . already, today, little by little penetrates the strictest, seemingly most objective sciences, and is allowed to do so; indeed, I think it has already become master of the whole of physiology and biology, to their detriment, naturally, by spiriting away their basic concept, that of actual activity. On the other hand, the pressure of this idiosyncrasy forces "adaptation" into the foreground, which is a second rate activity, just a reactivity, indeed life itself has been defined as an increasingly efficient inner adaptation to external circumstances (Herbert Spencer).
>
> But this is to misunderstand the essence of life, its will to power, we overlook the prime importance that the spontaneous, aggressive, expansive, re-interpreting, re-directing and formative forces have.
>
> (52)

We have followed in this chapter the loss of a human activity so central to Herder, Lessing, and Goethe from the genealogical fields of linguistics and evolution. Nietzsche returns us to it, but with a difference. It might seem that in attributing will to power a role in the transformation of physiology, Nietzsche is anthropomorphizing organisms or nature.[95] But Nietzsche quite spectacularly removed intent from *human* thinking, positing a spontaneous activity with only subsequent self-justifications. The process Nietzsche outlines, and which he adamantly labels historical (using both the terms *Geschichte* and *historisch/Historie*), applies to "any physiological organ (or legal institution, social custom, political usage, art form or religious rite)" (*Genealogy*, 51) and the will to power involves "a reinterpretation, a reformulation [*ein Neu-Interpretieren, ein Zurechtmachen*]" (KG, 6.2:330, my trans.) It is, in other words, a praxis rather than an intent.

If Nietzsche, in spite of his innovations, still works within the most prominent methodology of his century, there is one notable difference between his genealogy and those we have been exploring. Nietzsche's history of morality shows no signs of branching. After a century of the mapping of the complex kinship relations between humans and their cultural products, Nietzsche turns away from the sibling concept, the first sign of waning significance that will culminate in Sigmund Freud's restriction of the essential family to a reduced triad. Before we can understand Freud's motivations, however, we need to revisit the genealogical fields from another perspective, focusing in the next chapter not on language and evolution but on religion and race.

5

THE EAST COMES HOME

Race and Religion

The previous chapter explored the structure of two disciplines that established a similar set of methodologies in the nineteenth century—linguistics and evolutionary theory. One might be tempted to distinguish the two fields according to the mechanism of inheritance involved: cultural in the case of language, and biological in the case of species. Throughout the long nineteenth century, however, this perspective was deeply contested. Linguists and biologists both classified their disciplines as sciences, and both linked cultural heritage with biological descent. If the ethnologist James Cowles Prichard pleads in 1857 that the "use of languages really cognate must be allowed to furnish a proof, or at least a strong presumption, of kindred race," Darwin, as seen in the chapter 4, was still more insistent, in 1859, that "a genealogical arrangement of the races of man would afford the best classification of the various languages now spoken throughout the world."[1] The interaction of the physical and the spiritual that uniquely characterized the human animal had been the central focus of the study called *anthropology* already in eighteenth century.[2] By 1800 the investigation of humanity had ceased to be the study of a unified object, "man," and had become instead an exploration of diversity, of peoples. Looking back at the nineteenth century, it has become common to positively compare ethnology or *Völkerkunde* with a more problematic race theory or physical anthropology. As the citations demonstrate, however, absolute boundaries between these approaches were illusory. Just as ethnologists sought to derive descent from culture, race theorists sought to derive culture from descent, with the exact etiology for traits both tangible and intangible varying from practitioner to practitioner. If each of these fields was swept along by the genealogical method characterizing nineteenth-century epistemology, it became increasingly clear that the resulting genealogies of human groups failed to correspond across objects of study. As the philologist Ernest Renan would declare at the end of the nineteenth century, "these divisions of the Indo-European, Semitic, or other languages, created with such admirable sagacity by comparative philology, do not coincide with the divisions established by anthropology."[3] Not only did language fail to accord with race, it also failed to accord with religion.

While race theorists and ethnologists both used the comparative method, the diversification and diffusion model of genealogy discussed in chapter 4 proved inadequate to the types of observations and anxieties confronting genealogists of race and religion. Patrolling the boundaries of kinship required two distinct operations: establishing an appropriate line of descent and managing mergers. Linguistics and evolutionary theory had addressed the former through debates over monogenesis or polygenesis and had addressed the latter by excluding fusions from their developmental systems. The sexual mixing of "racial" populations, on the other hand, was a pervasive result of colonialism and slavery that was impossible for Europeans to overlook. Religious conversion, in addition, was seen by Europeans as a desirable outcome of cultural contact—as long as such conversion occurred in the "correct" direction. In fact, Europeans recognized as a formative moment in their own history a mass conversion from paganism to Christianity. Fusions and leaps were thus central to these fields. Moreover, not only descent from a common ancestor but also intermingling, established siblinghoods. As seen in chapter 3, in the nineteenth century in-laws were viewed as siblings, and the fusion that occurred in producing children linked the two families involved even in the absence of marriage. On a larger scale, pervasive sexual mixture eventually became joint ancestry for a population. Kinship at the level of race and religion was therefore acknowledged to be something it was possible to generate as well as to trace. The boundary setting of race, people, and religion was never a simple binary matter of distinguishing self from some clear other, least of all when a set of practitioners declared it to be so. While it may look, in other words, like genealogies map familial affiliations and kinships, the opposite is true—desired systems of kinship and affiliation produce genealogies. In the cases of both religion and race, the possibilities of merging, or skipping between, branches of the family tree were experienced both as a threat to and an opportunity for the imposition of reassuring boundaries.

This chapter will analyze the genealogical race theory that developed alongside, in competition, and also in constant exchange with genealogical ethnologies of religion and language. We will explore the constellations of anxiety surrounding the kinship of peoples in the nineteenth century as a matter of both descent and intermingling and also analyze their interrogation through fiction. Around 1800 literature explored European identity along its long-contested Muslim/Christian borderlands through the sibling relationship we have come to expect. Attention turned toward Southeast Asia during the so-called Oriental Renaissance, but Great Britain's involvement in its romanticizing tendencies were short-lived, as Muslim, Hindu, and Buddhist populations increasingly became objects of colonial power dynamics. The accompanying knowledge-formations shifted in ways that have been studied since Edward Said's foundational work. In Germany, on the other hand, a romanticized form of exoticism remained attached to India and to Buddhism in particular throughout the nineteenth century. Racial and religious theory soon replaced Muslims at the geographical periphery with a new primary liminal figure closer to home, namely, Jews dwelling within national borders. It is beyond the scope of a single chapter to provide a complete history of all these fields. Instead, I will illuminate fraught thresholds of kinships as Europe generated conflicting genealogies in attempts to regulate its brotherhoods.

GENEALOGY AND RACE: PHYSICAL ANTHROPOLOGY

Beginning at least as early as the tenth century, Jews, Christians, and Muslims had mobilized the biblical genealogy of Noah's sons both to identify their own lineage and to explain human diversity.[4] Jews and Arabs both identified themselves as descendants of Shem, the brother privileged by the biblical account.⁵ Europeans saw themselves as descendants of Japheth, whom Noah also blessed, and whom he prophesied would "dwell in the tents of Shem."⁶ After Ham saw his father's nakedness without covering him, however, Noah cursed the lineage of Ham's son Canaan to servitude. Over the centuries, Jews, Muslims, and Christians identified these descendants of Ham with whomever they currently enslaved. After the slave trade became concentrated in sub-Saharan Africa in the early modern period, the curse of Ham was associated with—indeed, from the aesthetically as well as culturally narcissistic perspective of white Europeans, came to *include*—a dark skin and other African features. The logic of such classification was both genealogical and geographical; it sometimes emphasized physical traits associated with whatever group it currently designated as Hamitic, and it often attributed innately "slavish" characteristics to the population in question. Nonetheless, it was not "racial" in a modern sense because the mechanism of differentiation and of transmission was embedded in a divine curse rather than in a theory of heredity subject to natural law. Race theory was an outgrowth of the Enlightenment move away from God as a causal explanation and sought instead to locate causal mechanisms in nature. The concept of "races," as it solidified over the long nineteenth century, did not have a single etiology.⁷ What these streams of thought had in common, however, was a commitment to a genealogical form of global mapping that imbued the kinship structures thus created with affective and ethical significance.

If the Noahdic genealogy accounted for variety as a form of diversification and diffusion, the new race theories of the late eighteenth century were equally obsessed with merger. Race theories arose in the late eighteenth century as mass migrations—both voluntary and coerced—performed a giant experiment on the persistence of human traits over multiple generations. This experiment was two-pronged: First, colonization brought Europeans to various continents as colonizers and settlers and brought colonial subjects to Europe in small numbers. Second, and more dramatically, the cross-Atlantic slave trade transported millions of Africans to the Americas. Both phenomena, but slavery in particular, created conditions of sexual exploitation for non-European women on a large scale and led to the birth of children with every conceivable degree of mixed heritage. Theories of race developed to account for three phenomena that appeared to be in tension in terms of new theories of heredity. First, the existence of human diversity given the inheritance of traits put pressure on the notion of a single human origin. Second, the sexual compatibility of humans from different parts of the world, measured by the viability and fertility of offspring, seemed to speak in favor of a common origin. Finally, the manner in which traits appeared, blended, and disappeared in children of mixed heritage was a matter of much debate. Race theories were thus always also theories about both natural kinds and sexual desire. In other words, they incorporated both poles of the dynamic by which kinship is generated.

The notion of merger lay at the heart of debates over heredity in general in the late eighteenth century. The dominant theory of reproduction in the eighteenth century, called preformation, held that the preformed embryos of all future generations were encapsulated, Russian-doll style, within the progenitor of each species and were usually held to be a feature of the maternal line. Maternal resemblances among humans were explicable as signs—not natural consequences—of belonging to a single lineage. Paternal resemblances were viewed as superficial imprints of the mother's desires and imagination on the developing fetus.[8] Quite in contrast to the theories of language influence discussed in the previous chapter, however, children of mixed descent were viewed as fundamentally mixed, not only in the frequent case of a white father but also in the case—infrequent but projected as a nightmarish threat—when the father was nonwhite and the mother white. The blending of traits among children of mixed heritage was understood as extending to deep structure. It is no surprise, then, that the emergence of race theory correlated with the rise of a competing reproductive theory, namely, epigenesis, which posited that each descendent constituted a truly new living being who fused the traits of both parents.[9] Within Europe, this new view was accompanied by the growing significance of love in the search for marriage partners, which was viewed as a natural sign of suitability that augured the health of the offspring. Children born under this new marriage regime became members of, and the responsibility of, families on both sides.[10] The children, as much as the marriage, merged families. Children of mixed heritage thus raised the specter of uncomfortable kinships. It is not surprising that the first epigenesists such as Johann Friedrich Blumenbach and Immanuel Kant were also among the earliest theorists of race.

If the debate between preformation and epigenesis considered merger, that between monogenesis and polygenesis arose around the question of common ancestry. Both monogenesists and polygenesists equated the natural kind with a lineage traceable to a common ancestor. For polygenesists, different races were therefore tantamount to different species.[11] For monogenesists, "human beings belong not merely to one and the same *species* but also to one *family*."[12] Most monogenesists posited adaptation to differing climates and foodstuffs as the cause of human variety, and therefore theorized that races had indistinct boundaries, blended into one another, and remained in flux.[13] In both Europe and the United States, however, polygenesis had become the dominant theory in the early nineteenth century and retained its status as the leading scientific hypothesis until Darwin rewrote the terms of the genealogical debate.[14]

The existence of mixed race children staged a confrontation over the terms of kinship—descent and sexual merger—presenting conservative naturalists with a vexatious choice: either acknowledge the common ancestry of all humans or reject the most common definition of natural kinds, according to which the ability to produce fertile offspring constituted the species boundary. Immanuel Kant provided a conservative solution to this dilemma that can only be called ingenious, using the very existence of mixed offspring as evidence for race as indelible natural kind. For Kant, Buffon's definition of the species provided the only viable grounding for natural categories without appeals to the divine and was thus essential to the conduct of natural history.[15] Species boundaries were simply a description of sexual compatibility that could be equated to common lineage (i.e., to a history of sexual compatibility). Idiosyncratically among monogenesists, however, Kant was unwilling to accept contingent adaptability in the species.[16] Kant therefore speculated that the first human pair possessed a limited number of given germs and endowments, each providing an advantage in a different climate. After humans had multiplied and groups had dispersed and settled, properties not utilized in their present setting died out, leaving in place only the suitable germs and endowments, and eliminating any potential either for further adaptation, or for regression. Unlike other monogenesists, who saw the same mechanism at work in racial mixing as in any merging of parental traits, Kant segregated these adaptive germs from characteristics whose transmission was contingent. He defined the former, "invariably heritable" characteristics as race ("Determination of the Concept of a Human Race," 136; AA 8:100). Rather than demonstrating the porous boundary between groups, then, Kant claimed that blended traits in mixed offspring proved the stubborn persistence of the racial heritage of each parent, as each inevitably attempted to express itself. It is because of the stark distinctness of racial traits that "when they interbreed with one another, [they] necessarily produce half-breed children, or *hybrids* [*Blendlinge*] (Mulatten)" ("Of the Different Human Races," 60; AA 2:430). Kant added a new type of natural kind to his classification system. Humans belong to the same lineage and are one species, as demonstrated by the natural evidence of their reproductive compatibility, and yet races are distinct kinds, as demonstrated by the natural evidence of incisively intermediate traits in offspring.

While Kant's combination of common descent with present racial immutability was idiosyncratic, his fascination with sexual mixing was shared across race theories. This preoccupation manifested an attraction-repulsion dynamic that Arthur de Gobineau in the mid-nineteenth century would explicitly formulate as driving interracial intercourse.[17] Kant only hinted discreetly at a theory of natural repulsion toward racial mixing, but such claims were commonplace throughout the following two centuries.[18] Kant himself also avoided using the language of aesthetics in this context, but he was in the minority. It is this sexual voyeurism at the heart of the discourse of race that accounts both for the pervasive language of beauty and ugliness in physical descriptions of the races and for the preoccupation with comparative cultural accounts of taste among various peoples.[19] The ranking of races through an aesthetic hierarchy, common from Pieter Camper's invention of the facial angle in 1770, finds both a culmination and a striking reversal in Darwin's theory, in *The Descent of Man*, that the races evolved through sexual selection as a *consequence* of differing human tastes.[20] Darwin's theory of sexual selection—his granting of natural efficacy to the forces of preference and desire—was met with still greater resistance than his theory of natural selection.[21] This visual aspect of racial theory will play a significant role in this chapter.

Through the production of children, then, human sexuality was both an arbiter of common descent and a producer of current kinships. By 1787, when Granville Sharp and Thomas Clarkson founded the Committee for the Abolition of the Slave Trade in London, the crucial question governing investigations of human diversity had become clear: "Am I Not a Man and a Brother?" appeared on the seal designed by board member and potter Josiah Wedgwood above an image of a kneeling black man in chains (see fig. 5.1).[22] The question was by no means rhetorical but a matter of active debate. This abolitionist seal, which Sam Margolin describes as the first forerunner of the political button, would appear on medallions, pottery, snuffboxes, and jewelry in Great Britain and the United States.[23] The

FIGURE 5.1 Antislavery Medallion, 1787, Wedgwood Manufactory, England, solid white jasper and black basalt, cut steel and ivory frame, 5.2×4.1×0.64 cm, Amelia Blanxius Memorial Collection, gift of Mrs. Emma B. Hodge and Mrs. Jene E. Bell, 1912.326, The Art Institute of Chicago. Photography © The Art Institute of Chicago.

discourse of brotherhood dominated understandings of race until the late nineteenth century. James Hunt, who became president of the Anthropological Society of London when it broke away from the Ethnological Society of London in 1863 to focus more exclusively on physical theories of race, declared proudly in his President's Address of 1867:

> Our science is dreaded, not because its deductions form the basis of all genuine political economy, but because it is supposed to threaten the destruction of a system of government which has for its goal the high sounding titles of universal equality, fraternity, and brotherhood. May it be the lot of our society to show that such chimeras are not supported by the indications of our science![24]

The separation of peoples into natural kinds undermined republicanism and economic equity as gravely as it threatened universal kinship claims, and, in colonial Britain, for much the same reason. The moral and affective imperative projected into the notion of brotherhood lacked enforcement even when rhetorically proffered, however, as Johann Gottfried Herder had already noted. While Johann Gottfried Gruber, who translated Blumenbach's influential monogenetic treatise on race from Latin to German, began the volume with a condemnation of slavery based on the pronouncement "all humans are brothers!" followed by the dictum "love your brother as yourself,"[25] the polygenesist abolitionist Georg Forster protested pointedly, "Let me rather ask if the thought that blacks are our brothers has ever, anywhere, even once, caused the raised whip of the slave driver to be lowered?" ("Something More," 165). The assertion of brotherhood that might, in some circles, serve as an injunction to equal treatment could, in others, drive policies of segregation to institutionally reinforce divisions not found in nature.

We have seen in previous chapters how sibling action endangers the integrity of terms even in parthenogenetic systems such as those of linguistics and evolution as they were formulated in the nineteenth century. This threat increases in sexual systems. The always indistinct interface of race was manifested in kin who frequently occupied radically different positions in the very same households. Incest and miscegenation were the twin fears of the nineteenth century not because they formed the inner and outer limits of a pool of acceptable sexual partners but because they so often coincided. One need look no further than Thomas Jefferson, whose slave and lover Sally Hemings was his wife's half-sister, or the family of Martha Washington, whose son by her first marriage, sources suggest, had an enslaved child with his mother's enslaved half-sister, or peer into any Faulkner novel to recognize that the lines demarcating race in slaveholding and colonial settings divided sibling from sibling and cousin from cousin, while simultaneously rendering one set sexually available to the other along a boundary in need of constant buttressing.[26]

GENEALOGIES OF RELIGIONS AND PEOPLES

Race theory came to supplement but not supplant simultaneous explorations of cultural history, comparative philology, and comparative religion. Herder, whose speculations on cultural variety we encountered in the last chapter, was not the only thinker writing on the diversity of *Völker* in the 1770s.[27] August Ludwig Schlözer, a historian at the University of Göttingen, which would become the institutional center of German anthropology, coined the terms *Völkerkunde* and its Latinized synonym *Ethnographie* in 1771.[28] Ten years later, Schlözer coined another word whose resonance has lasted still longer. Concluding from an examination of the language and wisdom (*Weisheit*), that is, religion and philosophy, of the Chaldeans that they descended from one of Shem's children, Schlözer referred to both them, and the language they spoke, as *Semitic*, for the two concepts are nearly interchangeable: "In the youth of the world (until Cyrus) there were not yet many languages, thus not a variety of *Völker*, or also vice versa."[29]

Ethnology throughout the nineteenth century largely overlapped with linguistics; while the interests of the field extended beyond language to include belief systems, worldview, and cultural practices, all these phenomena were presumed to be firmly linked. In 1808, when Friedrich Schlegel published his *On the Language and Wisdom of the Indians*, he followed a common pattern by discussing both language and religion. Schlegel's formative contribution to the developing field of comparative philology was the dichotomy he drew between two types of grammatical systems, which he correlated with two language families: the

Indo-European and the Semitic, to use currently accepted terms.[30] The first group, Schlegel noted, functioned through *inflection*, changing the roots of verbs and nouns in processes of conjugation and declination. The grammar of the second group, which Schlegel saw as "entirely distinct from the other, indeed entirely opposed to it" (44, trans. mine), worked through what Wilhelm von Humboldt later named *agglutination*, or the aggregation of suffixes and prefixes. In the value-laden interpretation of the field from Schlegel forward, the first set of languages was viewed as flexible and organic, the second as constraining and mechanic. As we saw in the philosophy of language outlined in the last chapter: as the language, so the speakers. For well over a century, the narrow, constrained, inflexible nature of Middle Easterners would be contrasted with the open-minded creativity of Indians and Europeans. In 1819 Schlegel coined the name *Aryan*, not only for a language family but also "the people [*Volke*, emphasis in original], which spoke it."[31] He justified his choice as an amalgamation of questionably related words from Persian, Sanskrit, and Greek used to identify one's own people (as in the case of *Iran* and *Iranian*, for example), and which he associated through a false etymology with the German word for *honor* (*Ehre*). While Schlegel does not use the term *Semitic* in this piece, he returns more than once to Noah's biblical blessing that Japhet " 'will dwell in the house of Shem'; which currently in modern times has been so richly fulfilled by the western peoples who for the most part are descended from Japhet" (499, trans. mine). Christianity, in other words, is a Semitic dwelling place for Japhetic peoples. To understand the pernicious reverberations of this constellation of ideas which fed modern anti-Semitism, we need to first tarry in the period between 1770 and 1820, a period in which genealogical approaches proliferated within this joint discourse of language, culture, religion, and people or race, while the method of transmission lay suspended between physical and cultural inheritance.

Most histories of comparative religion begin with Max Müller, who, after the philological work we have already discussed, delivered a series of lectures intended to found a "science of religion" in 1870. Eric Sharpe's classic history of comparative religion identifies Darwin's publication of *On the Origin of Species* in 1859 as the decisive moment in the formation of the discipline, when "an attempt was beginning to be made to view religion on the criteria provided by science, to judge its history and growth and evolution as one would judge the history, growth, and evolution of any organism—and to dissect it as one would dissect any organism." Darwinian evolution provided, in other words, "the principle of comparison."[32] We have already seen that the directionality and chronology of this methodological influence is far more complicated, however, as the comparative method developed in the fields of biblical scholarship, classical philology, and comparative philology in the late eighteenth and early nineteenth centuries. An attempt to analyze belief systems and order them into families had also begun by the end of the eighteenth century. Thinking of religions genealogically required a fundamental shift in the way religions were conceived as objects of inquiry and as objects of transmission, a transference of emphasis from evaluating truth value to exploring practices and traditions, although it was possible to combine these pursuits. As Guy Stroumsa notes, the secularization of the public sphere not only transformed religion into a private matter, it also converted religions into a cultural feature available to ethnology (*A New Science*, 8–9). Enlightenment figures such as David Hume and Hermann Samuel Reimarus began to historicize religion and to include Christianity within that historical paradigm. Such Enlightenment figures, however, still focused on the evaluation of truth claims. I will argue here that it was only Gotthold Ephraim Lessing's emphasis on affective experience over truth content that opened the door for a nonevaluative religious genealogy. Subsequent adaptations of his genealogy, however, reintroduced and intensified value-laden analysis.

MONOTHEISTIC SIBLINGS AND MECHANISMS OF INHERITANCE

Alongside political philosophy, aesthetics, economic theory, evolutionary theory, and the history of comparative linguistics, I have returned throughout this volume to literature that negotiates subjectivity, collective identities, and epistemological categories through the figure of the sibling as a permeable threshold. All the literary works discussed here circle around incestuous desire. There is another link between them, however, which we have not yet explicitly addressed. The majority of sibling-incest narratives around 1800, in British and in German literature, also deal in one way or another with Islam. Many of these works are narratives of cultural encounter set at a European border or within alternate multicultural geographies. Some take place entirely within a Muslim setting. We have seen the former constellation in Schiller's *Bride of Messina*, set in multicultural Sicily, and the latter in Percy Shelley's *Revolt of Islam*, set in the religiously diverse Ottoman Empire. The pattern recurs in works we will explore in this chapter, namely, Lessing's *Nathan the Wise* (set in Jerusalem during the Crusades) and Byron's *Bride of Abydos* (set along the Dardanelles). It also appears in literature we will not have space to examine, from Robert Southey's *Thalaba the Destroyer* (set in a fully Muslim Middle East) and Coleridge's *Remorse* (which takes place in diverse southern Spain), to Friedrich Maximilian Klinger's "Geschichte Giafars des Barmeciden" (set in Persia and India), Caroline von Günderrode's *Udohla*, in which Muslims and Hindus cohabit in India, and Mary Shelley's *Frankenstein*, which addresses Ottoman/European intermarriages.[33] Several narratives of sibling incest that do not explicitly address Islam retain a geographical connection to the religion: Goethe's *Iphigenia in Tauris* takes place in antiquity, but in an area, Crimea, that during Goethe's own era was home to a multicultural population that prominently included the Muslim Crimean Tatars. Byron's *Manfred*, meanwhile, is set in the Alps but evokes Zoroastrian mythology, prevalent in Persia, which was predominantly Muslim at the time Byron wrote.[34] Even Goethe's *Wilhelm Meister*, which situates incestuous siblings in Italy, alludes to more Eastern climes in the child Mignon's memory of her homeland, as we will discuss below.[35]

Islam presented a conundrum to Europeans at the turn of the nineteenth century. The military threat of the Ottoman Empire had receded after its defeat by the Holy Roman Empire in 1699. However, Turkey still constituted an anxious boundary with middle Europe. Europe had also existed in conflict with other Islamic populations at its southern borders, including in southern Spain, southern Italy (Sicily, in particular), and the southern border of Russia in the Crimea. At the turn of the nineteenth century, Napoleon invaded Egypt and Syria, still part of the Ottoman Empire. Great Britain, already at war with France, fought with the armies of the Ottomans, Egyptians, and Syrians against France, defeating Napoleon in 1801, and administered Egypt until returning it to the Ottomans in 1803. Just as the Ottoman Empire's reach receded, Great Britain found itself in a new relationship to Muslim populations, first as a powerful trading partner and then as a colonizer of Muslims and of Hindus in the Indian subcontinent, and eventually of Muslim and other populations in the Middle East. As knowledge of the vast diversity of belief systems around the world expanded in Europe, the common ancestry of Judaism, Christianity, and Islam stood out in stark relief.[36] Christian Europeans did not experience this familial relationship as a comfortable kinship. Sandwiched chronologically between the other two monotheistic religions, Christians could claim to be neither the recipients of the original revelation nor the most advanced purveyors of progressive truths. In an Enlightenment era committed both to progress and to global exploration, Islam seemed to present the greater and more germane challenge, a perspective that would change in a nineteenth century obsessed with the past.

In Germany, the emergence of comparative religion out of theology crystallized in a very public manner in 1777, when Lessing anonymously and posthumously published several fragments from a manuscript written by the deist Hermann Samuel Reimarus, a professor of oriental languages at an academic preparatory school (*Gymnasium*).[37] The infamous *Fragmentenstreit*, or fragment-controversy, that ensued engulfed Lessing in a series of polemical disputes with theologians.[38] At the center of the controversy was not only the acceptability of the idea of a rational or natural religion but also implicitly the application of ethnological methodologies to religion, including historical investigations of the events in the Gospels. As a result of the exchange, Lessing was officially censored from any further publications on religion by the Duke of Braunschweig. Lessing's most famous literary work, *Nathan the Wise*, has regularly been read as a barely covert continuation of this dispute in a literary form likely to circumvent the censors. Most Lessing critics interested in the fragments have focused on the advocacy of a religion of reason in the play, but *Nathan the Wise* also picks up Reimarus's comparative approach to understanding the relationship between the monotheistic religions and his cultural-geographical approach to belief systems around the world. The drama as a whole—which interrogates familial relations—and the famous ring parable at the literal center of the drama, which recasts the relationship between the monotheistic religions as a sibling relationship, can together be read as a particular variant of the eighteenth-century transition from patriarchy to fratriarchy under discussion in this book. The narrative structure of *Nathan the Wise* did more than help the piece elude censorship, however. The narrative form, with its attention to the significance of particulars and to modes of transmission involving affect, also facilitated the invention of a new kind of object and a new methodology for comparative religion and even for ethnology as a whole.

Lessing's *Nathan the Wise* thus becomes a paradigmatic text for reading classifications of human population groups through the structure of the family as it explores the role of physical and cultural transmission of traits. Willi Goetschel has noted Lessing's departure from norms represented by Johann David Michaelis, among others, who erected essentialist ethnic categories.[39] Similarly, Helmut Schneider reads Lessing's play as a valorization of the autogenesis of reason above the material morass of body, sex, race, and national identity, although one that also illustrates the inescapable material constraints obstructing such self-creation.[40] I would argue, however, that Lessing gives both more credence and more respect to inherited physical difference than Goetschel and Schneider allow for.[41] This material component of identity serves as a structural enabler of human worth, reframing the combined effects of physical and cultural determinants of group identity.

The play is not Lessing's only reflection on the relationship between the religions. In his theoretical responses to the fragment controversy, including the piece "The Education of the Human Race," Lessing's historiography takes a far different shape. This treatise can be read as a bridge from the older genre of history of "man" to the equally progressive philosophy of history of the nineteenth century. While "The Education of the Human Race" complicates the notion of universal human progress by connecting the nature of belief to historical circumstance, it does ultimately represent the Christian religion as a cultural advance. The universalizing tendency that seems in Lessing's treatise an argument for respectful coexistence has another side, therefore, and one that would take on a long and unpleasant afterlife. In his treatise, Lessing implies that Christianity has a moral imperative to leave behind a materialism envisioned as imparted by its Jewish roots. Indeed, even the notion of shared roots is too disturbing for Lessing, for whom "the Christian peoples ... were grafted onto the trunk/tribe [*Stamm*] of Judaism"[42] rather than growing organically out of it. This idea of grafting indicates that in spite of the transfer of nourishment or ideas, Christians and Jews are of separate kinds. If tolerance and progress in "The Education of the Human Race" conflate a divorce of spirit from letter and a move away from particularism with a repudiation of Judaism, then the essay becomes merely an acclamation of an understanding of Protestant Christianity that was coming to stand for the universal.[43] Islam, meanwhile, because it is subsequent to Christianity but deemed less advanced, fails to appear at all. Willi Goetschel is not wrong, however, when in his exploration of Lessing's drama *Nathan the Wise* he emphasizes Lessing's recognition of the debt owed by Christianity to the Judaism from which it sprang, a debt that amounts to an obligation for respect and acknowledgment and, more, an acceptance of national and civic equality without reference to religious identity ("Lessing's 'Jewish' Questions," 62–64). Lessing's depiction of religion and coexistence in the drama is predicated on characters with individual rather than universal histories and therefore constructs a more nuanced vision of community than does his philosophical treatise. Indeed, it is this narrative form that gestures toward an ethnological alternative to universal histories. Family histories are important to this new perspective.

The text by Reimarus that Lessing published characterizes religion as an arbitrary imposition by one generation on the next, which stunts the reason and subjects the child to a lasting irrational fear of damnation. Lessing himself contested this view, valorizing childhood education in religion as the necessary foundation of an ethical habit that was its salient feature. "Education is revelation imparted to the individual," he declares in "The Education of the Human Race."[44] *Nathan the Wise* spells out what Reimarus has overlooked in the parent-child relationship that Lessing finds redemptive, namely, *love*, which removes the *inherited religion* from the sphere of violence. Nonetheless, Lessing's ring parable illustrates how love can re-create the effect of fear as long as truth in religion is viewed as attached to a single doctrine. The three siblings in Nathan's famous parable are loved equally by their father but are unable to accept this equality. Their love leaves them equally blind to the truth and unable to judge the equal legitimacy of their siblings' claims to it. Nathan's ring parable can thus be read as a rebuke to the author's own philosophical treatise, which retains the notion of a progressive approach to religious truth.

While *Nathan the Wise* is often read as an appeal for universal brotherhood, Lessing's focus on the three monotheistic religions had long since become anachronistic as an indicator of universality. The European medieval and early modern division of the world into four religions, namely, Judaism, Christianity, Islam, and polytheism or heathenism, had given way over the course of the seventeenth and eighteenth centuries to an increasingly vast panoply of known religions, ancient and modern.[45] Alain Schnapp has outlined the result for the British and French context: "what emerges unmistakably . . . is the appeal to a new form of knowledge, uniting natural science with human history, theological inquiry with the study of antiquity."[46] This new approach soon expanded in scope, adopting the same methods in the study of more recent and indeed contemporary religious practice and belief. It is not a coincidence that Saladin, when countering Nathan's figuration of the three monotheistic religions as three identical rings, insists on their variety in "clothing, . . . food and drink" (Lessing, *Nathan*, 72),[47] while Nathan himself refers to differences between religious groups "in color [that is, skin color] and clothing, in form" (56). Both descriptions mix bodily and cultural elements, with skin color on one side and clothing on the other. Food traverses the boundary, for it, along with climate, was often thought to affect the physical characteristics of a people.[48]

If these external features generally characterize the religious groups, they nonetheless prove throughout the course of the play to be inadequate to their signifying task. Not only does Nathan mistake his Parsi friend al-Hafi for a Muslim once he has changed into the uniform of Saladin's court,[49] but the terms "Jud'" and "Christ" used as forms of address based on visual judgments of exteriors are shown to be indicative of a category mistake that equates individuals with their "Volk" (*Nathan*, 56–57).[50] Skin color and build can be similarly misleading. The adopted Recha, for example, passes as Jewish without problem although her inherited physical traits come from a European Christian mother and a Muslim-born, Middle Eastern father. Meanwhile Daja sees nothing odd about Curd's claim to be a simple Swabian in spite of the resemblance to his Muslim-born, Middle Eastern father noticed by both Saladin and Nathan (43).

Throughout the play, Lessing approaches this relationship between body and culture through objects of representation: coins, the famous ring, even the sultan's chess pieces. Reflecting on the relationship of age-old and new coin, Nathan establishes the value of transmission as dependent on material, while side-stepping an evaluation of the material itself, an approach in other words that allows him to assign worth to all three religions and escape the "tyranny" of a singular truth. It is worth comparing this genealogical view of truth to Nietzsche's extraordinarily similar definition of truth a century later as "coins that have lost their design and are now considered only as metal."[51] For Nietzsche, as for Reimarus before him, the genealogical reading discredits truth. For Lessing, however, the same procedure reveals and *validates* the source of truth as transmission rather than substance.[52] While in "The Education of the Human Race" Lessing was content to separate letter from spirit, in *Nathan the Wise* he finds a new way to combine them.[53]

This perspective finds its culmination in Nathan's famous ring parable, in which the original ring was passed down from father to best-loved son for generations until it was eventually replicated by a father who loved his three sons equally and who gave a ring to each of them. As the judge in Nathan's story notes, not only the knowledge of which ring is the original but the true ring itself may very well have been lost. All three rings are likely copies whose value now depends on faith in transmission. Significantly, the value of even the original ring lay in its role as a marker of a loving relationship between two people, rather than in its material.[54] After the proliferation of rings, one could still imagine authenticating the true ring or the true religion through its ostensible power to make its wearer beloved, if it is worn with that intention. While vertical transmission motivates the adoption of a particular religious truth-claim, therefore, it is horizontal affirmation of regard from siblings or contemporaries that distinguishes the bearer of the true ring. The competition over a singular version of truth in replaced by a competition in goodness, which can be shared without diminishing. As truth content devolves into process, and substance dissolves into a history of relationships, the replication of a single father in each generation proliferates into a complex set of affective kinship relations.

The central question of the play is posed by Nathan to Saladin just after coming to the end of his parable:

> After all, aren't they [religions] all grounded in history? Written or passed down [*überliefert* (Lessing, *Werke*, 9:557)]! And history can only

be accepted on faith and belief, right? Well, whose faith and belief is one least likely to call into question? Isn't it that of his own people? Of those of our own blood? Of the people who from childhood on have given us proof of their love?

(*Nathan*, 73, trans. mod.)

Belief, in other words, is not a rational judgment about truth but a question of assuming an identity, a membership. The passage raises the question that needs to be addressed to the entire late eighteenth century and the sciences that emerged from this period: religious studies, linguistics, race theory, ethnology, and anthropology. What does it mean to belong? Who are "his own people" ("die Seinen")—those of whose blood we are (to follow Nathan's sudden shift from third to first person here), *or* those who raise us with love? How do the material and the cultural inform each other? The parable, like the play as a whole, dismisses neither birth nor emotional ties as legitimate foundations for the transmission of belief and culture but intertwines them. The eventual discovery that the Templar and Recha are brother and sister by bloodline, and thus Saladin's nephew and niece, is not disregarded as irrelevant to their behavior, their emotions toward one another, or what one could call their cultural identity. Blood, however, is not a defining substance here. Saladin unexpectedly gets this right when he reassures Recha, "Truly blood, blood alone does not make the father! It hardly makes the father of an animal! At the most it confers the right to earn that name!" (113). True to this notion of *earning* value, the play dramatizes the way that inherited traits must enter a history of activity and relationships to shape their expression as deeds and to acquire meaning.[55] Moreover, blood alone does not communicate itself without a history of shared experience. Not only does Saladin recognize Curd because of his memory of his brother, but the drama also suggests that Curd recognizes Recha, although less distinctly, because of his vaguer memories of his parents. Significantly, Recha, orphaned as an infant, cannot reciprocally recognize him and therefore does not react to him with the same passion that he immediately feels for her.

While on a first acquaintance Saladin and Curd are each attracted to these new objects of affection, more interaction is required to solidify the bond. Lessing's commitment to moving beyond physical traits and first impressions is programmatic rather than accidental. The relationships must both develop a history and be recognized as historical by the participants. This process entails establishing a complex interaction of inherited and learned traits, through an integration of temporal and spatial experiences. While Curd's appearance, for example, highlights the persistence of inherited characteristics, these inherited characteristics are not limited to the physical and cannot be isolated from their lived contexts. While Recha's behavior, on the other hand, emphasizes the significance of learned characteristics, the effect of these learned characteristics is influenced by her innate traits. The plot of Nathan the Wise turns on Curd's resemblance to Nathan's friend and to Saladin's brother, who are, of course, revealed to be both one and the same and Curd's father. The traits Curd shares with his father range from the most concretely material to the intangible. Saladin pardons the Templar at first glance because of a visual resemblance and later notes that the tone of their voices also coincides (Werke, 9:582). Saladin also regularly compares the Templar's behavior, rash as well as brave, to that of his long-lost brother, while Nathan reasons without hesitation from appearance to character, and does so *against* its superficial indications. After just one look at the Templar and before their first conversation Nathan concludes, "The shell might be bitter; the core certainly isn't" (Nathan, 54).

Recha, unlike her brother, seems to be first and foremost the product of her education, and to resemble Nathan more than her biological parents. Her features are never described, and it would seem that her physical traits exist in no relationship, in no history. Mild and soft, as both her Jewish and Christian names suggest, she appears as the ideal imprintable blank slate.[56] And yet, as with Curd and Saladin, Recha awakens memories in the Templar through both her appearance and her voice. In an early draft of the play, Curd asks himself: "I have seen just such a heavenly form somewhere before—heard just such a heavenly voice.—But where? In a dream? Images from dreams do not impress themselves so deep" (Werke, 9:649, my trans.). The two most prominent rescues in the play are thus both motivated by recognition, whether conscious or not: visual in one case (when Saladin pardons Curd, who is a prisoner of war) and auditory in the other (when Curd rescues Recha from her burning house, prompted by her cry for help).[57] Curd's own bemusement over this action, which makes him a "mystery to me" (43), can be unraveled only once he has solved this mystery, that is, his relationship to Recha. Lessing removed such explicit allusions to Recha's resemblances from the final version, however, creating an initial tension between appearance and voice in Curd's perception of Recha that he must overcome.

Curd's first attachment to Recha seems to play out in the field of the visual. His defensive insistence after the rescue that "the girl's image disappeared long ago from my mind, if it was ever there in the first place," argues against its own import (43). A second meeting reinforces a bond created specifically through appearance: "seeing her, and the decision never to let her out of my sight.... Seeing her, and the feeling of being bound up with her, of being interwoven with her, were one and the same.... If that's love, then the Templar truly loves, the Christian truly loves the Jewish girl" (75–76).[58] After conversing with Recha, he feels a sense of disjunction, crying out, "How my soul is divided between eye and ear" (65). Educated exclusively orally by her foster father, who discouraged her from reading, her speech echoes his empirical bent. We must therefore surmise a glimmer of awareness on Curd's part, of the contrasting pull of her appearance toward her birth family, toward his own parents.

We soon realize, however, that the perceived division between eye and ear in Curd's reaction to Recha is another of his groping misinterpretations.[59] Recha's voice combines Nathan's instruction with the timbre of her ancestry, while visual traits such as her smile are integrated into a history of action and behavior. Curd himself recognizes that Recha's smile alone would not appeal to him, were it not for the thoughts that motivate its appearance, thoughts attributable to her upbringing.[60] The already mercurial image of a smile and the material timbre of voice, which might be inherited, are thus replaced by the actions of smiling and speaking, which represent the unique combinatorics of nature and nurture and complicate the discrepancy between time and space.

The split between eye and ear was at the center of Lessing's aesthetic treatise *Laocoön: An Essay on the Limits of Painting and Poetry*. Lessing's preference there for the thoughts and empathy awakened by the arbitrary signs of language above the beauty achieved by the natural signs of visual art reappears here, when Curd turns his head aside to hear Recha without distraction from his eyes. And yet Curd is unable to keep his eyes averted. While drama always combines visual and verbal material, Curd's and Saladin's reflections are more than cues for how the audience should interpret the play. Rather, they model how the audience should read bodies in action as signs in general. Lessing here expands his semiotics, merging aesthetics, ethics, and epistemology. Verbal discourse, because it is non-mimetic, creates a space necessary for the plastic to achieve meaning, enabling a material thing—whether tone or smile—to be freed from the pure mimesis of inheritance and to refer to the historical experience of a person in time. It is no accident that *Nathan the Wise*, like Goethe's *Iphigenia in Tauris* and George Eliot's *Mill on the Floss* discussed previously, dwells with such intensity on the meaning of objects, here the ring, the coin whose relationship to truth Nathan ponders, and the undifferentiated chess pieces that conform to the Islamic (and Jewish) image prohibition, but which Saladin throws aside in a precisely anti-iconoclastic frustration. Saladin would prefer mimesis, straightforward representation, unambiguous inheritance. Nathan is aware, however, of the inevitable difference that history, story, narrative make, without, however, repudiating the significance of material. For Saladin at the end of the drama, and in spite of his declaration about the insignificance of blood for fatherhood cited previously, Recha and Curd are now part of his own family because he has traced their bloodline. As Ruth Klüger Angress poignantly notes, however, it will eventually occur to Saladin, as it seems already to have occurred to Nathan, that his brother Wolf/Assad died a Christian Crusader fighting against Saladin's own army.[61]

It is these constellations of bodies and signification, of cultural and physical inheritance, of mixing and segregation of peoples that Lessing's text, like many others of the period, investigates through the figure of the sibling. As in so much later social and genetic science, siblings foreground questions of how shared or divergent upbringing interacts with shared biological origins. If with a coin, it is not only the stamp but also the metal itself whose value depends on convention, the matter/meaning constellation is still more complicated in humans. It is significant in this vein that the story's familial dénouement departs from traditions in which an orphan discovers a father who provides a name, a title, and often a fortune enabling a happy ending based on marriage. Here, the reunited family conspicuously excludes vertical lineage, extending the dismantling of reproductive relationships that has structured the story throughout. Even in the symbolic terms of church titles, the sympathetic and open-minded lay *brother* is clearly to be preferred to the fanatical *Patriarch*.[62] Discovering that the beloved Recha is his sister creates a moment of dismay for Curd, but only a moment, after which he declares to Nathan that in providing him with a sister rather than a wife, "You've given me more than you've taken from me! Infinitely more!" (117).

What are we to make of this preference for siblinghood over spousal and parent-child relations? In one of few attempts to account for this oddity, Helmut Schneider sees the affirmation of the sibling over the lover as an attempt to sublimate erotic interest into a vision of universal brotherhood (*Genealogy*, 197–99). But we should not forget that brotherhood has group-oriented as well as universal associations, and affective attachment to particulars is still affirmed in the play. Rather, I would argue, Lessing exploits a disparity between two versions of history, exemplified also in the discrepancy between Lessing's treatise on "The Education of the Human Race" and his drama *Nathan the Wise*. Any universal, progressive history requires abstracting ideas and cultural affiliations from individuals and positing a story of linear descent as supersession. Such descent, in order to be progressive and teleological, necessarily implies the preference of new over old, necessarily distorts by ignoring developments that do not fit the desired vision of advance. Hence Lessing's denigration of Judaism in comparison to Christianity, and his avoidance of Islam altogether, in his philosophical treatise. Narrative works differently, however. In the play, history is always personal, and the abstract becomes concrete and particular. Religious succession based on time of origin becomes religious coexistence in the present; the genealogy of the monotheistic religions metamorphoses from one of generational descent to one of common ancestry; and parental relationships with their emphasis on replication in inheritance melt away in favor of complex lateral and step-relationships that emphasize nuanced differentials of similarity and difference.[63] As we have seen, the dichotomy between universal laws and human history as agents of development came to structure the division between the sciences and the humanities. Lessing here grants the former significance only through the intervention and recognition of the latter.

Nathan the Wise has been read almost exclusively in terms of the Jewish-Christian dynamic.[64] Daniel Wilson, one of the few critics who have explored the relationship to Islam in the text, reads *Nathan the Wise* in the context of eighteenth-century Turkish operas in which abducted Christian women are rescued from the harem (most famously Mozart's

Abduction from the Seraglio).[65] As Wilson indicates, the negative traits typically associated with Muslims are omitted or transferred in Lessing: lust plays no part in the drama, and only the Christians—most notably the Patriarch—are violent religious fanatics. Lessing, however, not only reverses the traditional narrative of the rescue of Christian from Muslim (*Humanität*, 80); rather he transforms a narrative about the distinctions between peoples and religions into one in which multiple forms of crossing and merging make classification all but impossible. Thanks to the conversion of a Muslim husband by a Christian wife who abducts him to Europe, the adoption of their son by his fanatical Christian uncle, and of their daughter by a tolerant Jewish friend, their mixed children participate in multiple traditions. The figures actively produce kinship. Lessing's innovative genealogy of religion provided a template for a value-neutral investigation of cultural difference, but one that long lay dormant.[66] Unfortunately, by freeing later thinkers from the strict linear genealogy of the monotheistic traditions, Lessing also provided a starting point for later attempts to "Aryanize" Christianity.

ISLAMIC GEOGRAPHIC AND CULTURAL BORDERS

The prevalence of Muslims in narratives about sibling kinship was not limited to German literature of 1770s–1810s; it was also pervasive in British literature of the same period. By 1813, the year Byron published a poem called *The Bride of Abydos*, he was able to reference a literary tradition in which geographical, religious, and cultural difference was negotiated through sibling desire. The sibling relationship in Byron's poem continues to illustrate the perviousness of classifications, an ambiguity that Lessing embraced, but which Byron finds far more threatening. Here the border under interrogation is quite literally geographical, namely, the Hellespont or Dardanelles, although the geography overlays a cultural divide. While this boundary is breached in the mixed heritage of the protagonist, Selim fatally encounters the limits of its porousness when he attempts to make "home" portable in the form of a sister-bride.

The Bride of Abydos is one among a set of Byron's poems referred to interchangeably as Turkish Tales, Eastern Tales, or Oriental Tales, a confusion that illustrates the continuing centrality of the Ottoman Empire in British imaginings of the *Orient* in the early nineteenth century, even as India grew in significance. Abydos was a town adjacent to present-day Çanakkale on the eastern shore of the Dardanelles at its narrowest point. The Dardanelles marks a natural border between Europe and Asia, and yet one whose permeability Byron documented with his own body—in 1810 he became the first verified swimmer of the Hellespont, a feat he memorialized in the mock-heroic poem "Written After Swimming from Sestos to Abydos."[67] The crossing cannot be imaged as free of danger, however. Leander, the mythological lover Byron imitated, died on one of his swims across the channel when the lamp lit by his beloved Hero was extinguished in a storm. Byron came away from his swim merely with an ague, if we are to believe his poetic account. The status of the waterway continued to occupy Byron, however. Selim and Zuleika, his lovers in the poem written three years after his swim, never manage to embark on the ship Selim envisions as an escape from their childhood home. Indeed, Selim is killed just as his foot touches water, and Zuleika, like the mythical Hero, dies of grief. It is, of course, merely a coincidence that Byron actually died of an ague in 1824. It is significant, however, that the cause in which he was militarily and financially engaged when he became ill, namely, Greek independence from the Ottoman Empire, would have converted the Hellespont into a national boundary, realigning nationality with both landscape and a cultural divide Byron envisions as equally entrenched.[68]

Hero and Leander are not the only tragic pair invoked by Byron's verse; he weaves into the text a dense sibling heritage, both ancient and modern. Byron refers to the body of water between Europe and Asia as "Helle's wave," "Helle's Tide," and "Helle's Stream," foregrounding the mythical Helle, who lost her balance as she rode over the water on a flying golden ram.[69] The ram had been sent by her nymph mother to rescue Helle and her brother Phrixos from "their shared fate" at the hands of a murderous stepmother.[70] Phrixos nearly loses his own life in his attempt to save her, and he mourns "his partner in their twin peril" (3:873). The waterway itself manifests the bond between siblings while also gesturing toward the contiguous sibling myth that named the Bosphorus (cow-ford), a waterway just north of the Hellespont. The name memorializes the crossing of the princess Io, whom Zeus had transformed into a cow in order to hide their dalliance from his wife. Io's brother Cadmus, after an unavailing quest to find her, founded Thebes, the incestuous city of Oedipus and his children, to which we will return a final time briefly below. Thebes was also the murderous polis from which Phrixos and Helle were fleeing, completing the sibling circuit with a sister lost in each direction.

It was not the long nineteenth century alone, in other words, that envisioned fraught boundaries through the figure of the sibling, but Byron also frames his poem by two blatant allusions to a more recent tradition of sibling incest narratives familiar to us already from this volume.[71] First the title—*The Bride of Abydos*—echoes the title of Friedrich Schiller's play *The Bride of Messina* (1803). Second, the poem's opening verse is an adaptation of the song sung by Goethe's most famous character at the time, the mysterious and doomed Mignon, child of sibling incest from his novel *Wilhelm Meister*, discussed in chapter 3.[72] These allusions do not direct us away from the preoccupation with geography, shared by both other texts, but rather situate Abydos within a wider imagined borderland that reads both time and space through genealogy.

To understand the implications of the sibling figure for cultural geography, we must turn briefly again to Goethe's Mignon. Mignon's song draws her back into a mythological past that eventually swallows her up and lays her to rest in a collector's set of displaced ruins, providing a warning for the modern audience to leave behind her doomed version of attachment. The distance between readers and characters in Byron's *Bride* is of a different sort, one that follows the logic of the spatial, rather than temporal, boundary the poem erects between Europe and Asia. Mignon's song in Goethe's *Wilhelm Meister's Apprenticeship* begins:

> Know you the land where lemon blossoms blow,
> And through dark leaves the golden oranges glow,
> A gentle breeze wafts from an azure sky,
> The myrtle's still, the laurel tree grows high—
> You know it, yes? Oh there, oh there
> With you, O my beloved, would I fare.[73]

It has long been taken for granted that the land referred to here is Italy, the land of Mignon's birth and of Goethe's famous travels. This association takes Mignon's origins far too literally; she may be born, or reborn, in Italy before traveling to Germany, but as a personification of classical poetry, her symbolic roots are older.[74] The three-verse poem, I would argue, traces the figure of Mignon back first to the landscape of ancient

Greece, then to the temple of Apollo in Delphi where she serves as oracle, and finally to Thebes, her own incestuous point of origin. The landscape of the first verse, like the architecture of the second, is common to both Greece and Italy, but the second verse includes more specific allusions. The classical temple stands not as the ruin which visitors would have encountered in Goethe's time or our own, but intact and in use:

> Know you the house? Roof pillars over it,
> [Auf Säulen ruht sein Dach.]
> The chambers shining and the hall bright-lit,
> [Es glänzt der Saal, es schimmert das Gemach,]
> The marble figures gaze at me in rue:
> "You poor child, what have they done to you?"
> You know it, yes? Oh there, oh there,
> With you, O my protector, would I fare.
>
> (Goethe, *Apprenticeship*, 83; *Werke*, 9:503)

The verbs *schimmern* and *glänzen* are more extreme than would be called for by illumination from candles or torches and call to mind the flickering shimmer of vapors, which Plutarch reported were emitted through fissures in the floor of Apollo's temple at Delphi, and which were the acknowledged source of the Pythian priestess's inspiration.[75] The priestess was originally a young girl, a virgin, who left behind family and all other duties to take up this position (Scott, *Delphi*, 12–13). Like Mignon, then, she is isolated, and like Mignon, she speaks in ways both mysterious and inspired. Mignon's chaotic language practice echoes that of the priestesses, whose tumultuous oracles were translated into verse by priests (21). Wilhelm must ask her to sing the song twice and to explain it, after which he translates the result into a German that does "not even approximate the originality of the phrases" once the "broken language was smoothed over and the disconnectedness removed" (*Apprenticeship*, 83). Mignon's Delphic pronouncements include the assertion that Felix is Wilhelm's son before there is any evidence for it. Apollo was not only the god of song and poetry but also the inventor of Mignon's instrument the zither, which was sacred to him.[76]

The last verse of Mignon's song leads the listener away from Delphi through the mountains. It retraces the path of a famous petitioner of the priestess, Cadmus, who, following an oracle, encountered and slew the Ismenian Dragon, setting into motion a myth cycle discussed at length in chapter 1. "The dragon's ancient brood" (*Apprenticeship*, 83), the Spartoi, sprang from the ground where Cadmus had planted his teeth in accord with instructions from Athena, built Thebes, and became its inhabitants. The most famous descendants of Cadmus and the dragon-tooth autochthones were the incestuous family of Oedipus and his mother/wife Jocasta, with their children Antigone, Ismene, Polyneices, and Eteocles. Thebes is thus the paradigmatic home of the tragic and incestuous poetry Mignon embodies.

Mignon's song urges a temporal displacement, a return to an Apollonic land of tragedy and fate, to the world in which she still participates, a world, however, that the novel rejects. Mignon is not an authoritative guide but an unself-conscious participant in the mythological machinations of fate. The first verse of Byron's *Bride of Abydos* presents a far different epistemological relation between narrator, subject, and projected reader.

> Know ye the land where the cypress and myrtle
> Are emblems of deeds that are done in their clime,
> Where the rage of the vulture—the love of the turtle—
> Now melt into sorrow—now madden to crime?
> Know ye the land of the cedar and vine?
> Where the flowers ever blossom, the beams ever shine,
> Where the light wings of Zephyr, oppressed with perfume,
> Wax faint o'er the gardens of Gúl in her bloom;
> Where the citron and olive are fairest of fruit,
> And the voice of the nightingale never is mute.
>
> (107–8)

Replacing the laurel, lemons, and oranges with funereal cypress, Asian cedars, and the far older cultivated citron, Byron conjures a landscape that has moved slightly east, and which reflects the character that Byron assigns to its culture—sexualized, sensuous, oppressive, and violent. While the cypress was associated with mourning from ancient times, both it and the myrtle were sacred to Aphrodite, as was the turtle. The verse uses the Greek word *Zephyr* for breezes and the Persian word *Gúl* for roses, thereby demonstrating a mastery over multiple languages which contrasts strongly with Mignon's linguistic mélange. Byron's poem as a whole provides a veritable forest of allusions to Greek and Roman mythology, to Islam, to Turkish customs, and to Arabic literature with an air of sovereignty so persuasive that critics frequently refer to his detailed portrayal of "the East" in terms of its accuracy, which was just the impression he was aiming for.[77] The question the poem poses and tries to settle is how to circumscribe and delimit "the clime of the east" and "the land of the sun" (108) authoritatively, particularly in the test case of Asia's westernmost boundary, featuring a main character with a Greek mother and Turkish father.

Adopted by the uncle who killed his father, Selim is viewed by his foster father Giaffir with suspicion and hostility and derides Selim's sensitivity to poetry and love of nature as a Greek effeminacy that contrasts poorly with the masculine warrior pleasures of the Turks.[78] Once he discovers his history, Selim experiences his liberation from his uncle as a release from the narrow confines of place, a liberation from nationality. "I was Free!" he recalls to Zuleika, "Ev'n for thy presence ceased to pine— The World—nay—Heaven itself was mine!" (134). Selim finds refuge with, and eventually becomes the leader of, a band of pirates who embody the globe, representing "every creed, and every race" (135) so that their ship becomes a world in miniature. The opportunity for a kind of global cosmopolitanism might seem to suit Selim's mixed heritage, which is why it is all the more significant that he cannot maintain this attitude. After a brief escape, he does indeed begin to pine for his beloved sister/cousin, and this pining closely resembles a form of homesickness. In inviting her to join him, he envisions her as a fixed point, "the star that guides the wanderer" even as she would share the wanderings (135). Zuleika usurps and unites within her all the diverse trappings of identity: religion, upbringing, and homeland; her voice is described as

> Blest—as the Muezzin's strain from Mecca's wall
> To pilgrims pure and prostrate at his call;
> Soft—as the melody of youthful days,
> That steals the trembling tear of speechless praise;
> Dear—as his native song to Exile's ears.
>
> (136)

The sibling's voice recurs here in all its formative eminence. The terms chosen are significant not only because they circumscribe institutions and places that generally demand allegiance but also because they are not analogical—in each case evoking a position that Selim actually occupies: he is a Muslim, nostalgic, and an exile. Rather than reacting to Zuleika's voice the same way he reacts to each of the other sounds, as the verses might suggest, he positions her as the sole repository of all emotional ties and all allegiances, which should free them from geography. "With thee," he tells her, "all toils are sweet—each clime hath charms, Earth—sea alike—our world within our arms!" (138). Zuleika thus quiets all those anxieties in Selim to which Mignon, on the other hand, is exposed. If Zuleika inoculates against the unease of globalization, the intense sibling relationship could be seen as a necessary component of the successful negotiation of a new global, indeed a new imperial, economy, and hence allied with it. Such a sibling would serve, as Adam Smith's theories imply, as an anchor for a network of trade weaving together the world. Selim rebuffs this interpretation of his desired lifestyle, however. He abdicates any claim to "land beyond [his] Sabre's length" because "Power sways but by division" (137). In spite of this anticapitalist and anti-imperialist stance, he is no cosmopolitan; he identifies himself firmly within the cultural system in which he was raised. In his pirate garb, he calls himself a Galiongée, a word specifically designating Turkish sailors, and his weapon is a sabre inscribed with Koranic verses. If the depiction of the pirates in *The Bride of Abydos* oscillates between an idealization of landless roving and support for nationalist rebellions,[79] this ambivalence ends with Selim's inability to escape his homeland, and his love for his sister becomes a manifestation of conservative, nationalistic identification.

Both Nigel Leask and Saree Makdisi have compared Byron's *Bride of Abydos* to Percy Shelley's *Revolt of Islam*.[80] In both cases, a brother attempts to rescue a sister from the harem; both sibling pairs are erotically committed to each other; each poem features a kind of rebellion.[81] As Leask notes, however, Selim does not aspire to a grand political revolution but remains caught in a familial drama. On the other hand, by using an ahistorical version of the Ottoman Empire as a setting for a reprise or foreshadowing of the French Revolution, Shelley denies to his vague East the ability to execute its own political history. Makdisi discusses the contrast between the global temporalities formulated by Shelley and by Byron. For Shelley, as for Goethe, to travel east is simultaneously to travel back in time. For Byron, however, history runs forward everywhere simultaneously, so that for him there is "not a *pre-modern*, but an *anti-modern* Orient."[82] When Goethe's Mignon sings of returning to Greece, the ruins have been miraculously reconstituted. In Byron's Orient, Makdisi notes, the ruins are ruins (*Imperialism*, 126). The liminal spaces occupied by the incestuously inclined siblings thus vary in each of these three reflections on the East. In Goethe, the sibling dyad represents a premodern adherence to tragic fate that needs to be rejected in the modern world for history and exchange to proceed. For Byron, on the other hand, the siblings occupy a borderland whose integrity they threaten while alive; their sacrifice reinforces geography as the arbiter of culture. While Shelley denies a cultural and political identity to Osman's empire, he grants Cythna an active role in world history—a more active role, in fact than that of her brother Laon. His universalizing gesture breaks down discrete and complementary sexual roles for the brother-sister pair but also denies alterity on an individual and a global scale. In each case, however, the jointure of siblings reverberates onto the contemporary culture of its readership, challenging integral identities both individual and collective.

ARYAN AND SEMITIC BRETHREN

The European desire to explore Islamic-Christian relations through the lens of the sibling from the 1770s through the 1810s reflects the perception of these cultures as uncomfortably close relatives, both geographically contiguous and bound genealogically through a shared religious history. In the early nineteenth century, however, linguistic investigations began to rewrite the understanding of proximate relations. Hebrew and Arabic were classified as belonging to a language family unrelated to European languages yet tied to European heritage through religious affiliation and the ongoing cultural influence of the Hebrew Bible. Sanskrit and Persian came to be viewed as sisters to most European languages. Turkish, on the other hand, was situated among a set of languages unaffiliated with European heritage. Looking through the lens of language rather than geography shifted world relations as if a kaleidoscope had rotated, distancing Turkey and locating Europe at the intersection of two families, as "descendants of this providential couple at the root of the only civilization they considered worthy of the name: Semites by spiritual filiation, Aryans by historical vocation," in Maurice Olender's formulation.[83] In this new environment, the anxieties and enthusiasms of scholarly communities and of the cultural imaginary rearranged themselves around a new divide: *Aryans* and *Semites*.[84]

Over the course of the nineteenth century, the expectation that language groups were also related by blood slowly receded among both philologists and race theorists, but the rhetoric of blood, genealogy, and *Volk* persisted as the ground of linguistic discourse. In spite of contemporary expectations that "the linguistic community is open, whereas the race community appears in principle closed,"[85] cultural ideologies were perfectly capable of matching both the virulence and the exclusionary principles of their sibling discipline, race theory, as a quick glance at August Schleicher will demonstrate. Writing in 1865, Schleicher set the limits of the human at the ability to speak: those who lacked this capacity due to birth defect or injury were "not to be considered complete humans, true humans."[86] *True humans* were moreover divisible into two classes according to whether their language was suited or "unsuited to historical being" (ibid., 28). Unsurprisingly, the Indogermanic ranks highest among Schleicher's historical peoples and languages; Chinese and Native American languages bring up the linguistic rear. A polygenesist, Schleicher posited a differentiated "ability for development" (23) within each language family at its origin, and he precluded the possibility of bilingualism (11–14), in effect eliminating the potential for either cultural or individual movement in a direction he would have considered advancement. The slippage between race and ethnicity worked to particular advantage for anti-Semitic thinkers who imbued this group with undesirable inherited characteristics whether working with the term *Volk* or race. In fact, the self-declared anti-Semite Paul de Lagarde argued that it was the atavistic racial thinking of Jews themselves that created and preserved their racial designation through their rejection of intermarriage. The progressive national identity of modern nations like Germany, in contrast, lay "not in the blood, but in the mind [nicht im Geblüte, sondern im Gemüte]."[87] The boundaries between discourses of race and discourses of *Volk* remained entirely porous not only through the nineteenth century but through the Nazi period in Germany.[88]

Because language was perceived to be intricately related to all aspects of culture, and indeed to thought itself, the terms *Aryan* and *Semitic* referred to both character and cultural products, chief among them religion. Judaism was designated a Semitic religion not only because it arose in a population that spoke a Semitic language but because it sprang from a Semitic worldview understood to be arid and rigid; Hinduism, on the other hand, was an Aryan religion, rich in mythology and art. Islam, Buddhism, and Christianity presented more complicated cases as each had spread widely outside of its original, "national" setting.[89] While classifications were debated, there was consensus on historical outlines—Islam had preserved its Semitic roots by retaining Semitic adherents, even while converting through conquest. Buddhism and Christianity, on the other hand, had risen above their nationalist roots in acts of rebellion against their narrower progenitors, Hinduism and Judaism.

Pruning the family tree to control kinship was thus at issue for linguistic ethnology as it was for race theories. Given the fusions and migrations that played a large and visible role in both historical systems, ensuring purity required the two different forms of defense mentioned earlier, one focused on differentiating origins and one on managing later entanglements. In the United States, for example, where polygenesis dominated racial theory, anxiety over rampant intermingling dictated policies that first stipulated race through the mother alone, who was assumed to be black in mixed cases, then criminalized interracial marriages, and later shifted to a "one drop of blood" standard.[90] Within Europe, as the so-called Jewish Question became the dominant pressure point for policing kinship, ethnographic theories that bled into racial theories tackled the question of origin, while debates on intermarriage put Jews in a strangling double-bind: on the one hand, mingling was considered harmful to the Aryan population, while on the other, the preference of Jews to marry among themselves was targeted as a sexual perversion that repudiated wider kinship formations through recourse to incest. Christina von Braun has documented that the term *Blutschande* (blood shame), which referred to incest at the turn of the nineteenth century, had come to mean miscegenation by the turn of the twentieth.[91] In both cases, however, the term adhered to Jews, who were necessarily guilty of one or the other, whichever marriage choices they made. Rhetoric surrounding Jews increasingly merged this double-edged racial dynamic with the orientalizing tendencies formerly applied to Muslim populations in Turkey, the Middle East, and India. Suzanne Marchand argues that Islam was of less interest to German scholars than Sanskrit and Persian pasts sought as roots for Christianity. This claim points to a shift in the early nineteenth century, however, and applies primarily to German Christian scholars.[92] As Susannah Heschel has shown, Islamic studies in nineteenth-century Germany was disproportionately populated with Jewish researchers. Meanwhile, Jewish and Christian scholarship on Islam diverged sharply. While Christians characterized both Judaism and Islam as dry ritualistic and legalistic systems, Jews used Islamic studies as a tool for resituating Judaism in modern Europe, providing an opportunity to portray both as liberal, rational, and strictly monotheistic in contrast to a Christianity corrupted by superstition and pagan syncretism.[93]

Jewish scholars characterized the theological relationship of Judaism to Islam as a mother-daughter relationship or one of sisters (Heschel, "German Jewish Scholarship," 101). Christian efforts to discipline and redefine the genealogical relationship of Judaism to Christianity, meanwhile, were applied simultaneously and in intersecting ways to the history of religious ideas, the sexual history of peoples, and the figure of Jesus himself. The manipulation of common ancestry to Aryanize Christianity began very soon after the first attempts to historicize Jesus.[94] Reimarus, as we have seen, was among the earliest historicizers. While he provoked a storm of dissent by reading Jesus as a Jew who had not intended to break with his Jewish heritage, he initiated a debate over the extent to which Jesus could be read within rather than merely against Jewish tradition.[95] By 1804 Johann Gottlieb Fichte became the first thinker to suggest that Jesus was not Jewish, blaming Paul for syncretizing him into Jewish prophesy.[96] David Friedrich Strauss, who counted Reimarus and Lessing among his strongest influences, attributed the innovations of Jesus to Assyrian influences in his widely read *Life of Jesus* in 1835.[97] Confronting this anti-Jewish turn in biblical studies, the Jewish theologian (and Qur'an scholar) Abraham Geiger rejected the idea that Jesus was a rebel against the Jewish tradition. His reintegration of Jesus into the mainstream of Judaism represented earlier by Hillel provoked a widespread backlash.[98] By the time Ernest Renan published his *Life of Jesus* (1863), which sold 100,000 copies in the first few months and was translated into ten languages, Jesus's Jewish origin had become a matter of public debate (Poliakov, *Aryan Myth*, 208). Throughout the work, Renan fans the flames of anti-Semitism while couching his assertions in the language of tolerance. He grants Jesus "one of those lovely faces which sometimes appear in the Jewish race" but calls it "impossible ... to seek to ascertain what blood flowed in [his] veins."[99] While the comment is a tacit nod to anti-Semitic racism, Renan turns the tables, identifying the fulcrum of Jesus's overcoming of Judaism in a rejection of "pride of blood" (225) for which he substitutes love of "human brotherhood" (232).[100] By late century, the idea that Jesus had Jewish origins is controversial and "gets [Richard Wagner] heated" as it "has not been proven."[101] At the turn of the twentieth century, Houston Stewart Chamberlain strengthens a claim that Renan had only implied, namely that Jesus arose from a minority Aryan population in Galilee and thus had an Aryan "racial" heritage.[102] This position would become dogma under the Nazis (Heschel, *Aryan Jesus*, 68). Halvor Moxnes makes the fascinating suggestion that it is against this segregationist background that we should read Martin Buber's embrace of Jesus as "my big brother" to whom he claims a "fraternally open relationship" as well as similar claims by other post-Holocaust Jewish philosophers.[103]

The genealogizing of Jesus was augmented by a genealogizing of religion on the larger scale oriented toward disentangling Christianity from Judaism as kin. In 1870 Friedrich Max Müller delivered the lecture series *Introduction to the Science of Religion* at the Royal Institution. He hoped to repeat the foundational gesture for the field of comparative religion that his *Lectures on the Science of Language*, delivered in the same location in 1861, had played for comparative philology. Although Max Müller identified parallels between the fields in their comparative, genealogical approach, they were intertwined rather than analogous in his practice. He theorized the roots of mythological narrative in the gendering of nouns and the use of figurative language, while religion in turn stabilized language. Max Müller divided religions into three families or streams that aligned with the linguistic heritage of Noahdic genealogy: the Semitic "worship of *God in History*," the Aryan "worship of *God in Nature*," and the less world-historic Turanian worship of a host of spirits, including ancestral spirits:

> The only scientific and truly genetic classification of religions is the same as the classification of languages, and ... , particularly in the early

history of the human intellect, there exists the most intimate relationship between language, religion, and nationality—a relationship quite independent of those physical elements the blood, the skull, or the hair, on which ethnologists have attempted to found their classification of the human race.[104]

While Max Müller here calls such a human collective a *nation*, he elsewhere and frequently uses the word *race*. In his lectures on religion, he gives priority to religion in the consolidation of a people, so that nationality lies in a "common allegiance . . . to the great father of gods and men" (84–86). It is, one could say, a siblinghood of belief.

Having established that linguistic and religious classifications *should* correspond, Max Müller must account for their failure to do so and develop methods for classification when they diverge. His lip service to prioritizing religion over language proves impossible to reconcile with the actual genealogical trees he draws in the second lecture (fig 5.2). In this image and its elucidation, we see that one religion—Buddhism—jumps

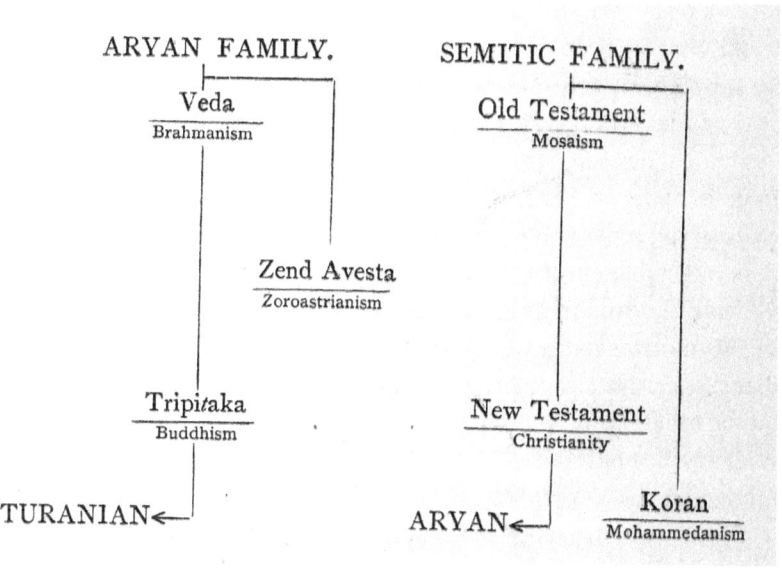

FIGURE 5.2 Friedrich Max Müller, diagram of history of religions, from *Introduction to the Science of Religion*, 1873. University of Pennsylvania Library.

from the language family in which it originated to the speakers of a different family of languages, the Turanians. Analogously, Christianity, "the offspring of Mosaism," was "transferred from Semitic to Aryan ground," only then coming to "develop its real nature and assume its world-wide importance" (55). Islam does not even retain the privilege of common descent alongside Christianity from Judaism, but, in Max Müller's formulation, "springs ... from the ancient fountain-head of the religion of Abraham," namely, from a Semitic root older than Judaism itself (54). Max Müller here reverses Lessing, for whom Christianity was figured as a graft attached to the Jewish stock, and instead arranges for Christianity to escape from its Jewish roots as a graft onto Aryan stock. His Christian Europeans fail to join the Semitic race through common religious heritage, as his theory suggests they should. Rather, it is sister languages that create "Aryan brethren":[105] "the Aryan languages together point to an earlier period of language, when the first ancestors of the Indians, the Persians, the Greeks, the Romans, the Slaves, the Celts, and the Germans were living together within the same enclosures, nay, under the same roof."[106]

This enclosure, this household economy, as much as any speculative geographical point of origin, was "the original home of the whole *Aryan race*," a term that Max Müller more than any other thinker of the nineteenth century brought into common use in English (ibid., emph. mine). By supplanting the family metaphor with that of the dwelling place, Max Müller grounds race in language and common culture rather than in physical descent, while still evoking a shared inheritance, one rooted in upbringing and experience.[107] In spite of his preference for cultural criteria, his organic metaphors and appropriation of the term *race* had the predictable effect of strengthening the racial discourse of the time. Thomas Trautmann has attempted to rehabilitate Max Müller by locating his motives in the desire to reveal the kinship of Europeans and Indians. Inclusivity on one side was inextricably linked to an exclusivity on the other, however. The ur-Aryans "were living together beneath the same roof, separate from the ancestors of the Semitic and Turanian races."[108]

By the late nineteenth century, the linguist Ernest Renan had brought the proposal of a science of religion to France, "a *comparative mythology*, where religions would be classed by races and families, and where the transformation of the primitive myths would be left to be described by various organic processes, and where the *arbitrary* would have no part."[109] Renan's races are tied to blood as little as Max Müller's and yet were just as predictably amalgamated to that discourse through shared rhetoric. Renan's descriptions of the relationship of Christianity to Judaism are similarly cagey; he both calls Judaism the "mother's bosom" of Christianity and, following Lessing quite directly, claims that "Israel has been the trunk upon which the faith of the human race [i.e., Christianity] has been engrafted."[110] These organic and genealogical metaphors establish the historical affiliation as a step-relationship.[111]

Renan integrates the linguistic consensus on Indo-European mental dexterity denied to the speakers of agglutinative languages with the environmental theories common to early physical anthropology.

> In the Arabic or Semitic conception . . . the desert is monotheistic—sublime in its immense uniformity, it reveals from the first moment the idea of the infinite, but not that sentiment of fertile activity which an incessantly creative nature has inspired in the Indo-European race. That is why Arabia has always been the bulwark of monotheism. Nature plays no part in the Semitic religions. . . . The extreme simplicity of the Semitic mind, without expansiveness, without diversity, without plastic arts, without philosophy, without mythology, without political life, without progress, has no other object.
>
> (Renan, "Religions of Antiquity," 48–49)

The image of the Semite as a desert dwelling, tribe-bound, religious fanatic is one that should sound jarringly familiar today, if we adjust its referent from Semites in general to Middle Eastern Muslims. It might be salutary to our own current prejudices to consider how each term of Renan's rhetoric resonated disturbingly, at the time he wrote, with the so-called Jewish Question, in spite of the fact that Renan himself did not apply his portrait to contemporary, European Jews. From Jewish alienation from the soil and from nature it is a small step to Jewish urban cosmopolitanism, shiftiness, and rootlessness.[112] Their fossilized creed prevents them from engaging in the political and philosophical life around them. Even Jewish monotheism, their one useful contribution, resulted from a flawed imagination, incapable of generating the mythological profusion of their neighbors. The very distinct Aryan mind, on the other hand, applied the expansiveness evident in their verb conjugations and noun declensions to the creation of art and culture, and to the triumphant conquest of inferior cultures.[113] The elevation of a sun, nature, and body worship identified with Aryan mythology became widespread in popular writers and figures from Wagner to Christian Lassen to Houston Stewart Chamberlain and spread throughout popular culture.[114]

Jewish thinkers contributed to debates over the markers of identity as well, generally disputing a commonality of physical descent as a precondition for a national collective.[115] Moritz Lazarus, the German Jewish founder of *Völkerpsychologie*, delivered and published a lecture entitled "What Is a Nation?" to the Academy of Jewish Knowledge in 1880. Lazarus dismisses physiological race, language, and religion as criteria for national identity, accepting the notion of a *Volk* by spiritualizing it: "The concept of the *Volk* rests on the subjective view of the members of the *Volk* itself about itself, about its identity and its sense of belonging together."[116] Such a formulation rests on the notion of a group psychology that forms the basis for the discipline Lazarus founded with his brother-in-law Heymann Steinthal. As a definition, however, it is hopelessly circular. The spiritual definition of the nation was not limited to Jewish thinkers. Renan, in his own lecture, "What Is a Nation?," delivered at the Sorbonne in 1882 and published several years later, comes very close to Lazarus's conclusions. Renan adds geography to Lazarus's list of rejected criteria for national identity and establishes the nation on "the possession in common of a rich legacy of memories; [and] . . . present-day consent, the desire to live together" (19). Even in this civic formulation, we should note, genealogy plays a role, although it is a genealogy that allows for voluntary joining. A nation is "a spiritual family" (ibid.; Lazarus, "Was heißt national?," 12), in which "the ancestors have made us what we are" (Renan, "What Is a Nation?," 19). While criteria for the foundation of collective identity thus ranged from race, religion, language, and geography to the joint desire for a common identity, the reigning episteme of kinship floated freely between the terms.

The idea of religion jumping from one stock to another merges a spiritual with a biological concept of collective identity. Genealogies of Jesus and of the passage of religious thought were intertwined with the genealogizing of peoples. It is in this last case that the construction of a preferred lineage requires augmentation through the regulation of mingling. This drive to police emerges from the genealogical epistemology, which generates paranoia, and does not require sociological facts to be provoked into operation. Even while attempting to prune the tendrils by which Judaism and Christianity were related, the same thinkers could thus reprove Jews as the purest practitioners of a segregationist mentality in their sexual habits. Moritz Lazarus notes and dismisses the idiosyncrasy by which "among the Jews, it is true, the borders of the unit of belief fall together with those of the unit of lineage" ("Was heißt national?," 25). He thus echoes the theorization of civic brotherhood independent of intermarriage that Moses Mendelssohn put forward a century earlier.[117] The Jewish reluctance to intermarry played a large role, however, in the influential midcentury race theory of Arthur de Gobineau, as in the virulently anti-Semitic theory of Paul de Lagarde ("Über die gegenwärtigen Aufgaben," 13–14) and would in fact be made the origin of racial thinking by the widely read turn of the century anti-Semite Houston Stewart Chamberlain (*Grundlagen*, 1:302).

Gobineau was a racial polygenesist whose *Inequality of Human Races* succinctly encapsulated the attraction-repulsion dynamic driving race theory throughout its history.[118] The "secret repulsion from the crossing of blood," which each tribe feels but only the Jews and several others tenaciously respect, is countered by the sexual drive that is strongest in the strongest races (ibid., 29), he claims. Jewish immutability, achieved through inbreeding, provides Gobineau's principal evidence for the indelibility of race. On the other hand, that "picked race of men, a sovereign people" who are driven to conquer other, weaker groups, possesses "the usual strong propensities of such a people to cross its blood with another" and degenerates (31). Gobineau here transfers chosen-ness from Jews to Aryans. Gobineau's race theory has been called "tragic" in its fatalism toward the possibility of ensuring racial purity even through a theory of polygenesis because he locates the motor for the ongoing deterioration of the so-called superior races in their superior drives (Rose, "Wagner," 139). Heterogeneous societies are proud to proclaim inequality, but they inevitably succumb to miscegenation, and once "the majority of the citizens have mixed blood flowing in their veins, they erect into a universal and absolute truth what is only true for themselves" (Gobineau, *Inequality of Human Races*, 36); "hybrid philosophers" such as, in Gobineau's example, Percy Shelley, then declare that "'All men are brothers'" (37).

Chamberlain, who read Gobineau at the urging of his future mother-in-law, Cosima Wagner, returns repeatedly to widespread racial mixing and the Jewish exception in his popular turn-of-the-century *Foundations of the Nineteenth Century* (1899). Unlike Gobineau, Chamberlain is not entirely opposed to race mixing. Following a eugenic analogy to animal breeding, he suggests that good human races can be bred through judicious hybridization followed by long periods of endogamy to preserve the desired traits. The Jewish practice of endogamy, on the other hand, preserves only an arid materialism (2:304) which can hardly be called a religion (1:251), and whose "fundamental law" (1:301) is racial purity. It is, in other words, the fault of the Jews themselves if they decline to enter into brotherhood with other peoples.

FROM LANGUAGE TO ART: REFLECTIONS AND DEPTH

It is not surprising that Richard Wagner befriended Arthur de Gobineau or reacted enthusiastically to his work after they met in 1876. It was a member of Wagner's circle, Ludwig Schemann, who translated Gobineau into German in 1902. In Germany, Wagner played a central role in strengthening ties between the notions of religion, people, language, and theories of creativity, although he only began to use the word "race" late in life. In his appropriately infamous essay "Jewishness in Music" (1840). Wagner preferred such terms as "co-religionists" (*Glaubensgenossen*), "members of the same lineage" (my trans.) (*Stammesgenossen*), and, most frequently, *Volk*, or *Stamm* (tribe, lineage, trunk [of tree]).[119]

In "Jewishness in Music," Wagner's main claim is linguistic and ethnographic: Jews are incapable of *creating*; they cannot bring forth authentically new ideas or forms. Tossing aside the graft-stock analogies of Lessing, Renan, and Max Müller, Wagner severs Judaism from its own roots as it is divided from its original soil. The Jew, an outsider, exists "in a dispersed and barren [*zersplitterten, bodenlosen*] stock [*Volksstamme*], incapable of real evolution, just as his own Hebraic language has been handed down as something dead" (Wagner, "Judaism," 27–28; "Judenthum," 5.2.305). Lest one might think only an unfortunate accident stranded the

Jews in a foreign language and culture, Wagner here establishes not a causal connection but an analogical one. Jews have no potential for original creation in the "foreign language" ("Judenthum," 5.2.305, trans. mine) represented by "our entire European civilization and art" ("Judaism," 28). But they have also proven incapable of keeping their own language alive; it is the principle of vitality that is lacking. Given the interdependence of language and spirit, the "impossib[ility] for [a Jew] ever to speak colloquially, authoritatively or from the depths of his being" (27), means "he is incapable of really deep feeling" (28). Like Gobineau (*Inequality*, 195), Wagner insists that "The Jew ... always speaks ... as a foreigner" ("Judaism," 27). Speaking but not speaking German, creating not art but artifice, the Jew is a mimic, engaged in *nachsprechen, nachkünsteln* (*Werke*, 5.2:306); his voice is less than humans, *nachgeplappert* as if by parrots and *nachäffend* (5.2:312): "aping." We see signs here of an "almost the same but not quite" dynamic, which Homi Bhabha has discovered in the relationship between colonized and colonizer. Such colonial mimicry, mocking the possibility of representation, triggers in the dominant or colonial power those "twin figures of narcissism and paranoia that repeat furiously, uncontrollably."[120] We certainly find signs of both in Wagner. A yearning for pure mimesis and a policing of purity is evident not only in Wagner's essay on Judaism in art but also in his aesthetic theory and in his operas themselves.

Just a year after publishing "Jewishness in Music," Wagner theorized the form of musical drama now generally referred to as a *Gesamtkunstwerk*, of which he saw himself the pioneer. One might associate Wagner's *Gesamtkunstwerk* with Lessing's discussion of drama as the ideal combination of verbal and visual art. For Lessing, narrative is ideally suited to action, and visual art to representing objects. The dramatic form thus provides a unique opportunity to introduce history, both collective and personal, into the interpretation of bodies, as seen earlier. Lessing used this dramatic capacity to undermine any direct notion of inheritance as a kind of mimesis. The visual and the verbal, in other words, do not complement but complicate each other for Lessing, by gesturing toward the reciprocal impingement of different kinds of inheritance and influence. Wagner nods to Lessing as the essay opens ("Opera and Drama," in *Werke*, 3.1:587), only to move in precisely the opposite direction, deploying musical echoes in the form of leitmotifs that reinforce the physical presence of the characters on stage, and leaning on physical evocations of identifiable types.[121] If Wagner appeals to many senses simultaneously, it would nonetheless be appropriate to say his art form leans toward the static Lessing related to visual art, producing a typology allied with the "visual ideology" of racism (Mosse, *Final Solution*, xii). Wagner explicitly repudiates Lessing's emphasis on imagination, instead prefiguring today's affective theories of film studies by theorizing the impact of the work of art as mediated through the senses rather than the intellect (*Werke*, 4.1:587–89). Reception is bodily; representation direct. The relationship between Wagner's aesthetic theory and his race theory is thus one of analogy. Inheritance, like representation, appears as a kind of direct mimesis, and vice versa. It is significant that Thomas Mann, in noting—and critiquing—Wagner's appeal to the "figure for display . . . [a] type," jumps to a racial figure so caricatured as to lose figurality: "Moor: he is black . . . he is no longer a type, he is an emblem, a symbol—the exalted representative of all who are in any sense 'black.'"[122] The Wagnerian *Gesamtkunstwerk* thus aims to erase the traces of its performativity, so prized by Lessing and by Goethe. Ideally for Wagner, the resonance between elements of the performance elicits a sense of inevitability, the artifice becomes invisible, and the portrayal takes on the aura of reality, a goal Thomas Mann dismisses as "the most futile of all ambitions" ("Versuch," 100).

In the final literary reading of this book, then, I want to turn to Mann's "Blood of the Walsungs" as a more comprehensive critique of Wagner than has previously been noticed, one that encompasses an interrogation of the genealogical structure of anti-Semitism. Mann's piece, like Wagner's *The Valkyrie* from which it draws its title, consummates the anxieties surrounding collective identity in a flagrant act of sibling incest. There has been some excellent criticism of this irritatingly mesmerizing story. Sander Gilman and Alan Levenson stress the role of sibling incest in the debate over Jewish endogamy, Marc Anderson analyzes mimicry as a mockery of assimilation, while Paul Levesque focuses on the aesthetic rivalry between Mann and Wagner.[123] What I will argue here is that the connection between these three threads of the story is a necessary rather than a contingent one, which challenges the current consensus on the anti-Semitism of Mann's novella. Mann, I claim, makes an argument against natural kinds through an aesthetic point about mimesis and vice versa. Both the aesthetic and the racial critique target Wagner equally.[124] As the figure of the sibling comes into focus, we will watch it metamorphose from narcissistic mirror image into the manifestation of interpenetrating and yet nonidentical subjectivity we have seen in action so frequently, here sabotaging the anti-Semitic stereotypes that Mann calls on.[125]

Mann's novella, I argue, creates a divide between surface and depth, visual ideology and psychology. This divide instantiates, respectively, the differing aesthetic modes Mann attributes to Wagnerian opera and narrative prose, and equally the distinction between a racial typology and a view of character as environmentally influenced, but not determined, by questions of collective identity. The story is full of reiterative reflections whose superficial conformity with anti-Semitic stereotypes is carefully built, only to be deconstructed. Because they are doubled in each other, its two main characters, the twins Siegmund and Sieglinde, can combine narcissistic self-absorption with exhibitionism and voyeuristic pleasures. The twins have been compared in their ostentation to the facing pair of peacocks on Sieglinde's dress.[126] But the peacock is not merely a symbol of preening and finery. According to Ovid, Hera set the hundred eyes of her watchman Argus in the peacock's tail feathers after Argus was slain by Hermes. The birds are thus simultaneously creatures of display and observers of it. Even Siegmund and Sieglinde's life consists of "richly laden days [that] glided past them with vacant eyes."[127] The two incestuous episodes in the story—the second of which is consummated—are culminations of Siegfried's self-examination before a mirror. Closing his eyes, which Sieglinde then kisses, he exchanges his visual likeness for the tactile assurances of his "likeness," his twin (170). He would seem to accomplish with her what Narcissus can only long for. Even Siegmund's stuttered words of seduction and their justification rest on the essential unity of the pair as mirror images, "'You're totally like me.... Everything is like me'" (283). The incest is hence transformed into a kind of masturbation, a refusal of intercourse with an "other" that would seem to justify an interpretation of the scene as an anti-Semitic indictment of Jewish inbreeding and sexual perversity.

Such a reading would gain strength from the numerous visual descriptions of the assimilated Jewish Aarenhold family that re-create a racial typology familiar from anthropological sources. Gobineau's, in particular, deserves some closer attention here:

The Jewish type has, however, remained much the same.... The warlike Rechabites of the Arabian desert, the peaceful Portuguese, French, German, and Polish Jews—they all look alike. I have had the opportunity of examining closely one of the last kind. His features and profile clearly betrayed his origin. His eyes especially were unforgettable. This denizen of the north, whose immediate ancestors had lived, for many generations, in the snow, seemed to have been just tanned by the rays of the Syrian sun. The Semitic face looks exactly the same, in its main characteristics, as it appears on the Egyptian paintings of three or four thousand years ago, and more; and we find it also, in an equally striking and recognizable form, under the most varied and disparate conditions of climate. The identity of descendant and ancestor does not stop at the features; it continues also in the shape of the limbs and the temperament. The German Jews are usually smaller and more slender in build than the men of European race among whom they have lived for centuries.

(Gobineau, *Inequality*, 122–23)

Every one of the physical traits enumerated by Gobineau in this paragraph makes an appearance in Mann's story, from Sieglinde's "big, dark eyes, probing, expecting, inquiring" (261) and shoulders, "a bit too high and horizontal, like the shoulders of Egyptian statues" (279), to the slim "ephebic" (256) build of Siegmund and the skin color of their mother, "as if she had withered under a torrid foreign sun" (255). While Gobineau does not specify the characteristic shape of Jewish limbs, Mann obsesses over the 'long, slender hands" of the two twins, constantly joined, as their greatest point of resemblance (256–57). The family sports a host of stereotypical traits beyond this description as well, from sister Margit's hooked nose to Siegmund's hirsuteness. Gobineau viewed the supposed indelibility of these characteristics as a consequence of Jewish endogamy. Predictably, the distinctiveness of racial markers is heightened during the moments before and after the incestuous act.

In its recourse to typology, as in the consummation of incest, the novella mirrors Wagner's opera, which is also narrated in the story as the twins named after Wagner's characters attend a performance of *The Valkyrie* before reenacting its sexual climax. And yet the repetition opens up discrepancies that complicate this simple unidirectional model of imitation. As Mann himself noted in his essay "On the Jewish Question"

(1921), the description of "the hated, disrespectful, and god-chosen breed, from which a pair of twins united their anguish and agony" ("Walsungs," 279), was intended to produce "Confusion: namely of the reader, who no longer knows, which lineage [*Geschlecht*] is being referred to."[128] In Wagner as in Gobineau, the ascription of chosen-ness has leapt from Jews to Aryans. Mann exposes Wagner caught in a double-bind and reflects his Aryan demigods back to him unmasked as Jews.[129] Levesque interprets Mann's method here as careless exploitation of the anti-Semitism of Wagner's audience, and his motive as retribution for Wagner's devaluation of prose in favor of his own musical art form. Mann's analysis of Wagner, however, goes further. "The Blood of the Walsungs" is an attempt not to avenge but to disprove Wagner's claim that prose is dilettantish, primarily by demonstrating through the novella a capacity unique to narrative fiction, which, for Mann, raises it above Wagner's art form. In "Tackling the Theater [Versuch über das Theater]," an essay written just two years after the story, Mann argues that the theater—by which he primarily means Wagner—leans on "stereotypes"; while the novel is "more precise, more complete, more knowledgeable, more conscientious, deeper than drama" (Mann, "Versuch," 89). In the novella, an attempt to dive deep while exploring surface effects and shallow prejudices, Jews are not just a means to an end. Mann is interested in demonstrating how certain reiterations in form can produce the impression of rigid and immutable structures, by eliciting this reaction himself, in imitation of Wagner. Through the figure of the Moor caricatured by the theater, he impugns both the desired Wagnerian effect and the art form built around it as complicit with a dangerous form of typological thinking that suspends interpretation and judgment. Mann is still more invested, however, in demonstrating how prose can surpass this superficial effect and introduce nuance through a play of ambiguities, a complex picture of psychology, and an open-endedness that signals aesthetic strength rather than weakness. If Mann correlates Wagnerian opera with racial typology, he sets up his own novella as an experiment in ambiguous cultural behaviors.

Siegmund's instigation of the incestuous encounter with Sieglinde is by no means a simple and direct transmission of affect from musical drama to life. The failure of the opera to transcend illusion is repeatedly noted in the description of operatic technique and stage effects, in Sieglinde's interruption of the action, and in the twins' critique of singers and orchestra. Nonetheless, contradicting Wagner's own theory, an impact succeeds. This impact is not a direct manipulation of the senses but an invitation to Siegmund to affective contemplation of his own entrapment in an isolation born of "lavishness and lucidity," wealth and insight (Mann, "Walsungs," 278). Returning home, he deliberates and decides, posing himself theatrically—and comically—on the luxurious polar bear rug in a mimicry of the rough bearskin in the opera. He is neither carried away by the opera nor need we assume he is subject to an innate sexual perversion; rather, he enacts an ironic interpellation of prejudice, simultaneously as revenge and as experiment. Looking at the Yiddish conclusion of the original version of the story, in which Siegfried says of Sieglinde's fiancé, "Beganeft haben wir ihn—den Goj"/"We swindled him, the Goy,"[130] critics have seen an irruption of a suppressed but indelible racial essence of a particularly ugly kind.[131] But the sentence, which is entirely out of keeping with Siegmund's linguistic habits up to that point, is more plausible as an ironic appropriation of the double-bind of assimilation, a self-conscious if grim and desperate *commentary* on the insurmountable gap that turns assimilation into mimicry by undermining *all* authenticity. The sentence is, after all, not Yiddish but High German in its grammar and in its vocabulary, with the exception of two words: *beganeft*, a word that refers to its own *theft*, and *Goy*.[132] It was grammar, linguists insisted, that linked speech to its ancestry and persisted for generations, rather than such easily borrowed vocabulary. Siegmund's locution here is not a reversion but a subversion. His artificial use of Yiddish demonstrates that he understands precisely the worst that is expected of him, in his language and his habits, and chooses to perform it. His lucidity evokes W. E. B. Du Bois's double-consciousness, through which a member of a devalued group is always aware of himself or herself also as seen through the lens of prejudice. Becoming one with the stereotype is simultaneously an act of irony and of frustration or despair.[133] The irony thus belongs both to character and to author, and it is not only an authorial technique but also the goal. In stark contrast to drama, the story features a relentlessly detached third-person narrator, demonstrating an "indirectness" Mann celebrates as the "condition and characteristic of all figurative art" ("Versuch," 92) in contrast to Wagner's desired "direct effect" (ibid., 115).

It is not only contemporary readers who find Mann's last sentence scurrilous—his concerned publisher forced him to alter it. Mann's substitute ending is revealing. While not equally pointed, Siegmund similarly turns the tables on Wagner with his concluding conviction that Sieglinde's future husband "ought to be grateful to us. He will lead a less trivial existence from now on" ("Walsungs," 284). The word *trivial* is not trivially chosen. Siegfried's own poor artistic forays may seem to embody Wagner's depiction of Jewish art as "indifferent and trivial, since his entire artistic impulse was to him an unnecessary luxury" (Wagner, "Judaism," 30). In fact, Siegfried recognizes his own art as "silly," impeded not by innate incapacity but by the "superfluous" richness of "the circumstances of his existence" ("Walsungs" 266). This existence itself, however, his life, his final line suggests, is not trivial. Living as a Jew in Germany has given him a depth of awareness, about self and others, about the influence of circumstance, that the ordinary German lacks. In "The Solution to the Jewish Question," an essay written two years after his story, Mann points to psychological pressure on Jews as a an explanation for the "exceptionality . . . that distinguishes them in a sublime or an ignominious sense from the base norm."[134] Siegmund falls certainly into the latter category. In either case, however, this inner conflict converts Jews for the artist into "Brothers," "a relationship [Verwandtschaft] for which he will love them" (130).

In stark contrast to the territorializing of race theorists such as Gobineau or ethnographers such as Renan, Mann in his novella simultaneously deterritorializes and shows his character in the act of doing the same. We see this same deterritorialization projected onto territory itself in the vastly overdetermined "East" named as Herr Aarenhold's place of origin.[135] This East conflates the Eastern Europe from which the elder Aarenholds emigrated not only with the Near East—the implied original homeland of the Aarenhold ancestors—but even with India.[136] It is precisely this multivalent "East" that ushers the reader into the story, as it ushers the family to lunch:

> Since it was seven minutes to twelve, Wendelin came into the second-floor vestibule and beat the gong [Tamtam]. Broad-legged, in his violet knee breeches, he stood on an old, faded prayer rug as be belabored the metal with his club. The brass clanging, savage, cannibalistic, and far too excessive for its purpose, penetrated everywhere. . . . The racket filled the entire house, whose evenly warmed atmosphere was thoroughly imbued with a sweet and exotic perfume.
>
> (Mann, "Walsungs," 255)

The dinner bell is a tam-tam, a gong that originates, according to the Grimms' dictionary, in either India or Turkey; it stands before a prayer rug, presumably Islamic.[137] The exotic perfume, as much as the club and savagery, points back to various primitive Easts. And yet the entire mise en scène is contrived. The prayer rug is desecrated when used as a mat; the club trivialized as a gong mallet; the tam-tam calls the family to a meal that is not in the least cannibalistic. The confused mélange in this description reveals the slippage and inconsistencies in the racial theories of origin. These Easts represent neither an authentic Jewish past nor a manifestation of the family's true identity; rather, this bric-a-brac firmly associates the family with, while exaggerating, European norms in collecting. The objects are fetishes, to return to a common theme throughout this study, not within the cultures where they originated but when, displaced into a fin-de-siècle context as commodities and décor, they become signs to demonstrate European mastery over "primitive" spaces and "primitive" beliefs. Anne McClintock has eloquently revealed the way such object relations enact instead the opposite power structure, granting agency to the objects.[138] Here the ambiguity about on which side of the divide the family stands opens up the mirror relationship into an endless set of fun-house reflections.

The hostile reception of Mann's novella reveals that he possessed too tenuous a grasp of the very real and justified sensitivities illuminated by the story itself, and that he may have had too much faith in an audience's ability to penetrate the indirectness he deployed. Mann, moreover, engages in a separation of body and mind that is not, I will argue in the epilogue, the most promising way out of the dilemma of human variety. Far from endorsing the racial stereotypes it evokes, however, "The Blood of the Walsungs" offers a glimpse at tortured attempts at self-identification. The fact that the twins consummate their relationship just before Sieglinde's marriage points not only toward Siegmund's resentment at losing her but also to his recognition of the narcissistic dynamic as an illusion. Sieglinde is not in the end his "likeness" (268) but "a Like unlike," to quote George Eliot from the previous chapter.[139] Her impending departure to present him with a "Teuton" as a brother-in-law forces him to confront notions of kind that are porous and yet intractable (270). Should Sieglinde find herself pregnant in the near future, the twins will not have succeeded in securing a pure Jewish heritage for the next generation but only in rendering paternity deeply uncertain.[140] Such a future remains, of course, a fictional projection far gentler than the reality of life and death would be for the next generation of German Jews. That future lurks threateningly just beyond its margins.

―――― ∞∞∞ ――――

The Holocaust also lies outside the bounds of this study. I want to end my exploration with one additional nod in its direction, however, by turning back to a rabid anti-Semite of the late nineteenth century encountered in this chapter already, Paul de Lagarde. The most infamous passage in his essay "Jews and Indogermans" (1887) transforms Jews into a virulent form of infection: "One does not negotiate with trichina and bacillus, one also does not educate trichina and bacillus, they are exterminated as quickly and as thoroughly as possible."[141] For our purposes, however, another passage is just as significant. Having been stateless for thousands of years, Lagarde claims, atavistic Jews are incapable of partaking in the life of a modern state. They "confront the tasks of, for example, German civic life [*Staatsleben*], with the detachment [*Unbefangenheit*] with which a jackdaw would fly over a copy [*Exemplar*] of the Antigone and Iphigenia lying open [*aufgeschlagen*] in a garden" (344).

The claim is formulated as an analogy, and yet the jackdaw is not haphazardly chosen. In *Aesop's Fables*, this bird attempts to mimic pigeons to steal from them but is unmasked, and in the Grimms' German legend of *The Councilor of Schweidnitz* it pilfers gold coins from the city coffers for its corrupt master.[142] Moreover, the jackdaw was known to mimic human language as well as the calls of other birds. It is neither attractive nor musical, managing therefore to unite a surprising number of anti-Semitic stereotypes. We must assume, then, that the Jews alluded to through the bird are similarly impervious to the specific culture Lagarde presents as exemplary, and which represents an Aryan amalgam of Classical Greek with German Classicism in a copy, or *example*, composed of two of the most famous sisters of the nineteenth century, Antigone and Iphigenia. For the epoch, these sisters radiated a kind of selfless love that both exemplified the family and enabled the civic sphere by providing its ground and its motivation, a role to which the un-civic Jew is said to be impervious. As sisters who would never become wives or mothers, Antigone and

Iphigenia were also symbols of sexual purity. Here, however, as they lie open in a garden, their sexual vulnerability is hard to overlook. The rapacious Jewish jackdaw overhead embodies a threat to Aryan women and to the Aryan culture they here represent, and yet he is accused primarily of disdaining the sexual invitation of the sister that would turn him into a *brother*, into a fellow citizen. I have argued throughout this book that the sibling reveals the precariousness of any boundaries that would ensure the integrity of self-identity. What registers here as the sister's need of protection is thus a screen for the threat to the narrator's own identity implicit both in the sister's ability, synecdochally entwined with him, to entangle him with another, and in her sexuality, which produces kinship and can convert the Jew into a brother. The paranoia on display in the passage merges anti-Semitic racism with a misogyny that polices female sexuality against miscegenation.

EPILOGUE

Spawning Disciplines

Throughout this study, we have followed the spread of genealogy as the dominant structure for organizing knowledge in the nineteenth century, with the sibling serving as a splinter in the system, simultaneously constitutive of terms and yet always promiscuously intermingling, undermining the very possibility of term-integrity and the establishment of natural kinds. In the genealogy of genealogical disciplines we have performed, comparative anatomy, comparative philology, cultural history, and race theory stand, jointly around 1800, as coprogenitors (often among others) of fields with as little obvious contemporary connection as biological and cultural anthropology, evolutionary biology, linguistics, religious studies, psychoanalysis, political science, national literary studies, and comparative literature. These domains have needed to demarcate their boundaries and distinguish themselves from their siblings, each other. In particular, as we saw in chapter 4, the "sciences" and the "humanities" diverged over the causal explanatory power assigned to accident, contingency, and agency in evolving systems, that is, over the purview of history versus natural law. Here, in the liminal spaces between disciplines, the sibling has continued to exercise its customary prerogatives. Family structure was not only a model for but also an object of the theoretical gaze we have explored, its imbrication in both nature and culture evident even to an age determined to separate the two. It is, fittingly, through speculations about the indistinct boundaries manifested in theories of incest that the genealogical disciplines and their heirs have defined themselves against each other. And it is by looking here that we can, perhaps, reemerge from the disciplinary di- or *trichotomy* and find ways to recognize and enact hybridity without devaluing divergent methodologies.

Theories about incest aversion were always already boundary markers in the self-definition of disciplines. Johann Heinrich Zedler, whose *Universallexicon* (1735) was the most comprehensive German encyclopedia of the eighteenth century, captures something of the present disciplinary problem when addressing incest, although his account predates modern disciplinary divisions. Having excluded the prohibition against incest from the status of natural *law* because the first humans could never have multiplied without engaging in incest, he erects a new category in an attempt to bind nature to culture, that of natural *right*. In his entry on *Blut-Schande*, he writes:

> I have no desire to engage in an argument over how broadly it is possible to set the boundaries of the rights of nature [dem Rechte der Natur], in consideration of its status as a discipline. The honorable, the beneficial, and the just are by no means opposites, but rather species and genus. [Honestum, utile, und justum sind keinesweges Opposita, sondern Species und Genus.] The honorable and beneficial, if it is truly useful, is also just. I have no objections to relegating the honorable and beneficial to a separate discipline [eine a parte Disciplin von dem honesto und utili machen], as long as one concedes that that which is honorable and beneficial is also right [dasjenige, was ehrlich und nützlich ist, auch recht sey]. We posit accordingly this claim as a foundation: That which furthers the benefit of society, is right.[1]

By the end of this passage about incest avoidance, in other words, Zedler has supplied a neat argument for stretching the boundaries of disciplines to correlate the *rights* of nature, the *right* of justice, and benefit to society. Of course, for Zedler, still operating in the shadow of natural law as outlined by Thomas Aquinas, the enabler of a disciplinary link between nature and ethics is God.

By the turn of the nineteenth century, the modern configuration of nature, culture, and ethics had begun to emerge, leading to a range of proposals surrounding incest that looks decidedly familiar. In the choice that developed between incest aversion as instinct or incest prohibition as custom, we see the rights of nature torn away from the right of justice, as nature and custom are drawn into decisively different sets of disciplines. As divine natural law segued into empirical natural laws, a new foundation was suggested for the supposition that the incest aversion was innate. No longer a divine injunction against debauchery, the aversion was interpreted, in Jeremy Bentham's account of contemporary perspectives, as a defense against the tendency of the species otherwise to degenerate.[2] Immanuel Kant, in "On the Use of Teleological Principles" (1788), adhered to such a view, arguing that nature had an interest in preserving variety among humans in order to retain traits adaptive to different environments, variety that would be threatened by inbreeding.[3] He hints on the same page at an analogous aversion to racial mixing for the same reason, as discussed in chapter 5. This proposition raises the pressing question of how purpose can regulate function in nature, as the title of his essay indeed suggests. Kant's contribution to the emerging field of biology was a philosophical legitimation of the use of teleological reasoning in explaining the function of parts, such as organs, in natural systems, such as organisms. While nature provides no compelling evidence to reason for the existence of God or an agency in or behind nature, science can proceed only if the understanding is permitted to theorize purpose *as if* such an author were present. Kant's bridge between purpose and nature did not stop short of human tendencies or abilities but indeed included them, as becomes clear from his racial classifications.[4] Nonetheless, Kant posited a human faculty of reason, and thus also the ethical imperatives governed by it, as utterly independent of natural forces. His proposed incest aversion thus remains stranded on the side of nature—an instinct with no ethical force.

Bentham affirmed this gulf between nature and culture in his claim that no instinctive reaction could constitute the foundation for an ethical prohibition:

> "Nature," it is said, "is repugnant to such alliances...." This argument alone never can furnish a satisfactory reason for prohibiting any action whatever. If the repugnance be real the law is useless. Why forbid what nobody wishes to do? If, in fact, there be no repugnance, the reason is at

an end; vulgar morality would have nothing more to say in favor of prohibiting the acts in question, since its whole argument, founded upon natural disgust, is overturned by the contrary supposition. If everything be referred to nature—that is, the bent of desire, we must equally conform to her decisions, whatever they may be.

(Bentham, *Theory*, 219–20)

Bentham advances two separate arguments here. First, laws are introduced as curbs to desire rather than codifications of aversions. And second, no natural reaction may either be confused with or taken to legitimate an ethical stance. Countering Zedler's assertion, he thus posits the relationship between morals and nature as both antagonistic and supervening. Nature is confined behind clear boundaries that deny its investigators jurisdiction over questions of ethics or customs. Those who would try to confuse these domains—*vulgar moralists*—are unmasked as charlatans.

There were, however, also attempts at the turn of the nineteenth century to take into account a perceived correlation between human repugnance and natural detriment.[5] Noah Webster (in 1789) and Samuel Taylor Coleridge (in 1803), on opposite sides of the Atlantic, came independently to the same explanation for incest aversions, one that conjectures the conversion of a natural imperative into an affective prohibition through cultural evolution. Relying no longer on the existence of God but instead on *belief* in the divine, Coleridge speculates that an early society practiced sibling marriage with disastrous and widely observed results.[6] As the human population spread around the globe, it carried with it the memory not of the evidence but of the trauma, interpreted as an expression of divine vengeance and performatively revitalized in each generation's injunction to the following one.[7] Or, as Webster phrases it more succinctly, "Superstition iz often awake, when reezon iz asleep."[8]

Coleridge combines this explanation with an account of the *social* benefits of the division of "the sisterly & fraternal from the conjugal affection" so that "the Heart has two loves instead of one."[9] Though he proclaims neither stronger than the other, it is the sibling bond that serves as a foundation for the gradations of attachment that bind each person into a wider community, initiating a sequence: "Sister, Wife, Child, Uncle, Cousin, one of our blood, &c. on to mere Neighbour—to

Townsman—to our Countrymen" (1:1637). The sister may precede the wife in this list at least partly for chronological reasons—the "practice" a man receives through his relationship with his sister refines and strengthens conjugal love (ibid). The difference is also structural, however, in precisely the ways explored in chapter 2—conjugal love is envisioned as unitary and particular, while sibling affection grounds more generalizable sympathetic attachments and guides ethics. In the midst of a Romantic embrace of fraternity, sorority, and lateral associations in general, Coleridge fully omits the filial relationship Robert Filmer had set at the foundation of governance and social order in the seventeenth century. When Percy Shelley declared the incest prohibition a matter of "convention" in 1817, he therefore followed the cultural reasoning common to the period, but he was certainly in the minority in "forbidding [the moral sense] to waste its energies in seeking to avoid actions which are only crimes of convention," thus allying the lifting of incest prohibitions with social and political revolution.[10]

As the modern disciplines became increasingly entrenched over the course of the nineteenth and twentieth centuries and into the twenty-first, the dispute over incest intensified: each assertion about aversions, taboos, or ethical prohibitions not only pits the powers of nature against the powers of culture but also stakes a claim to the jurisdiction and hence legitimacy of the discipline framing the argument. Incest theories thus ground and differentiate fields of inquiry on the most slippery of platforms. The enigma of incest is the enigma of *anthropology* in its original sense, the mystery of the human as spiritual and natural, as rational and animal. While eighteenth-century anthropology investigated the synthesis of these two elements, the profusion of institutional disciplines in the following centuries amounted to a centrifugal force that created what C. P. Snow would famously call *The Two Cultures*. These two cultures, however, did not simply occupy separate domains but engaged in disputes to annex territory behind a border considered equally solid by both sides. In the second half of the nineteenth century, then, the same alternatives for conceptualizing incest took on more robust forms along with the emergence of two new disciplines: kinship studies and sociobiology.

To claim that incest prohibitions are universal—as do fields on both sides of the disciplinary divide—is question begging, as incest is defined through its prohibition. Incest and kinship are mutually constitutive, their definitions interdependent. *Kin* is an old word in English that, until the late nineteenth century, indicated those individuals whom Europeans considered to be *kinsfolk*, namely, relatives linked by descent through both the maternal and paternal lines, and not including relations through marriage. The word *kinship*, on the other hand, is a late nineteenth-century development incorporating in its very coinage the notion that the production of kin depends on a theory, a theory newly acknowledged to differ from society to society. By the early twentieth century, a bifurcation had been established in the use of the word *kin* that is still in place. The field of genetics that arose in the twentieth century adapted the older meaning of the word into a designation of genetic relatives, a definition still in use among biologists and evolutionary psychologists. Cultural anthropologists beginning in the late nineteenth century instead came to define kinship through social recognition in explicit contrast to biological relatedness. It would be another century before David Schneider would offer his profound critique of kinship as a European template that blinds anthropologists to other ways of organizing interpersonal relations.[11] Kinship studies from the beginning built "social kinship" on or against "natural kinship" as a fictive form of the latter, without questioning the universality of the European privileging of blood as the basis for attachment.[12]

Kinship studies began with a triad of books published in a single decade that attempted to reconstruct cultural histories of familial relationships: *Mother Right* (1861) by the Swiss jurist Johann Jakob Bachofen, *Primitive Marriage* (1865) by the Scottish lawyer John Ferguson McLennan, and *Systems of Consanguinity & Affinity of the Human Family* (1871, followed in 1877 by *Ancient Society*) by the American lawyer Lewis Henry Morgan.[13] Confronted with a profusion of systems of organizing family relations over time and space, they were forced to use language creatively. These studies, out of which sprang modern anthropology, investigated current and past kinship formations through the comparative method discussed at such length in chapters 4 and 5, generating genealogies of kinship systems while conflating geography with history, following the logic encountered in Johann Gottfried Herder in chapter 4. As McLennan explicitly affirms of various non-European societies, "These facts of to-day are, in a sense, the most ancient history" (*Primitive Marriage*, 13), while Morgan in *Ancient Society* writes of "ethnical periods" dependent on condition rather than time (6). Cultural anthropology doubled as cultural history. It is no accident that the first word of Morgan's *Systems of Consanguinity & Affinity of the Human Family* is "Philology" (xxi). Like McLennan, Morgan hoped to extend the genealogical discoveries of philology by investigating a phenomenon posited as still more conservative and slower to change than language, namely, family structure: "Systems of relationship," he claimed, "have been handed down as transmitted systems, through the channels of the blood, from the earliest ages of man's existence upon the earth" (xxii). In spite of this beginning, Morgan, like McLennan, allows for a divergence between blood-relatedness and cultural kinship without relinquishing the expectation that any recognition of relatedness entails belief in a physical genealogical connection. Morgan thus uses the expression "systems of consanguinity" to emphasize the role of convention, while retaining the identification of a blood relationship as the presumed goal.[14] All three kinship studies focused on sexual relations as well as descent—both alliance and filiation—linked of course through reproduction. From the beginning, therefore, incest taboos played a pivotal role.

The ancient systems of relationship postulated by these three accounts contrasted strongly with the European family derived from Roman precedents, displacing or eliminating paternity in favor of matriarchal systems that placed siblings in the center of kinship arrangements. In Bachofen's "gynecocracy," for example, marriage plays no role, so that the most important relationship is that between sisters, and male kinship is determined through mother and sisters (*Mother Right*, 4). Maternality for Bachofen formed a kind of material substratum to history which, because of its lack of differentiation, levels relations; in the gynecocracy "all people are brothers and sisters" (5). Only the spiritual advance necessary for the recognition of paternity initiated both progress and individuation (12–13). Morgan concretely argued a decade later for a stage of cultural development at which McLennan had also hinted, in which every tribe was a family, and brothers and sisters of each generation were simultaneously husbands and wives.[15] In *Primitive Marriage*, McLennan not only introduced the terms "exogamy" and "endogamy" but also proposed a set of primary affections distinct from that of Coleridge: "The filial and fraternal affections may be instinctive. They are obviously independent of any theory of kinship, its origin or consequences; they are distinct from the perception of the unity of blood upon which kinship depends; and they may have existed long before kinship became an object of thought" (63).

McLennan's vertical and horizontal axes reflect the two poles that governed genealogical epistemology in the nineteenth century and would form the backbone of structural anthropology in the twentieth. In this case, they disclose a mystical existence predating and transcending the social practice of kinship in a period whose existence later structural anthropology would dispute. For Bachofen, McLennan, and Morgan, civilizational advance correlated with patrilineage, differentiation, ownership, and the privatizing of the family. The object of study around which the new field consolidated was thus gradual accession to civilization through the masculine transcendence of feminine nature. Kinship studies formed the kernel of new set of disciplines whose name marks their genesis out of a perimeter: the social sciences.

At the same moment, another field arose from this very same perimeter, which oriented its causal explanations in the opposite direction, namely, sociobiology, or eugenics. Sociobiologists embraced what Laura Otis has termed the "organic memory" of heredity, which "placed the past *in* the individual, *in* the body, *in* the nervous system."[16] Heredity, thinkers such as Cesare Lombroso and Francis Galton theorized, controlled not only physiology but also character and inclinations from criminality to intelligence. Following this logic, Edvard Westermarck argued in *The History of Marriage* in 1891 that the aversion to sexual intercourse among siblings was an innate, heritable adaptation. Westermarck was very aware that the forms of kinship and alliance covered by the incest taboo vary widely. Dismissing the transmission of an aversion through the kind of performative curse described by Coleridge and Webster, Westermarck insists that no advantage conveyed by exogamous marriages could be sufficient to account for the lack of *desire* to engage in nearest endogamy (319). He thus proposes "an innate aversion to sexual intercourse between persons living very closely together from early youth, and that, as such persons are in most cases related, this feeling displays itself chiefly as a horror of intercourse between near kin" (320). This repulsion first "provoked prohibition" (330) and then spread to more distant kin as well as others affiliated through marriage or adoption as a result of an "association of ideas" (331). Finally, Westermarck concludes that it is not in the first place by degrees of consanguinity, but by close living together, that prohibitory laws against intermarriage are determined.... The extent to which, among various nations, relatives are not allowed to intermarry, is obviously nearly connected with their close living together. There is so strong a coincidence (as statistical data prove) between exogamy and the "classificatory system of relationship"—which system springs, to a great extent, from the close living together of considerable numbers of kinsfolk—that they must, in fact, be regarded as two sides of one institution.

(544)

While this remarkable passage acknowledges that systems of relatedness and incest prohibitions are mutually constitutive, Westermarck grounds both in nature as the only causal agent. It is not a kinship system that determines living arrangements but rather living arrangements that determine relational classifications. Those living together are, however, "kinfolk," prior to and regardless of any system designating them as such. Indeed, they would have to be close genetic relatives in a significant number of cases for an aversion cued to cohabitation to be efficacious. Where the social seems inevitably to raise its head in law or classification systems, Westermarck provides an anchor in practices that are said to spring from nature. Indeed, so eager is Westermarck to erase the social as cause that he defines marriage itself as "a more or less durable connection between male and female, lasting beyond the mere act of propagation till after the birth of the offspring. It is found among many of the lower animals, it occurs as a rule among the anthropomorphous apes, and it is universal among mankind" (537). We encounter here a conflation consistent with what E. O. Wilson would a century later, in 1998, name *consilience*: "It is the custom of scholars when addressing behavior and culture to speak variously of anthropological explanations, psychological explanations, biological explanations, and other explanations appropriate to the perspectives of individual disciplines. I have argued that there is intrinsically only one class of explanation."[17]

Both Sigmund Freud and Claude Lévi-Strauss founded disciplines on their repudiation of nature as a unitary explanation and of Westermarck's logic about kinship, about incest aversions, and hence about the very constitution of the human. If Westermarck stressed human animality in the expression of an instinct that guided sexual behavior, Freud and Lévi-Strauss both invoked the incest taboo as the foundational moment in which culture supersedes nature. Freudian psychoanalysis posits both a pre-oedipal and an oedipal erotic attachment to the mother. The shift from one to the other marks the emergence of the *subject* through individuation, while the subsequent internalization of the incest prohibition originates *ethics* and *culture*, both ontogenetically and phylogenetically. The link between ontogeny and phylogeny through the incest taboo then legitimates both individual and group psychology as the objects of psychoanalysis. Modern anthropology too has been defined by kinship studies structured around the incest taboo. As Lévi-Strauss states unambiguously:

> Of course, the biological family is ubiquitous in human society. But what confers upon kinship its socio-cultural character is not what it retains from nature, but, rather, the essential way in which it diverges from nature. A kinship system does not consist in the objective ties of descent or consanguinity between individuals. It exists only in human consciousness.[18]

Such a statement makes claims not only about the jurisdiction of a study of human society and behavior but also about ability to delimit nature from culture, so that for cultural anthropology, "the incest prohibition is at once on the threshold of culture, in culture, and in one sense, as we shall try to show, culture itself."[19] It is crucial to note here that Lévi-Strauss situates the incest taboo both at the boundary between nature and culture *and* firmly on the cultural side of that boundary: "That it should provide a transition, in itself natural, between nature and culture would be inconceivable" (ibid.). For Lévi-Strauss, nature is a substratum, and culture supervenient. Jacques Lacan then reimagines both Freudian castration and Lévi-Straussian exchange to position the incest prohibition as the hinge between the real and the symbolic: the law of the father (as for Bachofen) is the initiation of difference, and hence of language and culture.

When, at the dawn of the twentieth century, Freud declared the mother the primary erotic object, he converted both of Samuel Coleridge's distinct loves into substitutes for the mother, fully subordinating the lateral to the vertical axis and shifting the incest debate from siblings to intergenerational intercourse.[20] We should not forget that it was not only cultural anthropology but also psychoanalysis that was indebted to kinship studies, which had already correlated civilization and the initiation of higher thought such as ethics with paternal ascendency and the establishment of an order in which sons succeeded to the place of a father. While older kinship studies also envisioned an earlier epoch of communal siblinghood, both Freud and Lévi-Strauss erased this human option from the imaginary, equating the human with culture, and culture with universal social formations that privileged the agent of exchange as a subject of patrilineage arrived at through abjection of the maternal.

Although we certainly owe to Freud the displacement of *Antigone* by *Oedipus Rex* as the exemplary Classical tragedy, Freud was, of course, not solely responsible for the waning of the sibling's theoretical and cultural significance in the early twentieth century. As the nineteenth century drew to a close, family size shrank, reducing the number of cousins available as a pool of marriage partners. Warnings from biologists and eugenists about the potential harmfulness of close-kin marriages increased in intensity. Women gained some degree of independence from their family units, meeting marriage partners at school or even in the workplace. Meanwhile, the early modern age of cultural encounter that had elicited the formation and entrenchment of new collective identities in the seventeenth through nineteenth centuries had segued into an age of colonialism and globalization that, by the turn of the twentieth century, left Europeans firmly ensconced in the scaffolding they had built to maintain their own supremacy. Simultaneously, the historicism that had dominated knowledge-formation for the previous century began to retreat. Structural linguistics, an approach that stressed nondevelopmental commonalities of language across both space and time, joined and soon succeeded comparative linguistics as the center of the discipline. Like the structural linguistics that inspired it, the structural anthropology founded by Lévi-Strauss sought timeless universals. As discussed in chapter 3, structural anthropology depended on the sister, but only as an object to be traded away in order to create exogamous ties, rather than as an agent whose activity mattered. If the sibling waned in significance in all these arenas, there was one new field in which it played a crucial role. The regime of genetics promoted twins to the status of preeminent experimental control group in one of its major endeavors, namely, the identification and segregation of innate from learned traits. Siblings thus continued to mark a fraught boundary, that between nature and culture, but they now embodied the expectation that such thorny problems could be solved. The convergence of these trends away from the sibling logic of the nineteenth century is evident.

In the second half of the twentieth century, sociobiology lost its institutional status as a result of its association with the eugenics of the Holocaust, but the basic shape of its arguments have not disappeared. Its current heir, evolutionary psychology, begins with the premise that elements of human behavior can be explained as evolutionary adaptations. Sociobiology looked at population statistics and analyzed large-scale trends; evolutionary psychology, while still interested in human universals arrived at through statistical analyses, tries to correlate purportedly evolved human behavior with individual mental experiences. Not only behavior but the beliefs and emotions that motivate it, evolutionary psychologists argue, affect fitness and survival, can be genetically coded for, and are hence open to adaptationist influence. Given the hereditary disadvantages attendant on inbreeding, the existence of an innate inbreeding-avoidance mechanism would seem to form a test case on which the plausibility of the field rests.[21] Unsurprisingly, then, evolutionary psychology has taken Edvard Westermarck as its patron saint.

In spite, or perhaps because, of the foundational status of inbreeding-avoidance to the discipline, great certainty of belief within the field rests on very precarious evidence, primarily studies by Arthur Wolf beginning in the 1960s on *sim pua* or minor marriages in Taiwan—in which a future wife is adopted into the family of her future husband when both are children—and those in the 1970s and 1980s by Joseph Shepher on Israeli kibbutzim where children were raised collectively. Wolf measured "aversion" through rates of fertility and divorce.[22] Shepher noted very low marriage rates in the kibbutz peer groups, and none between those raised together from before the age of six.[23] Alternate interpretations of these data, however, are also plausible.[24] Newer approaches to innate aversions focus on multiple potential cues for *kin recognition*, which include not only childhood cohabitation but also body odor, physical resemblance, and observations of one's mother nursing another child.[25] The (unconscious) estimation of kinship that results from these mechanisms triggers, evolutionary psychologists suggest, not only sexual aversion but also kin selection, that is, altruistic behavior toward genetic relatives.[26] Moreover, the incest taboo that Westermarck and contemporary evolutionary psychologists theorize as an extension of the innate aversion is now serving as the basis for a field of research on innate moral sentiment.[27] Such theories built on disgust function quite differently from the eighteenth-century theories of moral sentiments discussed in chapter 3, which unfolded from sympathy. Dodging the question of what constitutes the ethical, current research focuses on the development of prohibitions as codifications of aversions, reuniting Zedler's two rights in a new way.

Evolutionary psychology provides a kind of inverse sibling logic, returning to the sibling as the central focus of the incest taboo and to kinship as a pivotal motivation for behavior, and dissolving the subject along the way, but only by positing underlying innate mechanisms that in the end reify, rather than disrupting, gender and the self. The answer to such approaches cannot be a return to the abjection of materiality and maternality, and the invalidation of lateral bonds that haunt psychoanalysis and cultural anthropology. Many in the humanities, however, remain unwilling to enter the disciplinary borderlands by considering embodiment as more than a condition for disembodied mental cogitation. Permeable boundaries are productive sites, however, and thoughtful cross-disciplinary thinking has begun to emerge. In the sciences, the thriving field of epigenetics—from *beyond* genetics—investigates the ways in which the activity of genes is integrated into environmental flux. The great majority of the human genome is switched off at any given time, but the status of genes can change from active to dormant or vice versa during a single lifetime. This new on-off position is then bequeathed to offspring, returning us to Jean-Baptiste Lamarck's theory of the inheritance of acquired characteristics. The causes of such epigenetic changes are often referred to as "environmental cues," but the field takes account of the fact that the "environment" exists both internally and externally, that the strict conceptual maintenance of any strict boundary between organism and environment is unproductive in praxis. The wall between organism and environment, constantly retheorized over the history of biology, is currently being breached in other ways as well, for example, by the new emphasis on human symbiosis with the manifold microbiota inhabiting us.

Practitioners of the no-longer-properly-named humanities are also slowly relinquishing their defense of the purview of culture-alone, propagating theories of affect, the posthuman and the human animal, and philosophies of embodiment that focus on difference rather than identity, and action rather than stable essence.[28] The sibling adds something crucial to a philosophy of difference, however, offering instead a theory of differentials, an understanding of partial jointures recaptured within difference, a variety of differences and samenesses linking what is differentiated in a synecdochal network of actions, interactions, and intra-actions. I have shown throughout this book the ways in which sibling action generates rhizomes, disrupting genea-logic from the inside out without abandoning human embodiedness, embracing the material as well as the social elements of relatedness, transversing objects as well as subjects, and revealing the reciprocal interaction of history, contingency, and that which is materially given. The sibling performed these functions already at the dawn of humanism and the genealogical sciences before being overtaken by unproductive certainties and reifications. I am not advocating an anachronistic embrace of fraternal or sibling rhetoric, which can all too easily be absorbed into ideologies of nation or race, as we have seen. Reanimating the sibling dynamic, however, should enable us to reach beyond it in the interests of joint political action generated by patterns of alliance rather than identity; a democratic participatory politics that does not segregate itself from a material and erotic component coded familial; access to our shared animal and organismal processes; and the transformation of epistemological categories into epistemological activities. Sibling action, in other words, should be permitted to dissolve and release the genealogical it produces and that produces it.

NOTES

INTRODUCTION

1. In fact, among other disciplines, this book will revisit the three realms in Foucault's groundbreaking *The Order of Things*: economics, linguistics, and biology. I build on Foucault here not only by respecting the specificity and difference between fields, as he charged himself, but by taking his notion of causal historicity one step further. Developmental history does not entirely banish the horizontal in favor of the vertical, as Foucault suggests, but reconceptualizes the horizontal by grounding affinities on inheritance. The ties between similars are thus no longer simple analogies. Michel Foucault, *The Order of Things: An Archeology of the Human Sciences* (London: Routledge, 2007).
2. See Mona Ozouf, "Liberty, Equality, Fraternity," in *Realms of Memory: The Construction of the French Past*, 3 vols., ed. Pierre Nora and Lawrence Kritzman, trans. Arthur Goldhammer, 3:77–116 (New York: Columbia University Press, 1992); Anthony Black, *Guild & State: European Political Thought from the Twelfth Century to the Present* (New Brunswick, N.J.: Transaction, 2003), 43; and Jacques Derrida, *The Politics of Friendship*, trans. George Collins (London: Verso, 1997).
3. See Leila Silvana May's excellent introduction to *Disorderly Sisters* where she refers to "Victorian childhood as a kind of boot camp whose primary purpose was to inculcate future gender roles," while also discussing the productive failures of such nursery practices. Leila Silvana May, *Disorderly Sisters: Sibling Relations and Sororal Resistance in Nineteenth-Century British Literature* (Lewisburg, Pa.: Bucknell University Press, 2001), 20. See also Leonore Davidoff, *Thicker Than Water: Siblings and Their Relations, 1780–1920* (Oxford: Oxford University Press, 2012), esp. 109–23. Davidoff refers to the close kinship networks established through management of sibling marriages as a "lattice of kinship" (121).

4. Foucault is of course indebted to Nietzsche, and Nietzsche, as I will discuss in chapter 4, is indebted to comparative philology, so that I am myself implicated in the genealogy of methods under discussion.
5. The intersections of these narratives take on fascinating contours in Alexis Harley's recent *Autobiologies*, which explores the entanglement of narratives of self and species in autobiographical writings of evolutionary theorists. Alexis Harley, *Autobiologies: Charles Darwin and the Natural History of the Self* (Lewisburg, Pa.: Bucknell University Press, 2015).
6. Indeed, in his recent book, *The Age of Analogy*, Devin Griffiths depicts this process, which he calls "comparative historicism," as a method that "embraces similarity as well as difference" and moves "*between* histories . . . [to] articulate history as a tense composite rather than an organic whole" (15). Griffiths traces the transdisciplinary emergence of this narrative historical approach across and among literary and scientific ventures. While Griffith's insightful analysis reveals the theoretical underpinnings of historical comparative methodologies, not all genealogical fields or practitioners were willing to accept the historical contingency on which their reconstructions depended. Devin Griffiths, *The Age of Analogy: Science and Literature Between the Darwins* (Baltimore: Johns Hopkins University Press, 2016).
7. Donna Haraway, "Race: Universal Donors in a Vampire Culture," in *Modest_Witness@ Second_Millennium. FemaleMan©_Meets_OncoMouse™: Feminism and Technoscience*, 213–65 (New York: Routledge, 1997), 265.
8. Alys Eve Weinbaum, *Wayward Reproductions: Genealogies of Race and Nation in Transatlantic Modern Thought* (Durham, N.C.: Duke University Press, 2004).
9. Charles Taylor, *Sources of the Self: The Making of the Modern Identity* (Cambridge: Harvard University Press, 1989).
10. Dror Wahrman, *The Making of the Modern Self: Identity and Culture in Eighteenth-Century England* (New Haven: Yale University Press, 2004), 274–78.
11. Ian Watt, *The Rise of the Novel: Studies in Defoe, Richardson and Fielding* (Berkeley: University of California Press, 1957).
12. See Felicity A. Nussbaum, *The Autobiographical Subject: Gender and Ideology in Eighteenth-Century England* (Baltimore: John Hopkins University Press, 1989); Nancy Armstrong, *How Novels Think: The Limits of Individualism from 1719–1900* (New York: Columbia University Press, 2005); and Anthony J. Cascardi, *The Subject of Modernity* (Cambridge: Cambridge University Press, 1992).
13. John Locke, *An Essay Concerning Human Understanding*, ed. Peter H. Nidditch (Oxford: Clarendon Press, 1975), 335–40.
14. Harvie Ferguson, *Modernity and Subjectivity: Body, Soul, Spirit* (Charlottesville: University Press of Virginia, 2000), 3–19.
15. Raymond Martin and John Barresi, *Naturalization of the Soul: Self and Personal Identity in the Eighteenth Century* (London: Routledge, 2000), 44.
16. Locke, *Essay*, 342–45.
17. One could as easily think of two persons in one body as fusion; it is only if one starts from the perspective of the body as primary and integral and then split be-

tween two persons that Martin and Baresi's term fission for such a scenario makes sense.

18. See Hillel Schwarz, *The Culture of the Copy: Striking Likenesses, Unreasonable Facsimiles* (New York: Zone, 1996).

19. In one of the more scurrilous reflections on personal identity, the Scriblerus Club, which included Alexander Pope, John Arbuthnot, and Jonathan Swift, among others, published the satirical fictional *Memoirs of Martinus Schriblerus* in 1714, which included an episode in which Scriblerus falls in love with one conjoined twin, who shares sexual organs with her sister. The erotic relationship thus raises the specters of rape, bigamy, and incest, while opening a debate over the essence of female personhood as situated in her sexual organs. Scriblerus Club, *Memoirs of the Extraordinary Life, Works, and Discoveries of Martinus Scriblerus*, ed. Charles Kerby-Miller (New York: Oxford University Press, 1988), 143–63.

20. T. Row, Letter, *Gentleman's Magazine* 56, no. 2 (1786), 772. Wahrman mentions and compares the Parrau/Rudd case of fraud in the 1870s with the later statement but without analyzing the reference to brothers in particular.

21. Moreover, "brother-Twin[s] . . . [whose] outsides were so like, that they could not be distinguished" (*Essay*, 342), present for Locke an obvious example of why body cannot be equated with person. He reasons from the distinct personhood of these identical twins to the need to consider as separate a sleeping Socrates and a waking Socrates who were unaware of each other's thoughts and actions. If the invention of an unconscious by the Romantics complicates Locke's reflections on Socrates's two halves, this uncertainty begins to reach back through the analogy to contaminate the twins as well.

22. Adam Smith, *The Theory of Moral Sentiments*, ed. D. D. Raphael and A. L. Macfie, vol. 1 of *Glasgow Edition of the Works and Correspondence of Adam Smith* (Oxford: Clarendon, 1976), 9.

23. Lawrence Stone, *The Family, Sex and Marriage in England 1500–1800* (New York: Harper and Row, 1977).

24. See also Davidoff, *Thicker Than Water*, 14–18.

25. Johann Jakob Bachofen, *Mother Right: A Study of the Religious and Juridical Aspects of Gynecocracy in the Ancient World*, abridged and trans. David Partenheimer (Lewiston, Me.: Edwin Mellen, 2007); Johann Jakob Bachofen, *Das Mutterrecht. Eine Untersuchung über die Gynaikokratie der alten Welt nach ihrer religiösen und rechtlichen Natur* (Stuttgart: von Krais and Hoffmann, 1861); John Ferguson McLennan, *Primitive Marriage: An Inquiry Into the Origin of the Form of Capture in Marriage Ceremonies*, ed. Peter Rivière (Chicago: University of Chicago Press, 1970); and Lewis Henry Morgan, *Systems of Consanguinity & Affinity of the Human Family* (Lincoln: University of Nebraska Press, 1997). Although widely disparate in their histories of civilizations, both Friedrich Engels in *Origin of the Family, Private Property and the State* (1884) and Claude Lévi-Strauss in *Elementary Structures of Kinship* (1949), which he dedicated to Morgan, depended heavily on Morgan's conclusions (Engels) and methodology (Lévi-Strauss). This history will be discussed in more detail in chapter 3. Friedrich Engels, *The Origin of the Family, Private Property, and the State. In the Light of the*

Researches by Lewis H. Morgan, in vol. 26 of Karl Marx and Frederick Engels, *Collected Works*, 129–276 (New York: International, 1990); and Claude Lévi-Strauss, *The Elementary Structures of Kinship*, trans. James Harle Bell, John Richard von Sturmer, and Rodney Needham, ed. Rodney Needham (Boston: Beacon, 1969).

26. The *OED* does list some earlier uses of the word *kinship*, dating back to the late eighteenth century, but the word in those cases was used to indicate a specific "relationship by descent" between people rather than a system of designating such relationships. OED online, s. v. "kinship," http://www.oed.com.proxy.lib.duke.edu/view/Entry/103585?redirectedFrom=kinship#eid.

27. See David Warren Sabean, *Kinship in Neckarhausen, 1700–1870* (Cambridge: Cambridge University Press, 1998), as well as all his later work.

28. Adam Kuper, *Incest and Influence: The Private Life of Bourgeois England*, Cambridge, Mass.: Harvard University Press, 2009; Michaela Hohkamp, "Do Sisters Have Brothers? The Search for the 'rechte Schwester.' Brothers and Sisters in Aristocratic Society at the Turn of the Sixteenth Century," in *Sibling Relations and the Transformation of European Kinship, 1300–1900*, ed. David Warren Sabean and Christopher Johnson, 65–83 (Oxford: Berghan Books, 2011); Christopher Johnson, *Becoming Bourgeois: Love, Kinship, and Power in Provincial France, 1670–1880* (Ithaca, N.Y.: Cornell University Press, 2015); Margareth Lanzinger, *Verwaltete Verwandtschaft. Eheverbote, kirchliche und staatliche Dispenspraxis im 18./19. Jahrhundert* (Wien: Böhlau, 2015). Another line of critique of the traditional view has emerged from the analysis of significant same-sex bonds in the period. See, for example, Sharon Marcus, *Between Women: Friendship, Desire, and Marriage in Victorian England* (Princeton: Princeton University Press, 2007); and, for an analysis that includes as an afterword the political stakes of earlier historical arguments, Alan Bray, *The Friend* (Chicago: University of Chicago Press, 2003).

29. Davidoff speculates that the delayed formation of a middle class in eastern Europe and the prolongation of feudalism could be results of the ongoing prohibition on cousin marriages in the Orthodox churches, which hindered the building of a lattice of kinship. Davidoff, *Thicker Than Water*, 229–30. See also Johnson, *Becoming Bourgeois*.

30. For the German sphere, see Claudia Jarzebowski, *Inzest: Verwandtschaft und Sexualität im achtzehnten Jahrhundert* (Cologne: Böhlau Verlag, 2006), 11–12. See also Lanzinger, *Verwaltete Verwandtschaft*, 281–342. Lanzinger documents the requests for papal dispensations for cousin marriages, most often successful when there was a risk of the conversion or the civil marriage of petitioners (318–19). For the spread of these streamlined and reduced civil marriage restrictions through the Code Napoleon, see Kuper, *Incest and Influence*, 83.

31. See Lanzinger, *Verwaltete Verwandtschaft*, 223–80.

32. Mary Jean Corbett, *Family Likeness: Sex, Marriage, and Incest from Jane Austen to Virginia Woolf* (Ithaca: Cornell University Press, 2008), 6–19, 57–85; and Lanzinger *Verwaltete Verwandtschaft*, 254–80.

33. See Zedler's account of the reasons put forward for the prohibition of incest in his *Universallexicon* under "Blutschande." Theories of incest prohibition and aversions will be discussed at more length in the epilogue. Johann Heinrich Zedler, *Grosses vollständiges Universallexicon aller Wissenschaften und Künste* (1731–1754), 4:254, http://www.zedler-lexikon.de/index.html.
34. See Michaela Hohkamp, "Do Sisters Have Brothers?" 68–71. The word *Geschwister* originally meant sisters, but had begun including both sexes by the fourteenth century. See Grimm, Jakob, and Wilhelm Grimm. *Deutsches Wörterbuch*. 1854–1971. http://dwb.uni-trier.de/de/.
35. Around the same time, geneticists began using the word *sib* to indicate the same thing. Geneticists now sometimes use sib interchangeably with sibling, and sometimes to designate a sibling who shares both parents and is not an identical twin. See Michael Lynch and Bruce Walsh, *Genetics and Analysis of Quantitative Traits*, (Sunderland, Mass.: Sinauer, 1998), 553. Both terms were derived from the earlier use of sib in English to designate all kin, a word etymologically related to the German *Sippe* (OED online, s. v. "Sibling," http://www.oed.com/view/Entry/179145?redirectedFrom=Sibling).
36. For an illuminating overview of the shifting ethnicities to whom the genealogical descent of Noah's sons was assigned by various biblical peoples over two thousand years, see William McKee Evans, "From the Land of Canaan to the Land of Guinea: The Strange Odyssey of the 'Sons of Ham,'" in *American Historical Review* 85, no. 1 (1980): 15–43. We will also encounter the significance of the Noahdic genealogy in the philological theories of William Jones and Friedrich Max Müller in chapter 4, and in relation to race theory in chapter 5.
37. On the history of reproduction, see Clara Pinto-Correia, *The Ovary of Eve: Egg and Sperm and Preformationism* (Chicago: University of Chicago Press, 1997); and Shirley Roe, *Matter, Life, and Generation: Eighteenth-Century Embryology and the Haller-Wolff Debate* (Cambridge: Cambridge University Press, 1981).
38. The word derives from Greek for after origin and refers to the development of traits subsequent to conception. *Epi* can also mean outside of. Conrad Waddington was aware of the earlier use of epigenesis in contrast to preformationism when he recoined the word *epigenetics* in 1942 to indicate what lies outside of genetics, a coinage from which the contemporary use of the term derives. See Stefan Willer, "'Epigenesis' in Epigenetics: Scientific Knowledge, Concepts, and Words," in *The Hereditary Hourglass. Genetics and Epigenetics, 1868–2000*, ed. Ana Barahona, Edna Suarez-Díaz, and Hans-Jörg Rheinberger (Berlin: Max-Planck-Institut für Wissenschaftsgeschichte Preprint, 2010), 19, https://www.mpiwg-berlin.mpg.de/Preprints/P392.PDF.
39. Johann Friederich Blumenbach, *Über den Bildungstrieb und das Zeugungsgeschäfte* (Göttingen: Johann Christian Dieterich, 1781).
40. William Jones, *Discourses Delivered Before the Asiatic Society*, ed. James Elmes, 2 vols. (London: Charles S. Arnold, 1824), 2:36–37.
41. Friedrich Max Müller, *Introduction to the Science of Religion: Four Lectures Delivered at the Royal Institute in February and May, 1870* (London: Longmans, Green, 1882), 9.

42. Henry M. Hoenigswald, "On the History of the Comparative Method," *Anthropological Linguistics* 5, no. 1 (1963): 2.
43. Charles Darwin, *The Origin of Species*, ed. Gilliam Beer (Oxford: Oxford University Press, 1996), 351.
44. I do not, however, mean to suggest a strict dispersal model of descent similar to those discussed here. These disciplines may share a root, but they each possess more than one; every field arises out of a multitude of intersecting influences.
45. Chapters 4 and 5 will also discuss the early engagement of comparative religion with hybridity, since Christian scholars of northern Europe could scarcely ignore the fact that religions frequently spread through conversion and syncretism.
46. To use the word *aesthetic* in this context requires recognizing that Kant substantially failed in his attempt to segregate aesthetics from sexual desire. For the centrality of sexual desire to race theories, see Robert Young, *Colonial Desire: Hybridity in Theory, Culture and Race* (London: Routledge: 1995); and Ann Laura Stoler, *Race and the Education of Desire: Foucault's History of Sexuality and the Colonial Order of Things* (Durham: Duke University Press, 1995).
47. Naturalists such as the Comte de Buffon had defined hybrids out of existence by establishing the boundary of a species through the ability to produce fertile offspring. Darwin, however, notes to the contrary that some population groups cannot breed, which he still finds reasons to classify as subspecies, while other populations can, which he finds reasons to call separate species. This makes hybridity a particularly thorny issue for him. Darwin, *Origin of Species*, 246–79.
48. Ernst Mayr, "Speciation Phenomena in Birds," *American Naturalist* 74, no. 752 (1940): 258. *Sibling species* is still current usage. Darwin could not have used the term *sibling* because it did not yet exist. However, he could have coined a term himself for the relationship between descendent species of a common ancestor species. We will return to Darwin's strategies and the reasons for them in chapter 4.
49. See James O. McInerney, Davide Pisani, Eric Bapteste, and Mary J. O'Connell, "The Public Goods Hypothesis for the Evolution of Life on Earth," *Biology Direct* 6, no. 4 (2011), http://www.biology-direct.com/content/6/1/41.
50. See James H. Degnan and Noah A. Rosenberg, "Gene Tree Discordance, Phylogenetic Inference and the Multispecies Coalescent," *Trends in Ecology & Evolution* 24, no. 6 (June 2009): 332–40.
51. See Frédéric Bouchard, "Symbiosis, Lateral Function Transfer and the (Many) Saplings of Life," *Biology and Philosophy* 25 (2010): 623–41.
52. It is no coincidence that the most common alternative suggested for the tree in the past few years is the network, which currently dominates pattern formations from sociology to economics to university administration. I am of course guilty of utilizing the network structure to some extent in this book as well. For contemporary instantiations of the network model in evolutionary theory, see Eric Bapteste et al., "Networks: Expanding Evolutionary Thinking," *Trends in Genetics* 29, no. 8 (August 2013): 439–41. For the longer history of the network metaphor, which, however, lost ground against the tree metaphor, particularly because of the temporal element implied by growth, see

Mark A. Ragan, "Trees and Networks Before and After Darwin," *Biology Direct* 4, no. 43 (November 2009), http://www.biology-direct.com/content/4/1/43. See also Robert G. Beiko, "Gene Sharing and Genome Evolution: Networks in Trees and Trees in Networks," *Biology and Philosophy* 25 (2010): 659–73.

53. See George Steiner, *Antigones* (New York: Oxford University Press, 1984).
54. Otto Rank, *Das Inzest-Motiv in Dichtung und Sage. Grundzüge einer Psychologie des dichterischen Schaffens* (Leipzig: F. Deuticke, 1926).
55. Lynn Hunt, *The Family Romance of the French Revolution* (Berkeley: University of California Press, 1992).
56. In addition to Hunt, see W. Daniel Wilson, "Science, Natural Law, and Unwitting Sibling Incest in Eighteenth-Century Literature," *Studies in Eighteenth-Century Culture* 13 (1984): 249–70; Alan Richardson, "The Dangers of Sympathy: Sibling Incest in English Romantic Poetry," *Studies in English Literature* 25, no. 4 (1985): 737–54; and Richardson, "Rethinking Romantic Incest: Human Universals, Literary Representation, and the Biology of Mind," *New Literary History* 31, no. 3 (2000): 553–72.
57. There are some exceptions and borderline cases: Augustine in Goethe's *Wilhelm Meister's Apprenticeship* (1795) refuses at first to give up his lover after discovering she is his sister; a couple in love in "Die drei Nüsse" (1817) by Clemens Brentano believe that they are siblings; and Siegmund and Sieglinde in Wagner's *Valkyries* (1870) become lovers knowing that they are siblings but having spent much of their childhood separated. Thomas Mann's twentieth-century story "The Blood of the Walsungs" (1906) unambiguously depicts consummated incest between siblings raised together. For a typological breakdown of incest plots, see Michael Titzmann, "Literarische Strukturen und kulturelles Wissen: Das Beispiel inzestuöser Situationen in der Erzählliteratur der Goethezeit und ihrer Funktionen im Denksystem der Epoche," in *Erzählte Kriminalität. Zur Typologie und Funktion von narrative Darstellungen in Strafrechtspflege, Publizistik und Literatur zwischen 1770 und 1920*, ed. Jörg Schönert (Tübingen: Max Niemeyer Verlag, 1991).
58. Ellen Pollak, *Incest and the English Novel, 1684–1814* (Baltimore: Johns Hopkins University Press, 2003). In two works, Marc Shell has reflected on the implications of a Christian call for universal brotherhood. Any system that establishes kinship on a large scale, Shell notes, both renders erotic relationships incestuous and radicalizes exclusion—rendering those left outside the system nonhuman rather than merely unrelated. Shell's work does not historicize these trends, but his insights resonate in the more recent explorations mentioned here and will do so in my work as well. Marc Shell, *Children of the Earth: Literature, Politics, and Nationhood* (New York: Oxford University Press, 1993); and Shell, *The End of Kinship: Measure for Measure, Incest, and the Idea of Universal Siblinghood* (Stanford: Stanford University Press, 1988).
59. Sibling incest has received far less attention in the German cultural sphere than in the British. Exceptions are Sander Gilman, "Sibling Incest, Madness, and the 'Jews,'" *Jewish Social Studies* 4, no. 2 (1998): 157–79; and Titzmann, "Literarische Strukturen und kulturelles Wissen." Studies of incest in single authors are more common.

60. Johann Gottfried von Herder, "Treatise on the Origin of Language," in *Philosophical Writings*, trans. and ed. Michael N. Forster (Cambridge: Cambridge University Press, 2002), 127. For more, see chapter 4.
61. Johann Wolfgang von Goethe, "Observation on Morphology in General," in *Scientific Studies*, ed. and trans. Douglas Miller, vol. 12 of *The Collected Works* (Princeton: Princeton University Press, 1988), 57.
62. See chapter 4.
63. Elizabeth Grosz, *Becoming Undone: Darwinian Reflections on Life, Politics, and Art* (Durham: Duke University Press, 2011), 27. Grosz, however, situates Darwin's conception of activity at the beginning of a process she traces into the late nineteenth and early twentieth centuries, whereas I here explore the process's development a century earlier.
64. Eve Kosofsky Sedgwick, "Tales of the Avunculate," in *Tendencies* (Durham, N.C.: Duke University Press, 1993), 63, emphasis in original.
65. Friedrich Max Müller, "On the Relation of the Bengali to the Arian and Aboriginal Languages of India," *Report of the Meeting of the British Association for the Advancement of Science* 7 (1847): 349.

1. SIBLING LOGIC

1. George Steiner, *Antigones* (New York: Oxford University Press, 1984), 18.
2. Juliet Mitchell and Prophecy Coles, building on early work by Melanie Klein, have recently begun to address sibling relations within psychoanalytic theory. Juliet Mitchell, *Siblings: Sex and Violence* (Cambridge: Polity, 2003); Prophecy Coles, *The Importance of Sibling Relationships in Psychoanalysis* (London: Karnac, 2003).
3. Paul Allen Miller, "The Classical Roots of Poststructuralism: Lacan, Derrida, and Foucault," *International Journal of the Classical Tradition* 5, no. 2 (1998): 204–26.
4. While Percy Shelley declared in a letter to John Gisborne in 1821 that "Some of us have in a prior existence been in love with an Antigone" (Percy Bysshe Shelley, *The Letters of Percy Bysshe Shelley*, ed. Frederick L. Jones, 2 vols. [Oxford: Clarendon, 1964], 2:363), Antigone veneration in Great Britain was more marked in the Victorian than in the Romantic period. See, for example, Thomas de Quincey, "The Antigone of Sophocles as Represented on the Edinburgh Stage," in *The Collected Writings of Thomas de Quincey*, ed. David Masson (Edinburgh: Adam and Charles Black, 1890), 10:360–88, and the discussion of George Eliot in chapter 3. See also Steiner, *Antigones*, for an overview of *Antigone* reception.
5. See Jean Bethke Elshtain, "Antigone's Daughters Reconsidered: Continuing Reflections on Women, Politics, and Power," in *Life-World and Politics: Between Modernity and Postmodernity*, ed. Stephen K. White (Notre Dame: University of Notre Dame Press, 1989); and Elshtain, "Antigone's Daughters," *Democracy* 2, no. 2 (1982): 46–59.
6. Judith Butler, *Antigone's Claim: Kinship Between Life and Death* (New York: Columbia University Press, 2000), 57.

1. SIBLING LOGIC 247

7. Butler nonetheless opens the door to a relational reading of Antigone, as we shall see.
8. Jacques Lacan, *The Ethics of Psychoanalysis: 1959–1960*, trans. Dennis Porter (New York: Norton, 1992), 250.
9. Georg Wilhelm Friedrich Hegel, *Phenomenology of Spirit*, trans. A. V. Miller (Oxford: Oxford University Press, 1977); and Hegel, *Elements of the Philosophy of Right*, ed. Allen W. Wood, trans. H. B. Nisbet (Cambridge: Cambridge University Press, 1991).
10. In spite of its title, Cecilia Sjöholm's nuanced *The Antigone Complex* resists erecting a structure parallel to the oedipal. By limiting herself to the figure of Antigone, particularly within modern criticism, however, Sjöholm loses the ability to reach beyond pervasive misreadings. Cecilia Sjöholm, *The Antigone Complex: Ethics and the Invention of Feminine Desire* (Stanford: Stanford University Press, 2004).
11. There is no single defining relationship in this play. However, I will attend to the undertheorized relationship between Antigone and Ismene to unsettle readings and theories that resolve sibling relations into parent-child relations.
12. Bracha Ettinger, "Transgressing With-In-To the Feminine," in *Differential Aesthetics: Art Practices, Philosophy and Feminist Understandings*, ed. Penny Florence and Nicola Foster, 184–209 (Aldershot: Ashgate, 2000).
13. See Lacan, *Ethics*; Steiner, *Antigones*; and Simon Goldhill, "Antigone and the Politics of Sisterhood," in *Laughing with Medusa: Classical Myth and Feminist Thought*, ed. Vanda Zajko and Miriam Leonard, 141–61 (Oxford: Oxford University Press, 2006).
14. Eve Kosofsky Sedgwick, "Tales of the Avunculate," in *Tendencies* (Durham, N.C.: Duke University Press, 1993), 63.
15. Mitchell, *Siblings*, 12–13.
16. Barbara Maria Stafford, *Visual Analogy: Consciousness as the Art of Connecting* (Cambridge: MIT Press, 2001), 10, 86, 10.
17. Antigone's brothers, Polyneices and Eteocles, have killed each other in a struggle over the throne, leaving Creon (their mother/grandmother's brother and their father/half brother's uncle and brother-in-law) ruler of Thebes. Although Polyneices has attacked Thebes with a foreign army, Creon's interpretation of him as a vicious enemy of the city and Eteocles as its honorable defender is strained by the fact that Polyneices is the elder son. Sophocles, *Oedipus at Colonus*, in *Sophocles I*, trans. and intro. David Grene (Chicago: University of Chicago Press, 1991), lines 375–76. Unless otherwise indicated, all quotations of *Oedipus at Colonus* in English are from Grene's translation. References to the Greek are from Sophocles, *Oedipus at Colonus* (Greek), in *Sophocles Fabulae*, ed. Hugh Lloyd-Jones, 409–599 (Cambridge: Harvard University Press, 1994). In all cases I cite by Greek line number, to which the English largely corresponds.
18. *Antigone*, in *Sophocles I*, trans. and intro. David Grene (Chicago: University of Chicago Press, 1991), lines 909–12. Unless otherwise indicated, all quotations of *Antigone* in English are from Grene's translation. Quotations in Greek are from Sophocles, *Antigone*, ed. Mark Griffith, Cambridge Greek and Latin Classics, ed. P. E. Easterling, Philip Hardie, Richard Hunter, and E. J. Kenney (Cambridge: Cambridge University Press, 1999). In both cases I cite by Greek line number, to which the English largely corresponds. The oddity of these lines has prompted some commentators to hope

that they were a later interpolation. Goethe considered the tone of the passage too legalistic for a girl on the verge of death. Johann Wolfgang von Goethe, "From the Conversations of Goethe with Eckermann and Soret," in *Sophocles: The Classical Heritage*, ed. Roger David Dawe (New York: Garland, 1996), 175. Others have objected to the elevation of brother over husband and children. Contemporary philology supports their authenticity. For a history of the controversy and a justification of the lines' legitimacy, see Mark Griffith, "Commentary," in Sophocles, *Antigone*, ed. Griffith, 277–78.

19. Ettinger, "Transgressing," 193, 195.
20. Ettinger is particularly concerned with the transmission of trauma from Holocaust survivors to later generations. See Bracha Ettinger, *The Matrixial Borderspace*, ed. Brian Massumi (Minneapolis: University of Minnesota Press, 2006), esp. 123–57, 162–69; quote on 197.
21. Ettinger is not alone in stressing this emphasis. Lacan (*Ethics*, 255) notes the use of the word *adelphos*, which means womb-mate. Luce Irigaray also relates their "co-uterine attraction" to the power of shared blood (Luce Irigaray, *Speculum of the Other Woman*, trans. Gillian G. Gill [Ithaca: Cornell University Press, 1982], 216), which is, however, subordinated to the patronymic, the symbolic, so that in Lacan, as in Hegel, the sister exists as a medium through which the brother arrives at his individuating self without any benefit to her (*Speculum*, 221). Pushing on Irigaray's reading, Carol Jacobs rehabilitates Antigone as a threat to patronymy, seeing in her insistence on the womb a reenactment of motherhood that "leaves no room for a clear oppositional struggle, for she who would bury Polyneices and give him meaning and form also produces or rather has already produced the dispersal of that form-giving" (Carol Jacobs, "Dusting Antigone," *Modern Language Notes* 111 [1996]" 910). While I appreciate Jacobs's reading, I think there is much to be gained by following more assiduously the role of the sister without reverting to the role of the mother.
22. Aeschylus, *The Oresteia*, in *Aeschylus II*, ed. David Grene and Richmond Lattimore, trans. Richmond Lattimore (Chicago: University of Chicago Press, 1953). This is not the place to plumb the substantial history of criticism on the *Oresteia*. For brief discussions of Aeschylus's trilogy in the context of *Antigone*, see Goldhill, "Antigone," 149–52; and Sjöholm, *The Antigone Complex*, 31–34.
23. The concepts of identity and identity politics in relation to such identifications are major points of contention today, particularly in gender and queer studies. Engaging this debate lies outside the scope of this book. For a selection of views, see Jacqueline Rose, *Sexuality in the Field of Vision* (London: Verso, 1986), esp. 49–83; Jessica Benjamin, *The Bonds of Love: Psychoanalysis, Feminism, and the Problem of Domination* (New York: Pantheon, 1988), but especially Jessica Benjamin, *Shadow of the Other: Intersubjectivity and Gender in Psychoanalysis* (New York: Routledge, 1998), 35–78; Judith Butler, *Gender Trouble: Feminism and the Subversion of Identity* (New York: Routledge, 1990); Allison Wier, *Sacrificial Logics: Feminist Theory and the Critique of Identity* (New York: Routledge, 1996); and Tim Dean, *Beyond Sexuality* (Chicago: University of Chicago Press, 2000).

24. See Luce Irigaray, *This Sex Which Is Not One*, trans. Catherine Porter (Ithaca, N.Y.: Cornell University Press, 1985); and Irigaray, *Speculum of the Other Woman*.
25. See Naomi Schor, *Breaking the Chain: Women, Theory, and French Realist Fiction* (New York: Columbia University Press, 1985); and Schor, *Reading in Detail: Aesthetics and the Feminine* (New York: Methuen, 1987).
26. Luce Irigaray, *The Way of Love*, trans. Heidi Bostic and Stephen Pluháček (London: Continuum, 2002), 10.
27. Ettinger, "Transgressing," 197.
28. Jacques Lacan, "The Family Complexes," trans. Carolyn Asp, *Critical Texts* 5. 3 (1983): 17. Significantly, bridging the polarity of identification and object choice is central to Freud's discussion of group psychology, which will arise again in the next chapter.
29. Griffith, "Commentary," 211–12. Grene translates the line in question as "My nature is to join in love, not hate."
30. Mary Whitlock Blundell, *Helping Friends and Hurting Enemies: A Study in Sophocles and Greek Ethics* (Cambridge: Cambridge University Press, 1989), 40–42. Compare this list to Coleridge's chain of affection, reaching outward from the sister to all "Countrymen" (1637), discussed in the epilogue. Samuel Coleridge, *The Notebooks*, in vol. 1 of *The Complete Works of Samuel Taylor Coleridge* (New York: Pantheon, 1957), 1637.
31. Nussbaum in particular denies that Antigone is "a loving or passionate being in anything like the usual sense" (Martha Nussbaum, *The Fragility of Goodness: Luck and Ethics in Greek Tragedy and Philosophy* [Cambridge: Cambridge University Press, 1986], 65). Blundell argues persuasively, however, that Antigone's repetition of *phil*- words when speaking of Polyneices indicates "the special character of her devotion" (*Helping Friends*, 108).
32. Frequent polyptotons in which forms of the same word refer to two different family members reinforce the intertwinement of family members in this drama.
33. Antigone's self-law-giving characteristic is noted by the chorus with the word "autonomos / αὐτόνομος" (*Antigone*, line 821). While Grene folds this word into the phrase "it was your own choice," Griffith translates it directly as "observing your own law" ("Commentary," 268). Butler (*Antigone's Claim*, 11) and Gourgouris discuss this autonomy as well. Stathis Gourgouris, *Does Literature Think? Literature as Theory for an Antimythical Era* (Stanford: Stanford University Press, 2003), 146–47.
34. These plays form a loosely related collection rather than a trilogy, but reading between them is still a useful exercise. It is telling to observe how the same sets of lines uttered in one case by Antigone and in the other by Ismene are taken up differently by criticism. For more, see Stefani Engelstein, "Ismene on Horseback and Other Subjects," *Philosophy Today* 59, no. 3 (2015).
35. See Steiner, *Antigones*, 208–9; Goldhill, "Antigone," 145–46 and 151–53; and Simon Goldhill, *Sophocles and the Language of Tragedy* (Oxford: Oxford University Press, 2012), 240–41.
36. Antigone's rejection of Ismene also saves Ismene's life, and there are clear moments of reconciliation in their final scene together. The most interesting recent interpretation of their dialogue comes from Bonnie Honig, who argues that Ismene has performed

the first, nighttime burial and Antigone the second, daytime one. When they meet before Creon, they thus conduct an ambiguous conversation with one set of meanings for each other and a different set for Creon, as each attempts to understand what the other has done and to deflect blame away from the other sister. Honig's reading clears Antigone of the charge of brutality toward her sister. It does not depart drastically from traditional readings of Ismene, however, who is not granted her own motivations or independent decisions and is still depicted as timid and vacillating. Bonnie Honig, *Antigone, Interrupted* (Cambridge: Cambridge University Press, 2013). For a longer response to Honig, see my "Ismene on Horseback."

37. This situation has begun to change. In addition to my own work and that of Goldhill and Honig, see Lot Vekemans's powerful play, *Sister of*, performed in Berlin in March 2014 under the title *Ismene, Schwester von*. Lot Vekemans, *Schwester von*, trans. Eva Pieper (Berlin: Kiepenheuer-Medien, 2014).

38. Peggy Phelan recognizes this flaw when she reads *Antigone* in the context of queer theory (Phelan, *Mourning Sex: Performing Public Memories* [London: Routledge, 1997], 15). She finds it not only in Lacan but also in Sophocles, however, claiming that the two sisters inhabit an oedipal space within which no desire between women can be acknowledged (15–16). Phelan, like so many critics before her, misreads the dynamic of the opening dialogue between Ismene and Antigone, stating that Ismene's refusal to die for Polyneices is also a refusal to die for Antigone, to extend love beyond death (13–14). This reading fails to account for the fact that Ismene explicitly insists on her devotion to Antigone beyond death in lines 97–100, 548, and 568, and that she attempts to share her death.

39. David Grene, "Introduction," in *Sophocles I*, trans. and intro. David Grene (Chicago: University of Chicago Press, 1991), 1–2.

40. Griffith points out that Ismene here concedes Antigone's position of loyalty to family above all else ("Commentary," 138–39). I shift the emphasis to argue that Ismene is repeating with respect to Antigone, Antigone's attitude toward Polyneices.

41. Disregard for Ismene can be considered part of a larger blindness to relationships between women paradigmatically noted by Virginia Woolf, *A Room of One's Own* (San Diego: Harcourt, 1981), 82–85. With respect to antiquity, scholars have begun to redress this deficiency. See Nancy Sorkin Rabinowitz and Lisa Auanger, eds., *Among Women: From the Homosocial to the Homoerotic in the Ancient World* (Austin: University of Texas Press, 2002); and Goldhill, "Antigone" and *Sophocles*.

42. Irigaray, *Speculum*, 218. While many critics pass over Ismene in silence, Goethe considered her a "standard of the commonplace" against which Antigone's greatness would appear more striking ("Conversations," 177). In a similar move, Griselda Pollock has called Ismene "the unaffecting cipher to Antigone's tragic beauty" (Pollock, "Beyond Oedipus: Feminist Thought, Psychoanalysis, and Mythical Figuration of the Feminine," in *Laughing with Medusa: Classical Myth and Feminist Thought*, ed. Vanda Zajko and Miriam Leonard [Oxford: Oxford University Press, 2006], 100). Nussbaum alters the valence on Ismene's weeping by acknowledging it as an expression of "felt love" (*Fragility of Goodness*, 64).

43. Jonathan Strauss argues in a recent book that *Antigone* provided a crucial avenue to a notion of individuality made possible through personal and particular affection. His book gives Ismene barely a mention, locating the potential for such affection first in Antigone's attitude toward Polyneices and more cohesively in Haemon's attitude toward Antigone. Strauss's reading links affection through irreplaceable particularity to individuality, but as I argue here, neither particularity nor personhood requires a Hegelian version of the integral individual. Strauss's understanding of the individual revokes the radical potential of *Antigone* in favor of a Freudian oedipal version of selfhood. In his reading, Antigone is domesticated into a reproductive, heterosexual family by Haemon's affection. The transformation is crowned by Strauss's discussion of the funerary stele depicted on his cover, which shows a yearning infant, held by its father, reaching for its mournful mother, from whom death has parted it. He thus rewrites Antigone into the roles of wife and mother she refused. Jonathan Strauss, *Private Lives, Public Deaths: Antigone and the Invention of Individuality* (New York: Fordham University Press, 2013).
44. Françoise Meltzer, "Theories of Desire: Antigone Again," *Critical Inquiry* 37, no. 2 (2011): 169–86, quote on 186.
45. For more on sexual complementarity and wholeness in this context, see Londa Schiebinger, *The Mind Has No Sex? Women in the Origins of Modern Science* (Cambridge: Harvard University Press, 1989); and also my "The Allure of Wholeness: The Organism Around 1800 and the Same-Sex Marriage Debate," *Critical Inquiry* 39, no. 4 (2013): 754–76. We will also return to complementarity in the following two chapters.
46. Judith Butler, *Giving an Account of Oneself* (New York: Fordham University Press, 2005), 64.
47. Georg Wilhelm Friedrich Hegel, *Aesthetics: Lectures on Fine Art*, trans. T. M. Knox, 2 vols. (Oxford: Clarendon, 1974), 1214.
48. August Wilhelm Schlegel, "Life and Political Character of Sophocles—Character of His Different Tragedies," trans. John Black, in *Sophocles: The Classical Heritage*, ed. Roger David Dawe (New York: Garland, 1996), 163.
49. Friedrich Hölderlin, "Antigonae," in *Sämtliche Werke und Briefe*, ed. Jochen Schmidt (Frankfurt: Deutscher Klassiker Verlag, 1994), 2:905.
50. Translation mine. Hölderlin's translation of *Antigone* was greeted with derision when it was published but has since been acknowledged as an extraordinary interpretation of the original. For more, see Wolfgang Schadewaldt, "Antikes und Modernes in Schiller's *Braut von Messina*," *Jahrbuch der deutschen Schillergesellschaft* 13 (1989): 286–307; Schadewaldt, "Hölderlin's Translations," in *Sophocles: The Classical Heritage*, ed. Roger David Dawe, 101–10 (New York: Garland, 1996); and Kathrin Rosenfield, "Getting Inside Sophocles' Mind Through Hölderlin's Antigone," *New Literary History* 30, no. 1 (1999): 107–27.
51. Froma Zeitlin emphasizes the "double determination by which action is predicated on both internal and external agency" (Zeitlin, "Thebes: Theater of Self and Society in

Athenian Drama," in *Nothing to Do with Dionysus? Athenian Drama in Social Context*, ed. John Winkler and Froma Zeitlin [Princeton: Princeton University Press, 1990], 162n.44), and Rosenfield notes Antigone's "realization that her conscious desire . . . is inextricably linked to an even deeper, ancestral impulse" ("Getting Inside," 112). While Rosenfield's formulation gestures toward a joint fate, neither addresses the possibility of joint agency.

52. Bonnie Honig sensitively analyzes the horror of Ismene's situation, that of being asked to receive as a gift a life that no longer holds meaning (*Antigone Interrupted*, 177–81). Oddly, however, Honig does not accept Ismene's oft-repeated reason for no longer wanting to live, namely, that life without Antigone is utterly unthinkable. Instead, she invents as a reason the difficulty of living on in the household of her sister's killer, a psychological burden entirely unmentioned in the text (167, 180). However, Antigone is for Ismene a sufficiently motivating force for life and death, just as Polyneices is for Antigone.

53. For the two competing myths and Thebes as their combination, see Nicole Loraux, *Born of the Earth: Myth and Politics in Athens*, trans. Selina Stewart (Ithaca: Cornell University Press, 2000), 13–14.

54. Cadmus was instructed to follow a marked cow to the site where he should settle. Europa had been carried off by Zeus in the form of a bull, so that the cow symbolically gestures to a fulfillment of Cadmus's quest.

55. Miriam Leonard, "Lacan, Irigaray, and Beyond: Antigones and the Politics of Psychoanalysis," in *Laughing with Medusa: Classical Myth and Feminist Thought*, ed. Vanda Zajko and Miriam Leonard (Oxford: Oxford University Press, 2006), 122.

56. Hegel, by opposing a feminine familial to a masculine public sphere, famously renders woman the "everlasting irony [in the life] of the community" (*Phenomenology*, 288). Many objections to Hegel's interpretation have been raised, particularly the unsuitedness of Antigone to represent kinship given the muddled tangle of her incestuous relationships, and the inaptness of forcing Antigone into a model of femininity given the ambiguous and transgressive formulation of her gender in the play. As Butler argues, "There is no uncontaminated voice with which Antigone speaks" (*Antigone's Claim*, 88n.1). A similar list of difficulties exists for Hegel's positioning of Creon as representative of the civic sphere. See also Gourgouris, *Does Literature Think?*, 26; and Olga Taxidou, *Tragedy, Modernity and Mourning* (Edinburgh: Edinburgh University Press, 2004), 25–26.

57. Georg Wilhelm Friedrich Hegel, *Phänomenologie des Geistes*, vol. 9 of *Gesammelte Werke*, ed. Wolfgang Bonsiepen and Reinhard Heede, 240–63, Rheinisch-Westfälischen Akademie der Wissenschaften (Hamburg: Felix Meiner Verlag, 1980). In *Grundlinien der Philosophie des Rechts*, 237–62, Hegel briefly reprises his interpretation of *Antigone* and here uses the word *Staat*.

58. Steiner translates Hegel's term as "communal totality" (*Antigones*, 33). Stuart Elden provides a detailed commentary on the inadequacy both of Miller's use of *community* for Hegel's term and of Hegel's and Butler's focus on the *state* as a rendition of the *polis* (Elden, "The Place of the Polis: Political Blindness in Judith Butler's *Antigone's Claim*,"

Theory & Event 8, no. 1 [2005], *Project Muse* [Web]), July 22, 2010). My use of the word *community* here does not carry the sense of Hegel's abstracted *Gemeinwesen* but instead refers to a set of human beings living together.
59. Terry Pinkard, *Hegel: A Biography* (Cambridge: Cambridge University Press, 2000), 229–31.
60. For Hegel's relationship to the French Revolution and to contract theory, see Joachim Ritter's classic *Hegel und die französische Revolution* (Cologne: Westdeutscher Verlag, 1957); and Manfred Riedel, *Zwischen Tradition und Revolution. Studien zu Hegels Rechtsphilosophie* (Stuttgart: Klett-Cotta, 1982). Both are also available in English.
61. Hegel saw nationality as a subset of race, that is, embedded in the same natural, familial heritage. However, all such natural tendencies were capable of being superseded by spirit. Georg Wilhelm Friedrich Hegel, *Enzyklopädie der Philosophischen Wissenschaften im Grundrisse* (1830), ed. Wolfgang Bonsiepen and Hans-Christian Lucas, vol. 20 of *Gesammelte Werke* (Hamburg: Felix Meiner Verlag, 1992), § 392–95.
62. Martin Heidegger, *Hölderlin's Hymn "The Ister,"* trans. William McNeill and Julia Davis (Bloomington: Indiana University Press, 1991); and Heidegger, *Introduction to Metaphysics*, trans. Gregory Fried and Richard Polt (New Haven: Yale University Press, 2000).
63. On self-creation, see Cornelius Castoriadis, "Aeschylean Anthropology and Sophoclean Self-Creation of Anthropos," in *Agon, Logos, Polis: The Greek Achievement and Its Aftermath*, ed. Johann P. Arnason and Peter Murphy (Stuttgart: Franz Steiner, 2001), esp. 150–51.
64. For more on circularity and repetition in Thebes, see Zeitlin, "Thebes," 153–56.

2. THE SHADOWS OF FRATERNITY

1. European Union website, http://europa. eu/abc/symbols/anthem/index_en.htm (emphasis in original). While the website states that Beethoven has set to music "Friedrich von Schiller's lyrical verse from 1785," the iconic line "All humans shall become brothers" was part of Schiller's 1805 revision. Translations of the ode are mine. Friedrich Schiller, "An die Freude," in *Gedichte*, ed. Georg Kurscheidt, vol. 1 of *Werke und Briefe* (Frankfurt: Deutscher Klassiker Verlag, 1992), 248.
2. Schiller, "An die Freude," 1:251.
3. The idea that *woman* or the feminine is constitutive for a privileged space from which it is excluded is not unique to my argument. Julia Kristeva's diagnosis of the abjection of the maternal in the erection of the masculine subject works according to this same principle (Kristeva, *Powers of Horror: An Essay on Abjection*, trans. Leon Roudiez [New York: Columbia University Press, 1982]). In the political realm, Carole Pateman and Zillah Eisenstein have demonstrated the way that the division of labor inherent in the separation of public and private spheres enables the dominant masculine public space (Pateman, *The Disorder of Women: Democracy, Feminism, and Political Theory* [Stanford: Stanford University Press, 1989]; Pateman, *The Sexual Contract* [Stanford:

Stanford University Press, 1988]; Eisenstein, *The Radical Future of Liberal Feminism* [New York: Longman, 1981]). Joan Landes followed a similar argument in her exploration of the threat perceived in women's using, rather than serving as the objects of, symbolic political language (Landes, *Women and the Public Sphere in the Age of the French Revolution* [Ithaca: Cornell University Press, 1988]). In light of this structural problem, much feminist political theory has shifted away from consensual contractarianism to an ethics of care modeled on mothering, an arrangement that takes into account the complicated intertwining of will and emotional bonding. Some of the most influential thinkers in this large field include Carol Gilligan, *In a Different Voice: Psychological Theory and Women's Development* (Cambridge: Harvard University Press, 1982); Nel Noddings, *Caring: A Feminine Approach to Ethics and Moral Education* (Berkeley: University of California Press, 1984); Joan Tronto, *Moral Boundaries: A Political Argument for an Ethics of Care* (New York: Routledge, 1993); Virginia Held, *The Ethics of Care: Personal, Political, and Global* (Oxford: Oxford University Press, 2006); and Michael Slote, *The Ethics of Care and Empathy* (London: Routledge, 2007). As Sibyl Schwarzenbach points out, however, care as a model for feminist societal relations suffers from a troubling lack of reciprocity and equality (Schwarzenbach, *On Civic Friendship: Including Women in the State* [New York: Columbia University Press, 2009], xiii, 210–30). This chapter demonstrates that the concern with emotional investment in relationship to political choice was already present in the eighteenth century but was imagined in fraternal and sororal as well as maternal configurations.

4. For a fascinating reconstruction of the history of the terms of the motto, including the competing interpretations of each and the tensions between them, see Mona Ozouf, "Liberty, Equality, Fraternity," in *Realms of Memory: The Construction of the French Past*, ed. Pierre Nora and Lawrence Kritzman, trans. Arthur Goldhammer, 3:77–116 (New York: Columbia University Press, 1992). Anthony Black has pointed out that fraternity is most frequently evoked as a collectivist alternative to civic society, "a tightly-knit, warm, charismatic community, *Gemeinschaft* or fraternity" (Black, *Guild & State: European Political Thought from the Twelfth Century to the Present* [New Brunswick, N.J.: Transaction, 2003], 43). Black overlooks the gender issues involved in this communal image.

5. Annette Timm and Joshua Sanborn, *Gender, Sex and the Shaping of Modern Europe: A History from the French Revolution to the Present Day* (Oxford: Berg, 2007), 40.

6. Pateman, *Disorder* and *The Sexual Contract*. See also Juliet Flower MacCannell, *The Regime of the Brother: After the Patriarchy* (Routledge: London, 1991); Lynn Hunt, *The Family Romance of the French Revolution* (Berkeley: University of California Press, 1992); and Jacques Derrida, *Politics of Friendship*, trans. George Collins (London: Verso, 1997).

7. Marc Shell's fascinating reflections on incest and kinship remain limited by a conflation of universal brotherhood with universal siblinghood, and by his ahistorical approach. Marc Shell, *Children of the Earth: Literature, Politics, and Nationhood* (New York: Oxford University Press, 1993); and Shell, *The End of Kinship: Measure for Mea-*

sure, Incest, and the Idea of Universal Siblinghood (Stanford: Stanford University Press, 1988).

8. Marquis de Sade, *Philosophy in the Bedroom*, in *Justine, Philosophy in the Bedroom, and Other Writings*, ed. and trans. Richard Seaver and Austryn Wainhouse (New York: Grove, 1965), 324.
9. Sir Robert Filmer, *Patriarcha and Other Writings*, ed. Johann Sommerville (Cambridge: Cambridge University Press, 1991), 11. See also Silke-Maria Weineck's powerful study of the haunting of politics by the figure of the father. *The Tragedy of Fatherhood: King Laius and the Politics of Paternity in the West* (New York: Bloomsbury, 2014).
10. Although referring to the creation of Eve out of Adam's rib, Filmer, in *The Anarchy of a Limited or Mixed Monarchy*, calls Adam "the father of all flesh." Filmer, *Patriarcha*, 139.
11. John Locke, *Two Treatises of Government*, ed. Peter Laslett (Cambridge: Cambridge University Press, 1988), 143.
12. Carole Pateman discusses Filmer and Locke in readings in *Disorder* (esp. 35–40) and *The Sexual Contract* (esp. 21–25), to which my own argument is indebted. While Pateman stresses Locke's division of a natural conjugal from a consensual political sphere and thus interprets his inclusion of consent in the domestic relationship as a sign of hypocrisy, I read Locke's two spheres as structurally analogous throughout: consent superimposed on a natural law foundation. I agree with Pateman, however, that the division itself is a specious political move that attempts to erase its own traces.
13. Sophocles, *Antigone*, in *Sophocles I*, trans. and intro. David Grene (Chicago: University of Chicago Press, 1991), line 569.
14. See esp. Pateman, *Disorder*, 39–40 and 213–14; and *The Sexual Contract*, 52–55.
15. Jean-Jacques Rousseau, "On the Social Contract," in *The Basic Political Writings*, trans. Donald Cress (Indianapolis: Hackett, 1987), 144.
16. Jean-Jacques Rousseau, *Emile or On Education*, trans. Allan Bloom (New York: Basic Books, 1979), 424.
17. Although Rousseau frequently described the differences between the sexes as natural, his work can be read convincingly as an attempt to shore up dangerously permeable gender roles. Linda Zerilli, Sarah Kofman, and Elizabeth Wingrove in particular have explored the ways "Rousseau clearly reveals, even if he then re-veils, the social and political expediency that drives his account of femininity and masculinity." Elizabeth Wingrove, "Republican Romance," in *Feminist Interpretations of Jean-Jacques Rousseau*, ed. Lynda Lange (University Park: Pennsylvania State University Press, 2002), 319. See also Linda Zerilli, *Signifying Women: Culture and Chaos in Rousseau, Burke, and Mill* (Ithaca: Cornell University Press, 1994); and Sarah Kofman, "Rousseau's Phallocratic Ends," trans. Mara Dukats, in *Feminist Interpretations of Jean-Jacques Rousseau*, ed. Lynda Lange, 229–44 (University Park: Pennsylvania State University Press, 2002).
18. Idiosyncratically, Rousseau locates the victim of rape neither in the assaulted woman nor in the interested parties of husband or father but rather in the rapist himself, who, because of a lack of control over the woman's other sexual partners, will be unable to establish paternity. This reinterpretation, by rendering rape counterproductive to its perpetrator, reinforces Rousseau's argument that it does not exist.

19. Linda Zerilli focuses instead on the equally troubling converse of this claim, that the absence of women from the "Social Contract" indicates their inability to assume "legitimate chains," that is, those of willing submission to the terms of the communal contract (*Signifying Women*, 50–55).
20. Jean-Jacques Rousseau, *Politics and the Arts: Letter to M. D'Alembert on the Theatre*, trans. Allan Bloom (Ithaca: Cornell University Press, 1960), 85.
21. Georg Wilhelm Friedrich Hegel, *Phenomenology of Spirit*, trans. A. V. Miller (Oxford: Oxford University Press, 1977), 270.
22. Max Horkheimer and Theodor Adorno first called attention to Sade as a critic of the Enlightenment, focusing on the analogous architecture of Sade's and Kant's moral reasoning. They also note that Sade exposes the competition between civil society and familial love under discussion here. Horkheimer and Adorno, *Dialectic of Enlightenment*, trans. John Cumming (New York: Continuum, 1994), 137–39.
23. Even the language of the political treatise clearly specifies a male readership. Jane Gallop notes, for example, the gesture toward equality of the sexes in the choice of a male and a female teacher for the ingénue in the novel, which is then betrayed by a fundamental inequality of access and privilege. Gallop, "The Liberated Woman," *Narrative* 13, no. 2 (May 2005): 89–104.
24. Gilles Deleuze, *Masochism: An Interpretation of Coldness and Cruelty*, trans. Jean McNeil (New York: Braziller, 1971), 67. Sade, as Deleuze points out (esp. 69, 75–76), sees contracts and the laws they create and authorize as mystifications of power that uphold and obscure a complicity of masters and slaves.
25. Sade serves as evidence that one need not elevate the maternal above the Law of the Father to endorse incest. Sade attacks not just the mother as normative educator but, as Angela Carter notes, "the mothering function" (Carter, *The Sadeian Woman and the Ideology of Pornography* [New York: Pantheon, 1978], 36). As Carter points out, Sade goes so far as to endorse spermaticism, which held that the father alone is responsible for the child's form, which the mother merely nurtures (Sade, *Philosophy in the Bedroom*, 206; Carter, *Sadeian Woman*, 120). Carter is mistaken in assuming that this was a common view in 1795, however. By the late eighteenth century, the epigenetic view of a merging of maternal and paternal traits in the formation of a child was gaining ground. Even in the heyday of preformationism, however, most people assigned responsibility for the fetus to the mother, not the father. See Clara Pinto-Correia, *The Ovary of Eve: Egg and Sperm and Preformationism* (Chicago: University of Chicago Press, 1997), 85–104. Sade therefore goes out of his way to ally himself with Aeschylus in denying motherhood as kinship altogether. On Sade's hatred of mothers, see also Deleuze, *Masochism*, esp. 52 and 107; and Gallop, "Liberated Woman," esp. 96.
26. Sade, *Philosophy in the Bedroom*, 321–22. While Rousseau assigns a different affect to the maternal, one could say that Sade merely pushes to its logical conclusions Rousseau's almost identical argument for a public education to replace "the prejudices of . . . fathers" with allegiance to a mother-state: "If children are raised in common and in the bosom of equality, if they are imbued with the laws of the state and the maxims of the general will, if they are instructed to respect them above all things, if they are sur-

rounded by examples and objects that constantly speak to them of the tender mother who nourishes them, of the love she bears for them, of the inestimable benefits they receive from her, and in turn of the debt they owe her, doubtlessly they thus will learn to cherish one another as brothers, never to want anything but what the society wants." Jean-Jacques Rousseau, "Discourse on Political Economy," in *The Basic Political Writings*, trans. Donald Cress (Indianapolis: Hackett, 1987), 125–26.

27. Jacques Rancière, *The Politics of Aesthetics: The Distribution of the Sensible*, trans. Gabriel Rockhill (London: Continuum International, 2012).

28. Marc Redfield, *The Politics of Aesthetics: Nationalism, Gender, Romanticism* (Stanford: Stanford University Press, 2003), 59.

29. In fact, outside of a very specific philosophical tradition, beauty remained firmly ensconced in the discourse of female sexual attractiveness. See, for example, race theory and evolutionary theory, which will be discussed in chapter 5.

30. Jonathan Hess has illustrated "aesthetic autonomy and the public sphere as functionally interdependent" in late-Enlightenment German discourse, as both reinvent themselves as organic in reciprocally reinforcing ways in an attempt to mask their mechanistic underpinnings (Hess, *Reconstituting the Body Politic: Enlightenment, Public Culture and the Invention of Aesthetic Autonomy* [Detroit: Wayne State University Press, 1999], esp. 137–48, 215–22, 243–46; quote on 26). See also Redfield, *Politics of Aesthetics*, 9–22, for the paradox of the aesthetic as "a discourse of framing that violates its own frame" (quote on 10).

31. Friedrich Schiller, "Concerning the Sublime," trans. Daniel O. Dahlstrom, in *Essays*, ed. Walter Hinderer and Daniel O. Dahlstrom (New York: Continuum, 1993), 71.

32. Peter Uwe Hohendahl, "German Classicism and the Law of the Father," in *Literary Paternity, Literary Friendship: Essays in Honor of Stanley Corngold*, ed. Gerhard Richter (Chapel Hill: University of North Carolina Press, 2002), 82–83; and Gerhard Kaiser, *Väter und Brüder: Weltordnung und gesellschaftlich-politische Ordnung in Schillers Werk* (Leipzig: Verlag der Sächsischen Akademie der Wissenschaften zu Leipzig, 2007), 12. Juliet Mitchell has posited a psychoanalytic sibling complex based on rivalry and the fear of displacement. Such a fear would still depend on viewing identity through a stable positionality. I believe siblings hold the potential for a more nuanced confrontation with versions of joint or partial identity, however. See Mitchell, *Siblings: Sex and Violence* (Cambridge: Polity Press, 2003). I addressed the deficit of sibling forms in psychoanalysis in more detail in chapter 1.

33. Friedrich Schiller, *Schillers Werke. Nationalausgabe* [hereafter *NA*], 43 vols., ed. Norbert Oellers and Siegfried Seidel (Weimar: Hermann Böhlaus Nachfolger), 29:141. See Florian Prater, *Schiller und Sophokles* (Zurich: Atlantis, 1954); and Günter Oesterle, "Friedrich Schiller: *Die Braut von Messina*. Radikale Formrückgriff angesichts eines modernen kulturellen Synkretismus oder fatale Folgen kleiner Geheimnisse," in *Schiller und die Antike*, ed. Paolo Chiarini and Walter Hinderer, 167–75 (Würzburg: Königshausen & Neumann, 2008). In looking as well to Euripides's *Phoenician Women*, I follow Wolfgang Schadewaldt, "Antikes und Modernes in Schillers *Braut von Messina*," *Jahrbuch der deutschen Schillergesellschaft* 13 (1989): 286–307.

258   2. THE SHADOWS OF FRATERNITY

34. Schiller's engagement with these plays around the time of his writing can be documented. All these tragedies follow the fate of the children of Oedipus and Jocasta: the fratricidal brothers Polyneices and Eteocles and their sisters Ismene and Antigone, the latter of whom is executed for her proscribed attempt to bury her intensely beloved brother Polyneices. It is clear that Schiller is familiar with Sophocles's *Antigone* from his mention of it in a letter to Goethe on April 4, 1797 (NA 29:56). He translated two acts of Euripides's *Phoenician Women* (Schadewaldt, "Antikes," 290) and mentioned Euripides's *Seven Against Thebes* in relation to his composition of *Die Braut von Messina* in a letter to Humboldt (NA 32:11).

35. Friedrich Schiller, *Die Braut von Messina*, in *Dramen IV*, ed. Matthias Luserke, vol. 5 of *Werke und Briefe* (Frankfurt am Main: Deutscher Klassiker Verlag, 1992). All translations from the play are mine. Citations are given in line numbers. Schiller composed *The Bride of Messina* in the year between *The Virgin of Orleans* and *William Tell*, both dramas concerned with political upheaval and the tensions between an indigenous population and irresponsible foreign rulers, and *Tell* in particular also concerned with fraternity. See Albrecht Koschorke et al., *Vor der Familie. Grenzbedingungen einer modernen Institution* (Munich: Konstanz University Press, 2010). During the period of composition, Schiller also worked on adaptations of Gotthold Ephraim Lessing's *Nathan the Wise* for the Weimar Theater, a play that also features unwitting incestuous attraction between siblings and hidden family identities. See Johannes Endres, "Nathan Disenchanted: Continuity and Discontinuity of Enlightenment in Schiller's *The Bride of Messina*," in *Historical Reflections/Reflexions Historiques* 26, no. 3 (2000): 410; and Francis Lamport, "Virgins, Bastards and Saviors of the Nation: Reflections on Schiller's Historical Dramas," in *Schiller: National Poet—Poet of Nations*, ed. Nicholas Martin (Amsterdam: Rodopi, 2006), 172. We will return to Lessing in chapter 5.

36. Thomas Paine, *Common Sense, The Rights of Man, and Oher Essential Writings* (New York: New American Library, 1969), 163.

37. Jocasta also attempts to reconcile the warring sons she bears Oedipus in *The Phoenician Women*. The two speeches diverge in significant ways, however. While Isabella upholds a structural hierarchy and tries unsuccessfully to place both sons simultaneously at its peak, Jocasta offers a paean to equality, which "ties friends to friends, cities to cities, allies to allies" (Sophocles, *Antigone*, lines 536–37). It is not unusual to see covert justifications of democracy in the tragedies, which are written about monarchies by and for Athenians proud of their democratic form of government.

38. Frank Fowler notes that "something about the girl's stance and stature subconsciously reminds [Cesar] of his mother" ("Matters of Motivation: In Defence of Schiller's *Die Braut von Messina*," *German Life and Letters* 39, no. 2 [1986]: 135), but not much attention has been paid to the question of family resemblance in the play. Don Cesar describes his first glimpse of Beatrice by comparing her to his mother (Schiller, NA, line 1485), while Don Manuel recognizes a resemblance between Beatrice and his brother Cesar (line 504). Manuel also associates his first encounter with her as "like a dream image . . . from the half-lit days of early childhood" (lines 711–12) and describes falling in love with her as "kin converging with kin [sich Verwandtes zum Verwandten fin-

det]" (line 71). Horst Daemmrich notes some of these lines but reads them only as a suggestion of possible early childhood memories that the siblings have of each other. Daemmrich, "The Incest Motif in Lessing's *Nathan der Weise* and Schiller's *Braut von Messina*," *Germanic Review* 42, no. 3 (1967): 192.

39. The legitimate complaints of the Sicilians combined with their evident inability to self-govern reflect Schiller's much-discussed ambivalence about republicanism and the mob.
40. Schiller, "Concerning the Sublime," 71. Schechter's simpler rendition in his translation of *Nathan* reads, "No one has to have to." Gotthold Ephraim Lessing, *Nathan the Wise*, trans. and ed. Ronald Schechter (Boston: Bedford, 2004), 33.
41. From Jean-Jacques Rousseau, *Julie, or The New Heloise*, trans. Philip Stewart and Jean Vaché, in vol. 6 of *The Collected Writings of Rousseau*, ed. Roger D. Masters and Christopher Kelly (Hanover, N.H.: University Press of New England, 1997), 262. Reproduced by Friedrich Schiller, *On the Aesthetic Education of Man in a Series of Letters*, ed. and trans. Elizabeth Wilkinson and L. A. Willoughby (Oxford: Clarendon Press, 1982).
42. In that same year, two other relevant commentaries on the revolution appeared: Sade's *Philosophy in the Bedroom*, discussed earlier, and Johann Wolfgang von Goethe's *Wilhelm Meister's Apprenticeship*, to which we will turn in the next chapter.
43. Plato, *The Symposium*, trans. Alexander Nehamas and Paul Woodruff, in *Complete Works*, ed. John M. Cooper, 457–505 (Indianapolis: Hackett). See Richard Foley for more on the conflict between universality and particularity as the appropriate basis for love in the *Symposium*. Foley, "The Order Question: Climbing the Ladder of Love in Plato's Symposium," *Ancient Philosophy* 30 (2010): 57–72.
44. See Foley, "Order Question," 70–72.
45. We will return shortly to the question of the role played by sex in inspiring love or in marking difference.
46. For a discussion of civic affect in *Laon and Cythna* and the Jacobin novelists, see Anahid Nersessian, "Radical Love and Political Romance: Shelley After the Jacobin Novel," *Journal of English Literary History* (hereafter *ELH*) 79, no. 1 (2012): 111–34. Nersessian, however, reads Shelley's poem as more inclusive of diversity than I will below.
47. Richard Sha similarly notes the correlation between sibling incest and "aesthetic disinterest or selflessness" and identifies "Shelley's problem" as "how to make the immediacy of sexual passion disinterested without emptying it of passion" (Sha, *Perverse Romanticism: Aesthetic and Sexuality in Britain, 1750–1832* [Baltimore: Johns Hopkins University Press, 2009], 7). For Shelley's importation of passion into state formation, see also Cian Duffy, *Shelley and the Revolutionary Sublime* (Cambridge: Cambridge University Press, 2005), 134; and Nersessian, "Radical Love."
48. Percy Bysshe Shelley, *Laon and Cythna*, in *The Poems of Shelley*, ed. Kelvin Everest and Geoffrey Matthew (New York: Longman, 2000), 2:47.
49. Percy Bysshe Shelley, *Shelley's Poetry and Prose*, ed. Donald Reiman and Sharon Powers (New York: Norton, 1977), 2:222.
50. Denis Flannery, *On Sibling Love, Queer Attachment and American Writing* (Hampshire, UK: Ashgate, 2007), 18. I prefer throughout this study to think of the relationship

in terms of a mutual synecdoche, in which shared parts refer siblings to each other while leaving them open to further sharings with other partial others. For the use of the term for queer relationships in the eighteenth century, see also Robert Tobin, *Warm Brothers: Queer Theory and the Age of Goethe* (Philadelphia: University of Pennsylvania Press, 2000).

51. Percy Shelley was already married when he and sixteen-year-old Mary Godwin fell in love. They remained abroad for two years, until the suicide of Percy's first wife allowed them to marry.

52. Percy Bysshe Shelley, *The Letters of Percy Bysshe Shelley*, ed. Frederick L. Jones, 2 vols. (Oxford: Clarendon, 1964), 1:361.

53. See in particular P. M. S. Dawson, *The Unacknowledged Legislator: Shelley and Politics* (Oxford: Clarendon Press, 1980); Duffy, *Shelley and the Revolutionary Sublime*, 123–48; and Hugh Roberts, *Shelley and the Chaos of History: A New Politics of Poetry* (University Park: Pennsylvania State University Press, 1997), 160–98.

54. Laon and Cythna grow up in the region of Argolis (Shelley, *Poems*, 2:676) in the Aegean Sea, placing *The Revolt of Islam* at the borderlands of Europe and at the meeting point of Christianity and Islam. The setting bears comparison to that of Bryon's sibling-incest poem, *The Bride of Abydos*, which is situated at the narrowest point of the Dardanelles that separate Europe from Asia, as well as Coleridge's sibling-incest play *Osorio*, located in Grenada during the Inquisition. I will return to the connection between sibling incest and the relationship of Christianity to Islam in chapter 5.

55. In his preface to the poem, Shelley refers to religion generally as a fraud that serves to "delude . . . into submission" (*Poems*, 2:33). I do not mean to deny the anti-Islamic bent of the poem or the title but to contextualize it within Shelley's contempt for all organized religions. The new title was chosen after the recall of the first edition for its atheistic tendencies, as well as for the sibling incest it depicted. Islam thus serves as a cover for the more general critique of religion.

56. While Thomas Frosch notes that "Laon's first recollections are of maternal sweetness and nourishment" (Frosch, *Shelley and the Romantic Imagination: A Psychological Study* [Newark: University of Delaware Press, 2007], 118), Jerrold Hogle sees in these same lines evidence that Laon is "so dissociated from his mother . . . that he recalls frantically searching for a responsive 'nurse'" in the larger world (Hogle, *Shelley's Process: Radical Transference and the Development of His Major Works* [New York: Oxford University Press, 1988], 97). I would argue that both critics misunderstand the tenor and purpose of these lines.

57. These lines recall those of Goethe's Wilhelm Meister to his alleged son, Felix, which we will return to in the next chapter. Wilhelm too converts child into sibling.

58. The fact that the affect Laon and Cythna promulgate in the wider social world originates in a sibling bond rooted in biology complicates the disaffiliating move and demonstrates the paradox of a universal siblinghood.

59. In the original version of the poem, Laon and Cythna are biological siblings. After outrage at the first print run, Shelley's publisher, Charles Ollier, recalled the edition and insisted Shelley change the nature of the relationship, transforming Cythna into an

orphan raised with Laon. Shelley resisted, but changes were eventually made during a weekend collaboration among a reluctant Shelley, his friend the author Thomas Love Peacock, and Ollier himself. The critique of religion as a tyrannical illusion was also toned down, and the poem was republished under the title *The Revolt of Islam*. The changes were so hasty that now-nonsensical remnants like the physical resemblance of Laon and Cythna remained. See John Donovan's introduction to Laon and Cythna in the Everest/Matthews edition of Shelley's *Poems* (Shelley, *Laon and Cythna*, 10–29), and also his "Incest in Laon and Cythna: Nature, Custom, Desire," *Keats-Shelley Review* 2 (1987): 42–90.

60. Roberts addresses the paradox that "the revolutionaries [are] sharing in the forms of power they hope to overthrow" (*Shelley and the Chaos of History*, 175) by suggesting that Shelley differentiates the imposition of lies from the imposition of truths, justifying the latter (175–77). I would argue that there is a larger critique here—Laon's early engagement with injustice is incomplete, affecting only his reason; sympathy meanwhile is something he hopes to inspire in others to his own benefit, not something he feels for others, until after he is transformed by Cythna's love.

61. The designation of religion as "foul worship" is clearly anti-Islamic, but all the explicit religious critique in the poem is nondenominational, as applicable to Christianity as to Islam.

62. See, for example, Friedrich Schlegel, *Lucinde and the Fragments*, ed. and trans. Peter Firchow (Minneapolis: University of Minnesota Press, 1971), 48; and Karoline von Günderrode, "Die Malabarischen Witwen," in *Gesammelte Werke* (Berlin: Goldschmidt-Gabrielli, 1920), 2:12–13.

63. Cannibalism arises at two other points in the poem, when at moments of deepest madness, Laon and Cythna each imagine feeding off the corpse of the other. Roberts, without referring to the return to cannibalism at the end of the poem, remarks on the threat inherent in the earlier instances, of collapse into a solipsistic economy of death (*Shelley and the Chaos of History*, 185).

64. Sigmund Freud, "Group Psychology and the Analysis of the Ego," in vol. 18 of *Standard Edition of the Complete Psychological Works of Sigmund Freud*, ed. and trans. James Strachey (London: Hogarth, 1955), 105–7.

65. Moses Mendelssohn, *Jerusalem, or, on Religious Power and Judaism*, trans. Allan Arkush (Hanover, N.H.: Brandeis University Press, 1983), 134.

66. We will return to the Jewish proscription on intermarriage in definitions of nationhood in chapter 5. For an excellent reading of brotherly vs. conjugal love in Mendelssohn, see Katja Garloff, *Mixed Feelings: Tropes of Love in German Jewish Culture* (Ithaca: Cornell University Press, 2016).

3. ECONOMIZING DESIRE

1. Friedrich Schiller, *On the Aesthetic Education of Man in a Series of Letters*, ed. and trans. Elizabeth Wilkinson and L. A. Willoughby (Oxford: Clarendon, 1982).

2. Adam Smith, *An Inquiry into the Nature and Causes of the Wealth of Nations*, ed. R. H. Campbell and A. S. Skinner, vol. 2 of *Glasgow Edition of the Works and Correspondence of Adam Smith* (Oxford: Clarendon, 1976), quote on 22. Smith does return to the negative effects of such division on individuals later in the *Wealth of Nations*, arguing in nearly Schillerian terms both that societies called barbarous generally allow and demand a greater range of fields of knowledge and activity from their members than does "a civilized and commercial society" (784), and that some remedy is therefore necessary for the mental and physical incapacity that results from a life spent merely repeating without innovation "a few very simple operations" (781). Smith suggests state-subsidized education as such a remedy, without detailing how such an education would combat the deleterious effects of overspecialization (784–86).

3. Adam Smith, *The Theory of Moral Sentiments*, ed. R. H. Campbell and A. S. Skinner, vol. 1 of *Glasgow Edition of the Works and Correspondence of Adam Smith* (Oxford: Clarendon, 1976), 220, emphasis added.

4. David Marshall has written on the "instability of self" (177) embedded in Smith's theory of sympathy, in *The Figure of the Theater: Shaftesbury, Defoe, Adam Smith, and George Eliot* (New York: Columbia University Press, 1986), esp. 177–81.

5. There are limits to this network, set at the boundary of the "civilized" world. Cultures that have not yet begun to organize labor through division are isolated from other cultures, and internally individuals within such a culture are isolated from each other, since each bears much greater responsibility for outfitting him or herself with all of life's necessities. The boundaries of the human fabric of commerce and industry are however potentially extendable throughout the globe by spreading the production method of division of labor in a process that Smith, in the very first sentence of book 1, referred to as "improvement" (*Wealth*, 1.13).

6. Mary Poovey, "Aesthetics and Political Economy in the Eighteenth Century: The Place of Gender in the Social Constitution of Knowledge," in *Aesthetics and Ideology*, ed. George Levine (New Brunswick, N.J.: Rutgers University Press, 1994), 86.

7. Claude Lévi-Strauss, *The Elementary Structures of Kinship*, ed. Rodney Needham, trans. James Harle Bell, John Richard von Sturmer, and Rodney Needham (Boston: Beacon, 1969), 479–80. Lévi-Strauss's comment provides a critique of the nineteenth-century practices we will investigate in this chapter.

8. In *The Regime of the Brother*, Juliet Flower MacCannell emphasizes the gendered power relations that continued to structure the postmonarchical world. Without disputing that fact, I would argue that the concepts of the sister and of siblings as groups, as well as of the brother, together played a constitutive role in developing economic and political structures, epistemological systems, and the modern subject. See MacCannell, *The Regime of the Brother: After the Patriarchy* (Routledge: London, 1991).

9. Engels follows the trajectory of Morgan's universal history but not his evaluation of its stages. Whereas Morgan sees the establishment of property and a settled agricultural life as the welcome breakthrough from barbarism to civilization, Engels and Marx see the concept of ownership and the related domination inherent in the family system as a decisive ethical decline. See Frederick Engels, *The Origin of the Family, Private Prop-*

erty, and the State. In the Light of the Researches by Lewis H. Morgan, vol. 26 of Karl Marx and Frederick Engels, *Collected Works*, 129–276 (New York: International, 1990). For an excellent analysis of Morgan's attitude toward private property, see Thomas Trautmann, *Lewis Henry Morgan and the Invention of Kinship* (Berkeley: University of California Press, 1987).

10. Lewis Henry Morgan, *Ancient Society, or, Researches in the Lines of Human Progress from Savagery through Barbarism to Civilization* (Chicago: Charles H. Kerr, 1877), 454.
11. For a good overview of the afterlife of Engels's theory and feminist Marxian approaches, see Alys Eve Weinbaum, *Wayward Reproductions: Genealogies of Race and Nation in Transatlantic Modern Thought* (Durham: Duke University Press, 2004), 106–44.
12. Edward Aveling and Eleanor Marx, "Shelley and Socialism," *Marx To-day: Monthly Magazine of Scientific Socialism* 53 (April 1888): 108, 109.
13. See Stephanie Coontz, *Marriage, a History: From Obedience to Intimacy or How Love Conquered Marriage* (New York: Viking, 2005); and Stefani Engelstein, "The Allure of Wholeness: The Organism Around 1800 and the Same-Sex Marriage Debate," *Critical Inquiry* 39, no. 4 (2013): 754–76.
14. Sharon Marcus, *Between Women: Friendship, Desire, and Marriage in Victorian England* (Princeton: Princeton University Press, 2007), 4–5.
15. Michael Hardt and Antonio Negri, *Empire* (Cambridge: Harvard University Press, 2000), 364–67; and Michael Hardt and Antonio Negri, *Multitude: War and Democracy in the Age of Empire* (New York: Penguin, 2004), 108–15, 146–48.
16. Michel Foucault, *The History of Sexuality: An Introduction*, trans. Robert Hurley (New York: Vintage, 1978), 138–45, 108–10; Foucault, *The Birth of Biopolitics: Lectures at the Collège de France, 1978–1979* (New York: Palgrave Macmillan, 2008).
17. Karl Marx, *Capital: A Critique of Political Economy*, trans. Ben Fowkes (New York: Vintage, 1977), 1:183. All citations from Marx are from this edition and translation unless otherwise noted.
18. Early twentieth-century theorists of the *Bildungsroman* saw in the genre a story of intense individuation. See Wilhelm Dilthey, *Poetry and Experience*, in *Selected Works*, ed. Rudolf Makkreel and Frithjof Rodi (Princeton: Princeton University Press, 1985), esp. 5:335; Thomas Mann, "Der Entwicklungsroman," in *Aufsätze. Reden. Essays*, ed. Henry Matter (Berlin: Aufbau-Verlag, 1983), 2:116–17. In the 1970s and 1980s critics were attracted to theories of socialization. See Jerome Buckley, *Season of Youth: The Bildungsroman from Dickens to Golding* (Cambridge: Harvard University Press, 1974); Franco Moretti, *The Way of the World: The Bildungsroman in European Culture* (London: Verso, 1987); and Friedrich Kittler, "Über die Sozialisation Wilhelm Meisters," in *Dichtung als Sozialisationsspiel*, ed. Gerhard Kaiser and Friedrich Kittler (Göttingen: Vanderhoeck & Ruprecht, 1979). More recent criticism has contested the very existence of the genre, a genre without exemplars or a phantom genre (Jeffrey Sammons, "Heuristic Definition and the Constraints of Literary History," in *Dazwischen*, ed. Andreas Härter, Edith Anna Kunz, and Heiner Weidmann [Göttingen: Vandenhoeck & Ruprecht, 2003]; and Sammons, "The Mystery of the Missing

Bildungsroman, or: What Happened to Wilhelm Meister's Legacy?" *Genre* 14, no. 1 [1981]: 229–46). The term *phantom* was first used by Sammons ("Mystery", 239) and was developed by Marc Redfield in *Phantom Formations: Aesthetic Ideology and the Bildungsroman* (Ithaca: Cornell University Press, 1996). Beginning in the 1980s, a line of criticism also developed criticizing the exclusion of stories of female development, which often follow very different patterns. For further reflection on the term in this vein, see Elizabeth Abel, Marianne Hirsch, and Elizabeth Langland, "Introduction," in *The Voyage In: Fictions of Female Development*, 1–19 (Hanover, N.H.: University Press of New England, 1983); Marianne Hirsch, "Spiritual *Bildung*: The Beautiful Soul as Paradigm," in *The Voyage In*; Susan Fraiman, "*The Mill on the Floss*, the Critics, and the Bildungsroman," *PMLA* 108, no. 1 (January 1993): 136–50; Carol Lazzaro-Weiss, "The Female 'Bildungsroman': Calling It Into Question," in *NWSA* 2, no. 1 (1990): 16–34; Joshua Esty "Nationhood, Adulthood, and the Ruptures of *Bildung*: Arresting Development in *The Mill on the Floss*," in *The Mill on the Floss and Silas Marner: George Eliot*, ed. Nahem Yousaf and Andrew Maunder (Basingstoke: Palgrave, 2002); and Sammons, "Heuristic Definition." For the connection between the theory of the *Bildungsroman* and perceptions of history, see also Tobias Boes, *Formative Fictions: Nationalism, Cosmopolitanism, and the Bildungsroman* (Ithaca: Cornell University Press, 2012).

19. Friedrich Schlegel, Athenaeum Fragment 216, in *Lucinde and the Fragments*, ed. and trans. Peter Firchow (Minneapolis: University of Minnesota Press, 1971), 191.
20. Georg Lukács, *Goethe and His Age*, trans. Robert Anchor (London: Merlin, 1968), 61.
21. Kittler, "Über die Sozialisation Wilhelm Meisters," 124; my translation.
22. Lawrence Stone, *The Family, Sex and Marriage in England 1500–1800* (New York: Harper and Row, 1977).
23. Johann Wolfgang von Goethe, *Wilhelm Meister's Apprenticeship*, ed. and trans. Eric A. Blackall, vol. 9 of *The Collected Works* (Princeton: Princeton University Press, 1989), 6, 7, 9, 10. Michael Minden notes that the protagonists of *Bildungsromane* tend to be only-children and are always oldest sons (Michael Minden, *The German* Bildungsroman*: Incest and Inheritance* [Cambridge: Cambridge University Press, 1997], 3). Wilhelm is the oldest son. Such identificatory genre characteristics can be circular, however. Beginning in the 1980s, calls to view works about women's development alongside those about men's have broadened significantly the range of family types recognized as appearing in novels of development. See note 4, this chapter. Siblings, older and younger, often play a large role in these works. We will return below to the question of why Wilhelm Meister's siblings fade from the action of the novel.
24. While Kittler analyzes the condensing of Wilhelm's family in the transition from the draft version of the novel, *Wilhelm Meister's Theatrical Calling* (1777–85), to the final version, Thomas Saine notes that much of what Goethe added to the novel as he revised it consists of the newly developed family backgrounds of all the other significant characters. Saine, "Was *Wilhelm Meisters Lehrjahre* Really Supposed to Be a Bildungsroman?," in *Reflection and Action: Essays on the* Bildungsroman, ed. James N. Hardin (Columbia: University of South Carolina Press, 1991), 136.
25. Friedrich Kittler inaugurated the interest in family constellations in the novel in 1978, followed by Jochen Hörisch's Lacanian reading in 1983 in *Gott, Geld, und*

Glück: Zur Logik der Liebe in den Bildungsromanen Goethes, Kellers und Thomas Mann (Frankfurt am Main: Suhrkamp, 1983), but it is particularly since the 1990s that the family has emerged as one of the principle avenues of research into the novel. Studies fall into two general categories: First, those arguing that the novel experiments playfully with a variety of familial types. See Heidi Schlipphacke, " 'Die Vaterschaft beruht nur überhaupt auf der Überzeugung': The Displaced Family in *Wilhelm Meisters Lehrjahre,*" *Journal of English and Germanic Philology* 102 (2003): 390–412; Ingrid Broszeit-Rieger, "Paintings in Goethe's Wilhelm Meister Novels: The Dynamics of Erecting and 'Eroding' the Paternal Law," *Goethe Yearbook* 13 (2005): 105–24; Broszeit-Rieger, "Transgressions of Gender and Generation in the Families of Goethe's Meister," in *Romantic Border Crossings,* ed. Jeffrey Cass and Larry Peer (Aldershot, UK: Ashgate), 75–85; and Robin Tobin, *Warm Brothers: Queer Theory and the Age of Goethe* (Philadelphia: University of Pennsylvania Press, 2000). Second are those who see in the novel an attempt to curtail such experimentation and to strengthen a patriarchally centered nuclear family. See Barbara Becker-Cantarino, "Patriarchy and German Enlightenment Discourse: From Goethe's *Wilhelm Meister* to Horkheimer and Adorno's *Dialectic of Enlightenment,*" in *Impure Reason: Dialectic of Enlightenment in Germany,* ed. W. Daniel Wilson and Robert Holub (Detroit: Wayne State University Press, 1993), 48–64; Elisabeth Krimmer, "Mama's Baby, Papa's Maybe: Paternity and Bildung in Goethe's Wilhelm Meisters Lehrjahre," *German Quarterly* 77, no. 3 (2004): 257–77; Krimmer, "Abortive *Bildung*: Women Writers, Male Bonds, and Would-Be Fathers," in *Challenging Separate Spheres: Female* Bildung *in Eighteenth- and Nineteenth-Century Germany,* ed. Marjanne Goozé (Oxford: Peter Lang, 2007), 235–59; and Martha B. Helfer, "Wilhelm Meister's Women," *Goethe Yearbook* 11 (2002): 229–54. Thomas Saine also concludes that Goethe favors strongly patriarchal families but sees this preference in a less critical light.

26. David Warren Sabean, *Kinship in Neckarhausen, 1700–1870* (Cambridge: Cambridge University Press, 1998); Leonore Davidoff, *Thicker Than Water: Siblings and Their Relations, 1780–1920* (Oxford: Oxford University Press, 2012); Christopher Johnson, *Becoming Bourgeois: Love, Kinship, and Power in Provincial France, 1670–1880* (Ithaca: Cornell University Press, 2015); Margareth Lanzinger, *Verwaltete Verwandtschaften. Eheverbote, kirchliche und Staatliche Dispenspraxis im 18. und 19. Jahrhundert* (Vienna: Böhlau, 2015).

27. David Warren Sabean and Christopher Johnson, *Sibling Relations and the Transformation of European Kinship, 1300–1900* (Oxford: Berghan, 2011), 12.

28. Kittler, "Über die Sozialisation Wilhelm Meisters," 8–9; Tobin, *Warm Brothers,* 8–9.

29. See Hans Jaeger, "Generations in History: Reflections on a Controversial Concept," *History & Theory* 24, no. 3 (1985): 273–92; and Ohad Parnes, "Generationswechsel—eine Figur zwischen Literatur und Mikroskopie," in *Fülle der Combination: Literaturforschung und Wissenschaftsgeschichte,* ed. Bernhard J. Dotzler and Sigrid Weigel, 127–42 (Munich: Wilhelm Fink, 2005).

30. Michaela Hohkamp, "Do Sisters Have Brothers? The Search for the 'rechte Schwester.' Brothers and Sisters in Aristocratic Society at the Turn of the Sixteenth Century," in

Sibling Relations and the Transformation of European Kinship, 1300–1900, ed. David Warren Sabean and Christopher Johnson (Oxford: Berghan, 2011), 68.

31. *OED Online*, s.v. "sibling," http://www.oed.com/view/Entry/179145?redirectedFrom =Sibling.

32. Albrecht Koschorke et al. depict family relations in the nineteenth century as a manifestation of tension between the newly significant nuclear family and the older model of the extended household in which more distant relations such as uncles, aunts, and cousins were important. While their nuclear family includes multiple children in relation to parents, they oddly locate siblings in the second category of distant relations, rather than in the closer familial category (Koschorke et al., *Vor der Familie. Grenzbedingungen einer modernen Institution* [Munich: Konstanz University Press, 2010], 49). Such a distorted view is a result of a century of accepting the Freudian triad as the nuclear family. A more productive way to understand this dynamic is recognize that related nuclear families blend into each other through the sibling bond, which over a life cycle creates the relationships of aunts, uncles, in-laws, and cousins.

33. Leonore Davidoff refers to such kinship networks as lattices of kinship; Christopher Johnson, as sibling archipelagos. See Davidoff, *Thicker Than Water*, 121; and Johnson, *Becoming Bourgeois*, 22–24, 125–70.

34. Johann Wolfgang von Goethe, *Wilhelm Meisters Lehrjahre*, vol. 9 of *Sämtliche Werke* (Frankfurt: Deutscher Klassiker Verlag, 1991), 469.

35. Remember the similar line discussed in the previous chapter, in which Percy Shelley has Cythna describe her daughter as her twin sister.

36. See Lynn Hunt, *The Family Romance of the French Revolution* (Berkeley: University of California Press, 1992); W. Daniel Wilson, "Science, Natural Law, and Unwitting Sibling Incest in Eighteenth-Century Literature," *Studies in Eighteenth-Century Culture* 13 (1984): 249–70; Alan Richardson, "The Dangers of Sympathy: Sibling Incest in English Romantic Poetry," *Studies in English Literature* 25, no. 4 (1985): 737–54; and Richardson, "Rethinking Romantic Incest: Human Universals, Literary Representation, and the Biology of Mind," *New Literary History* 31, no. 3 (2000): 553–72.

37. Peter Uwe Hohendahl, "German Classicism and the Law of the Father," in *Literary Paternity, Literary Friendship: Essays in Honor of Stanley Corngold*, ed. Gerhard Richter, 63–85 (Chapel Hill: University of North Carolina Press, 2002).

38. Goethe, *Apprenticeship*, 357. Achim Aurnhammer was the first to note the way this figure of the lilies marks a shift from myth to empirical data as a guide to identification and self-justification (Achim Aurnhammer, *Androgynie. Studien zu einem Motiv in der europaischen Literatur* [Cologne: Böhlau, 1986], 178–79). As Daniel Wilson revealed, however, Goethe had read Christian Konrad Sprengel's botanical work from 1793, which demonstrated the rarity of self-pollination in even hermaphroditic plants like the lily (Wilson, "Science," 262). Goethe, however, disapproved of Sprengel's portrayal of nature as an agency capable of deploying an organism for a purpose external to it (Goethe, Letter 5061 to August Batsch [February 26, 1794], in *Briefe, Tagebücher, Gespräche*, CD_ROM, ed. Mathias Bertram [Berlin: Directmedia, 2000]). Augustin's

own reference to nature as an ethical guide, Wilson notes, leads to a naturalistic argument *against* incest, given Mignon's physical incapacities and early death. I would argue that Goethe, however, does not succumb to this naturalist fallacy either to justify or to condemn incest. Incest is not viable for Goethe as a social structure, a concern in which Goethe prefigures Lévi-Strauss. The question of accounting for innate predispositions is neither more nor less pressing in the case of Mignon than in the recurring emphasis on family resemblances throughout the novel. Natalie and her sister the Countess both look like their aunt, the author of the "Confessions of a Beautiful Soul." Natalie, moreover, takes after this aunt's personality, while her sister favors their mother's. Wilhelm meanwhile shares the aesthetic taste of his grandfather. For more on how Goethe accounts for resemblances in nature, see Stefani Engelstein, *Anxious Anatomy: The Conception of the Human Form in Literary and Naturalist Discourse* (Albany: State University of New York Press, 2008), 23–58. On family resemblances in *Wilhelm Meister*, see also Saine, "Bildungsroman?"; and Andreas Gailus "Forms of Life: Nature, Culture, and Art in Goethe's Wilhelm Meister's Apprenticeship," *Germanic Review* 87 (2012).

39. Critical work on gender in *Wilhelm Meister* falls roughly into two camps. On the one hand, scholars such as Helfer and Krimmer trace the novel's drive toward normalized, heterosexual gender relations that involve the suppression of androgyny and the sacrifice of female autonomy and desire (see Helfer, "Meister's Women"; Krimmer, "Abortive *Bildung*"). On the other hand, critics such as Tobin, Redfield, and Catriona MacCleod interpret this affirmation of gender complementarity as one aspect of the manipulative program of the Tower Society, toward which the novel exhibits a critically ironic attitude (see Tobin, *Warm Brothers*; Redfield, *Phantom Formations*; and MacLeod, *Embodying Ambiguity: Androgyny and Aesthetics from Winckelmann to Keller* [Detroit: Wayne State University Press, 1998]). The essential question, here as elsewhere, is whether the novel's ironic handling of the Tower Society amounts to a critique. We will return to this question below.

40. Maternity is here revealed to be cultural-symbolic rather than natural. While Redfield argues that the elimination of the maternal body as a natural sign allows Goethe to escape from a violent aestheticization of the feminine (*Phantom Formations*, 1–73, 93), others read this erasure of maternity as a hostile takeover of the creative power of women by male discourse. See Gail Hart, *Tragedy in Paradise: Family and Gender Politics in German Bourgeois Tragedy 1750–1850* (Columbia, S.C.: Camden House, 1996); Becker-Cantarino, "Patriarchy"; and Krimmer, "Abortive *Bildung*" and "Mama's Baby, Papa's Maybe."

41. For insightful analyses of the oedipal in the novel, see Hörisch, *Gott, Geld*; Redfield, *Phantom Formations*; and Minden, *The German Bildungsroman*.

42. André Lottmann also sees in the Tower a surveillance agency, but a bureaucratic one that appropriates the functions of a weak state (Lottmann, *Arbeitsverhältnisse. Der arbeitende Mensch in Goethes Wilhelm Meister-Romanen und in der Geschichte der Politischen Ökonomie* [Würzburg: Königshausen & Neumann, 2011], 139). Tobias Boes notes that the Tower anticipates the conversion of narrative subjects into

risk management calculations while also following the logic of the eighteenth-century family romance (*Formative Fictions*, 66–68). As I argue in this chapter, it is precisely the blending of surveillance, insurance, and affective familial relations that characterizes the modern political economy.

43. See Thomas Wegmann, *Tauschverhältnisse. Zur Ökonomie des Literarischen und zum Ökonomischen in der Literatur von Gellert bis Goethe* (Würzburg: Königshausen & Neumann, 2002), 197–98; Joseph Vogl, *Kalkül und Leidenschaft: Poetik des ökonomischen Menschen* (Zurich: Diaphanes, 2004), 35–38, 87–95; and Gailus, "Forms of Life," 165. Andre Lottmann, on the other hand, notes the clear disparity between Smith's invisible hand and Goethe's Tower Society (*Arbeitsverhältnisse*, 143–44). Bernd Mahl has documented Goethe's engagement with Adam Smith, at least through the medium of Johann Georg Büsch, during the composition of Wilhelm Meister (Mahl, *Goethes ökonomisches Wissen. Grundlagen zum Verständnis der ökonomischen Passagen im dichterischen Gesamtwerk und in den 'Amtlichen Schriften'* [Frankfurt am Main: Peter Lang, 1982]). Vogl does quite rightly recognize the "*Wilhelm-Meister*-Problem" as the question of how "a personal substrate as well as the management of a mass of contingent events can be guaranteed in a world of unpredictable accidents and embroilments" (*Kalkül*, 87, my trans.).

44. Jane Brown draws a particularly productive connection between *Wilhelm Meister's Apprenticeship* and Rousseau's novel of education, namely, *Emile*, in which the notion of control over the student is figured through the puppet theater (Brown, "Faust als Revolutionär: Goethe zwischen Rousseau und Hannah Arendt," *Goethe-Jahrbuch* 126 [2009]: 84). Brown sees a strong contrast, however, between the need to control and surveil the pupil in Rousseau and the withdrawal of such control in favor of a natural unfolding of character in Goethe. I see far more similarities here than Brown does.

45. Andreas Gailus aptly refers to a "bioaesthetics" ("Forms of Life," 153) in *Wilhelm Meister*.

46. See in particular Michel Foucault, *The Birth of Biopolitics: Lectures at the Collège de France, 1978–1979*, ed. Michel Sennelart, trans. Graham Burchell (New York: Palgrave Macmillan, 2008), 130–31 and 239–48.

47. Foucault notes that the turn of the nineteenth century brought a change in the relationship of family to state, in which the family was no longer seen as a viable model for state organization but became instead an instrument of state policies. This shift occurred at the same moment, and because governance adjusted its understanding of its own jurisdiction toward managing population through what we now call the economy. Michel Foucault, *Security, Territory, Populations: Lectures at the Collège de France, 1977–1978*, ed. Michel Sennelart, trans. Graham Burchell (New York: Palgrave Macmillan, 2007), 101–10. See also Foucault, *The Birth of Biopolitics*.

48. Hörisch rightly unsettles the absoluteness of this declaration by pointing out the logic of exchange still implied by it (*Gott, Geld*, 83–84), but the point here is precisely that in such a logic of exchange there must be a projected absolute for the system to work.

49. Krimmer, "Mama's Baby," 266. Martha Helfer notes that "Natalie does not represent an aesthetic, an erotic, or an economic ideal. She merely completes a textual economy"

("Meister's Women," 247). Krimmer ("Mama's Baby," 265); Hannelore Schlaffer, *Wilhelm Meister: Das Ende der Kunst und die Wiederkehr des Mythos* (Stuttgart: J. B. Metzlersche Verlagsbuchhandlung, 1980), 88; and Anneliese Dick, *Weiblichkeit als natürliche Dienstbarkeit. Eine Studie zum klassischen Frauenbild in Goethes Wilhelm Meister* (Frankfurt: Peter Lang, 1986), 104, 123, all also allude to Natalie's voidlike role in the novel.

50. Jane Brown has analyzed irony in Goethe as a way of infusing the subjective into "traditional forms of aristocratic public representativity" ("Goethe: The Politics of Allegory and Irony," in *The Politics of Irony: Essays in Self-Betrayal*, ed. Daniel W. Conway and John E. Seery [New York: St. Martin's, 1992], 67). Such irony involves not merely ambiguous but "ambivalent intent" (68), as it opens a door to self-reflection without stepping through that door. Redfield reads Goethe more programmatically, claiming that the novel's irony "disarticulates the aesthetic and naturalizing illusion that composes all ideologies, thus opening them to critique by accounting for their occurrence" (*Phantom Formations*, 93). I agree that Goethe casts a critical eye on the social machinations of the Tower Society, but he does not move beyond this step, so that the novel posits such biopolitics as distasteful but unavoidable.
51. Davidoff, *Thicker Than Water*, 6, 60.
52. See Claudia Jarzebowski, *Inzest: Verwandtschaft und Sexualität im achtzehnten Jahrhundert* (Cologne: Böhlau, 2006). Catholics still required a dispensation to marry a cousin, which could be hard to come by. See Lanzinger, *Verwaltete Verwandtschaft*. Adam Kuper, *Incest and Influence: The Private Life of Bourgeois England* (Cambridge: Harvard University Press, 2009), and Davidoff, *Thicker Than Water*, both discuss the best-known cases of multiple cousin marriages within and in successive generations, namely, those of the Darwin-Wedgwood clan and of the Rothschild family.
53. Elizabeth Langland, *Nobody's Angels: Middle-Class Women and Domestic Ideology in Victorian Culture* (Ithaca: Cornell University Press, 1995), 6–61.
54. Davidoff, *Thicker Than Water*, 53–56; and Rebekka Habermas, *Frauen und Männer des Bürgertums* (Göttingen: Vanderhoeck & Ruprecht, 2000), 99.
55. See, among others, Elisabeth Joris, "Kinship and Gender: Property, Enterprise, and Politics," in *Kinship in Europe: Approaches to Long-Term Development (1300–1900)*, ed. David Warren Sabean, Simon Teuscher, and Jon Mathieu (New York: Berghahn Books, 2007), 231–57; Elizabeth Langland (*Nobody's Angels*); and Leonore Davidoff and Catherine Hall, *Family Fortunes*, rev. ed. (London: Routledge, 2002), 193–315.
56. David Warren and Simon Teuscher, "Kinship in Europe: A New Approach to Long-Term Development," in *Kinship in Europe: Approaches to Long-Term Development (1300–1900)*, ed. David Warren Sabean, Simon Teuscher, and Jon Mathieu (New York: Berghahn Books, 2007), 20. For an analysis of the political stakes of earlier historical arguments, see the Afterward in Alan Bray, *The Friend* (Chicago: University of Chicago Press, 2003). In her book on the family and the novel from 1748 to 1818, Ruth Perry depends on the older idea, arguing that the increasing importance of the conjugal family lessened the importance of the consanguineal family—that wives and mothers became more important than sisters and daughters (Perry, *Novel Relations. The*

Transformation of Kinship in English Literature and Culture, 1748–1818 (Cambridge: Cambridge University Press, 2004), esp. 1–37, 107–89). She projects this trend forward into the long nineteenth century. Her efforts to fit family roles into this bifurcated classification runs into problems, however, as sisters, mothers, and daughters are all consanguineal, and she acknowledges the increasing significance of in-laws at this time (119–21). In-laws maintain importance, however, only insofar as the spouse retains a relationship to them. Where Perry sees the tensions between sister-rights and wife-rights as the sign of a shift from the former to the latter (part of a larger move from lateral to linear inheritance; 111), such tensions could also be read as the manifestation of the social need to maintain both simultaneously. Moreover, while female inheritance rights waned during the second half of the eighteenth century, actual female inheritance waxed during the first half of the nineteenth (Kuper, *Incest and Influence*, 16). The main problem with Perry's line of argumentation is that she assumes that a weakening legal economic position for daughters correlates with a weakened affective attachment to sisters. Economic dependence, however, created a social imperative to maintain affective bonds. Running economy through channels of affect rather than through channels of law significantly alters social roles in ways this chapter addresses.

57. Niklas Luhmann, *Love as Passion: The Codification of Intimacy*, trans. Jeremy Gaines and Doris L. Jones (Cambridge: Polity, 1986).
58. The recent work of Sabean, Davidoff, and others directly contradicts Luhmann's claim that "the differentiation of other functional systems made it possible to do without family ties (created by marriage) as the pillar of political, religious or economic functions" (ibid., 145).
59. David Warren Sabean, "Kinship and Class Dynamics in Nineteenth-Century Europe," in *Kinship in Europe: Approaches to Long-Term Development (1300–1900)*, ed. David Warren Sabean, Simon Teuscher, and Jon Mathieu (New York: Berghahn, 2007), 302 (emphasis added).
60. For more on the conversion of sibling-affect into conjugal love, see in particular Davidoff, *Thicker Than Water*, 109–10; Leonore Davidoff, "Where the Stranger Begins: The Question of Siblings in Historical Analysis," in *Worlds Between: Historical Perspectives on Gender and Class*, ed. Leonore Davidoff (New York: Routledge, 1995), 210–11; Perry, *Novel Relations*, 111; Leila Silvana May, *Disorderly Sisters: Sibling Relations and Sororal Resistance in Nineteenth-Century British Literature* (Lewisburg, Pa.: Bucknell University Press, 2001), 18–25; and David Sabean, "Inzestdiskurse vom Barock bis zur Romantik," *L'Homme* 13, no. 1 (2002): 7–28. On the literary explorations of this dynamic, see Joseph Boone and Deborah E. Nord, "Brother and Sister: The Seductions of Siblinghood in Dickens, Eliot, and Brontë," *Western Humanities Review* 46, no. 2 (1992): 164–88; Valerie Sanders, *The Brother-Sister Culture in Nineteenth-Century Literature* (Basingstoke: Palgrave, 2002); and May, *Disorderly Sisters*. On the shift from egalitarian nursery relations to differing educations, see, in addition, Charlotte Goodman, "The Lost Brother, The Twin: Women Novelists and the Male-Female Double Bildungsroman," *Novel* 17, no. 1 (Autumn 1983): 28–43.

61. George Eliot, *The Mill on the Floss*, ed. Gordon S. Haight (Oxford: Clarendon, 1980), 295.
62. Annette B. Weiner, *Inalienable Possessions: The Paradox of Keeping-While-Giving* (Berkeley: University of California Press, 1992), 67.
63. It lies outside the scope of this chapter to review in detail the long history of engagements with commodity fetishism. For a summary of past approaches, see William Pietz's thorough retrospective, "Fetishism and Materialism: The Limits of Theory in Marx," in *Fetishism as Cultural Discourse*, ed. Emily Apter and William Pietz (Ithaca: Cornell University Press, 1993). In addition to the 1993 volume on the fetish edited by Apter and Pietz in which this article appears, foundational examples of different theoretical approaches can be found in Jean Baudrillard, "Fetishism and Ideology: the Semiological Reduction," in *For a Critique of the Political Economy of the Sign*, trans. Charles Levin (St. Louis: Telos Press, 1981); Slavoj Žižek, *The Sublime Object of Ideology* (London: Verso, 1989); Arjun Appadurai, "Introduction: Commodities and the Politics of Value," in *The Social Life of Things: Commodities in Cultural Perspective* (Cambridge: Cambridge University Press, 1986); and W.J.T. Mitchell, *What Do Pictures Want? The Lives and Loves of Images* (Chicago: University of Chicago Press, 2005). Other interesting approaches include that of Anne McClintock, *Imperial Leather: Race, Gender, and Sexuality in the Colonial Contest* (London: Routledge, 1995); Jon Stratton, *The Desirable Body: Cultural Fetishism and the Erotics of Consumption* (Manchester: Manchester University Press, 1996); and Johanna Malt, *Obscure Objects of Desire: Surrealism, Fetishism and Politics* (Oxford: Oxford University Press, 2004).
64. On the ethno-religious origin of the term that will primarily occupy us here, see, in addition to William Pietz, "Fetishism and Materialism," Mitchell, *What Do Pictures Want?*; and Falko Schmieder, "Zur Kritik der Rezeption des Marxschen Fetischbegriffs," *Marx-Engels-Jahrbuch* (2005): 106–27. On its adaptation by the British Romantics, see David Simpson, *Fetishism and Imagination: Dickens, Melville, Conrad* (Baltimore: Johns Hopkins University Press, 1982).
65. William Pietz, "The Problem of the Fetish, II: The Origin of the Fetish," *RES: Anthropology and Aesthetics*, no. 13 (Spring 1987): 23.
66. See in particular the excellent article by Jack Amariglio and Antonio Callari on the Marxian subject in relation to the fetish, "Marxian Value Theory and the Problem of the Subject: The Role of Commodity Fetishism," in *Fetishism as Cultural Discourse*, ed. Emily Apter and William Pietz, 186–216 (Ithaca: Cornell University Press, 1993).
67. I will return in the next chapter to Mitchell's discussion of the historical progression in the Western naming of cult objects: from idol to fetish to totem (*What Do Pictures Want?*). Many of the associations Mitchell claims for the totem will arise here in reference to the kind of fetish that I see George Eliot theorizing, which runs counter to the use of the word at the time but builds on it, just as Mitchell's progression from the Fetish to the Totem does.
68. Bruno Latour, *On the Modern Cult of the Factish Gods*, partial trans. Catherine Porter and Heather MacLean (Durham: Duke University Press, 2010), 35 (emphasis in original).

69. Mitchell correlates the idol with the father, the fetish with the mother, and the totem with "sister, brother, or kinfolk" (*What Do Pictures Want?*, 165). As mentioned earlier, Mitchell's use of totem approaches the range of meanings of the fetish in my discussion.
70. Auguste Comte, *The Positive Philosophy*, trans. and condensed by Harriet Martineau (London: Kegan Paul, Trench, Trübner, 1893), 2:157. See also George Henry Lewes, "Ages of Fetishism and Polytheism," in *Comte's Philosophy of the Sciences*, 273–87 (London: Henry G. Bohn, 1853). Lewes was writing this volume on Comte during the first years of his acquaintance with Eliot and completed it shortly before they moved in together in a relationship they considered marriage.
71. Comte is somewhat inconsistent here, as he insists on the fetish as a worshipped object that does not allow for the abstraction of symbolization and yet also believes the fine arts would have flourished in the fetish stage because imagination had so free a range (*Positive Philosophy*, 2:163–64). Critics have contested the extent of Eliot's acceptance of Comte's positivism. She certainly considered him a strong and lifelong influence, but that need not mean she accepted his ideas without emendation. See in particular James Scott, "George Eliot, Positivism, and the Social Vision of 'Middlemarch,'" *Victorian Studies* 16, no. 1 (1972): 59–76; T. R. Wright, "George Eliot and Positivism: A Reassessment," *Modern Language Review* 76, no. 2 (1981): 257–72; and James McLaverty, "Comtean Fetishism in Silas Marner," *Nineteenth-Century Fiction* 36, no. 3 (December 1981): 318–36.
72. Deanna Kreisel notes the fetishistic attachment to hard cash in the novel ("Superfluity and Suction: The Problem with Saving in *The Mill on the Floss*," *Novel* 35, no. 1 [2001]: 85–87). For Eliot's engagement with contemporary discussions of fetishism, see also Peter Melville Logan, "George Eliot and the Fetish of Realism," *Studies in the Literary Imagination* 35, no. 2 (2002): 27–51; and McLaverty, "Comtean Fetishism."
73. George Eliot was a translator of David Strauss and Ludwig Feuerbach and an avid reader of Comte. She and Marx therefore shared the same background on the theory of the fetish.
74. Marx, in contrast, gestures in *Capital* toward a natural form of family relationship, one in which a division of labor develops spontaneously as a result of evidently natural affinities and rhythms based on gender, age, and season. Both the Penguin and International Publishers translations of *Capital* obscure the way Marx naturalizes gender by translating *naturwüchsig* as "spontaneous" rather than "through a natural outgrowth." Marx, *Capital* (Vintage), 1:171; *Capital: A Critique of Political Economy*, in *Karl Marx, Frederick Engels: Collected Works* (New York: International, 1996), 1:77–78; and *Das Kapital: Kritik der politischen Ökonomie, Vol. 1*, vol. 23 of *Werke*, by Karl Marx und Friedrich Engels (Berlin: Dietz, 1970), 92.
75. John Kucich, "George Eliot and Objects: Meaning as Matter in *The Mill on the Floss*," *Dickens Studies Annual* 12 (1983): 321.
76. Kucich derives this understanding of Maggie's relationship to objects primarily by analogy to discussion of language with her brother, in which she explains that words have multiple meanings. Margaret Homans, in contrast, believes that Maggie loses this

ability to perceive and create multivalency as she attempts to retain Tom's love by adapting to his masculine desire to exert mastery over objects. Homans, "Eliot, Wordsworth, and the Scenes of the Sisters' Instruction," *Critical Inquiry* 8, no. 2 (Winter 1981): 223–41.

77. Neil Hertz, *George Eliot's Pulse* (Stanford: Stanford University Press, 2003), 68.
78. Kathleen Blake finds two conflicting economic systems in *Mill on the Floss*, a gift economy in which Maggie operates and a modern economy best exemplified by Uncle Glegg (Blake, "Between Economies in The Mill on the Floss: Loans Versus Gifts, or, Auditing Mr. Tulliver's Accounts," *Victorian Literature and Culture* 33 [2005]: 219–37). Many of the characters drift between the two in her analysis, however, and debt is a feature of both economies. As Marcel Mauss first clarified, gifts awaken a reciprocal obligation. A more productive division of the novel is Mary Poovey, "Writing About Finance in Victorian England: Disclosure and Secrecy in the Culture of Investment," in *Victorian Investments: New Perspectives on Finance and Culture*, ed. Nancy Henry and Cannon Smith (Bloomington: Indiana University Press, 2009). Poovey sees a split between two plots—an economic and a sentimental—woven together by the migration of secrecy and disclosure from the impersonal and inaccessible collective sphere of economics into the sentimental, interpersonal relations. Poovey analyzes the way that "unlike the inheritance plots that dominated eighteenth-century novels, financial plots allowed writers to explore matters involving personal agency and individual will" within a world of opaque agency (52). Hence, I would add, such horizontal plots reveal the imbrication of personal lives within collective networks.
79. See Molstad, "'The Mill on the Floss' and 'Antigone,'" *PMLA* 85, no. 3 (May 1970): 527–31; Sandra M. Gilbert and Susan Gubar, *The Madwoman in the Attic: The Woman Writer and the Nineteenth-Century Literary Imagination* (New Haven: Yale University Press, 1979), 497; and May, *Disorderly Sisters*, 80, for comparisons of Tom and Creon. Marianne Hirsch does not analyze Tom, but her claim that Maggie adheres to a circular pattern of development peculiar to women in the nineteenth-century novel, and following in the footsteps of Antigone, participates in an ongoing gendering of Antigone that Eliot herself tried to move away from ("Spiritual *Bildung*").
80. See Gerhard Joseph, "The Antigone as Cultural Touchstone: Matthew Arnold, Hegel, George Eliot, Virginia Woolf, and Margaret Drabble," *PMLA* 96, no. 1 (January 1981): 22–35; and Hirsch, "Spiritual *Bildung*." See also August Böckh, *Über die Antigone des Sophokles. Nebst Nachträgliche Bemerkungen* (n.p., 1826).
81. George Eliot, "The Antigone and Its Moral," *Leader* 7 (March 29, 1856): 306, C19: The Nineteenth-Century Index.
82. One exception is Esty, who notices that both siblings fall into a "familial and historical trap" as they try to restore an earlier economic model, which prevents both from marrying or acquiring the other trappings of maturity (Esty, "Nationhood," 111).
83. There is some ambiguity in this sentence, and it is not entirely clear if it is Maggie's character or the harsh treatment he feels forced to exercise toward her that makes him bitter, but such ambiguity reflects his feelings toward her.

84. The *millstone* as a figurative burden or weight dates back to the Bible and was current in the nineteenth century (*OED Online*, s.v. "millstone," http://www.oed.com/view /Entry/118596?redirectedFrom=millstone). Most critics are more interested, however, in the nature of the wooden machinery that sinks the skiff and causes the siblings to drown. Homans, "Dinah's Blush, Maggie's Arm: Class, Gender, and Sexuality in George Eliot's Early Novels," *Victorian Studies* 36, no. 2 (Winter 1993): 172; and May, *Disorderly Sisters*, 77, see the machinery as a symbol of industrial capitalism, and Esty reads the flood itself as excessive expression of the river's role as a "conduit for economic modernity" ("Nationhood," 113). Kathleen Blake, however, notes that as part of a wooden wharf, the equipment is as much a part of long-established trade patterns as of newer capitalistic trends ("Between Economies," 232). Their death is induced not by a shift to a new economy but by their withdrawal from economies altogether.

85. Nina Auerbach in particular has drawn out the demonic resonances of Maggie's character as death-bringing, in "The Power of Hunger: Demonism and Maggie Tulliver," *Nineteenth-Century Fiction* 30, no. 2 (September 1975): 150–71.

86. The oscillation between extremes of desire and renunciation fits into an important nineteenth-century economic debate between adherents of Say's Law such as Ricardo and Mill and its detractors, primarily Malthus. Kreisel has perceptively analyzed the way Maggie challenges both the assumption that there can never be a glut because demand is always sufficient to account for supply (Say's Law) and the insistence on the propriety of moderation (see "Superfluity"). While a detailed analysis of the debate over the law of supply and demand lies outside the scope of this chapter, it is worth noting that the debate highlights problems of individual agency and general laws of collectives that we touch on here.

87. Gillian Beer notes the correspondence between this interest in Eliot and in Darwin, in *Darwin's Plots: Evolutionary Narrative in Darwin, George Eliot and Nineteenth-Century Fiction* (London: Routledge & Kegan Paul, 1983), 154. *The Mill on the Floss* was published just a year after *The Origin of Species*, which Eliot read immediately after publication (ibid., 156). The joint concern with roots and branches, that is, with genealogical structures, predates both Eliot and Darwin, however. We will return to the genealogical tree in the next chapter. In *George Eliot*, Beer builds on this insight, noting that Eliot counters the drive to recognize origins with "an equally intense movement towards differentiation, expansion, lateral kinning, fostering and foster-parenting, and sympathetic generalization, which all create new and multiple relationships." Gillian Beer, *George Eliot* (Brighton: Harvester, 1986), 54.

88. See Sigmund Freud, "Fetischismus," in *Gesammelte Werke*, ed. Anna Freud (Frankfurt: S. Fischer, 1976).

89. Critics have noted this recurrence. See Homans on Maggie's "renewed love of those identical objects" ("Eliot," 231) and Kucich's note that "The mill reminds the Tullivers mainly of itself" ("George Eliot," 331).

90. George Eliot, "Notes on Form in Art," in *Essays of George Eliot*, ed. Thomas Pinney (New York: Columbia University Press, 1963), 433.

91. Neil Hertz notes that at this moment the narrator resembles not only Maggie and Tom in their childhood loves but also their father, and that the narrator's voice multiplies identification—with Maggie, with George Eliot, and with the child who became her—Mary Ann Evans (*Pulse*, 68). For Hertz, narration—that of the novel itself and scenes within it—enacts a transfer of emotional attachment stripped of the passions that render it dangerous. I think this is both an over- and understatement that unnecessarily domesticates the novel. The narration presents a way of reconciling attachment and survival but not of rendering emotion safe or minimizing passion. The narrator's voice is not one of renunciation. On the other hand, the emotion is not transferred but shared. This is a case of keeping-while-giving, a form of debt that is equivalent with life.
92. Devin Griffiths arrives at a similar conclusion in his analysis of Eliot's use of what he calls sympathetic analogy, which reaches toward a "shared subjectivity," but within a "more complex network of social relationships" that disrupt a collapse into complete identification. Griffiths, *The Age of Analogy: Science and Literature Between the Darwins* (Baltimore: Johns Hopkins University Press, 2016), 166–210, quote on 195.
93. Gilles Deleuze and Félix Guattari, *Anti-Oedipus: Capitalism and Schizophrenia* (Minneapolis: University of Minnesota Press, 1983), 146–47.
94. Goethe, *Wilhelm Meister's Apprenticeship*, 19. See also, for example, Gustav Freytag's Anton Wolfahrt in *Soll und Haben*, who swoons over the global network of relations represented by the goods traded by the company in which he works and interprets the attraction of commodities as a by-product of these interactions: "We live in the midst of a colorful fabric composed of countless threads stretching from one person to another over land and sea from one part of the world to another. These threads attach themselves to every individual and connect each to the whole world. Everything we wear on our body and everything that surrounds us brings before our eyes the most curious occurrences in all foreign lands and also every human activity; thus everything becomes attractive. And because I feel myself to be of assistance in this process and, however small my contribution, because I do have a hand in ensuring that every person is maintained in an enduring relationship to every other person, I can be well pleased by my own occupation." Freytag, *Soll und Haben*, in *Gesammelte Werke* (Leipzig: von S. Hitzel, 1887), 4:274 (my trans.).
95. There is some affinity here between Smith's description and Baudrillard's account of fetishism as inhering in system. For Baudrillard, however, the system in question is the process of signification that he has emptied of all history (Baudrillard, "Fetishism"). Smith's system, on the other hand, still operates in time; it has "motions" whose regularity on a clock marks its smooth functioning.
96. Marc Redfield, *The Politics of Aesthetics: Nationalism, Gender, Romanticism* (Stanford: Stanford University Press, 2003), 22.
97. See Howard Caygill's excellent discussion of Smith in the *Art of Judgment* (Cambridge: Basil Blackwell, 1989), 85–98.
98. The bleeding of economics into aesthetics was not an innovation of Smith's but, as Mary Poovey discusses, emblematic of the incomplete process by which these two

sciences of desire split off from moral theory in the second half of the eighteenth century. Poovey argues, moreover, that Smith completes the move from aesthetics to acquisitive desire in *The Wealth of Nations*. See Poovey, "Aesthetics and Political Economy."

99. Gotthold Ephraim Lessing, *Laocöon: An Essay on the Limits of Painting and Poetry*, trans. Edward Allen McCormick (Baltimore: Johns Hopkins University Press, 1982).

100. Ibid. It is noteworthy, then, that the protagonists of both the novels under discussion in this chapter are incapable of the form of aesthetic abstraction embraced by Schiller. As Marc Redfield has noted, Wilhelm's inability to act stems from the same source as his misguided attraction to a painting of a sick prince, who has become ill through pining for his father's fiancée. Unable to universalize himself, Wilhelm identifies with the king's sick son as he does with Hamlet when he plays him on stage (*Phantom Formations*, 75–76). The brunette Maggie also experiences art through character identification, tossing aside Madame de Stael's novel *Corinne* when she realizes that a blond character will end up stealing the lover and hence the happiness of a dark-haired woman in the text (*Mill*, 292). These aesthetic failings are related to the fate of both characters. Wilhelm's penchant for identification facilitates the power exerted over him by the symbol-wielding Tower Society. Maggie, on the other hand, unable to find a way to negotiate particulars either by abstraction or integration, perishes.

101. George Eliot, "The Morality of Wilhelm Meister," *Leader* (July 21, 1855): 703, C19: The Nineteenth-Century Index.

102. Eliot was certainly familiar with Smith's writings. Imraan Coovadia discusses correspondences with Smith in Eliot's later work that are also relevant here, such as the web of human interdependence ("George Eliot's Realism and Adam Smith," *Studies in English Literature, 1500–1900* 42, no. 4 [Autumn 2002]: 819–35). Rae Greiner sees Smith's legacy in the combination of the aesthetic and the ethical manifest in the realist novel in general, and in Eliot in particular. Greiner understands Smithian sympathy as inherently aesthetic because of its dependence on imagination enabled by a narrative epistemological structure. Here Greiner convincingly supplements the traditional understanding of Smith's sympathy as specular and theatrical ("Sympathy Time: Adam Smith, George Eliot, and the Realist Novel," *Narrative* 17, no. 3 [October 2009]: 291–311). See also David Marshall, *The Figure of the Theater: Shaftesbury, Defoe, Adam Smith, and George Eliot* (New York: Columbia University Press, 1986).

4. LIVING LANGUAGES

1. For comprehensive histories of comparative philology and linguistics in the nineteenth century, see Tuska Benes, *In Babel's Shadow: Language, Philology and the Nation in Nineteenth-Century Germany* (Detroit: Wayne State University Press, 2008); Andreas Gardt, *Geschichte der Sprachwissenschaft in Deutschland vom Mittelalter bis ins 20. Jahrhundert* (Berlin: Walter de Gruyter, 1999); and Anna Morpurgo Davies, *Nineteenth-Century Linguistics*. History of Linguistics IV, ed. Giulio Lepschy (London: Longman, 1992). For a history of the reciprocal influence of linguistics and evolution-

ary thinking, see Joseph Errington, *Linguistics in a Colonial World: A Story of Language, Meaning, and Power* (Malden, Mass.: Blackwell, 2008); and Stephen G. Alter, *Darwinism and the Linguistic Image: Language, Race, and Natural Theology in the Nineteenth Century* (Baltimore: Johns Hopkins University Press, 1999).

2. In addition to Errington and Alter, see Peter Bowler, *Evolution: The History of an Idea* (Berkeley: University of California Press, 1983); and Jan Sapp, *Genesis: The Evolution of Biology* (Oxford: Oxford University Press, 2003).

3. See Michael Carhart, *The Science of Culture in Enlightenment Germany* (Cambridge, Mass.: Harvard University Press, 2007); and John Garber, "Von der Menschheitsgeschichte zur Kulturgeschichte. Zum geschichtstheoretischen Kulturbegriff der deutschen Spätaufklärung," in *Kultur zwischen Bürgertum und Volk*, ed. Jutta Held (Berlin: Augument-Verlag, 1983), 76–97, for discussions of the late eighteenth-century development of a science of culture in Germany in the context of anthropology and ethnography. Peter Burke places this development in a longer historical context in "Reflections on the Origins of Cultural History," in *Interpretation and Cultural History*, ed. Joan H. Pittock and Andrew Wear, 5–24 (New York: St. Martin's, 1991).

4. See Tomoko Masuzawa, *The Invention of World Religions, or, How European Universalism Was Preserved in the Language of Pluralism* (Chicago: University of Chicago Press, 2005); Stefan Arvidsson, *Aryan Idols: Indo-European Mythology as Ideology and Science*, trans. Sonia Wichmann (Chicago: University of Chicago Press, 2006); and Maurice Olender, *The Languages of Paradise: Race, Religion, and Philology in the Nineteenth Century*, trans. Arthur Goldhammer (Cambridge: Harvard University Press, 1992).

5. See Robert Bernasconi, "Who Invented the Concept of Race? Kant's Role in the Enlightenment Construction of Race," in *Race*, ed. Robert Bernasconi (Malden, Mass.: Blackwell, 2001); Nancy Stepan, *The Idea of Race in Science: Great Britain 1800–1960* (Basingstoke: Macmillan, 1982); and Robert Young, *Colonial Desire: Hybridity in Theory, Culture and Race* (London: Routledge: 1995). This chapter focuses on philology and evolution, and the next one will explore race theory and comparative religion.

6. We might compare this defensiveness to the discourse on cell boundaries and the threat of infiltration that arose in reciprocal interaction with political discussions of individual responsibilities and national boundaries, analyzed so acutely by Laura Otis in *Membranes: Metaphors of Invasion in Nineteenth-Century Literature, Science, and Politics* (Baltimore: Johns Hopkins University Press, 1999).

7. See the introduction for a discussion of the comparative method. Henry Hoenigswald defines this method as "a process whereby original features can be separated from recent ones and where the aim of classification is subordinated to the aim of reconstruction. Thus, genealogical reconstruction, arrived at by the Comparative Method, may well be at variance with typological classification" (Hoenigswald, "On the History of the Comparative Method," *Anthropological Linguistics* 5, no. 1 [1963]: 2). I would only quibble here that classification is still the goal of this process, but classification now coincides with genealogical position. Moreover, comparison between terms was the major avenue for arriving at the knowledge of chronological development.

8. August Schleicher, "The Darwinian Theory and the Science of Language," in *Linguistics and Evolutionary Theory: Three Essays by August Schleicher, Ernst Haeckel, and Wilhelm Bleck*, ed. Konrad Koerner, trans. Alexander Bikkers (Amsterdam: John Benjamins, 1983), 16–17.
9. Stephen Alter provides an excellent and extended account of the reciprocal development of genealogical thought between biology and linguistics, but with more emphasis on the mid- to late nineteenth century than on pre-Darwinian concepts (Alter, *Darwinism*).
10. Friedrich Schlegel, *Über die Sprache und die Weisheit der Indier* (Amsterdam: John Benjamins, 1977), 28 (trans. mine).
11. Lyle Campbell and William J. Poser, *Language Classification: History and Method* (Cambridge: Cambridge University Press, 2008), 2.
12. Herder uses the word *genetisch* to refer to origins and derivation (Johann Gottfried von Herder, "Über den Ursprung der Sprache," in *Frühe Schriften*, vol. 1 of *Werke in zehn Bänden*, ed. Ulrich Gaier [Frankfurt am Main: Deutscher Klassiker Verlag, 1985], 716, 733, 752). The OED cites only one occurrence of *genetic* in English prior to its appearance in a Herder translation (*OED Online*, s.v. "genetic," http://www.oed.com/view/Entry/77550?rskey=Hi2GfR&result=1.
13. August Ludwig Schlözer, *Vorstellung seiner Universal-Historie*, 2 vols. (Göttingen: Dieterich, 1772), 1:102. Schlözer also coined the terms *Völkerkunde* and *Ethnologie* in this work, fields we will return to in the next chapter. See also Han F. Vermeulen, "The German Invention of Völkerkunde: Ethnological Discourse in Europe and Asia, 1740–1798," in *The German Invention of Race*, ed. Sara Eigen and Mark Larrimore (Albany: State University of New York Press, 2006), 127–29. In 1781 Schlözer coined the word *Semitisch* for the languages related to Hebrew and Arabic and for the peoples who spoke them, in "Von den Chaldäern," vol. 8 of *Repertorium für biblische und morgenländische Literatur*, ed. Johann Gottfried Eichhorn (1781).
14. Etienne Bonnot de Condillac, *Essay on the Origin of Human Knowledge*, trans. and ed. Hans Aarsleff (Cambridge: Cambridge University Press, 2001), 120.
15. Jean-Jacques Rousseau, *The First and Second Discourses and Essay on the Origin of Languages*, ed. and trans. Victor Gourevitch (New York: Harper and Row, 1986), 240.
16. See Michel Foucault, *The Order of Things: An Archeology of the Human Sciences* (London: Routledge, 2007).
17. See Claus Ahlzweig for a thorough history of the word *Muttersprache* as "native language" (*Muttersprache-Vaterland: Die deutsche Nation und ihre Sprache* [Opladen: Westdeutscher Verlag, 1994]). Strangely, Ahlzweig does not consider the second, phylogenetic, meaning of mother tongue, even when discussing authors like Herder who used the term in this sense. See also Gardt, *Geschichte*, 47–48.
18. Johann Heinrich Zedler, *Grosses vollständiges Universallexicon aller Wissenschaften und Künste* (1731–1754), 22:846 (my trans.), http://www.zedler-lexikon.de/index.html.
19. Johann Christoph Adelung, *Grammatisch-kritisches Wörterbuch der hochdeutschen Mundart* (Vienna: Bauer, 1811), 349–50 (my trans.), http://lexika.digitale-sammlungen.de/adelung/online/angebot. Friedrich Kittler has analyzed this constellation of

mother, nature, and language, through which language was imbued with the mystical aura of the mother's voice around 1800. See *Discourse Networks: 1800/1900*, trans. Michael Metteer with Chris Cullens (Stanford: Stanford University Press, 1990). While some aspects of Kittler's analysis remain compelling, I question here his investment in aligning the romantic commitment to speech with the psychoanalytic family romance, hence dissolving siblings into a triangular model. It is worth noting that Kittler's primary example, Hoffmann's "The Golden Pot," identifies the lovely green snake with blue eyes who facilitates the writing of the main character Anselmus not as a mother but as one of three sisters. Kittler dismisses this appellation with a psychoanalytic wave of the hand: "The story of the poet princes and poets that we have from the pens of the fairy tale's hero and writer need not refer to the two other sisters of Serpentina as single, individual figures. Because the sisters all appear to men in the shape of their mother, it is enough to elevate Serpentina as the one signified" (*Discourse Networks*, 105). He goes on to identify Serpentina with the spirit of Sanskrit, which he posits as the mother language. The three sisters in question, however, could very well correlate with Greek, Latin, and Sanskrit, none of which is a mother language of the others nor a direct ancestor of German.

20. George Metcalf, "The Indo-European Hypothesis in the Sixteenth and Seventeenth Centuries," in *Studies in the History of Linguistics: Traditions and Paradigms*, ed. Dell Hymes (Bloomington: Indiana University Press, 1974).

21. Ephraim Chambers, *Cyclopaedia or, A Universal Dictionary of Arts and Sciences* (London: James and John Knapton et al., 1728), 2:586, http://artfl-project.uchicago.edu/content/chambers-cyclopaedia.

22. Ephraim Chambers et al., *A Supplement to Mr. Chambers's Cyclopedia: or, Universal Dictionary of the Arts and Sciences*, ed. George Scott Lewis, 2 vols. (n.p., 1753), 1: s.v. "Bible., Rhemish."

23. See Johann Gottfried Herder, "Treatise on the Origin of Language," in *Philosophical Writings*, trans. and ed. Michael N. Forster (Cambridge: Cambridge University Press, 2002); and Herder, "This too a Philosophy of History for the Formation of Humanity," in ibid.

24. In 1782 Johann Christoph Adelung coined the name *cultural history* for a phenomenon recently put into practice by Herder. In the "Origin of Language" (1772) and again two years later in "This Too a Philosophy of History," Herder embeds "culture" in a list of characteristics that define a particular people in a particular age and that vary over time: "*arts, science, culture and language*" ("Origin," 160; emphasis in orig.). In the later work, "culture" has moved up to the front of the list (288).

25. Herder, "This too a Philosophy," esp. 285–86 and 325–26. I am indebted to Helge Jordheim for pointing out this appearance of twins in Herder.

26. For a foundational analysis of the temporal distortion involved in creating the "primitive," see Johannes Fabian, *Time and the Other: How Anthropology Makes Its Object* (New York: Columbia University Press, 2002).

27. Gottfried Wilhelm Leibniz was the most widely read proponent of this theory, which identified Greek, Latin, Celtic (including Germanic), Slavic, and Tatar (including

Turkish) as descendants of Scythian (Leibniz, *Neue Abhandlungen über den menschlichen Verstand*, vol. 3 of *Philosophische Werke in vier Bänden*, trans. and ed. Ernst Cassirer [Hamburg: Feliz Meiner, 1996], 276). For more on the Scythian hypothesis, see Jean-Claude Muller, "Early Stages of Language Comparison," *Kratylos* 1956 (31): 1–31; Jack Fellman, "On Sir William Jones and the Scythian Language," *Language Sciences* 34 (1975): 37–38; Fellman, "Further Remarks on the Scythian Language," *Language Sciences* 41 (1976): 19; Gardt, *Geschichte*, 220–21; and Campbell and Poser, *Language Classification*, 18–23. Fellman in particular argues that William Jones adapted the Scythian theory, which he mentions in letters, into his Indo-European theory. Since Jones identifies Scythian with Tartar, however, which constitutes one of his major non-European language families, it makes more sense to say that he is replacing the idea of a Scythian origin for European languages with that of a "Hindu" origin that includes Sanskrit. For more on Leibniz and comparative philology, see Robert H. Robins, "Leibniz and Wilhelm von Humboldt and the History of Comparative Linguistics," in *Leibniz, Humboldt, and the Origins of Comparativism*, ed. Tullio de Mauro and Lia Formigari (Amsterdam: John Benjamins, 1990). For more on the relationship of Goethe to Leibniz, see Mathias Mayer, "Kraft der Sprache: Goethes 'Lebenslied' im Kontext monadischen Denkens," in *Monadisches Denken un Geschichte und Gegenwart*, ed. Sigmund Bonk (Würzburg: Königshausen & Neumann, 2003); and the Leibniz entry in Gero von Wilpert's *Goethe-Lexikon* (Stuttgart: Alfred Kröner, 1998).

28. The English and German words for *barbarian* derive from the Greek word, which was meant to replicate the sound of unintelligible muttering.
29. The orientalist and philologist Johann Gottfried Eichhorn was a close friend of Herder's and met Goethe as a result as well. In 1777 Eichhorn presented Goethe with a copy of Jones's *Poeseos Asiaticś Commentariorum*, as Goethe recalled in his commentary to the *West-östlicher Divan* (Goethe, *Sämtliche Werke* [hereafter SW], 40 vols. Frankfurt am Main: Deutscher Klassiker Verlag, 1991), 1:3.1, 270–71).
30. Goethe, SW, 2.3.220, letter dated January 13, 1787 (trans. mine).
31. Johann Wolfgang von Goethe, *Iphigenia in Tauris*, in *Plays*, trans. Frank Ryder (New York: Continuum, 1993), 136, line 2113. All quotations from *Iphigenia* in English are taken from this translation. German is from Johann Wolfgang von Goethe, *Iphigenie auf Tauris* in SW, 5:553–619, and indicated by line numbers.
32. Since German often uses definite articles instead of possessive pronouns, the slippage between "my sister" and "your sister" is easy to obscure in the original.
33. Impossible to translate, *Bildlichkeit* refers to the figurative nature of language or of an image or object.
34. The drama is thus related to Goethe's 1773 drama fragment Prometheus, in which Prometheus's voice develops through his loving and inner relationship to his sister Minerva. David Wellbery, influenced by Kittler (see note 19, this chapter), interprets this fragment as an expression of the primordial orality that emanates from the mother/child dyad and thus escapes a Law of the Father by predating it (Wellbery, *The Specular Moment: Goethe's Early Lyric and the Beginnings of Romanticism* [Stanford: Stanford

University Press, 1996], 199–212). Like Kittler, Wellbery dismisses the possibility of reading a sister apart from a mother: "Of course, Minerva is not actually ... Prometheus's mother, but she appears in what will become the mother function, much as Psyche in Wieland's *Agathon*, likewise a sister, is transformed into a maternal imago" (201). The sister will indeed be converted into the mother, but not until twentieth-century Freudian theory erased the more complex dynamics of the sibling predominating in the era before it.

35. Iphigenia's revelation of her identity leads Orestes into a hallucination or dream of his family happily reunited and reconciled in Hades. But, as Walter Erhart has suggested, the vision is not what heals him for the vision ends with the progenitor of the family, Tantalus, still in chains (Erhart, "Drama der Anerkennung. Neue gesellshcatstheoretische Überlegungen zu Goethes *Iphigenie auf Tauris*," *Jahrbuch der deutschen Schillergesellschaft* 51 [2007]: 140–65). He recovers because of his "neue Bindungsfähigkeit" to sister and friend (158). Kathryn Brown and Anthony Stephens also see the continued torment of Tantalus in the vision as a sign that the curse has not yet been broken (Brown and Stephens, "'Hinübergehn und unser Haus entsühnen.' Die Ökonomie des Mythischen in Goethes Iphigenie," *Jahrbuch der deutschen Schillergesellschaft* 32 [1988]: 103–5).

36. Goethe, SW, 1:15:1, 221 (trans. mine). For more on the production history of the sketch, see Waltraud Maierhofer, "Angelica Kauffmann Reads Goethe: Illustrations in the Goeschen Edition," *Sophie Journal* 2, no. 1 (2012), http://digitalcommons.mcmaster.ca/sophiejournal/vol2/iss1/1.

37. She and others also consistently refer to this figure as a *Bild* and never as an *idol*, a *fetish*, or even a *statue*. See 112, line 1095; 122, line 1437; 126, line 1564; 130, line 1708; 136, line 1929; 141, line 2100; and 141, line 2106.

38. This work appeared in German translation by Christian Pistorius in 1785.

39. William Pietz, "The Problem of the Fetish, II: The Origin of the Fetish," *RES: Anthropology and Aesthetics*, no. 13 (Spring 1987): 23.

40. According to Hartmut Böhme, Goethe uses the term "fetish" in letters and published work after 1800 (Böhme, *Fetishism and Culture: A Different Theory of Modernity* [Berlin: Walter de Gruyter, 2014], 164). While Böhme speculates that he learned the word from Christoph Meiners around 1800, the term was not rare earlier.

41. Oskar Seidlin once declared Iphigenia "not a man's sister, but *the* sister of man" ("Goethe's *Iphigenia* and the Humane Ideal," in *Goethe: A Collection of Critical Essays*, ed. Victor Lange [Englewood Cliffs, N.J.: Prentice-Hall, 1968], 54). Seidlin finds in her not a human or humane example but a benign ethical tendency, "in which the 'must' and 'shall' are one and the same" (55), a synecdoche indeed, but one in which Iphigenia is "a part" (57) and the brother the whole. I argue here that Goethe is more nuanced than this reading allows for. The brother and sister partake in each other without one subsuming the other. In addition, however, Goethe takes more seriously the threat of incest that Seidlin waves away.

42. See Katja Garloff, "Sublimation and Its Discontents: Christian-Jewish Love in Lessing's Nathan der Weise," *Lessing Yearbook/Jahrbuch* 36 (2004/2005)," for a reading of the

familial denouement as a mechanism for avoiding a mixed marriage without demonstrating intolerance.
43. We will return to Mignon's song in the next chapter.
44. Ernst Cassirer, *The Logic of the Cultural Sciences*, trans. S. G. Lofts (New Haven: Yale University Press, 2000), 75.
45. William Jones, *Discourses Delivered Before the Asiatic Society*, ed. James Elmes, 2 vols. (London: Charles S. Arnold, 1824), 1:28.
46. See Raymond Schwab's classic *The Oriental Renaissance: Europe's Rediscovery of India and the East, 1660–1880*, trans. Gene Patterson-Black and Victor Reinking (New York: Columbia University Press, 1984); and Arvidsson, *Aryan Idols*.
47. Thomas Trautmann also notes the exclusion of mixture from segmentary systems such as the genealogical tree as it developed in the nineteenth century and its social correlates, in *Aryans and British India* (Berkeley: University of California Press, 1997), 11.
48. Some good overviews of the recent debate include Eric Bapteste et al., "Networks: Expanding Evolutionary Thinking," *Trends in Genetics* 29, no. 8 (August 2013), 439–41; L. R. Franklin-Hall, "Trashing Life's Tree," *Biology and Philosophy* 25 (2010): 689–709; and William Martin O'Malley and John Dupré, "The Tree of Life: Introduction to an Evolutionary Debate," *Biology and Philosophy* 25 (2010): 441–53.
49. For a classic account of the evolutionary tree, see Howard E. Gruber, "Darwins's 'Tree of Nature' and Other Images of Wide Scope," in *On Aesthetics in Science*, ed. Judith Wechsler (Cambridge: MIT Press, 1978). Much research has recently appeared about the history of this image. See Julia Voss, *Darwin's Bilder. Ansichten der Evolutionstheorie 1837–1874* (Frankfurt: Fischer Taschenbuch Verlag, 2007); Horst Bredekamp, *Darwins Korallen. Frühe Evolutionsmodelle und die Tradition der Naturgeschichte* (Berlin: Klaus Wagenbach, 2006); Sigrid Weigel, *Genea-Logik. Generation, Tradition und Evolution zwischen Kultur- und Naturwissenschaften* (Munich: Wilhelm Fink, 2006); Theodore W. Pietsch, *Trees of Life: A Visual History of Evolution* (Baltimore: Johns Hopkins University Press, 2012); Nathalie Gontier, "Depicting the Tree of Life: The Philosophical and Historical Roots of Evolutionary Tree Diagrams," *Evolution: Education and Outreach* 4 (2011): 515–38; Mary Bouquet, "Family Trees and Their Affinities: The Visual Imperative of the Genealogical Diagram," *Journal of the Royal Anthropological Institute* 2, no. 1 (March 1996): 43–66; and Nils Petter Hellström, "Darwin and the Tree of Life: The Roots of the Evolutionary Tree," *Archives of Natural History* 39, no. 2 (2012): 234–52. For histories that include the connection between genealogical methods in biology and comparative philology, see John van Wyhe, "The Descent of Words: Evolutionary Thinking 1780–1880," *Endeavour* 29, no. 3 (September 2005); Quentin D. Atkinson and Russell D. Gray, "Curious Connections—Phylogenetic Thinking in Biology and Historical Linguistics," *Systematic Biology* 54, no. 4 (2005): 513–26; and Alter, *Darwinism and the Linguistic Image*.
50. Weigel, *Genea-Logik*, 21–54.
51. For more on the form of family trees as early as sixteenth century, see Volker Bauer, *Wurzel, Stamm, Krone: Fürstliche Genealogie in frühneuzeitlichen Druckwerken* (Wolfenbuuttel, 2013).

52. For a detailed account of the development of this methodology, see Sebastiano Timpanaro, *The Genesis of Lachmann's Method*, ed. and trans. Glenn W. Most (Chicago: University of Chicago Press, 2005). Errington notes the influence of manuscript studies on William Jones (*Linguistics*, 58–64).
53. For more on Zumpt, see Timpanaro, *The Genesis of Lachmann's Method*, 91-94. Schlyter was neither a biblical nor Classical scholar but a Swedish lawyer who published a history of Swedish law. It is unclear if any connections in either direction existed between his manuscript studies and those of the biblical scholars and philologists. See Gösta Holm, "Carl Johan Schlyter and Textual Scholarship," in *Saga Och Sed*, ed. Dag Strömbäck (Uppsala: A. B. Lundequistska Bokhandelsn, 1972).
54. This expression appears in Ritschl's notes from 1837, cited in Timpanaro, *Genesis*, 93n.10. See Timpanaro for this history of stemmata (90–101).
55. Hoenigswald ("On the History of the Comparative Method") points out that Ritschl was the first to pinpoint a copying error made in a manuscript as the site of divergence, of branching. August Schleicher introduced to comparative linguistics the analogous idea that branching accords with innovation in a language (Schleicher, "The Darwinian Theory," 8). One might add that deviation plays the same role in evolutionary theory. See Timpanaro, *Genesis*, as well for Ritschl's influence on Schleicher, and the general correspondence between textual philology and comparative historical linguistics.
56. On the other hand, Schleicher and Čelakovský were both professors at Charles University in Prague for two years, during which the trees in question were published. For conjectures about possible influences between the two, see T. M. S. Priestly, "Schleicher, Čelakovský, and the Family-Tree Diagram," *Historigraphia Linguistica* 2, no. 3 (1975): 299–333.
57. For differing interpretations, see Bowler, *Evolution*, 79–83; Weigel, *Genea-Logik*, 209–15, Bredekamp, *Darwins Korallen*,15–16; and Pietsch, "Trees of Life," 34–35.
58. Charles Darwin, *The Origin of Species*, ed. Gilliam Beer (Oxford: Oxford University Press, 1996), 171–72.
59. The question of one versus many origins—monogenesis or polygenesis—is still active in linguistics and played a major role in in race theory before Darwin. We will return to this debate in the next chapter.
60. Johannes Schmidt, *Die Verwandtschaftsverhältnisse der Indogermanischen Sprachen* (Weimar: Hermann Böhlau, 1872), 19 (trans. mine).
61. Sarah Grey Thomason and Terrence Kaufman, *Language Contact, Creolization, and Genetic Linguistics* (Berkeley: University of California Press, 1988), 255.
62. See, for example, George Lang's insistence that "creoles and creolization are perfectly natural phenomena," in *Entwisted Tongues: Comparative Creole Literatures* (Amsterdam: Rodopi, 2000), 2; and Thomason and Kaufman's study of contact languages as departures from the genetic model. Thomason and Kaufman claim that it is impossible for a language to have multiple ancestors, and that therefore contact languages have no genetic relations (*Language Contact*, 11). See Peter Mühlhäusler, *Pidgin and Creole Languages* (London: University of Westminster Press, 1997), 1–21 and 222–43; and Suzanne Romaine, *Pidgin & Creole Languages* (London: Longman, 1988), 1–24, for

contemporary overviews and histories of the field of pidgin and creole studies. For more on Schuchardt, see A. V. Issatschenko, "Allegmeine Fragestellungen bei H. Schuchardt und in der heutigen Sprachwissenschaft," in *Hugo Schuchardt. Schuchardt-Symposium 1977 in Graz*, ed. Klaus Lichem and Hans Joachim Simon (Vienna: Verlag der Österreichischen Akademie der Wissenschaften, 1980). See also Hugo Schuchardt, "Zu meiner Schrift, Slawo-deutsches und Slawo-italienisches," *Zeitschrift für die österreichischen Gymnasien* 37 (1886): 321–51; Schuchardt, "Review of Max Grünbaum: Mischsprachen und Sprachmischungen," *Internationale Zeitschrift für allgemeine Sprachwissenschaft* 3 (1887): 291; and Schuchardt, *The Ethnography of Variation: Selected Writings on Pidgins and Creoles*, ed. and trans. T. L. Markey (Ann Arbor, Mich.: Karoma, 1979).

63. One exception is Max Grünbaum's *Mischsprachen und Sprachmischungen* (1886), which used Yiddish as one of several examples (*Mischsprachen und Sprachmischungen*, no. 473 in *Sammlung Gemeinverständlicher Wissenschaftlicher Vorträge*, ed. Rudolf Virchow and Fr. von Holtzendorff [Berlin: Verlag von Carl Habel, 1885]). Schuchardt dismissed the volume as unscientific (*Internationale Zeitschrift für allgemeine Sprachwissenschaft*) and as "absolutely without value" (Zeitschrift für die österreichischen Gymnasien) without offering grounds for the judgment. For the ways in which Yiddish did enter German discourse, see Jeffrey A. Grossman, *The Discourse on Yiddish in Germany from the Enlightenment to the Second Empire* (Rochester, NY: Camden House, 2000).

64. See Georg Toepfer on the uses of the words *history* and *evolution* in the nineteenth century. As fervidly as linguists repudiated the term history, those in fields that were becoming the humanities embraced it. Toepfer, "Terminologische Entdifferenzierung in zwei gegenläufigen Übertragungsvorgängen: 'Geschichte' und 'Evolution' der Kultur und Natur," *Forum Interdisziplinäre Begriffsgeschichte* 3 (2014): 28–46. Wilhelm Dilthey, in theorizing the different goals of the humanities and the sciences in 1910, not only referred to the object of the humanities as „human-socio-historical reality" (103), but credited the humanities with creative powers: „the formation of the historical world occurs in the humanities" (109). Wilhelm Dilthey, "The Formation of the Historical World in the Human Sciences," Trans. Rudolf A. Makkreel and John Scanlon, *Selected Works*, ed. Rudolf A. Makkreel and Frithjof Rodi (Princeton: Princeton University Press, 2002) III: 101–211.

65. See the *Wörterbücher* of Adelung and of the Grimms.

66. Wilhelm von Humboldt, "Über die Verschiedenheit des menschlichen Sprachbaues und ihren Einfluss auf die geistige Entwicklung des Menschengeschlechts," in *Werke in Fünf Bänden*, ed. Andreas Flitner and Klause Giel (Stuttgart: J. G. Cotta'sche Buchhandlung, 1965), 382.

67. Wilhelm von Humboldt, *On Language: The Diversity of Human Language Structure and Its Influence on the Mental Development of Mankind*, trans. Peter Heath (Cambridge: Cambridge University Press, 1988), 20.

68. Jakob and Wilhelm Grimm, *Deutsches Wörterbuch (1854–1971)*, s.v. Verzweigung, http://dwb.uni-trier.de/de/.

69. While linguistics focused on diversification, the groupings of languages into families also joined various groups of speakers into kinship constellations. These will be discussed in the next chapter.

70. I conform to Friedrich Max Müller's own formulation of his surname as Max Müller.
71. Friedrich Max Müller, *Lectures on the Science of Language* (London: Longmans, Green, 1866), 1:76–78.
72. Max Müller describes change in language as neither history (which requires will) nor organic growth but instead like geological change—a physical rather than a biological science (*Science of Language*, 1:73–74), an indication also of deep disagreements between Max Müller, on the one hand, and Schlegel and Humboldt, on the other. See Masuzawa's excellent discussion in *World Religions*, especially 218–27, which establishes these differences persuasively. On the other hand, Max Müller's consistent metaphorical language of blood and race had predictable consequences, which he was willing to risk in order to borrow their rhetorical power.
73. Stephen Alter claims that after 1860 Max Müller retreats from a story of genealogical branching toward one of unification in order to disrupt the increasingly popular analogy between linguistics and evolutionary theory, which Max Müller rejected. Alter misinterprets Max Müller's writings on dialects, however, which in no way depart from the commitment to outward diversification. Max Müller rejects the idea that a written, stable language is the mother of the dialects surrounding it, in favor of the claim that every language is a dialect. A recognized or written language is a dialect that has been favored by a cultural or political development. Max Müller also rejects the idea that an ideal language typus could be said to have existed. At every historical moment, a language, to borrow terminology Max Müller would have shied away from, is already a species and never a genus. See Alter, *Darwinism and the Linguistic Image*, 79–96, for his interpretation. Max Müller denies language mixing in the passage cited, just after his discussion of dialects in the same lecture.
74. William Dwight Whitney, "Strictures on the Views of August Schleicher Respecting the Nature of Language and Kindred Subjects," *Transactions of the American Philological Association* 2 (1871): 51.
75. See also Benes, *Babel's Shadow*, 269–82.
76. William Dwight Whitney, *Language and the Study of Language: Twelve Lectures on the Principles of Linguistic Science* (1867; Hildesheim: Georg Olms Verlag, 1973), 198–99.
77. Humboldt called language an "internally connected organism" (*On Language*, 21) in his Kawi work, and Schlegel, Franz Bopp, and Jakob Grimm also used organic terms to describe language. Schleicher referred to words as organisms in *Die Sprachen Europas in systematischer Übersicht*, ed. Konrad Koerner, 1850 (Amsterdam: John Benjamins, 1983), 9). By 1860 he would claim that "the languages, these highest of all natural organisms, [are] formed out of the material of sound [aus lautlichem Stoffe]" (*Die deutsche Sprache* [Stuttgart: J. G. Cotta'scher Verlad, 1860], 33). See Errington, *Linguistics*, 70–92, for an overview of the rhetoric of organicism in reference to languages. When Errington interprets Schleicher's move as one of literalizing what were previously organic metaphors, however, he overlooks the conceptual history of the word *organism*, which derived from "organized being." Languages, like living beings, were thought to be organized in a similarly integral fashion, with reciprocal bonds between parts and between parts and the whole, and therefore to deserve equal access

to the word organism. While using the word strongly linked living beings with languages as possessing a shared quality, as late as midcentury it did not quite designate a language a living being. By the time Schleicher uses the word, however, it has lost this ambiguity and he is indeed designating a language a living being.

78. Errington, *Linguistics*, 83; see also 2.
79. Darwin states repeatedly "that there is no fundamental distinction between species and varieties" (*Origin*, 290; see also 104, 266, 288).
80. Elizabeth Grosz, *Becoming Undone: Darwinian Reflections on Life, Politics, and Art* (Durham: Duke University Press, 2011), 17. Devin Griffiths turns to Darwin's "comparative understanding of the past" precisely for his ability to reconstruct "the complexity and indeterminacy of previous events" (*The Age of Analogy* 235). Griffiths recognizes comparison in this sense as a process for working through analogies within changing historical contexts, a capacity that Darwin shares with the historical fiction that composed much of his reading. Devin Griffiths, *The Age of Analogy: Science and Literature between the Darwins* (Baltimore: Johns Hopkins University Press, 2016).
81. Friedrich Max Müller, "Max Muller on Darwin's Philosophy of Language," *Nature*, December 26, 1872, 145, http://digital.library.wisc.edu/1711.dl/HistSciTech.Nature18721226. Max Müller's choice of black and white overlays racial with epistemological concerns.
82. Darwin could have had additional motives for shying away from the term *sister species*. Evolution focused on reproduction and existential competition, two pursuits Victorians would have been reluctant to associate with sisters. Moreover, Darwin acknowledged the possibility of hybridization between closely related species, which would have translated into sororal incest.
83. Ernst Mayr, "Speciation Phenomena in Birds," *American Naturalist* 74, no. 752 (1940): 258, 259.
84. Johann Wolfgang von Goethe, *Wilhelm Meister's Apprenticeship*, ed. and trans. Eric A. Blackall, vol. 9 of *The Collected Works* (Princeton: Princeton University Press, 1989), 357.
85. George Eliot, "Brother and Sister," in *The Complete Shorter Poems*, ed. A. G. van den Broek (London: Pickering & Chatto, 2005), 2:5. Eliot read Darwin's *On the Origin of Species* when it first appeared, and reverberations throughout her work have been explored by Gillian Beer, *Darwin's Plots: Evolutionary Narrative in Darwin, George Eliot and Nineteenth-Century Fiction* (London: Routledge & Kegan Paul, 1983); Mary Jean Corbett, *Family Likeness: Sex, Marriage, and Incest from Jane Austen to Virginia Woolf* (Ithaca, N.Y.: Cornell University Press, 2008), 115–44; and Nancy Paxton, *George Eliot and Herbert Spencer: Feminism, Evolutionism, and the Reconstruction of Gender* (Princeton: Princeton University Press, 1991).
86. Isaac Evans cut off all contact with Eliot after she began living openly with the married George H. Lewes and did not resume contact until, after Lewes's death, Eliot married John Cross.
87. One exception is Margaret Homans, who looks beyond the roughly autobiographical import to give an immanent reading in which the narrator's "transformation of perception into love prevents the transformation of perception into the Wordsworthian,

visionary imagination" and thus forecloses the becoming-poet of a sister too invested in the "brother tongue" (Homans, "Eliot, Wordsworth, and the Scenes of the Sisters' Instruction," *Critical Inquiry* 8, no. 2 [Winter 1981]: 223–41). I argue here, to the contrary, that such sibling interaction in the poem fosters linguistic creativity on both sides.

88. In his "Studies in Animal Life" (1860), written in the wake of Darwin's *Origin of Species*, Lewes embarks on an extended discussion of the "extreme vagueness" of the concept "species" (G. H. Lewes, "Studies in Animal Life," *Cornhill Magazine* 1, no. 4 [1860]: 442–47) and concludes that "the thing Species does not exist" (443). Lewes goes on to compare evolution to philology (445–47) and calls the "anatomical investigation of the internal structure of animals" a "reading of the contents" (439) in an extended analogy between the classification of organisms and that of books. It seems likely that Lewes has been reading Melville's *Moby Dick* (1851), in which the narrator, tongue in cheek, classifies whales into folio sizes; Lewes uses whales as his example.

89. The connection between philology and philosophy for Nietzsche was neglected for a century before scholars began to look at the issue in the late 1980s. James Porter, *Nietzsche and the Philology of the Future* (Stanford: Stanford University Press, 2000); and Christian Benne, *Nietzsche und die historisch-kritische Philologie* (Berlin: Walter de Gruyter, 2005), are useful books on the topic published in the early 2000s. A handful of articles have also appeared, but the field has not attracted as much critical attention as it deserves. See excellent, though opposing, articles by Alan Schrift, "Genealogy and the Transvaluation of Philology," *International Studies in Philosophy* 20, no. 2 (1988): 85–95; and Anthony Jensen, "Meta-Historical Transitions from Philology to Genealogy," *Journal of Nietzsche Studies* 44, no. 2 (2013): 196–212. Richard Gray's reflections on similarities between Schlegel and Nietzsche on the goals on philology are insightful but incomplete as they do not include thoughts on those aspects of philology that became linguistics ("Skeptische Philologie: Friedrich Schlegel, Friedrich Nietzsche und eine Philologie der Zukunft," *Nietzsche-Studien* 38 [2009]: 39–64). Porter's groundbreaking book similarly neglects connections between classical philology and linguistics. Benne corrects this oversight.

90. The history of philology has become a topic of increasing interest. See most recently James Turner, *Philology: The Forgotten Origins of the Modern Humanities* (Princeton: Princeton University Press, 2015); Geoffrey Galt Harpham, "Roots, Races, and the Return to Philology," *Representations* 106, no. 1 (Spring 2009): 34-62; and the essays in Sean Gurd, *Philology and Its Histories* (Columbus: Ohio State University Press, 2010) and in Sheldon Pollock, Benjamin Elman, and Ku-ming Kevin Chang, *World Philology* (Cambridge: Harvard University Press, 2015).

91. Friedrich Nietzsche, *Nietzsches Werke. Kritische Gesamtausgabe* [KG], ed. Giorgio Colli and Mazzino Montinari (Berlin: Walter der Gruyter, 1967), 4.1:91.

92. With Ritschl as their joint Doktorvater—literally Doctoral Father—Nietzsche and August Schieicher were academic brothers. For Ritschl's influence on Nietzsche, see Benne, *Nietzsche*. For Ritschl's influence on Schleicher, see Hoenigswald, "On the

History of the Comparative Method"; and Timpanaro, *Genesis*. Schleicher was among his earliest and Nietzsche among his last students.

93. Michel Foucault, "Nietzsche, Genealogy, History," in *Language, Counter-memory, Practice: Selected Essays and Interviews*, ed. Donald F. Bouchard, trans. Donald F. Bouchard and Sherry Simon (Ithaca: Cornell University Press, 1977), 140.

94. Friedrich Nietzsche, *On the Genealogy of Morality*, ed. Keith Ansell-Pearson, trans. Carol Diethe (Cambridge: Cambridge University Press, 2007), 5, 6.

95. Dirk Johnson has recently analyzed Nietzsche's reaction against the Spencerian Social Darwinism Nietzsche and contemporaries associated with Darwin. While Johnson focuses on human culture in his discussion of evolution, see his discussion of Will to Power as an explanation of nonhuman transformation in *Nietzsche's Anti-Darwinism* (Cambridge: Cambridge University Press, 2010), 45–66. John Richardson, in addition to offering a more nuanced reading of Nietzsche on Social Darwinism, takes seriously Nietzsche's critique of Darwinian evolution in organisms generally. After putting aside Nietzsche's misunderstandings of Darwin, Richardson explores the similarities between Nietzsche's concept of organic change and that theorized by Darwin as Richardson understands him. See Richardson, *Nietzsche's New Darwinism* (Oxford: Oxford University Press, 2004).

5. THE EAST COMES HOME

1. James Cowles Prichard, *The Eastern Origin of the Celtic Nations Proved by a Comparison of Their Dialects with the Sanskrit, Greek, Latin, and Teutonic Languages* (London: Houlston and Wright, 1857), 9; Charles Darwin, *The Origin of Species*, ed. Gilliam Beer (Oxford: Oxford University Press, 1996), 406.

2. See Catherine Minter, *The Mind-Body Problem in German Literature, 1770–1830: Wezel, Moritz, and Jean Paul* (Oxford: Clarendon, 2002), 1–8; and Hans-Peter Nowitzki, *Der wohltemperierte Mensch: Aufklärungsanthropologien im Widerstreit* (Berlin: Walter de Gruyter, 2003).

3. Ernest Renan, "What Is a Nation?," trans. Martin Thom, in *Nation and Narration*, ed. Homi Bhabha (London: Routledge, 1990), 16–17.

4. For an illuminating overview of the shifting ethnicities to whom genealogical descent was assigned by various biblical peoples over two thousand years, see William McKee Evans, "From the Land of Canaan to the Land of Guinea: The Strange Odyssey of the 'Sons of Ham,'" *American Historical Review* 85, no. 1 (1980): 15–43. We have already encountered the significance of the Noahdic genealogy in the philological theories of William Jones and Max Müller in the previous chapter.

5. See Zoltán Szombathy, "Genealogy in Medieval Muslim Societies," *Studia Islamica* 95 (2002), esp. 19–21.

6. Gen. 9:27, *Oxford Annotated Bible*, ed. Herbert May and Bruce Metzger (New York: Oxford University Press, 1977).

7. There has been a tendency to "blame" race on Johann Friedrich Blumenbach, or more recently on Immanuel Kant. See, for example, Robert Bernasconi, "Who Invented the Concept of Race? Kant's Role in the Enlightenment Construction of Race," in *Race*, ed. Robert Bernasconi (Malden, Mass.: Blackwell, 2001). While Kant had a large impact on race theory and Blumenbach on racial designations, I would agree with John Zammito's warning against presuming a "'monogenetic'" origin of race theory, not least because of the tendency of older Biblical genealogies to intertwine with the newer theories. See "Policing Polygeneticism in Germany 1775: (Kames,) Kant, and Blumenbach," in *The German Invention of Race*, ed. Sara Eigen and Mark Larrimore (Albany: State University of New York Press, 2006), 35.
8. For overviews of this history, see Shirley Roe, *Matter, Life, and Generation: Eighteenth-Century Embryology and the Haller-Wolff Debate* (Cambridge: Cambridge University Press, 1981); and Clara Pinto-Correia, *The Ovary of Eve. Egg and Sperm and Preformationism* (Chicago: University of Chicago Press, 1997).
9. For more on race and the preformationism-epigenesis debate, see my *Anxious Anatomy: The Conception of the Human Form in Literary and Naturalist Discourse* (Albany: State University of New York Press, 2008), 224–32.
10. Leonore Davidoff, *Thicker Than Water: Siblings and Their Relations, 1780–1920* (Oxford: Oxford University Press, 2012), 58.
11. The polygenetic argument arose with the discovery of the Americas and the attempt to place Native Americans in a biblical history. The view was brought to popular attention by two British writers in 1774: the Scottish Enlightenment author Henry Homes, Lord Kames, tentatively espoused polygenesis, still embedding the story in a biblical narrative, while Edward Long in the same year converted polygenesis into a naturalist claim and used it to legitimate slavery. Voltaire and David Hume both repeated polygenetic claims in hierarchical forms that denigrated Africans, while Georg Forster advanced a somewhat more egalitarian polygenetic view. For more on the development of polygenesis as a theory, see Richard Popkin, *The High Road to Pyrrhonism* (Indianapolis: Hackett, 1980), 79–102; and Robert Bernasconi, "Who Invented the Concept of Race?" For the rise of polygenesis in the nineteenth century, see Nancy Stepan, *The Idea of Race in Science: Great Britain 1800–1960* (Basingstoke: Macmillan, 1982); Martin Staum, *Labeling People: French Scholars on Society, Race and Empire, 1815–1848* (Montreal: McGill-Queen's University Press, 2003); and B. Ricardo Brown, *Until Darwin: Science, Human Variety and the Origins of Race* (London: Pickering & Chatto, 2010).
12. Immanuel Kant, "Of the Different Human Races" (1777), in *Kant and the Concept of Race: Late Eighteenth-Century Writings*, trans. and ed. Jon M. Mikkelsen (Albany: State University of New York Press, 2013), 60. Early monogenesists included the Comte de Buffon, Johann Friedrich Blumenbach, Kant, William Lawrence, and James Cowles Prichard.
13. The extent of theorized flexibility varied, and some races were thought to be more distinct than others. In general, Europeans perceived white and black as the most divergent races, with concomitant places in their self-devised hierarchies.

14. Significant European polygenesists included Edward Long, Charles White, Christoph Meiners, Georg Forster, and Julien-Joseph Virey. Polygenesis was also embraced by prominent apologists for slavery in the United States, such as Samuel Morton, George Gliddon, and Josiah Nott. See Ricardo Brown for more on the American school. Brown rightly points out that there were monogenist defenders of slavery and polygenist abolitionists (such as George Squire and, although Brown does not mention him, Georg Forster). Brown, *Until Darwin*, 60.
15. Buffon adapted this definition from the sixteenth-century English naturalist John Ray. The definition was complicated by several known exceptions that even Buffon mentioned, however. Blumenbach therefore preferred a definition based on morphological similarity and breeding behavior in the wild, although he acknowledged the difficulties in specifying what counted as similar enough in the former criterion and the difficulty in testing the latter criterion among animals geographically separated. (Blumenbach, *Über die natürlichen Verschiedenheiten im Menschengeschlechte* [Leipzig: Breitkopf und Härtel, 1798], vol. 5 of *Concepts of Race in the Eighteenth Century*, ed. Robert Bernasconi [Bristol: Thoemmes Press, 2001]), 59–60). Kant held tenaciously to Buffon's definition in spite of its known problems, rejecting Blumenbach's first criterion because he was committed to generation over morphology in classification, and rejecting Blumenbach's second criterion because he tended towards a view of natural repulsion from interracial intercourse, as discussed above. As seen in the previous chapter, Darwin agreed with Blumenbach here.
16. Immanuel Kant, "Determination of the Concept of a Human Race" (1785), in *Kant and the Concept of Race: Late Eighteenth-Century Writings*, 134; AA 8:97.
17. Robert Young has described the way race theories were also theories of sexuality and of desire in the mid- to late nineteenth century, and Ann Laura Stoler has recorded the ways in which the sexual biopolitics of the nineteenth century was thoroughly implicated in the creation and maintenance of racial categories. This constellation had an earlier origin, however. See Robert Young, *Colonial Desire: Hybridity in Theory, Culture and Race* (London: Routledge: 1995); and Ann Laura Stoler, *Race and the Education of Desire: Foucault's History of Sexuality and the Colonial Order of Things* (Durham: Duke University Press, 1995).
18. See Immanuel Kant, "On the Use of Teleological Principles in Philosophy," in *Kant and the Concept of Race*, 179; AA 8:166–67. Georg Forster described this aversion in nearly the same language Gobineau would use some seventy-five years later, noting "disgust from the raw, unsophisticated peasant . . . [who] will avoid the Negro woman" ("Something More About the Human Races" [1786], in *Kant and the Concept of Race*, 157). Forster supports his view in the face of actual mixing by borrowing from his rival Kant a detailed description of how humans may acquire desires that go against their natural instincts, which Kant refers to as "lasciviousness" ("Conjectures on the Beginning of Human History," in *Kant: Political Writings*, ed. Hans Reiss and trans. H. B. Nisbet [Cambridge: Cambridge University Press, 1991], 223).
19. See David Bindman, *Ape to Apollo: Aesthetics and the Idea of Race in the Eighteenth Century* (Ithaca: Cornell University Press, 2002); and George Mosse, *Towards the*

Final Solution: A History of European Racism (Madison: University of Wisconsin Press, 1985), 17–34 in particular.

20. Pieter Camper was a Dutch sculptor, physician, and naturalist who created a scale of facial proportions with Greek statuary at the apex and Africans at the nadir. Charles Darwin, *The Descent of Man, and Selection in Relation to Sex* (London: Penguin, 2004), 621–75.
21. See Elizabeth Grosz's fascinating discussion of sexual selection, *Becoming Undone: Darwinian Reflections on Life, Politics, and Art* (Durham: Duke University Press, 2011), 115–42.
22. This question evolved into the protest slogan "I *am* a man" used in the Memphis Sanitation Strike of 1968 and later civil rights protests. See Steve Estes, *"I Am A Man." Race, Manhood, and the Civil Rights Movement* (Chapel Hill: University of North Carolina Press, 2005). It appeared again in 2015, where it was joined by "I am a woman," until "Black lives matter" emerged as the more popular motto. Interestingly, siblinghood has disappeared from these mottos, perhaps because "brother" and "sister" in American English can tend to mean "black." C. Dallett Hemphill records that African Americans used the terms widely for each other—whether related or not—as far back in American history as can be determined. Hemphill, *Siblings: Brothers and Sisters in American History* (Oxford: Oxford University Press, 2011), 186.
23. For the history of this image, see Sam Margolin, "'And Freedom to the Slave': Antislavery Ceramics, 1787–1865," *Ceramics in America* (2002): 81–109. Josiah Wedgwood, who designed the abolitionist medallion, was Darwin's grandfather (and that of his wife and cousin, Emma Wedgwood. Charles Darwin's sister Caroline Sarah Darwin married Emma Wedgwood's brother, Josiah Wedgwood III, so that the Darwin-Wedgwood clan is a prime example of the kind of sibling network described in chapter 3).
24. James Hunt, "The President's Address," *Journal of the Anthropological Society of London* 5 (1867): lxiii.
25. Johann Friedrich Blumenbach, *On the Natural Varieties of Mankind*, trans. Thomas Bendyshe (1865) (New York: Bergman, 1969), vii.
26. See Annette Gordon-Reed, *Thomas Jefferson and Sally Hemings: An American Controversy* (Charlottesville: University of Virginia Press, 1997); Marie Jenkins Schwartz, *Ties that Bound: Founding First Ladies and Slaves* (Chicago: University of Chicago Press, 2017), 64–65.
27. In fact, the word *Kultur* itself was introduced to German at this time by Johann Christoph Adelung. For a history the emergence of a new "science of culture" in the 1770s and 1780s in Germany, see Michael Carhart, *The Science of Culture in Enlightenment Germany* (Cambridge: Harvard University Press, 2007), 1–2.
28. August Ludwig Schlözer, *Vorstellung seiner Universal-Historie*, 2 vols. (Göttingen: Dieterich, 1772), 1:102. See also Han Vermeulen, "The German Invention of Völkerkunde: Ethnological Discourse in Europe and Asia, 1740–1798," in *The German Invention of Race*, ed. Sara Eigen and Mark Larrimore (Albany: State University of New York Press, 2006), 128–31; and Vermeulen, "Origins and Institutionalization of Ethnography and

Ethnology in Europe and the USA, 1771–1845," in *Fieldwork and Footnotes: Studies in the History of European Anthropology*, ed. Han Vermeulen and Arturo Alvarez Roldán (London: Routledge, 1995).

29. August Ludwig Schlözer, "Von den Chaldäern," vol. 8 of *Repertorium für biblische und morgenländische Literatur*, ed. Johann Gottfried Eichhorn (1781), 119, 161 (trans. mine). Herder soon picked up the term *Semitic* in his treatise on "The Spirit of Hebrew Poetry." See Maurice Olender, *The Languages of Paradise: Race, Religion, and Philology in the Nineteenth Century*, trans. Arthur Goldhammer. (Cambridge: Harvard University Press, 1992), 11–12.

30. Friedrich Schlegel, *Über die Sprache und die Weisheit der Indier* (Amsterdam: John Benjamins, 1977).

31. Friedrich Schlegel, "Über J. G. Rhode," in *Kritische Friedrich-Schlegel-Ausgabe*, ed. Ernst Behler (1819) (Zürich: Thomas-Verlag, 1975), 518.

32. Eric Sharpe, *Comparative Religion: A History* (New York: Charles Scribner's Sons, 1975), 32. This year 1859 is frequently accepted as the beginning of the discipline. See also Arie Molendijk, *The Emergence of the Science of Religion in the Netherlands* (Leiden: E. J. Brill, 2005); and Sigurd Hjelde, *Die Religionswissenschaft & das Christentum* (Leiden: E. J. Brill, 1994). For accounts that move the origin back into the eighteenth and sixteenth centuries, respectively, see Robert Baird, "How Religion Became Scientific," in *Religion in the Making*, ed. Arie Molendijk and Peter Pels (Leiden: E. J. Brill, 1998); and Guy Stroumsa, *A New Science: The Discovery of Religion in the Age of Reason* (Cambridge: Harvard University Press, 2010). In an excellent article, Peter Byrne delineates three ways to conceive the neutral, "scientific" approach to religion: naturalistically, phenomenologically, and through a cultural-symbolic approach. He traces the naturalistic approach back to David Hume. Byrne attributes the phenomenological method—in which Christian doctrine is justified through comparison—to Rudolf Otto and finds the origin of the cultural-symbolic approach in Herder and Hegel. I claim here, however, that in *Nathan the Wise*, Lessing applies Herder's cultural methodology more directly to religion, and that he provides a less hierarchical cultural approach than Hegel. Peter Byrne, "The Study of Religion: Neutral, Scientific, or Neither?," in *Method & Theory in the Study of Religion* 9, no. 4 (1997): 339–51. See also David Hume, "The Natural History of Religion," *A Dissertation on the Passions and The Natural History of Religion*, ed. Tom L. Beauchamp (Oxford: Clarendon, 2007), 33–87.

33. For an analysis of *Udohla* within a set of concerns also germane to this chapter, see Stefani Engelstein, "*Sibling Incest and Cultural Voyeurism in Günderode's* Udohla *and Thomas Mann's* Wälsungenblut," *German Quarterly* 77, no. 3 (July 2004): 278–99.

34. Persia is also the site of Baron de Montesquieu's *Persian Letters* (1721), which contains a tale of sibling incest in which the sister is also named Astarte. This tale takes place in a setting cohabited by Zoroastrians, who permit sibling marriage, and Muslims, who prohibit it.

35. The identification of Mignon as the daughter of Augustine and Sperata remains tenuous in this novel of uncertain parentage. There are of course some narratives that handle sibling incest without invoking the Muslim margins of Europe, from the

mid-eighteenth-century *Das Leben der Schwedischen Gräfin von G**** by Christian Gellert, to Gothic novels like Matthew Gregory Lewis's *The Monk*, to Ludwig Tieck's Romantic novella *Der blonde Eckbert*. Others, such as Jane Austen's *Mansfield Park*, play out against a slaveholding colonial Caribbean. The combination of sibling eroticism with Muslim-Christian relations is pervasive enough, however, to require explanation.

36. See Stroumsa, *A New Science*, 124–44.
37. Lessing first published a less controversial segment of Reimarus's manuscript in 1774 without much public reaction and then issued the five fragments that instigated the controversy in 1777 and a seventh fragment in 1778. For more, see Jonathan Hess, *Germans, Jews and the Claims of Modernity* (New Haven: Yale University Press, 2002), 114–118; Toshimasa Yasukata, *Lessing's Philosophy of Religion and the German Enlightenment: Lessing on Christianity and Reason* (New York: Oxford University Press, 2002), 1–43; and Charles H. Talbert, *Introduction to Fragments by Hermann Samuel Reimarus*, trans. Ralph S. Fraser (Philadelphia: Fortress, 1970).
38. For a more detailed analysis of Lessing and Reimarus that expands on my reading here, see my "Coining a Discipline: Lessing, Reimarus, and a Science of Religion," in *Fact and Fiction: Literature and Science in the European Context*, ed. Christine Lehleiter (Toronto: University of Toronto Press, 2016), 221–46.
39. Willi Goetschel, "Lessing's 'Jewish' Questions," *Germanic Review* 78, no. 1 (2003), esp. 63.
40. Helmut Schneider, "Der Zufall der Geburt: Lessings Nathan der Weise und der imaginäre Körper der Geschichtsphilosophie," in *Körper / Kultur: Kalifornische Studien zur deutschen Moderne*, ed. Thomas W. Kniesche (Würzburg: Königshausen and Neumann, 1995), esp. 176.
41. Carl Niekerk demonstrates Lessing's familiarity with the climatological anthropology of the time and demonstrates its influence on *Nathan the Wise*. One of the most popular such works in Germany was Cornelius de Pauw's account of the Americas, translated by Lessing's brother, Karl Lessing. Carl Niekerk, "Der Anthropologische Diskurs in Lessings *Nathan der Weise*," *Neophilologus* 88 (2004): 229.
42. We will encounter the significant word *Stamm* throughout this chapter. I generally translate it as lineage, but it equally means *tribe* and the *trunk* of a tree. I will note the German when the word arises. (Gotthold Ephraim Lessing, "Commentary on the Fragments of Reimarus," *Philosophical and Theological Writings*, ed. and trans. H. B. Nisbet [Cambridge: Cambridge University Press, 2005], 70, trans. modified.) Note the similarity to Schlegel's later claim, cited previously, that the Japhetic peoples dwell in the house of Shem.
43. For the anti-Jewish elements of the maturation of civilization argument Lessing employs, see Martha B. Helfer, *The Word Unheard: Legacies of Anti-Semitism in German Literature and Culture* (Evanston, Ill.: Northwestern University Press, 2011), 4–8.
44. Gotthold Ephraim Lessing, "The Education of the Human Race," in *Philosophical and Theological Writings*, 218.
45. See Karl Guthke, "Die Geburt des Nathan aus dem Geist der Reimarus-Fragmente," *Lessing Yearbook/Jahrbuch* 36 (2004/2005): 17–18. Guthke notes that both Reimarus

and Lessing focus on the monotheistic religions while acknowledging the much greater diversity around the world. As he mentions, in Lessing's Jerusalem one encounters "'Franken,' Inder, 'Mohren,' Agypter, Araber, Parsen ('Gheber'), Juden und Mohammedaner, selbstverständlich, aber auch ein 'Wilder'" (24). The "savage" is, with Lessing's typical irony, a European Christian.

46. Alain Schnapp, "Antiquarian Studies in Naples at the End of the Eighteenth Century: From Comparative Archaeology to Comparative Religion," in *Naples in the Eighteenth Century: The Birth and Death of a Nation State*, ed. Girolamo Imbroglia (Cambridge: Cambridge University Press, 2000), 162.

47. English citations to the play are taken from Gotthold Ephraim Lessing, *Nathan the Wise*, trans. and ed. Ronald Schechter (Boston: Bedford, 2004).

48. See also Niekerk, "Der Anthropologische Diskurs," on the impact and reach of climate as a medium of change in anthropology of the period. Interestingly, language is missing from this ethnological description. The common language in which the characters communicate is never thematized, although Nathan mentions that Wolf von Filnek preferred to speak Persian, and we learn that he inscribed his genealogy in his Christian breviary in Arabic. Even before William Jones, Persian was recognized as related to European languages, while Arabic, like Hebrew, was classified into a different family.

49. Al-Hafi is variously described as a Parsi, a Gheber, and a Dervish. The last of these designations conflicts with the first two, however. The Parsis are a Zoroastrian sect in India, which al-Hafi also mentions as his homeland (*Nathan*, 61). Gheber is a European word for a Zoroastrian, and there is evidence in the text that al-Hafi considers his religion to be other than the three monotheistic religions (51). On the other hand, Dervishes constitute a Muslim Sufi sect. R. H. Farquharson provides a convincing reading of Lessing's sources on Dervishes and Zoroastrians to suggest that he likely intended the character to be Zoroastrian rather than Muslim. Farquharson, "Lessing's Dervish and the Mystery of the Dervish-Nachspiel," *Lessing Yearbook* 18 (1986): 47–67.

50. Gotthold Ephraim Lessing, *Werke und Briefe*, 12 vols., ed. Wilfried Barner (Frankfurt am Main: Deutscher Klassiker Verlag, 1989), 9:533. All references to the German are from this source. The fact that Nathan rejects the identification of the individual with the group does not constitute a rejection of the idea of belonging to a group. Nathan wears identifiably Jewish clothing or other outward indicators, as evidenced by the Templar's identification of him as Jewish as he approaches (*Nathan*, 54), and during his interview with the Sultan he is determined not to convert. Moreover, while he points out that evidence of goodness, which inspires the Christian lay brother to call a person a Christian, simultaneously inspires *Nathan himself* to call that person a Jew (98), he does not reject either label in favor of a more universal designation. Nathan is committed to elucidating what religions share, and also to maintaining their distinctness. See Benjamin Bennett for a related but not identical argument that *Nathan the Wise* promotes belonging to a tradition—which Bennett, however, equates with blood-relatedness—as "rationally arbitrary but realistically necessary." Bennett, "Reason,

Error and the Shape of History: Lessing's Nathan and Lessing's God," *Lessing Yearbook* 9 (1977): 70.

51. Friedrich Nietzsche, "On Truth and Lie in an Extra-Moral Sense," in *The Portable Nietzsche*, ed. and trans. Walter Kaufmann (New York: Penguin, 1976), 357.

52. Eva Knodt also reads Lessing as "proto-Nietzschean" in his views of truth. Critics have long noted Lessing's intervention into the understanding of truth (Knodt, "Herder and Lessing on Truth: Toward an Ethics of Incommunicability," *Lessing Yearbook* 28 [1996]: 125–46). See also Axel Schmitt, "'Die Wahrheit ruht unter mehr als einer Gestalt': Versuch einer Deutung der Ringparabel in Lessings 'Nathan der Weise' 'more rabbinico,'" in *Neues zu Lessing Forschung*, ed. Eva J. Engel and Claus Ritterhoff (Tübingen: Max Niemeyer, 1998); Helmut Schneider, *Genealogie und Menschheitsfamilie: Dramaturgie der Humaniät von Lessing bis Büchner* (Berlin: Berlin University Press, 2011), 157–60; Willi Goetschel, "Negotiating Truth: On Nathan's Business," *Lessing Yearbook/Jahrbuch* 28 (1996): 115; Robert Leventhal, "The Parable as Performance: Interpretation, Cultural Transmission and Political Strategy in Lessing's *Nathan der Weise*," *German Quarterly* 61, no. 4 (1988): 502–27; Daniel Fulda, *Schau-Spiele des Geldes* (Tübingen: Max Niemeyer, 2005), 4; and Arno Schilson, "Dichtung und (religiöse) Wahrheit: Überlegungen zu Art und Aussage von Lessings Drama *Nathan der Weise*," *Lessing Yearbook* 27 (1995): 1–18.

53. Robert Leventhal similarly points out the shift from the disregard for the "letter" or means of religious tradition in "Education" to the respect for historical specificity of traditions in Nathan (Leventhal, "The Parable as Performance: Interpretation, Cultural Transmission and Political Strategy in Lessing's Nathan der Weise," *German Quarterly* 61, no. 4 [1988]: 515, emphasis in original). Schneider attempts to reunite the two views by claiming that the gulf between object and meaning sets both free by allowing the universal core to shine through the diverse particulars (*Genealogie*, 169–70). I would add, however, that the particulars are not merely conduits to higher abstract universals but instead that the sought-after meaning continues to integrate the bodily and particular with universal foundations.

54. Martin Buber takes up the idea that faith is a relationship to a person or people whom one trusts as one of two possible types of faith. He associates this relationship-based faith with Judaism, particularly in its earliest stage, and the other type—trust that an idea is true—with Christianity. See Buber, *Two Types of Faith*, trans. Norman P. Goldhawk (New York: Collier, 1951).

55. And does so through monetary metaphors. See my "Coining a Discipline."

56. For the etymology of Recha's names, see Hendrik Birus, "Das Rätsel des Namen in Lessings 'Nathan der Weise,'" in *Lessings "Nathan der Weise,"* ed. Klaus Bohnen (Darmstadt: Wissenschaftliche Buchgesellschaft, 1984).

57. The two rescues are also parallel in risk. While the jeopardy of rushing into a burning building is obvious, the Patriarch renders the threat to Saladin explicit when he attempts to recruit Curd to assassinate his benefactor. It is Curd's special protected status that would make him the ideal choice for the job.

296 5. THE EAST COMES HOME

58. The formulation implies that the novel emotion caused by a visual impression could be something other than erotic love. Curd's life is after all intertwined with Recha's biologically and historically. We see here how even natural signs such as resemblance require the intervention of education before they can be properly understood.

59. As Katja Garloff has argued, "the integration of visual, aural, and tactile impressions" in the play distinguishes successful moments of cognitive intuition from less mature infatuations dependent on vision alone. Garloff, "Sublimation and Its Discontents: Christian-Jewish Love in Lessing's Nathan der Weise," *Lessing Yearbook/Jahrbuch* 36 (2004/2005): 56.

60. Helmut Schneider reads the emphasis on paternal instruction in the evaluation of Recha's smile as a male appropriation of female generative abilities (*Genealogy*, 196). Schneider is right to critique the absence or inadequacies of maternal education here and throughout Lessing's work. It is noteworthy, if not exculpatory, however, that no dichotomy is established between maternal matter and paternal spirit: the paternal inhabits both body and mind.

61. Ruth Klüger Angress, "'Dreams That Were More than Dreams' in Lessing's Nathan," *Lessing Yearbook* 3 (1971): 108–27.

62. So that the point not be lost, the lay brother corrects the Templar's mistaken appellation of "father" to "brother" in their first encounter (37).

63. As Jakob Feldt notes in his discussion of Jewish repositionings of Judaism within a history of particularism, universalism, and trans/nationalism, the "strong historical attitude" that "set the Jew as either a fossil, a pariah, a parasite, or a prophecy of the world to come . . . did not have an interest in the actual lives of actual Jews; it was in many ways the opposite of an ethnography" (141). Jakob Egholm Feldt, *Transnationalism and the Jews: Culture, History, and Prophecy* (London: Rowman & Littlefield, 2016).

64. Until Thomas Mann's twentieth-century "Wälsungenblut," discussed below, it is the only sibling-incest narrative to include Jews, as far as I am aware, and yet critical responses to Lessing have overwhelmingly focused on Jewish-Christian relations to the exclusion of Islam. Exceptions are work by W. Daniel Wilson, *Humanität und Kreuzzugsideologie um 1780* (New York: Peter Lang, 1984); Karl-Joseph Kuschel, *Vom Streit zum Wettstreit der Religion. Lessing und die Herausforderung des Islam* (Düsseldorf: Patmos, 1998); Kuschel, *"Jud, Christ und Muselmann vereinigt"? Lessings "Nathan der Weise"* (Düsseldorf: Patmos, 2004); and David G. John, "Lessing, Islam and Nathan der Weise in Africa," *Lessing Yearbook/Jahrbuch* 32 (2000): 245–57. Performances of the play have initiated an engagement with Islam since the terrorist attacks in the United States in 2001 and subsequent attacks in Europe, although an unfortunately biased one. See Kuschel, *"Jud, Christ und Muselmann vereinigt"?*, 9–32.

65. Wilson persuasively locates Goethe's *Iphigenia auf Tauris* in this tradition as well. One can see echoes of it in Schiller's *Bride of Messina* also; when Beatrice disappears, her family is first convinced she has been abducted by pirates.

66. For Lessing's role in current theological debate, see Terry Foreman "Lessing and the Quest for Religious Truth 200 Years On: His Role in the Current Anglophone Culture-War," *Lessing Yearbook* 32 (2000): 391–405.

67. Byron, "Written After Swimming from Sestos to Abydos. May 9, 1810," in vol. 1 of *The Complete Poetical Works*, ed. Jerome McGann (Oxford: Clarendon, 1981).
68. Susan Oliver notes that all of Byron's so-called Turkish Tales take place at or on watery borderlands (*Scott, Byron and the Poetics of Cultural Encounter* [Basingstoke, UK: Palgrave Macmillan, 2005]). Today both sides of the Dardanelles lie within Turkey, but the Greek goal at the time Byron joined the fight for independence was to align the border here with the traditional break between Europe and Asia.
69. Lord Byron, "The Bride of Abydos. A Turkish Tale," in vol. 3 of *The Complete Poetical Works*, 123, 123, 124. This ram was the source of the golden fleece.
70. Ovid, *Times and Reasons*, trans. Anne and Peter Wiseman (Oxford: Oxford University Press, 2011), 3:863.
71. Like Shelley, Byron altered the original relationship of his characters under pressure, so that in the published version they are cousins rather than siblings. The relationship within the poem is scarcely less tabooed after Byron's revisions, however, since Zuleika believes that Selim is her brother until near the end of the narrative, and Selim's discovery of his identity seems to postdate his love for Zuleika.
72. Mohammed Sharafuddin notes the allusion with a brief mention that each illustrates the discovery of the East (*Islam and Romantic Orientalism: Literary Encounters with the Orient* [London: I. B. Tauris, 1994], 230–31). He is in the minority in this opinion, however, as Goethe scholarship has uniformly located the referent of Mignon's song in Italy. I will return to this geographical question below.
73. Johann Wolfgang von Goethe, *Wilhelm Meister's Apprenticeship*, ed. and trans. Eric A. Blackall, vol. 9 of Goethe's *Collected Works* (Princeton, N.J.: Princeton University Press, 1989), 83.
74. Even Mignon's literal origins and birthplace are identified only tentatively.
75. Archeological work done in Delphi since the 1980s has largely confirmed the presence of flowing water and fissures under the temple, which is located in a volcanic area directly above the intersection of two major fault lines. Current scholarship assumes that chemicals in the sporadically emitted steam could have induced trances. See Michael Scott, *Delphi: A History of the Center of the Ancient World* (Princeton.: Princeton University Press, 2014), 20–24.
76. The zither, from Greek kithara, was, like the laurel of the first verse, sacred to Apollo, the god of poetry. While Hermes created the lyre and gave it to Apollo as a gift, Apollo himself, according to Pausanias, invented the zither.
77. See, for example, Sharafuddin, *Islam*, 228–30. Peter Kitson provides a good overview of criticism on Byron's Eastern Tales in light of his knowledge of and attitude toward the region. Kitson, "Byron and Post-Colonial Criticism: The Eastern Tales," in *Palgrave Advances in Byron Studies*, ed. Jane Stabler (Basingstoke: Palgrave Macmillan, 2007).
78. This dichotomy complicates the prevalent critical assumption that Romantic writers feminized the East, allowing for cultural distinctions in the assignation of gendered terms.
79. Gerard Cohen-Vrignaud suggests that Byron might have had the anti-Ottoman intrigues of the Greek Lambros Katsoni in mind. Gerard Cohen-Vrignaud, "Becoming

Corsairs: Byron, British Property Rights and Orientalism Economics," *Studies in Romanticism* 50 (Winter 2011): 709.
80. Nigel Leask, *British Romantic Writers and the East* (Cambridge: Cambridge University Press, 1992); and Saree Makdisi, *Romantic Imperialism: Universal Empire and the Culture of Modernity* (Cambridge: Cambridge University Press, 1998).
81. Marilyn Butler notes that Moore's *Lalla Rookh*, Percy Shelley's *Prometheus Unbound* and *Hellas*, and Mary Shelley's *The Last Man* all displace revolutions onto Eastern regimes that share properties with European ones. Butler, "Byron and the Empire in the East," in *Byron: Augustan and Romantic*, ed. Andrew Rutherford (New York: St. Martin's Press, 1990), 68.
82. Makdisi, *Imperialism*, 125 (emph. orig.); see also 122–53.
83. Olender's *Languages of Paradise* offers an extended reflection on study of these two heritages in the nineteenth century, which has influenced my own.
84. Excellent histories of the categories include Mosse, *Towards the Final Solution*; Léon Poliakov, *The Aryan Myth: A Hisotry of Racist and Nationalist Ideas in Europe*, trans. Edmund Howard (London: Chatto Heinemann for Sussex University Press, 1971); Olender, *Languages of Paradise*; Ruth Römer, *Sprachwissenschaft und Rassenideologie in Deutschland* (Munich: Wilhelm Fink, 1985); and Stefan Arvidsson, *Aryan Idols: Indo-European Mythology as Ideology and Science*, trans. Sonia Wichmann (Chicago: University of Chicago Press, 2006).
85. Etienne Balibar and Immanuel Wallerstein, *Race, Nation, Class: Ambiguous Identities*, trans. Chris Turner (London: Verso, 1991), 103. Although Balibar and Wallerstein go on to note the divisiveness that can correlate with distinguishing linguistic communities, he maintains its basic openness because it is learned. Johann Gottlieb Fichte, Balibar declares in a more recent essay, thus dispenses thoroughly with genealogical thinking by tying nationality to language in his *Address to the German Nation* ("Fichte and the Internal Border: On Addresses to the German Nation," in *Masses, Classes, Ideas: Studies on Politics and Philosophy Before and After Marx*, trans. James Swenson [New York: Routledge, 1994]). The problem with such a reading of language communities in general, and of Fichte in particular, is that ideology is always a function of the imaginary subject to its own logic. In this chapter we will see August Schleicher, Arthur de Gobineau, and Richard Wagner all deny the possibility of entering a language community, even over many generations. Fichte reasons similarly. While on the one hand he transfers genealogical thinking from the bloodline to the language itself (which lives only so long as it retains continuity through its developmental history), he also claims that a people who take on a new language introduce a caesura into the genealogical development of that language from which it cannot recover, so that it ceases to be a living language (Johann Gottlieb Fichte, *Addresses to the German Nation*, trans. Isaac Nakhimovsky, Béla Kapossy, and Keith Tribe [Indianapolis: Hackett, 2013], 50–51). Language continuity thus remains dependent in practice on a sufficient correlation between the genealogy of the blood and that of the language (45–46). It can survive the gradual intermingling of peoples but not wholesale adoption by another bloodline. In other words, Fichte constructs his theory to allow for the historical mix-

ing of Teutons and Slavs within the German nation, while excluding the Jewish population that was transitioning from Yiddish to German before his eyes.

86. August Schleicher, *Über die Bedeutung der Sprache für die Naturgeschichte des Menschen* (Weimar: Hermann Böhlau, 1865), 15 (trans. mine).

87. Paul de Lagarde, "Über die gegenwärtigen Aufgaben der deutschen Politik," in *Deutsche Schriften* (Berlin: Verlag der Freunde, 1994), 24.

88. On the discourse of *Volk* in official Nazi documents, see Christopher Hutton, *Linguistics and the Third Reich: Mother-tongue Fascism, Race and the Science of Language* (London: Routledge, 1999); and Hutton, *Race and the Third Reich: Linguistics, Racial Anthropology and Genetics in the Dialectic of Volk* (Cambridge: Polity, 2005).

89. See Tomoko Masuzawa's fascinating history of the emergence of the category of world religions to help classify belief systems that migrated and expanded: *The Invention of World Religions, or, How European Universalism Was Preserved in the Language of Pluralism* (Chicago: University of Chicago Press, 2005).

90. For the dynamics of race as a maternal inheritance, see Alys Weinbaum, *Wayward Reproductions: Genealogies of Race and Nation in Transatlantic Modern Thought* (Durham: Duke University Press, 2004).

91. Christina von Braun, "Blutschande: From the Incest Taboo to the Nuremberg Racial Laws," in *Encountering the Other(s): Studies in Literature, History, and Culture*, ed. Gisela Brinker-Gabler (Albany: State University of New York Press, 1995), 127–48.

92. See Suzanne Marchand, *German Orientalism in the Age of Empire: Religion, Race, and Scholarship* (Washington, D.C.: German Historical Institute; New York: Cambridge University Press, 2009).

93. See Susannah Heschel, "German Jewish Scholarship on Islam as a Tool for De-Orientalizing Judaism," *New German Critique* 117, no. 39 (2012): 91–107; and Heschel, "The Rise of Imperialism and the German Jewish Engagement in Islamic Studies," in *Colonialism and the Jews*, ed. Ethan B. Katz, Lisa Moses Leff, and Maud S. Mandel (Bloomington: Indiana University Press, 2017): 54–80.

94. For more on the Aryanizing of Jesus, see Halvor Moxnes, "Jesus the Jew: Dilemmas of Interpretation," in *Fair Play: Diversity and Conflicts in Early Christianity*, ed. Ismo Dunderberg, Christopher Tuckett, and Kari Syreeni (Leiden: Brill, 2001); Arvidsson, *Aryan Idols*; Paul Lawrence Rose, *Wagner: Race and Revolution* (London: Faber and Faber, 1992), 50–58 and 142–50; and Susannah Heschel, *The Aryan Jesus: Christian Theologians and the Bible in Nazi Germany* (Princeton: Princeton University Press, 2008).

95. See Hess, *Germans, Jews*, 112–18; and Susannah Heschel, "The Image of Judaism in Nineteenth-Century Christian New Testament Scholarship in Germany," in *Jewish-Christian Encounters Over the Centuries: Symbiosis, Prejudice, Holocaust, Dialog*, ed. Marvin Perry and Frederick M. Schweitzer (New York: Peter Lang, 1994), 215–17.

96. Johann Gottlieb Fichte, *Die Grundzüge des gegenwärtigen Zeitalters* (Hamburg: Felix Meiner, 1978), 102–3.

97. For more on investigations into the life of Jesus by Reimarus, Schleiermacher, and Strauss, see Roy A. Harrisville and Walter Sundberg, *The Bible in Modern Culture: Baruch Spinoza to Brevard Childs* (Grand Rapids, Mich.: Eerdmans, 2002).

98. See Heschel, "Image of Judaism," 225–32.
99. Ernest Renan, *The Life of Jesus* (New York: Modern Library, 1955), 126, 83.
100. In a similarly hypocritical move, Renan chastises anti-Semites who blame all modern Jews for the death of Jesus, while concluding, as if reluctantly, "But nations, like individuals, have their responsibilities, and if ever crime was the crime of a nation, it was the death of Jesus" (358).
101. Cosima Wagner, *Diaries*, ed. Martin Gregor-Dellin and Dietrich Mack, 2 vols. (London: Collins, 1980), 2:211–12. Entry from 1878.
102. Chamberlain claimed it was certain Jesus was not Jewish by birth, that Aryans also lived in Galilee, and that only the Jews held themselves separate from racial mixing. While he declared speculations about whether Jesus was an Aryan were impossible to answer, his description makes some "Aryan" heritage the most probable conclusion. Houston Stewart Chamberlain, *Die Grundlagen des Neunzehnten Jahrhunderts*, 10th ed. (Munich: Verlagsantalt F. Bruckmann, 1912), 1:256–57.
103. Martin Buber, *Two Types of Faith*, trans. Norman P. Goldhawk (New York: Collier, 1951), 12 (trans. modified). Discussed in Halvor Moxnes, "Jesus the Jew: Dilemmas of Interpretation," in *Fair Play: Diversity and Conflicts in Early Christianity*, ed. Ismo Dunderberg, Christopher Tuckett, and Kari Syreeni (Leiden: Brill, 2001), 95.
104. Friedrich Max Müller, *Introduction to the Science of Religion: Four Lectures delivered at the Royal Institute* (London: Longmans, Green, 1882), 41, 82, 91, 92, 93.
105. Friedrich Max Müller, "On the Relation of the Bengali to the Arian and Aboriginal Languages of India," *Report of the Meeting of the British Association for the Advancement of Science* 7 (1847): 349. As Trautmann notes, this term was Max Müller's contribution to the "Orientalist love story of British India" (Trautmann, *Aryans and British India* [Berkeley: University of California Press, 1997], 179). Late in life, Max Müller converts the word *brethren* to its related word *brother*, claiming that Indians "have been recognised as our brothers in language and thought" (*Address Delivered at the Opening of the Ninth International Congress of Orientalists* [Oxford: Oxford University Press, 1892], 34). I am indebted to Trautmann for citing both formulations. Max Müller also refers here to a "brotherhood of Semitic speech" (*Address*, 33).
106. Friedrich Max Müller, *Lectures on the Science of Language* (London: Longmans, Green, 1866), 237.
107. Masuzawa and Trautmann emphasize this nonphysicalist element in Max Müller's thought.
108. Friedrich Max Müller, *Suggestions for the Assistance of Officers in Learning the Languages of the Seat of War in the East* (London: Longman, Green, and Longmans, 1854), 30.
109. Ernest Renan, "Religions of Antiquity," in *Studies in Religious History*, trans. William M. Thomson (London: Mathieson., 1895), 29n1.
110. Ernest Renan, "History of the People of Israel," in ibid., 94, 95.
111. The more rabidly anti-Semitic Paul de Lagarde repudiated all such organic metaphors, insisting "that Judaism and Evangelism . . . are not related as the bud to the tree or the tree to the root or the root to the seed, but as a thing to an entirely different second

thing." Lagarde, "Die Religion der Zukunft," in *Deutsche Schriften* (Berlin: Verlag der Freunde, 1994), 225.

112. Note Max Müller's similar classification of religions above, in which Aryans worship God in nature, and Semites, God in history.
113. See Ardivsson, *Aryan Idols*; Poliakov, *Aryan Myth*; Olender, *Languages of Paradise*; and Römer, *Sprachwissenschaft*, for a fuller history of these stereotypes.
114. See Arvidsson, *Aryan Idols*, in particular for the history of re-creating Christianity as an Aryan nature mythology.
115. Sander Gilman has analyzed the way many Jewish writers embraced negative stereotypes of Jewish characteristics, including linguistic particularities, and programs to expunge them. Gilman, *Jewish Self-Hatred: Anti-Semitism and the Hidden Language of the Jews* (Baltimore: Johns Hopkins University Press, 1986).
116. Moritz Lazarus, "Was heißt national? Ein Vortrag" (Berlin: Ferdinand Dümmlers Verlagsbuchhandlung, 1880), 13.
117. Moses Mendelssohn, *Jerusalem, or, on Religious Power and Judaism*, trans. Allan Arkush (Hanover, N.H.: Brandeis University Press, 1983), 135–39.
118. Arthur de Gobineau, *The Inequality of Human Races*, preface George Mosse, trans. not named (New York: Howard Fertig, 1999), 30.
119. Richard Wagner, *Werke, Schriften und Briefe*, ed. Sven Friedrich (Berlin: Directmedia, 2004), 5.2:310, 5.2:329; Wagner, "Judaism in Music," in *Stories and Essays*, ed. and trans. Charles Osborne (London: Peter Owen, 1973), 30. See Jens Malte Fischer, "Richard Wagners Das Judenthum in der Musik," in *Richard Wagner und die Juden*, ed. Dieter Borchmeyer, Ami Maayani, and Susanne Vill (Stuttgart: J. B. Metzler, 2000); and Rose, *Wagner*, 80, who notes that while Wagner still thinks of Jews as a Volk rather than a race at this period, his attitude is not "wholly lacking in what might be called a 'genetic' element."
120. Homi Bhabha, "Of Mimicry and Man: The Ambivalence of Colonial Discourse," *October* 28 (1984): 128, 130, 132. While there are significant social and political distinctions between living as part of a colonized population and living as part of a minority population, there are also commonalities in the expectations toward conformity and assimilation, which has made postcolonial and minority studies reciprocally productive.
121. See Leon Botstein, "German Jews and Wagner," in *Richard Wagner and His World*, ed. Thomas S. Grey (Princeton, N.J.: Princeton University Press, 2009), 171, for the convergence of sound and narrative achieved through surface effects. On the body as ideology, on musical mimesis, and on the evocation of Jewish stereotypes in Wagner, see in particular Marc Weiner, *Richard Wagner and the Anti-Semitic Imagination* (Lincoln: University of Nebraska Press, 1995). It is hardly surprising that Wagner had an aversion to Lessing—he once suggested, tongue in cheek according to Cosima Wagner, that all Jews should be invited to a performance of *Nathan the Wise* and the theater burned down. Cosima Wagner, *Diaries*, 2:772. See also Peter Gay, "Wagner aus psychoanalytischer Sicht," in *Richard Wagner und die Juden*, ed. Dieter Borchmeyer, Ami Maayani, and Susanne Vill (Stuttgart: J. B. Metzler, 2000), 253.

122. Thomas Mann, "Versuch über das Theater [Tackling the Theater]," in *Aufsätze, Reden, Essays*, 3 vols. (Berlin: Aufbau-Verlag, 1986), 1:113, 1:114–15. All translations from Mann's essays are mine.
123. See Sander Gilman, "Sibling Incest, Madness, and the 'Jews,'" *Jewish Social Studies* 4, no. 2 (1998): 157–79, as well as *Jewish Self-Hatred*, 292; Alan Levenson, "Thoman Mann's Wälsungenblut in the Context of the Intermarriage Debate and the 'Jewish Question,'" in *Insiders and Outsiders: Jewish and Gentile Culture in Germany and Austria*, ed. Dagmar Lorenz and Gabriele Weinberger (Detroit: Wayne State University Press, 1994), 135–43; Mark Anderson, "'Jewish' Mimesis? Imitation and Assimilation in Thomas Mann's 'Wälsungenblut' and Ludwig Jacobowski's Werther, der Jude," in *German Life and Letters* 492 (1996): 191–204; and Paul Levesque, "The Double-Edged Sword: Anti-Semitism and Anti-Wagnerianism in Thomas Mann's Wälsungenblut," *German Studies Review* 20, no. 1 (1997): 9–21.
124. See also my "Sibling Incest and Cultural Voyeurism in Günderode's Udohla and Thomas Mann's Wälsungenblut," *German Quarterly* 77, no. 3 (July 2004): 278–99), in which I read Mann's story in light of a century of Orientalism. In that article, however, I came to the conclusion that Mann is replicating a theory of racial types, a reading I no longer find convincing.
125. Since this story began to attract critical attention in the 1990s, it has been read consistently as anti-Semitic, although with varying degrees of mitigation either in Mann's identification with Siegmund as a failed artist or in parallels established between incest and Mann's own homosexual tendencies. For the former, see, for example, Todd Kontje, "Thomas Mann's "Wälsungenblut": The Married Artist and the 'Jewish Question,'" *PMLA* 123, no. 1 (2008): 109–24; and for the latter, Mark Anderson, "'Jewish' Mimesis?"
126. See, for example, Gail Finney, "Self-Reflexive Siblings: Incest as Narcissism in Tieck, Wagner, and Thomas Mann," *German Quarterly* 56, no. 2 (1983): 252.
127. Thomas Mann, "The Blood of the Walsungs," in *Death in Venice and Other Tales*, trans. Joachim Neugroschel (New York: Penguin Books, 1998), 268.
128. Thomas Mann, "Zur jüdischen Frage," in *Aufsätze, Reden, Essays* (Berlin: Aufbau-Verlag, 1986), 1:170.
129. For a forceful reading of the story's attitude toward both targets as vituperative, see Levesque, "Double-Edged Sword."
130. Line cited in Hans Rudolf Vaget, "Sang réservé in Deutschland: Zur Rezeption von Thomas Manns Wälsungenblut," *German Quarterly* 57, no. 3 (1984): 368. Vaget gives a good overview of the reception history.
131. See Gilman, "Sibling Incest, Madness," 164.
132. Yiddish for we is *mir*, rather than *wir*, and *ihm* is both accusative and dative masculine. In other words, Siegmund uses German rather than Yiddish inflection.
133. W. E. B. Du Bois, *The Souls of Black Folk* (New York: Norton, 1999), 11.
134. Thomas Mann, "Die Lösung der Jüdenfrage," in *Aufsätze, Reden, Essays* (Berlin: Aufbau-Verlag, 1986), 1:129.

135. Thomas Mann, "Wälsungenblut," in *Sämtliche Erzählungen* (Frankfurt am Main: S. Fischer, 1963), 305. Neugroschel translates *im Osten* misleadingly as in "Eastern Europe" (Mann, "Walsungs," 260).
136. Todd Kontje notes the "proximity of European orientalism and the language of anti-Semitism" ("Thomas Mann," 114).
137. The alternation between the barbaric and the refined in Mann's story has been noted by critics, particularly G. R. Kluge, "Wälsungenblut oder Halbblut? Zur Kontroverse um die Schlußsätze von Thomas Manns Novelle," *Neophilologus* 76 (1992): 237–55.
138. Anne McClintock, *Imperial Leather: Race, Gender, and Sexuality in the Colonial Contest* (London: Routledge, 1995).
139. George Eliot, "Brother and Sister," in *The Complete Shorter Poems*, ed. A. G. van den Broek (London: Pickering & Chatto, 2005), 2:323.
140. Contrast with John Whitton's assumption that the twins are here generating pure-blooded offspring, in "Thomas Mann's Wälsungenblut: Implications of the Revised Ending," *Seminar* 25, no. 1 (1989): 42–43.
141. Paul de Lagarde, *Juden und Indogermanen. Eine Studie nach dem Leben* (Göttingen: Dieterische Universitatätsbuchhandlung, 1887), 339 (my trans.).
142. Jakob and Wilhelm Grimm, *The German Legends of the Brothers Grimm*, ed. and trans. Donald Ward, 2 vols. (Philadelphia: Institute for the Study of Human Issues, 1981), story 359, 1:282–83.

EPILOGUE

1. Johann Heinrich Zedler, *Grosses vollständiges Universallexicon aller Wissenschaften und Künste* (1731–1754), 4:253, http://www.zedler-lexikon.de/index.html (my trans.). As Christina von Braun has documented, the term *Blutschande* (blood shame), which referred to incest at the turn of the nineteenth century, had generally come to mean miscegenation by the turn of the twentieth. It is of course relevant that *Blutschande* was in turn applied to each of the only two marriage choices available to Jews in the Diaspora. See von Braun, "*Blutschande*: From the Incest Taboo to the Nuremberg Racial Laws," in *Encountering the Other(s): Studies in Literature, History, and Culture*, ed. Gisela Brinker-Gabler (Albany: State University of New York Press, 1995).
2. Jeremy Bentham, *Theory of Legislation*, trans. R. Hildreth, French ed. Pierre Étienne Louis Dumont (London: Kegan Paul, Trench, Trübner, 1896), 221. See also Alfred Owen Aldridge, "The Meaning of Incest from Hutcheson to Gibbon," *Ethics* 61, no. 4 (1951): 309–13; and W. Daniel Wilson, "Science, Natural Law, and Unwitting Sibling Incest in Eighteenth-Century Literature," *Studies in Eighteenth-Century Culture* 13 (1984): 249–70, for more on early speculations on incest aversions.
3. Immanuel Kant, "On the Use of Teleological Principles in Philosophy," in *Kant and the Concept of Race: Late Eighteenth-Century Writings*, trans. and ed. Jon M. Mikkelsen (Albany: State University of New York Press, 2013), 179–80.

4. See, for example, ibid., 186–87, and Kant's notes for his anthropology lectures, *Kants gesammelte Schriften*, ed. Königlich Preußischen Akademie der Wissenschaften (Berlin: Walter de Gruyter and predecessors, 1902–), 25.2.1187 and 15.2.878, where he presents a starkly hierarchical view of what each race is capable (and incapable) of. See also my *Anxious Anatomy: The Conception of the Human Form in Literary and Naturalist Discourse* (Albany: State University of New York Press, 2008), 228–32.
5. The idea that close-kin marriages led to birth defects, ill health, or reduced fertility was common, though not universally accepted, in the late eighteenth century. The assumption that inbreeding was frequent and unproblematic among animals and plants was just beginning to be challenged, by Christian Conrad Sprengel in 1793, for example, who proved through meticulous observation that hermaphroditic plants have a number of mechanisms to prevent self-fertilization. In 1891 Edvard Westermarck noted that inbreeding is detrimental for animals (*The History of Human Marriage* [London: Macmillan, 1891], 334–38), and in his later editions he argued against a popular belief that animals inbreed regularly (*The History of Human Marriage*, 5th ed. [New York: Allerton, 1922], 2:223–24).
6. Unlike Webster, Coleridge does not clearly identify these negative consequences as physiological. Given his premise about the social significance of separating sibling love from conjugal love, discussed below, it would be possible to speculate on a cultural catastrophe if the two became conflated.
7. Samuel Taylor Coleridge, *The Notebooks*, in vol. 1 of *The Complete Works of Samuel Taylor Coleridge*, Bollingen Series (New York: Pantheon, 1957), 1:1637, entry of November 1803.
8. Noah Webster, *A Collection of Essays and Fugitiv Writings: On Moral, Historical, Political and Literary Subjects* (Boston: I. Thomas and E. T. Andrews, 1790), 322.
9. Coleridge, *Notebooks*, 1:1636.
10. Percy Bysshe Shelley, *Laon and Cythna*, in vol. 2 of *The Poems of Shelley*, ed. Kelvin Everest and Geoffrey Matthew (New York: Longman, 2000), 47. William Paley, even while labeling the avoidance of sexual relations between closest kin "a law of nature" (*Principles of Moral and Political Philosophy* [New York: Harper, 1860], 126), called for it to be instilled "by every method possible to inculcate an abhorrence of incestuous conjunctions" (125), since without it, there would be no guarantee of chastity within families. His law of nature, in other words, either was not innate or was insufficiently strong without external reinforcement. Paley, like many writers on the topic, commented on the societies known to have engaged in sibling marriages: the Egyptians, the Phoenicians, and the Hebrews—as evidenced by Abraham's marriage to his half-sister Sarah. This last example would become particularly popular in the anti-Semitic late nineteenth through mid-twentieth centuries. See, for example, Westermarck, *History of Human Marriage* (1891), 295.
11. See David Schneider, *A Critique of the Study of Kinship* (Ann Arbor: University of Michigan Press, 1984).

12. Excellent new work on kinship has followed Schneider's critique, often applied to new practices of relatedness that come out of reproductive technologies and same-sex relations, particularly before the Supreme Court decision in July 2015 to legalize same-sex marriage. See Marilyn Strathern, *Kinship, Law, and the Unexpected: Relatives Are Always a Surprise* (New York: Cambridge University Press, 2005); Janet Carsten, *After Kinship* (Cambridge: Cambridge University Press, 2004); Sarah Franklin, *Dolly Mixtures: The Remaking of Genealogy* (Durham, N.C.: Duke University Press, 2007); Judith Butler, "Is Kinship Always Already Heterosexual?," in *Undoing Gender* (New York: Routledge, 2004); Sarah Franklin and Susan McKinnon, eds., *Relative Values: Reconfiguring Kinship Studies* (Durham, N.C.: Duke University Press, 2001); and Ryan Conrad and Yasmin Nair, eds., *Against Equality: Queer Critiques of Gay Marriage* (Lewiston, Me.: Against Equality Pub. Collective, 2010).

13. Johann Jakob Bachofen, *Mother Right: A Study of the Religious and Juridical Aspects of Gynecocracy in the Ancient World*, abr. and trans. David Partenheimer (Lewiston, Me.: Edwin Mellen, 2007); John F. McLennan, *Primitive Marriage: An Inquiry Into the Origin of the Form of Capture in Marriage Ceremonies*, ed. Peter Rivière (Chicago: University of Chicago Press, 1970); Lewis Henry Morgan, *Systems of Consanguinity & Affinity of the Human Family* (Lincoln: University of Nebraska Press, 1997); Morgan, *Ancient Society, or, Researches in the Lines of Human Progress from Savagery Through Barbarism to Civilization* (Chicago: Charles H. Kerr, 1877). It is not merely coincidence that McLennan, Morgan, and Bachofen all studied law. As mentioned in chapter 4, the first pictorial genealogical tree was drawn to illustrate the development of legal systems. Kinship systems as imagined and adopted into anthropological fieldwork were juridical in concept, focusing on inheritance and distribution of rights, privileges, and prohibitions. Both McLennan and Morgan were influenced by the work of British lawyer Henry Maine on *Ancient Law* (1861), which included detailed accounts of Roman family law. Maine, however, remained focused on ancient Rome, not attributing to human history a greatly longer duration. Bachofen's book, which appeared simultaneously with Maine's, and the works by McLennan and Morgan that followed opened longer vistas into the ancient past.

14. This leads to some oddities, of course, as when Morgan notes that the "earliest system of consanguinity" (*Ancient Society*, 394) is the "consanguine" (393), that is, in the earliest family system, those Europeans and Americans might now call genetic siblings and cousins formed a group marriage with each other.

15. McLennan notes that any primitive endogamous tribe, "an ungoverned fraternity" (*Primitive Marriage*, 22), would not engage in the purchase or exchange of women because all property would be held in common. If such a group was not to be divided by quarrels over women, they must have maintained harmony through "indifference and promiscuity" (69).

16. Laura Otis, *Organic Memory: History and the Body in the Late Nineteenth & Early Twentieth Centuries* (Lincoln: University of Nebraska Press), 3.

17. Edward O. Wilson, *Consilience: The Unity of Knowledge* (New York: Knopf, 1998), 266.

18. Claude Lévi-Strauss, *Structural Anthropology*, trans. Claire Jacobson and Brooke Grundfest Schoepf (New York: Basic Books, 1963), 50.
19. Claude Lévi-Strauss, *The Elementary Structures of Kinship*, ed. Rodney Needham, trans. James Harle Bell, John Richard von Sturmer, and Rodney Needham (Boston: Beacon Press, 1969), 12.
20. Sander Gilman has argued convincingly that the revolution in incest discourse Freud accomplished was an act of deflection motivated by the race theory of the time, which, as discussed in chapter 5, associated Jews with sibling incest ("Sibling Incest, Madness, and the 'Jews,'" *Jewish Social Studies* 4, no. 2 [1998]: 172). The parent-child orientation of the Oedipal Complex thus served to protect psychoanalysis from one avenue of attack against it as a Jewish science.
21. The claim that human incest is necessarily detrimental to populations is still a question of debate. Alan Bittles has written on the difficulty of collecting data for a statistical analysis of the effect of parent-child or sibling incest on offspring due to the very small number of reported births resulting from such relations, and the disproportionate percentage among this small sample that need to be ruled out for control reasons ("Genetic Aspects of Inbreeding and Incest," in *Inbreeding, Incest, and the Incest Taboo: The State of Knowledge at the Turn of the Century*, ed. Arthur Wolf and William Durham [Stanford, Calif.: Stanford University Press, 2005]). Because of the abuse associated with such cases, the victimized party is disproportionately likely to be mentally disabled and to give birth at an age lower than is healthy. The abuser is also more likely to have genetic or nongenetic conditions that could negatively affect offspring. Bittles was able to perform a statistical analysis of cousin marriages in areas where such marriages are not held in disregard, however, and found mortality rate for children to the age of ten to be 4.4 percent higher than in nonconsanguineous unions. Gregory C. Leavitt, on the other hand, recounts the history of evidence that inbreeding in small populations may not be deleterious and could even be advantageous because harmful genes eliminate themselves so quickly ("The Incest Taboo? A Reconsideration of Westermarck," *Anthropological Theory* 7 [2002]: 393–418). Cultures with mixed marriage preferences would then be most detrimental.
22. Arthur P. Wolf and Chieh-shan Huang, *Marriage and Adoption in China, 1845–1945* (Stanford, Calif.: Stanford University Press, 1980).
23. Joseph Shepher, *Incest: A Biosocial View* (New York: Academic, 1983).
24. A more recent sociological study by Eran Shor and Dalit Simchai has shown how the unique bonds of the intense peer group of the kibbutz exerted pressure against pairing off. Through interviews of the former kibbutz children, Shor and Simchai found that self-reported sexual attraction frequently existed, along with very little self-reported sexual aversion. Shor and Simchai, "Incest Avoidance, the Incest Taboo, and Social Cohesion: Revisiting Westermarck and the Case of the Israeli Kibbutzim," *American Journal of Sociology* 114, no. 6 (2009): 1803–42.
25. See in particular Debra Lieberman, John Tooby, and Leda Cosmides, "The Architecture of Human Kin Detection," *Nature* 445 (February 15, 2007): 727–31; and Markus J. Rantala and Urszula M. Marcinkowska, "The Role of Sexual Imprinting and the Wes-

termarck Effect in Mate Choice in Humans," *Behavioral Ecology and Sociobiology* 65 (2011): 859–73. Interestingly, there are now also studies suggesting that family resemblances increase sexual attractiveness. R. Chris Fraley and Michael J. Marks postulate an aversion overlaying an attraction, which together act to direct sexual preferences at a band between incest and exogamy ("Westermarck, Freud, and the Incest Taboo: Does Familial Resemblance Activate Sexual Attraction?," *Personality and Social Psychology Bulletin* 36 [2010]: 1202–12). Shades of Kant.

26. As J. B. S. Haldane is purported to have quipped while explaining how kin selection functions, he would not lay down his life for his brother but would do so for two brothers or eight cousins. Maynard Smith, "Letters: Haldane," in *New Scientist* 7, no. 101 (July 29, 1976): 247.

27. See Debra Lieberman, John Tooby, and Leda Cosmides, "Does Morality Have a Biological Basis? An Empirical Test of the Factors Governing Moral Sentiments Relating to Incest," *Proceedings of the Royal Society London* 270 (2003): 819–26; Daniel Fessler and David Navarrete, "Third-Party Attitudes Toward Sibling Incest. Evidence for Westermarck's Hypotheses," *Evolution and Human Behavior* 25 (2004): 277–294; and Jana Schaich Borg, Debra Liebermann, and Kent A. Kiehl, "Infection, Incest, and Iniquity: Investigating Neural Correlates of Disgust and Morality," *Journal of Cognitive Neuroscience* 20, no. 9 (2008): 1529–46. For some of the problems with such an approach, see William Durham, "Assessing Gaps in Westermarck's Theory," in *Inbreeding, Incest, and the Incest Taboo: The State of Knowledge at the Turn of the Century*, ed. Arthur P. Wolf and William H. Durham (Stanford: Stanford University Press, 2005); and Martha Nussbaum, *From Disgust to Humanity: Sexual Orientation & Constitutional Law* (Oxford: Oxford University Press, 2010).

28. Foundational work includes that by Félix Guattari and Gilles Deleuze, Katherine Hayles, Donna Haraway, Carey Wolfe, Jacques Derrida, and most recently Elizabeth Grosz.

WORKS CITED

Able, Elizabeth, Marianne Hirsch, and Elizabeth Langland. Introduction to *The Voyage In: Fictions of Female Development*, 1–19. Hanover, N.H.: University Press of New England, 1983.

Adelung, Johann Christoph. *Grammatisch-kritisches Wörterbuch der hochdeutschen Mundart*. Wien: Bauer, 1811. http://lexika.digitale-sammlungen.de/adelung/online/angebot.

Aeschylus. *The Oresteia*. In *Aeschylus II*. Translated by Richmond Lattimore. Edited by David Grene and Richmond Lattimore. Chicago: University of Chicago Press, 1953.

Ahlzweig, Claus. *Muttersprache-Vaterland: Die deutsche Nation und ihre Sprache*. Opladen: Westdeutscher Verlag, 1994.

Aldridge, Alfred Owen. "The Meaning of Incest from Hutcheson to Gibbon." *Ethics* 61, no. 4 (1951): 309–13.

Alter, Stephen G. *Darwinism and the Linguistic Image: Language, Race, and Natural Theology in the Nineteenth Century*. Baltimore: Johns Hopkins University Press, 1999.

Amariglio, Jack, and Antonio Callari. "Marxian Value Theory and the Problem of the Subject: The Role of Commodity Fetishism." In *Fetishism as Cultural Discourse*, edited by Emily Apter and William Pietz, 186–216. Ithaca: Cornell University Press, 1993.

Anderson, Mark. "'Jewish' Mimesis? Imitation and Assimilation in Thomas Mann's 'Wälsungenblut' and Ludwig Jacobowski's *Werther, der Jude*." *German Life and Letters* 49, no. 2 (1996): 191–204.

Angress, Ruth Klüger. "'Dreams That Were More Than Dreams' in Lessing's Nathan." *Lessing Yearbook* 3 (1971): 108–27.

Appadurai, Arjun. "Introduction: Commodities and the Politics of Value." In *The Social Life of Things: Commodities in Cultural Perspective*, 3–63. Cambridge: Cambridge University Press, 1986.

Apter, Emily, and William Pietz. *Fetishism as Cultural Discourse*. Ithaca: Cornell University Press, 1993.

Armstrong, Nancy. *How Novels Think: The Limits of Individualism from 1719–1900*. New York: Columbia University Press, 2005.

Arvidsson, Stefan. *Aryan Idols: Indo-European Mythology as Ideology and Science*. Translated by Sonia Wichmann. Chicago: University of Chicago Press, 2006.

Atkinson, Quentin D., and Russell D. Gray. "Curious Parallels and Curious Connections—Phylogenetic Thinking in Biology and Historical Linguistics." *Systematic Biology* 54, no. 4 (2005): 513–26.

Auerbach, Nina. "The Power of Hunger: Demonism and Maggie Tulliver." *Nineteenth-Century Fiction* 30, no. 2 (September 1975): 150–71.

Aurnhammer, Achim. *Androgynie. Studien zu einem Motiv in der europaischen Literatur*. Cologne: Böhlau, 1986.

Bachofen, Johann Jakob. *Das Mutterrecht. Eine Untersuchung über die Gynaikokratie der alten Welt nach ihrer religiösen und rechtlichen Natur*. Stuttgart: von Krais and Hoffmann, 1861.

———. *Mother Right: A Study of the Religious and Juridical Aspects of Gynecocracy in the Ancient World*. Abridged and translated by David Partenheimer. Lewiston, Me.: Edwin Mellen, 2007.

Baird, Robert J. "How Religion Became Scientific." In *Religion in the Making*, edited by Arie L. Molendijk and Peter Pels, 205–30. Leiden: E. J. Brill, 1998.

Balibar, Etienne. "Fichte and the Internal Border: On Addresses to the German Nation." In *Masses, Classes, Ideas: Studies on Politics and Philosophy Before and After Marx*, translated by James Swenson, 61–84. New York: Routledge, 1994.

Balibar, Etienne, and Immanuel Wallerstein. *Race, Nation, Class: Ambiguous Identities*. Translated by Chris Turner. London: Verso, 1991.

Bapteste, Eric, Leo van Iersel, Axel Janke, Scot Kelchner, Steven Kelk, James O. McInerney, David A. Morrison, Luay Nakhleh, Mike Stell, Leen Stougie, and James Whitfield. "Networks: Expanding Evolutionary Thinking." *Trends in Genetics* 29, no. 8 (August 2013): 439–41.

Baudrillard, Jean. "Fetishism and Ideology: the Semiological Reduction." In *For a Critique of the Political Economy of the Sign*, translated by Charles Levin, 88–101. St. Louis: Telos, 1981.

Bauer, Volker. *Wurzel, Stamm, Krone: Fürstliche Genealogie in frühneuzeitlichen Druckwerken*. Wolfenbuuttel, 2013.

Becker-Cantarino, Barbara. "Patriarchy and German Enlightenment Discourse: From Goethe's *Wilhelm Meister* to Horkheimer and Adorno's *Dialectic of Enlightenment*." In *Impure Reason: Dialectic of Enlightenment in Germany*, edited by W. Daniel Wilson and Robert Holub, 48–64. Detroit: Wayne State University Press, 1993.

Beer, Gillian. *Darwin's Plots: Evolutionary Narrative in Darwin, George Eliot and Nineteenth-Century Fiction*. London: Routledge and Kegan Paul, 1983.

———. *George Eliot*. Brighton: Harvester, 1986.

Beiko, Robert G. "Gene Sharing and Genome Evolution: Networks in Trees and Trees in Networks." *Biology and Philosophy* 25 (2010): 659–73.

Benes, Tuska. *In Babel's Shadow: Language, Philology and the Nation in Nineteenth-Century Germany*. Detroit: Wayne State University Press, 2008.
Benjamin, Jessica. *The Bonds of Love: Psychoanalysis, Feminism, and the Problem of Domination*. New York: Pantheon, 1988.
———. *Shadow of the Other: Intersubjectivity and Gender in Psychoanalysis*. New York: Routledge, 1998.
Benne, Christian. *Nietzsche und die historisch-kritische Philologie*. Berlin: Walter de Gruyter, 2005.
Bennett, Benjamin. "Reason, Error and the Shape of History: Lessing's Nathan and Lessing's God." *Lessing Yearbook* 9 (1977): 60–80.
Bennett, Jane. *Vibrant Matter: A Political Economy of Things*. Durham: Duke University Press, 2010.
Bentham, Jeremy. *Theory of Legislation*. Translated by R. Hildreth. Edited by Pierre Étienne Louis Dumont (French ed). London: Kegan Paul, Trench, Trübner, 1896.
Bernasconi, Robert. "Who Invented the Concept of Race? Kant's Role in the Enlightenment Construction of Race." In *Race*, edited by Robert Bernasconi. Malden, Mass.: Blackwell, 2001.
Bhabha, Homi. "Of Mimicry and Man: The Ambivalence of Colonial Discourse." *October* 28 (1984): 125–33.
Bible. *Oxford Annotated Bible*. Edited by Herbert G. May and Bruce M. Metzger. New York: Oxford University Press, 1977.
Bindman, David. *Ape to Apollo: Aesthetics and the Idea of Race in the Eighteenth Century*. Ithaca: Cornell University Press, 2002.
Birus, Hendrik. "Das Rätsel des Namen in Lessings 'Nathan der Weise.'" In *Lessings "Nathan der Weise,"* edited by Klaus Bohnen, 290–327. Darmstadt: Wissenschaftliche Buchgesellschaft, 1984.
Bittles, Alan. "Genetic Aspects of Inbreeding and Incest." In *Inbreeding, Incest, and the Incest Taboo: The State of Knowledge at the Turn of the Century*, edited by Arthur Wolf and William Durham. Stanford: Stanford University Press, 2005.
Black, Anthony. *Guild & State: European Political Thought from the Twelfth Century to the Present*. New Brunswick, N.J.: Transaction, 2003.
Blake, Kathleen. "Between Economies in *The Mill on the Floss*: Loans Versus Gifts, or, Auditing Mr. Tulliver's Accounts." *Victorian Literature and Culture* 33 (2005): 219–37.
Blumenbach, Johann Friedrich. *On the Natural Varieties of Mankind*. Translated by Thomas Bendyshe. New York: Bergman, 1969. First published 1865 by Longman, Green, Longman, Roberts and Green (London).
———. *Über den Bildungstrieb und das Zeugungsgeschäfte*. Göttingen: Johann Christian Dieterich, 1781.
———. *Über die natürlichen Verschiedenheiten im Menschengeschlechte*. Vol. 5 of *Concepts of Race in the Eighteenth Century*, edited by Robert Bernasconi. Bristol: Thoemmes, 2001. First published 1798 by Breitkopf und Härtel (Leipzig).
Blundell, Mary Whitlock. *Helping Friends and Hurting Enemies: A Study in Sophocles and Greek Ethics*. Cambridge: Cambridge University Press, 1989.

Böckh, August. *Über die Antigone des Sophokles. Nebst Nachträgliche Bemerkungen.* N.p., 1826.
Boes, Tobias. *Formative Fictions: Nationalism, Cosmopolitanism, and the Bildungsroman.* Ithaca: Cornell University Press, 2012.
Böhme, Hartmut. *Fetishism and Culture: A Different Theory of Modernity.* Berlin: Walter de Gruyter, 2014.
Boone, Joseph, and Deborah E. Nord. "Brother and Sister: The Seductions of Siblinghood in Dickens, Eliot, and Brontë." *Western Humanities Review* 46, no. 2 (1992): 164–88.
Borg, Jana Schaich, Debra Lieberman, and Kent A. Kiehl. "Infection, Incest, and Iniquity: Investigating Neural Correlates of Disgust and Morality." *Journal of Cognitive Neuroscience* 20, no. 9 (2008): 1529–46.
Botstein, Leon. "German Jews and Wagner." In *Richard Wagner and His World*, edited by Thomas S. Grey, 151–97. Princeton: Princeton University Press, 2009.
Bouchard, Frédéric. "Symbiosis, Lateral Function Transfer and the (Many) Saplings of Life." *Biology and Philosophy* 25 (2010): 623–41.
Bouquet, Mary. "Family Trees and Their Affinities: The Visual Imperative of the Genealogical Diagram." *Journal of the Royal Anthropological Institute* 2, no. 1 (March 1996): 43–66.
Bowler, Peter. *Evolution: The History of an Idea.* Berkeley: University of California Press, 1983.
Braun, Christina von. "*Blutschande*: From the Incest Taboo to the Nuremberg Racial Laws." In *Encountering the Other(s): Studies in Literature, History, and Culture*, edited by Gisela Brinker-Gabler, 127–48. Albany: State University of New York Press, 1995.
Bray, Alan. *The Friend.* Chicago: University of Chicago Press, 2003.
Bredekamp, Horst. *Darwins Korallen. Frühe Evolutionsmodelle und die Tradition der Naturgeschichte.* Berlin: Klaus Wagenbach, 2006.
Broszeit-Rieger, Ingrid. "Paintings in Goethe's Wilhelm Meister Novels: The Dynamics of Erecting and 'Eroding' the Paternal Law." *Goethe Yearbook* 13 (2005): 105–24.
———. "Transgressions of Gender and Generation in the Families of Goethe's Meister." In *Romantic Border Crossings*, edited by Jeffrey Cass and Larry Peer. Aldershot: Ashgate, 75–85.
Brown, B. Ricardo. *Until Darwin, Science, Human Variety and the Origins of Race.* London: Pickering and Chatto, 2010.
Brown, Jane K. "Faust als Revolutionär: Goethe zwischen Rousseau und Hannah Arendt. *Goethe-Jahrbuch* 126 (2009): 79–89.
———. "Goethe: The Politics of Allegory and Irony." In *The Politics of Irony: Essays in Self-Betrayal*, edited by Daniel W. Conway and John E. Seery, 53–71. New York: St. Martin's, 1992.
Brown, Kathryn, and Anthony Stephens. "'Hinübergehn und unser Haus entsühnen.' Die Ökonomie des Mythischen in Goethes Iphigenie." *Jahrbuch der deutschen Schillergesellschaft* 32 (1988): 94–115.
Buber, Martin. *Two Types of Faith.* Translated by Norman P. Goldhawk. New York: Collier 1951.
Buckley, Jerome. *Season of Youth: The* Bildungsroman *from Dickens to Golding.* Cambridge: Harvard University Press, 1974.
Burckhardt, Sigurd. "'Die Stimme der Wahrheit und der Menschlichkeit': Goethes 'Iphigenie.'" *Monatshefte* 48, no. 2 (February 1956): 49–71.

Burke, Peter. "Reflections on the Origins of Cultural History." In *Interpretation and Cultural History*, edited by Joan H. Pittock and Andrew Wear, 5–24. New York: St. Martin's, 1991.
Butler, Judith. *Antigone's Claim: Kinship Between Life and Death*. New York: Columbia University Press, 2000.
———. *Gender Trouble: Feminism and the Subversion of Identity*. New York: Routledge, 1990.
———. *Giving an Account of Oneself*. New York: Fordham University Press, 2005.
———. "Is Kinship Always Already Heterosexual?" In *Undoing Gender*, 102–30. New York: Routledge, 2004.
Butler, Marilyn. "Byron and the Empire in the East." In *Byron: Augustan and Romantic*, edited by Andrew Rutherford, 63–81. New York: St. Martin's, 1990.
Byrne, Peter. "The Study of Religion: Neutral, Scientific, or Neither?" *Method & Theory in the Study of Religion* 9, no. 4 (1997): 339–51.
Byron, George Gordon, Lord. "The Bride of Abydos. A Turkish Tale." In vol. 3 of *The Complete Poetical Works*, edited by Jerome McGann, 107–47. Oxford: Clarendon 1981.
———. *The Complete Poetical Works*. 7 vols. Edited by Jerome McGann. Oxford: Clarendon, 1981.
Campbell, Lyle, and William J. Poser. *Language Classification: History and Method*. Cambridge: Cambridge University Press, 2008.
Camper, Petrus (Peter). *On the Connexion between the Science of Anatomy and the Arts of Drawing, Painting, Statuary*. Translated by T. Cogan. London: C. Dilly, 1794.
Carhart, Michael. *The Science of Culture in Enlightenment Germany*. Cambridge: Harvard University Press, 2007.
Carsten, Janet. *After Kinship*. Cambridge: Cambridge University Press, 2004.
Carter, Angela. *The Sadeian Woman and the Ideology of Pornography*. New York: Pantheon, 1978.
Cascardi, Anthony J. *The Subject of Modernity*. Cambridge: Cambridge University Press, 1992.
Cassirer, Ernst. *The Logic of the Cultural Sciences*. Translated by S. G. Lofts. New Haven: Yale University Press, 2000.
Castoriadis, Cornelius. "Aeschylean Anthropology and Sophoclean Self-Creation of Anthropos." In *Agon, Logos, Polis: The Greek Achievement and Its Aftermath*, edited by Johann P. Arnason and Peter Murphy, 138–54. Stuttgart: Franz Steiner, 2001.
Caygill, Howard. *Art of Judgment*. Cambridge, Mass.: Basil Blackwell, 1989.
Chamberlain, Houston Stewart. *Die Grundlagen des Neunzehnten Jahrhunderts*. 2 vols. 10th edition. Munich: Verlagsantalt F. Bruckmann, 1912.
Chambers, Ephraim. *Cyclopaedia or, A Universal Dictionary of Arts and Sciences*. London: James and John Knapton et al., 1728. http://artfl-project.uchicago.edu/content/chambers-cyclopaedia.
Chambers, Ephraim, et al. *A Supplement to Mr. Chambers's Cyclopedia: or, Universal Dictionary of the Arts and Sciences*. 2 vols. Edited by George Scott Lewis. N.p., 1753.
Cohen-Vrignaud, Gerard. "Becoming Corsairs: Byron, British Property Rights and Orientalism Economics." *Studies in Romanticism* 50 (Winter 2011): 685–714.
Coleridge, Samuel Taylor. *The Notebooks*. Vol. 1 of *The Complete Works of Samuel Taylor Coleridge*. Bollingen Series. New York: Pantheon, 1957.

Coles, Prophecy. *The Importance of Sibling Relationships in Psychoanalysis*. London: Karnac, 2003.
Comte, Auguste. *The Positive Philosophy*. Translated and condensed by Harriet Martineau. 2 vols. London: Kegan Paul, Trench, Trübner, 1893.
Condillac, Etienne Bonnot de. *Essay on the Origin of Human Knowledge*. Translated and edited by Hans Aarsleff. Cambridge: Cambridge University Press, 2001.
Conrad, Ryan, and Yasmin Nair, eds. *Against Equality: Queer Critiques of Gay Marriage*. Lewiston, Me.: Against Equality Pub. Collective, 2010.
Coontz, Stephanie. *Marriage, a History: From Obedience to Intimacy or How Love Conquered Marriage*. New York: Viking, 2005.
Coovadia, Imraan. "George Eliot's Realism and Adam Smith." *Studies in English Literature, 1500–1900* 42, no. 4 (Autumn 2002): 819–35.
Corbett, Mary Jean. *Family Likeness: Sex, Marriage, and Incest from Jane Austen to Virginia Woolf*. Ithaca: Cornell University Press, 2008.
Daemmrich, Horst S. "The Incest Motif in Lessing's *Nathan der Weise* and Schiller's *Braut von Messina*." *Germanic Review* 42, no. 3 (1967): 184–96.
Darwin, Charles. *The Descent of Man, and Selection in Relation to Sex*. London: Penguin, 2004.
———. *The Origin of Species*. Edited by Gilliam Beer. Oxford: Oxford University Press, 1996.
Davidoff, Leonore. *Thicker Than Water: Siblings and Their Relations, 1780–1920*. Oxford: Oxford University Press, 2012.
———. "Where the Stranger Begins: The Question of Siblings in Historical Analysis." In *Worlds Between: Historical Perspectives on Gender and Class*, edited by Leonore Davidoff, 206–26. New York: Routledge, 1995.
Davidoff, Leonore, and Catherine Hall. *Family Fortunes*. Revised edition. London: Routledge, 2002.
Dawe, Roger David, ed. *Sophocles: The Classical Heritage*. New York: Garland, 1996.
Dawson, P.M.S. *The Unacknowledged Legislator: Shelley and Politics*. Oxford: Clarendon Press, 1980.
Dean, Tim. *Beyond Sexuality*. Chicago: University of Chicago Press, 2000.
Degnan, James H., and Noah A. Rosenberg. "Gene Tree Discordance, Phylogenetic Inference and the Multispecies Coalescent." *Trends in Ecology & Evolution* 24, no. 6 (June 2009): 332–40.
Deleuze, Gilles. *Masochism: An Interpretation of Coldness and Cruelty*. Translated by Jean McNeil. New York: George Braziller, 1971.
Deleuze, Gilles, and Félix Guattari. *Anti-Oedipus: Capitalism and Schizophrenia*. Minneapolis: University of Minnesota Press, 1983.
———. *Kafka: Toward a Minor Literature*. Translated by Dana Polan. Minneapolis: University of Minnesota Press. 1986.
Derrida, Jacques. *The Politics of Friendship*. Translated by George Collins. London: Verso, 1997.
Dick, Anneliese. *Weiblichkeit als natürliche Dienstbarkeit. Eine Studie zum klassischen Frauenbild in Goethes* Wilhelm Meister. Frankfurt: Peter Lang, 1986.

Dickinson, Sara. "Russia's First 'Orient': Characterizing the Crimea in 1787." *Kritika: Explorations in Russian and Eurasian History* 3, no. 1, New Series (2002): 3–25.
Dilthey, Wilhelm. *Poetry and Experience*. Edited by Rudolf Makkreel and Frithjof Rodi. In *Selected Works*. 6 vols. Princeton: Princeton University Press, 1985.
Donovan, John. "Incest in *Laon and Cythna*: Nature, Custom, Desire." *Keats-Shelley Review* 2 (1987): 42–90.
Du Bois, W.E.B. *The Souls of Black Folk*. New York: Norton, 1999.
Duffy, Cian. *Shelley and the Revolutionary Sublime*. Cambridge: Cambridge University Press, 2005.
Durham, William. "Assessing Gaps in Westermarck's Theory." In *Inbreeding, Incest, and the Incest Taboo: The State of Knowledge at the Turn of the Century*, edited by Arthur P. Wolf and William H. Durham, 121–38. Stanford: Stanford University Press, 2005.
Eigen, Sara, and Mark Larrimore. *The German Invention of Race*. Albany: State University of New York Press, 2006.
Eisenstein, Zillah. *The Radical Future of Liberal Feminism*. New York: Longman, 1981.
Elden, Stuart. "The Place of the Polis: Political Blindness in Judith Butler's *Antigone's Claim*." *Theory & Event* 8, no. 1 (2005).
Eliot, George. "The Antigone and its Moral." *Leader* 7 (March 29, 1856): 306. C19: The Nineteenth-Century Index.
———. "Brother and Sister." In *The Complete Shorter Poems*, edited by A. G. van den Broek, 2:5–11. London: Pickering & Chatto, 2005.
———. *The Mill on the Floss*. Edited by Gordon S. Haight. Oxford: Clarendon, 1980.
———. "The Morality of Wilhelm Meister." *Leader* (July 21, 1855): 703. C19: The Nineteenth-Century Index.
———. "Notes on Form in Art." In *Essays of George Eliot*, edited by Thomas Pinney, 431–36. New York: Columbia University Press, 1963.
Elshtain, Jean Bethke. "Antigone's Daughters." *Democracy* 2, no. 2 (1982): 46–59.
———. "Antigone's Daughters Reconsidered: Continuing Reflections on Women, Politics, and Power." In *Life-World and Politics: Between Modernity and Postmodernity*, edited by Stephen K. White. Notre Dame, Ind.: University of Notre Dame Press, 1989.
Endres, Johannes. "Nathan Disenchanted: Continuity and Discontinuity of Enlightenment in Schiller's The Bride of Messina." *Historical Reflecitons/Reflexions Historiques* 26, no. 3 (2000): 405–27.
Engels, Frederick. *The Origin of the Family, Private Property, and the State. In the Light of the Researches by Lewis H. Morgan*. Vol. 26 of Karl Marx and Frederick Engels, *Collected Works*, 129–276. New York: International, 1990.
Engelstein, Stefani. "The Allure of Wholeness: The Organism Around 1800 and the Same-Sex Marriage Debate." *Critical Inquiry* 39, no. 4 (2013): 754–76.
———. *Anxious Anatomy: The Conception of the Human Form in Literary and Naturalist Discourse*. Albany: State University of New York Press, 2008.
———. "Coining a Discipline: Lessing, Reimarus, and a Science of Religion." In *Fact and Fiction: Literature and Science in the European Context*, edited by Christine Lehleiter, 221–46. Toronto: University of Toronto Press, 2016.

———. "Ismene on Horseback and Other Subjects." *Philosophy Today* 59, no. 3 (2015).

———. "Sibling Incest and Cultural Voyeurism in Günderode's *Udohla* and Thomas Mann's *Wälsungenblut*." *German Quarterly* 77, no. 3 (July 2004): 278–99.

Erhart, Walter. "Drama der Anerkennung. Neue gesellshcatstheoretische Überlegungen zu Goethes *Iphigenie auf Tauris*." *Jahrbuch der deutschen Schillergesellschaft* 51 (2007): 140–65.

Errington, Joseph. *Linguistics in a Colonial World: A Story of Language, Meaning, and Power*. Malden, Mass.: Blackwell, 2008.

Estes, Steve. *"I Am A Man." Race, Manhood, and the Civil Rights Movement*. Chapel Hill: University of North Carolina Press, 2005.

Esty, Joshua. "Nationhood, Adulthood, and the Ruptures of *Bildung*: Arresting Development in *The Mill on the Floss*." In *The Mill on the Floss and Silas Marner: George Eliot*, edited by Nahem Yousaf and Andrew Maunder, 101–21. Basingstoke: Palgrave Macmillan, 2002.

Ettinger, Bracha. *The Matrixial Borderspace*. Edited by Brian Massumi. Minneapolis: University of Minnesota Press, 2006.

———. "Transgressing With-In-To the Feminine." In *Differential Aesthetics: Art Practices, Philosophy and Feminist Understandings*, edited by Penny Florence and Nicola Foster, 184–209. Aldershot: Ashgate, 2000.

European Union website. http://europa.eu/abc/symbols/anthem/index_en.htm.

Evans, William McKee. "From the Land of Canaan to the Land of Guinea: The Strange Odyssey of the 'Sons of Ham.'" *American Historical Review* 85, no. 1 (1980): 15–43.

Fabian, Johannes. *Time and the Other: How Anthropology Makes Its Object*. New York: Columbia University Press, 2002.

Farquharson, R. H. "Lessing's Dervish and the Mystery of the Dervish-Nachspiel." *Lessing Yearbook* 18 (1986): 47–67.

Feldt, Jakob Egholm. *Transnationalism and the Jews: Culture, History, and Prophecy*. London: Rowman & Littlefield, 2016.

Fellman, Jack. "Further Remarks on the Scythian Language." *Language Sciences* 41 (1976): 19.

———. "On Sir William Jones and the Scythian Language." *Language Sciences* 34 (1975): 37–38.

Ferguson, Harvie. *Modernity and Subjectivity: Body, Soul, Spirit*. Charlottesville: University Press of Virginia, 2000.

Fessler, Daniel M. T., and C. David Navarrete. "Third-Party Attitudes Toward Sibling Incest. Evidence for Westermarck's Hypotheses." *Evolution and Human Behavior* 25 (2004): 277–94.

Fichte, Johann Gottlieb. *Addresses to the German Nation*. Translated by Isaac Nakhimovsky, Béla Kapossy, and Keith Tribe. Indianapolis: Hackett, 2013.

———. *Die Grundzüge des gegenwärtigen Zeitalters*. Hamburg: Felix Meiner, 1978.

Filmer, Robert. *Patriarcha and Other Writings*. Edited by Johann Sommerville. Cambridge: Cambridge University Press, 1991.

Finney, Gail. "Self-Reflexive Siblings: Incest as Narcissism in Tieck, Wagner, and Thomas Mann." *German Quarterly* 56, no. 2 (1983): 243–56.

Fischer, Jens Malte. "Richard Wagners Das Judenthum in der Musik." In *Richard Wagner und die Juden*, edited by Dieter Borchmeyer, Ami Maayani, and Susanne Vill, 35–54. Stuttgart: J. B. Metzler, 2000.

Flannery, Denis. *On Sibling Love, Queer Attachment and American Writing*. Hampshire: Ashgate, 2007.
Foley, Richard. "The Order Question: Climbing the Ladder of Love in Plato's Symposium." *Ancient Philosophy* 30 (2010): 57–72.
Foreman, Terry. "Lessing and the Quest for Religious Truth 200 Years On: His Role in the Current Anglophone Culture-War." *Lessing Yearbook* 32 (2000): 391–405.
Forster, Georg. "Something More About the Human Races." 1786. In *Kant and the Concept of Race: Late Eighteenth-Century Writings*. Translated and edited by Jon M. Mikkelsen, 143–68. Albany: State University of New York Press, 2013.
Foucault, Michel. *The Birth of Biopolitics: Lectures at the Collège de France, 1978–1979*. Edited by Michel Sennelart. Translated by Graham Burchell. New York: Palgrave Macmillan, 2008.
———. *The History of Sexuality: An Introduction*. Translated by Robert Hurley. New York: Vintage, 1978.
———. "Nietzsche, Genealogy, History." In *Language, Counter-memory, Practice: Selected Essays and Interviews*, edited by Donald F. Bouchard, translated by Donald F. Bouchard and Sherry Simon, 139–64. Ithaca: Cornell University Press, 1977.
———. *The Order of Things: An Archeology of the Human Sciences*. London: Routledge, 2007.
———. *Security, Territory, Populations: Lectures at the Collège de France, 1977–1978*. Edited by Michel Sennelart. Translated by Graham Burchell. New York: Palgrave Macmillan, 2007.
Fowler, Frank M. "Matters of Motivation: In Defence of Schiller's *Die Braut von Messina*." *German Life and Letters* 39, no. 2 (1986): 134–47.
Fraiman, Susan. "*The Mill on the Floss*, the Critics, and the Bildungsroman." *PMLA* 108, no. 1 (January 1993): 136–50.
Fraley, R. Chris, and Michael J. Marks. "Westermarck, Freud, and the Incest Taboo: Does Familial Resemblance Activate Sexual Attraction?" *Personality and Social Psychology Bulletin* 36 (2010): 1202–12.
Franklin, Sarah. *Dolly Mixtures: The Remaking of Genealogy*. Durham: Duke University Press, 2007.
Franklin, Sarah, and Susan McKinnon, eds. *Relative Values: Reconfiguring Kinship Studies*. Durham: Duke University Press, 2001.
Franklin-Hall, L. R. "Trashing Life's Tree." *Biology and Philosophy* 25 (2010): 689–709.
Freud, Sigmund. "Fetischismus." In *Gesammelte Werke*, edited by Anna Freud. Frankfurt: S. Fischer, 1976.
———. "Group Psychology and the Analysis of the Ego." In *Standard Edition of the Complete Psychological Works of Sigmund Freud*. Vol. 18. Edited and translated by James Strachey, 65–144. London: Hogarth, 1955.
Freytag, Gustav. *Soll und Haben*. Vols. 4–5 of *Gesammelte Werke*. Leipzig: von S. Hitzel, 1887.
Frosch, Thomas. *Shelley and the Romantic Imagination: A Psychological Study*. Newark: University of Delaware Press, 2007.
Fulda, Daniel. *Schau-Spiele des Geldes*. Tübingen: Max Niemeyer, 2005.
Gailus, Andreas. "Forms of Life: Nature, Culture, and Art in Goethe's Wilhelm Meister's Apprenticeship." *Germanic Review* 87 (2012): 138–74.

Gallop, Jane. "The Liberated Woman." *Narrative* 13, no. 2 (May 2005): 89–104.
Garber, John. "Von der Menschheitsgeschichte zur Kulturgeschichte. Zum geschichtstheoretischen Kulturbegriff der deutschen Spätaufklärung." In *Kultur zwischen Bürgertum und Volk*, edited by Jutta Held, 76–97. Berlin: Augument-Verlag, 1983.
Gardt, Andreas. *Geschichte der Sprachwissenschaft in Deutschland vom Mittelalter bis ins 20. Jahrhundert*. Berlin: Walter de Gruyter, 1999.
Garloff, Katja. *Mixed Feelings: Tropes of Love in German Jewish Culture*. Ithaca: Cornell University Press, 2016.
——. "Sublimation and Its Discontents: Christian-Jewish Love in Lessing's Nathan der Weise." *Lessing Yearbook/Jahrbuch* 36 (2004/2005): 51–68.
Gay, Peter. "Wagner aus psychoanalytischer Sicht." In *Richard Wagner und die Juden*, edited by Dieter Borchmeyer, Ami Maayani, and Susanne Vill, 251–60. Stuttgart: J. B. Metzler, 2000.
Gilbert, Sandra M., and Susan Gubar. *The Madwoman in the Attic: The Woman Writer and the Nineteenth-Century Literary Imagination*. New Haven: Yale University Press, 1979.
Gilligan, Carol. *In a Different Voice: Psychological Theory and Women's Development*. Cambridge: Harvard University Press, 1982.
Gilman, Sander. "Sibling Incest, Madness, and the 'Jews.'" *Jewish Social Studies* 4, no. 2 (1998): 157–79.
Gilman, Sander. *Jewish Self-Hatred: Anti-Semitism and the Hidden Language of the Jews*. Baltimore: Johns Hopkins University Press, 1986.
Gobineau, Arthur de. *The Inequality of Human Races*. Preface by George Mosse. Translator not named. New York: Howard Fertig, 1999.
Goethe, Johann Wolfgang von. *Briefe, Tagebücher, Gespräche*. CD_ROM. Edited by Mathias Bertram. Berlin: Directmedia, 2000.
——. "From The Conversations of Goethe with Eckermann and Soret." In *Sophocles: The Classical Heritage*, edited by Roger David Dawe, 171–77. New York: Garland, 1996.
——. *Iphigenie auf Tauris*. In *Sämtliche Werke*, 5:553–619. Frankfurt: Deutscher Klassiker Verlag, 1991.
——. *Iphigenia in Tauris*. In *Plays*, translated by Frank Ryder, 81–143. New York: Continuum, 1993.
——. "Observation on Morphology in General." In *Scientific Studies*, edited and translated by Douglas Miller. Vol. 12 of *The Collected Works*. Princeton: Princeton University Press, 1988.
——. *Sämtliche Werke*. 40 vols. Frankfurt: Deutscher Klassiker Verlag, 1991.
——. *Wilhelm Meister's Apprenticeship*. Edited and translated by Eric A. Blackall. Vol. 9 of *The Collected Works*. Princeton: Princeton University Press, 1989.
——. *Wilhelm Meisters Lehrjahre*. In vol. 9 of *Sämtliche Werke*, 355–992. Frankfurt: Deutscher Klassiker Verlag, 1991.
Goetschel, Willi. "Lessing's 'Jewish' Questions." *Germanic Review* 78, no. 1 (2003): 62–73.
——. "Negotiating Truth: On Nathan's Business." *Lessing Yearbook/Jahrbuch* 28 (1996): 105–23.
Goldhill, Simon. "Antigone and the Politics of Sisterhood." In *Laughing with Medusa: Classical Myth and Feminist Thought*, edited by Vanda Zajko and Miriam Leonard, 141–61. Oxford: Oxford University Press, 2006.

———. *Sophocles and the Language of Tragedy*. Oxford: Oxford University Press, 2012.

Gontier, Nathalie. "Depicting the Tree of Life: The Philosophical and Historical Roots of Evolutionary Tree Diagrams." *Evolution: Education and Outreach* 4 (2011): 515–38.

Goodman, Charlotte. "The Lost Brother, the Twin: Women Novelists and the Male-Female Double Bildungsroman." *Novel* 17, no. 1 (Autumn 1983): 28–43.

Gordon-Reed, Annette. *Thomas Jefferson and Sally Hemings: An American Controversy*. Charlottesville: University of Virginia Press, 1997.

Gourgouris, Stathis. *Does Literature Think? Literature as Theory for an Antimythical Era*. Stanford: Stanford University Press, 2003.

Gray, Richard. "Skeptische Philologie: Friedrich Schlegel, Friedrich Nietzsche und eine Philologie der Zukunft." *Nietzsche-Studien* 38 (2009): 39–64.

Greiner, Rae. "Sympathy Time: Adam Smith, George Eliot, and the Realist Novel." *Narrative* 17, no. 3 (October 2009): 291–311.

Grene, David. "Introduction." In Sophocles, *Sophocles I: Oedipus the King. Oedipus at Colonus. Antigone*, translated and introduced by David Grene, 1–8. The Complete Greek Tragedies, edited by David Grene and Richard Lattimore. Chicago: University of Chicago Press, 1991.

Griffith, Mark. Commentary. In Sophocles, *Antigone*, edited by Mark Griffith, 119–355. Cambridge Greek and Latin Classics, edited by P. E. Easterling, Philip Hardie, Richard Hunter, and E. J. Kenney. Cambridge: Cambridge University Press, 1999.

Griffiths, Devin. *The Age of Analogy: Science and Literature Between the Darwins*. Baltimore: Johns Hopkins University Press, 2016.

Grimm, Jakob, and Wilhelm Grimm. *Deutsches Wörterbuch*. 1854–1971. http://dwb.uni-trier.de/de/.

———. *The German Legends of the Brothers Grimm*. Edited and translated by Donald Ward. 2 vols. Philadelphia: Institute for the Study of Human Issues, 1981.

Grossman, Jeffrey A. *The Discourse on Yiddish in Germany from the Enlightenment to the Second Empire*. Rochester, NY: Camden House, 2000.

Grosz, Elizabeth. *Becoming Undone: Darwinian Reflections on Life, Politics, and Art*. Durham: Duke University Press, 2011.

Gruber, Howard E. "Darwins's 'Tree of Nature' and Other Images of Wide Scope." In *On Aesthetics in Science*, edited by Judith Wechsler, 121–42. Cambridge: MIT Press, 1978.

Grünbaum, Max. *Mischsprachen und Sprachmischungen*. No. 473 in Sammlung Gemeinverständlicher Wissenschaftlicher Vorträge, edited by Rudolf Virchow and Fr. von Holtzendorff. Berlin: von Carl Habel, 1885.

Günderrode, Karoline von. *Gesammelte Werke*. 3 vols. Berlin: Goldschmidt-Gabrielli, 1920.

Gurd, Sean. *Philology and Its Histories*. Columbus: Ohio State University Press, 2010.

Guthke, Karl S. "Die Geburt des Nathan aus dem Geist der Reimarus-Fragmente." *Lessing Yearbook/Jahrbuch* 36 (2004/2005): 13–49.

Habermas, Rebekka. *Frauen und Männer des Bürgertums*. Bürgertum: Beiträge zur europäischen Gesellschaftsgeschichte 14. Edited by Niethard Bulst, Wolfgang Mager, Peter Lundgreen, and Hans-Ulrich Weher. Göttingen: Vanderhoeck and Ruprecht, 2000.

Haraway, Donna J. "Race: Universal Donors in a Vampire Culture." In *Modest_Witness@ Second_Millennium. FemaleMan©_Meets_OncoMouse™: Feminism and Technoscience*, 213–65. New York: Routledge, 1997.

Hardt, Michael, and Antonio Negri. *Empire*. Cambridge: Harvard University Press, 2000.

——. *Multitude: War and Democracy in the Age of Empire*. New York: Penguin, 2004.

Harley, Alexis. *Autobiologies: Charles Darwin and the Natural History of the Self*. Lewisburg, Pa.: Bucknell University Press, 2015.

Harpham, Geoffrey Galt. "Roots, Races, and the Return to Philology." *Representations* 106, no. 1 (Spring 2009): 34–62.

Harrisville, Roy A., and Walter Sundberg. *The Bible in Modern Culture: Baruch Spinoza to Brevard Childs*. Grand Rapids, Mich.: Eerdmans, 2002.

Hart, Gail. *Tragedy in Paradise: Family and Gender Politics in German Bourgeois Tragedy 1750–1850*. Columbia, S.C.: Camden House, 1996.

Hayles, Donna Haraway. "Race: Universal Donors in a Vampire Culture." In *Modest_Witness@ Second_Millennium.FemaleMan©_Meets_OncoMouse™: Feminism and* Technoscience, 213–66. New York: Routledge, 1997.

Hegel, Georg Wilhelm Friedrich. *Aesthetics: Lectures on Fine Art*. Translated by T. M. Knox. 2 vols. Oxford: Clarendon, 1974.

——. *Elements of the Philosophy of Right*. Edited by Allen W. Wood. Translated by H. B. Nisbet. Cambridge: Cambridge University Press, 1991.

——. *Enzyklopädie der Philosophischen Wissenschaften im Grundrisse*. Edited by Wolfgang Bonsiepen and Hans-Christian Lucas. Vol. 20 of *Gesammelte Werke*. Rheinisch-Westfälischen Akademie der Wissenschaften. Hamburg: Felix Meiner, 1992.

——. *Grundlinien der Philosophie des Rechts*. Vol. 7 of *Sämtliche Werke*, edited by Hermann Glockner. Stuttgart: Friedrich Fromann, 1964.

——. *Phänomenologie des Geistes*. Vol. 9 of *Gesammelte Werke*, edited by Wolfgang Bonsiepen and Reinhard Heede. Rheinisch-Westfälischen Akademie der Wissenschaften. Hamburg: Felix Meiner, 1980.

——. *Phenomenology of Spirit*. Translated by A. V. Miller. Oxford: Oxford University Press, 1977.

Heidegger, Martin. *Hölderlin's Hymn "The Ister."* Translated by William McNeill and Julia Davis. Bloomington: Indiana University Press, 1991.

——. *Introduction to Metaphysics*. Translated by Gregory Fried and Richard Polt. New Haven: Yale University Press, 2000.

Held, Virginia. *The Ethics of Care: Personal, Political, and Global*. Oxford: Oxford University Press, 2006.

Helfer, Martha B. "Wilhelm Meister's Women." *Goethe Yearbook* 11 (2002): 229–54.

——. *The Word Unheard: Legacies of Anti-Semitism in German Literature and Culture*. Evanston, Ill.: Northwestern University Press, 2011.

Hellström, Nils Petter. "Darwin and the Tree of Life: The Roots of the Evolutionary Tree." *Archives of Natural History* 39, no. 2 (2012): 234–52.

Hemphill, C. Dallett. *Siblings: Brothers and Sisters in American History*. Oxford: Oxford University Press, 2011.

Herder, Johann Gottfried von. "Auch eine Philosophie der Geschichte zur Bildung der Menschheit." In Vol. 4 of *Werke in zehn Bänden*, edited by Martin Bollacher, 9–107. Frankfurt: Deutscher Klassiker Verlag, 1994.

———. "This too a Philosophy of History for the Formation of Humanity." In *Philosophical Writings*, translated and edited by Michael N. Forster, 272–358. Cambridge: Cambridge University Press, 2002.

———. "Treatise on the Origin of Language." In *Philosophical Writings*, translated and edited by Michael N. Forster, 65–164. Cambridge: Cambridge University Press, 2002.

———. "Über den Ursprung der Sprache." In *Frühe Schriften*. Vol. 1 of *Werke in zehn Bänden*, edited by Martin Bollacher, 695–810. Frankfurt: Deutscher Klassiker Verlag, 1985.

Hertz, Neil. *George Eliot's Pulse*. Stanford: Stanford University Press, 2003.

Heschel, Susannah. *The Aryan Jesus: Christian Theologians and the Bible in Nazi Germany*. Princeton: Princeton University Press, 2008.

———. "The Image of Judaism in Nineteenth-Century Christian New Testament Scholarship in Germany." In *Jewish-Christian Encounters Over the Centuries: Symbiosis, Prejudice, Holocaust, Dialog*, edited by Marvin Perry and Frederick M. Schweitzer, 215–40. New York: Peter Lang, 1994.

Hess, Jonathan. *Germans, Jews and the Claims of Modernity*. New Haven: Yale University Press, 2002.

———. *Reconstituting the Body Politic: Enlightenment, Public Culture and the Invention of Aesthetic Autonomy*. Detroit: Wayne State University Press, 1999.

Hirsch, Marianne. "Spiritual *Bildung*: The Beautiful Soul as Paradigm." In *The Voyage In: Fictions of Female Development*, edited by Elizabeth Abel, Marianne Hirsch, and Elizabeth Langland, 23–48. Hanover, N.H.: University Press of New England, 1983.

Hjelde, Sigurd. *Die Religionswissenschaft & das Christentum. Eine historische Untersuchung über das Verhältnis von Religionswissenschaft & Theologie*. Leiden: E. J. Brill, 1994.

Hoenigswald, Henry M. "On the History of the Comparative Method." *Anthropological Linguistics* 5, no. 1 (1963): 1–11.

Hogle, Jerrold E. *Shelley's Process: Radical Transference and the Development of His Major Works*. New York: Oxford University Press, 1988.

Hohendahl, Peter Uwe. "German Classicism and the Law of the Father." In *Literary Paternity, Literary Friendship: Essays in Honor of Stanley Corngold*, edited by Gerhard Richter, 63–85. Chapel Hill: University of North Carolina Press, 2002.

Hohkamp, Michaela. "Do Sisters Have Brothers? The Search for the 'rechte Schwester.' Brothers and Sisters in Aristocratic Society at the Turn of the Sixteenth Century." In *Sibling Relations and the Transformation of European Kinship, 1300–1900*, edited by David Warren Sabean and Christopher Johnson, 65–83. Oxford: Berghan, 2011.

Hölderlin, Friedrich. "Antigonae." In vol. 2 of *Sämtliche Werke und Briefe*, edited by Jochen Schmidt, 859–912. Frankfurt: Deutscher Klassiker Verlag, 1994.

Holm, Gösta. "Carl Johan Schlyter and Textual Scholarship." In *Saga Och Sed*, edited by Dag Strömbäck, 48–80. Uppsala: A. B. Lundequistska Bokhandelsn, 1972.

Homans, Margaret. "Dinah's Blush, Maggie's Arm: Class, Gender, and Sexuality in George Eliot's Early Novels." *Victorian Studies* 36, no. 2 (Winter 1993): 155–78.

———. "Eliot, Wordsworth, and the Scenes of the Sisters' Instruction." *Critical Inquiry* 8, no. 2 (Winter 1981): 223–41.

Honig, Bonnie. *Antigone, Interrupted*. Cambridge: Cambridge University Press, 2013.

Hörisch, Jochen. *Gott, Geld, und Glück: Zur Logik der Liebe in den Bildungsromanen Goethes, Kellers und Thomas Mann*. Frankfurt: Suhrkamp, 1983.

Horkheimer, Max, and Theodor Adorno. *Dialectic of Enlightenment*. Translated by John Cumming. New York: Continuum, 1994.

Humboldt, Wilhelm von. *On Language: The Diversity of Human Language Structure and Its Influence on the Mental Development of Mankind*. Translated by Peter Heath. Cambridge: Cambridge University Press, 1988.

———. *Über die Verschiedenheit des menschlichen Sprachbaues und ihren Einfluss auf die geistige Entwicklung des Menschengeschlechts*. Vol. 3 of *Werke in Fünf Bänden*, edited by Andreas Flitner and Klause Giel, 368–756. Stuttgart: J. G. Cotta'sche Buchhandlung, 1965.

Hume, David. "The Natural History of Religion." *A Dissertation on the Passions and The Natural History of Religion*, edited by Tom L. Beauchamp. Oxford: Clarendon, 2007.

Hunt, James. "The President's Address." *Journal of the Anthropological Society of London* 5 (1867): xliv–lxxi.

Hunt, Lynn. *The Family Romance of the French Revolution*. Berkeley: University of California Press, 1992.

Hutton, Christopher M. *Linguistics and the Third Reich: Mother-Tongue Fascism, Race and the Science of Language*. London: Routledge, 1999.

———. *Race and the Third Reich: Linguistics, Racial Anthropology and Genetics in the Dialectic of Volk*. Cambridge: Polity, 2005.

Irigaray, Luce. *Speculum of the Other Woman*. Translated by Gillian G. Gill. Ithaca: Cornell University Press, 1985.

———. *This Sex Which Is Not One*. Translated by Catherine Porter. Ithaca: Cornell University Press, 1985.

———. *The Way of Love*. Translated by Heidi Bostic and Stephen Pluháček. London: Continuum, 2002.

Issatschenko, A. V. "Allgemeine Fragestellungen bei H. Schuchardt und in der heutigen Sprachwissenschaft." In *Hugo Schuchardt. Schuchardt-Symposium 1977 in Graz*, edited by Klaus Lichem and Hans Joachim Simon. Vienna: Verlag der Österreichischen Akademie der Wissenschaften, 1980.

Jacobs, Carol. "Dusting Antigone." *Modern Language Notes* 111 (1996): 889–917.

Jaeger, Hans. "Generations in History: Reflections on a Controversial Concept." *History & Theory* 24, no. 3 (1985): 273–92.

Jarzebowski, Claudia. *Inzest: Verwandtschaft und Sexualität im achtzehnten Jahrhundert*. Cologne: Böhlau, 2006.

Jensen, Anthony K. "Meta-Historical Transitions from Philology to Genealogy." *Journal of Nietzsche Studies* 44, no. 2 (2013): 196–212.

John, David G. "Lessing, Islam and Nathan der Weise in Africa." *Lessing Yearbook/Jahrbuch* 32 (2000): 245–57.

Johnson, Christopher. *Becoming Bourgeois: Love, Kinship, and Power in Provincial France, 1670–1880*. Ithaca: Cornell University Press, 2015.

Johnson, Dirk R. *Nietzsche's Anti-Darwinism*. Cambridge: Cambridge University Press, 2010.

Jones, William. *Discourses Delivered Before the Asiatic Society*. 2 vols. Edited by James Elmes. London: Charles S. Arnold, 1824.

Joris, Elisabeth. "Kinship and Gender: Property, Enterprise, and Politics." In *Kinship in Europe: Approaches to Long-Term Development (1300–1900)*, edited by David Warren Sabean, Simon Teuscher, and Jon Mathieu, 231–57. New York: Berghahn, 2007.

Joseph, Gerhard. "The Antigone as Cultural Touchstone: Matthew Arnold, Hegel, George Eliot, Virginia Woolf, and Margaret Drabble." *PMLA* 96, no. 1 (January 1981): 22–35.

Kaiser, Gerhard. *Väter und Brüder: Weltordnung und gesellschaftlich-politische Ordnung in Schillers Werk*. Leipzig: Verlag der Sächsischen Akademie der Wissenschaften zu Leipzig, 2007.

Kant, Immanuel. "Conjectures on the Beginning of Human History." In *Kant: Political Writings*, edited by Hans Reiss and translated by H. B. Nisbet, 221–34. Cambridge: Cambridge University Press, 1991.

———. "Determination of the Concept of a Human Race." 1785. In *Kant and the Concept of Race: Late Eighteenth-Century Writings*, translated and edited by Jon M. Mikkelsen, 125–141. Albany: State University of New York Press, 2013.

———. *Kants gesammelte Schriften*. Edited by Königlich Preußischen Akademie der Wissenschaften. Berlin: Walter de Gruyter and predecessors, 1902–.

———. "Of the Different Human Races." 1777. In *Kant and the Concept of Race: Late Eighteenth-Century Writings*, translated and edited by Jon M. Mikkelsen, 55–71. Albany: State University of New York Press, 2013.

———. "On the Use of Teleological Principles in Philosophy." 1788. In *Kant and the Concept of Race: Late Eighteenth-Century Writings*, translated and edited by Jon M. Mikkelsen, 169–94. Albany: State University of New York Press, 2013.

Kitson, Peter. "Byron and Post-Colonial Criticism: The Eastern Tales." In *Palgrave Advances in Byron Studies*, edited by Jane Stabler, 106–29. Basingstoke: Palgrave Macmillan, 2007.

Kittler, Friedrich. *Discourse Networks: 1800/1900*. Translated by Michael Metteer, with Chris Cullens. Stanford: Stanford University Press, 1990.

———. "Über die Sozialisation Wilhelm Meisters." In *Dichtung als Sozialisationsspiel*, edited by Gerhard Kaiser and Friedrich Kittler. Göttingen: Vanderhoeck and Ruprecht, 1979.

Kluge, G. R. "Wälsungenblut oder Halbblut? Zur Kontroverse um die Schlußsätze von Thomas Manns Novelle." *Neophilologus* 76 (1992): 237–55.

Knodt, Eva M. "Herder and Lessing on Truth: Toward an Ethics of Incommunicability." *Lessing Yearbook* 28 (1996): 125–46.

Kofman, Sarah. "Rousseau's Phallocratic Ends." Translated by Mara Dukats. In *Feminist Interpretations of Jean-Jacques Rousseau*, edited by Lynda Lange, 229–44. University Park: Pennsylvania State University Press, 2002.

Kontje, Todd. "Thomas Mann's 'Wälsungenblut': The Married Artist and the 'Jewish Question.'" *PMLA* 123, no. 1 (2008): 109–24.

Koschorke, Albrecht, Nacim Ghanbari, Eva Eßlinger, Sebastian Susteck, and Michael Thomas Taylor. *Vor der Familie. Grenzbedingungen einer modernen Institution*. Munich: Konstanz University Press, 2010.

Kreisel, Deanna. "Superfluity and Suction: The Problem with Saving in *The Mill on the Floss*." *Novel* 35, no. 1 (2001): 69–103.

Krimmer, Elisabeth. "Abortive *Bildung*: Women Writers, Male Bonds, and Would-Be Fathers." In *Challenging Separate Spheres: Female Bildung in Eighteenth- and Nineteenth-Century Germany*, edited by Marjanne Goozé, 235–59. Oxford: Peter Lang, 2007.

———. "Mama's Baby, Papa's Maybe: Paternity and Bildung in Goethe's Wilhelm Meisters Lehrjahre." *German Quarterly* 77, no. 3 (2004): 257–77.

Kristeva, Julia. *Powers of Horror: An Essay on Abjection*. Translated by Leon Roudiez. New York: Columbia University Press, 1982.

Kucich, John. "George Eliot and Objects: Meaning as Matter in *The Mill on the Floss*." *Dickens Studies Annual* 12 (1983): 319–40.

Kuper, Adam. *Incest and Influence: The Private Life of Bourgeois England*. Cambridge: Harvard University Press, 2009.

Kuschel, Karl-Josef. *"Jud, Christ und Muselmann vereinigt"? Lessings "Nathan der Weise."* Düsseldorf: Patmos, 2004.

———. *Vom Streit zum Wettstreit der Religion. Lessing und die Herausforderung des Islam*. Düsseldorf: Patmos, 1998.

Lacan, Jacques. *The Ethics of Psychoanalysis: 1959–1960*. Book 7 of *The Seminar of Jacques Lacan*. Edited by Jacques-Alain Miller. Translated by Dennis Porter. New York: Norton, 1992.

———. "The Family Complexes." Translated by Carolyn Asp. *Critical Texts* 5, no. 3 (1983): 12–29.

Lagarde, Paul de. "Die Religion der Zukunft." In *Deutsche Schriften*, 209–58. Berlin: Verlag der Freunde, 1994.

Lagarde, Paul de. "Über die gegenwärtigen Aufgaben der deutschen Politik." In *Deutsche Schriften*, 3–33. Berlin: Verlag der Freunde, 1994.

Lagarde, Paul de. *Juden und Indogermanen. Eine Studie nach dem Leben*. Göttingen: Dieterische Universitätsbuchhandlung, 1887.

Lamport, Francis. "Virgins, Bastards and Saviors of the Nation: Reflections on Schiller's Historical Dramas." In *Schiller: National Poet—Poet of Nations*, edited by Nicholas Martin, 159–77. Amsterdam: Rodopi, 2006.

Landes, Joan. *Women and the Public Sphere in the Age of the French Revolution*. Ithaca: Cornell University Press, 1988.

Lang, George. *Entwisted Tongues: Comparative Creole Literatures*. Amsterdam: Rodopi, 2000.

Langland, Elizabeth. *Nobody's Angels: Middle-Class Women and Domestic Ideology in Victorian Culture*. Ithaca: Cornell University Press, 1995.

Latour, Bruno. *On the Modern Cult of the Factish Gods*. Translated by Catherine Porter, Heather MacLean, et al. Durham: Duke University Press, 2010.

Lanzinger, Margareth. *Verwaltete Verwandtschaft. Eheverbote, kirchliche und staatliche Dispenspraxis im 18./19. Jahrhundert*. Wien: Böhlau, 2015.

Lazarus, Moritz. *Was heißt national? Ein Vortrag*. Berlin: Ferdinand Dümmlers Verlagsbuchhandlung, 1880.

Lazzaro-Weis, Carol. "The Female 'Bildungsroman': Calling It Into Question." *National Women's Studies Association Journal* 2, no. 1 (1990): 16–34.

Leask, Nigel. *British Romantic Writers and the East*. Cambridge: Cambridge University Press, 1992.

Leavitt, Gregory C. "The Incest Taboo? A Reconsideration of Westermarck." *Anthropological Theory* 7 (2002): 393–418.

Leibniz, Gottfried Wilhelm. *Neue Abhandlungen über den menschlichen Verstand*. Vol. 3 of *Philosophische Werke in vier Bänden*, translated and edited by Ernst Cassirer. Hamburg: Feliz Meiner, 1996.

Leonard, Miriam, "Lacan, Irigaray, and Beyond: Antigones and the Politics of Psychoanalysis." In *Laughing with Medusa: Classical Myth and Feminist Thought*, edited by Vanda Zajko and Miriam Leonard, 121–40. Oxford: Oxford University Press, 2006..

Lessing, Gotthold Ephraim. "Commentary on the Fragments of Reimarus." In *Philosophical and Theological Writings*, edited and translated by H. B. Nisbet, 61–82. Cambridge Texts in the History of Philosophy. Cambridge: Cambridge University Press, 2005.

———. "The Education of the Human Race." In *Philosophical and Theological Writings*, edited and translated by H. B. Nisbet, 217–40. Cambridge Texts in the History of Philosophy. Cambridge: Cambridge University Press, 2005.

———. *Laocöon: An Essay on the Limits of Painting and Poetry*. Translated by Edward Allen McCormick. Baltimore: Johns Hopkins University Press, 1982.

———. *Nathan the Wise*. Translated and edited by Ronald Schechter. Boston: Bedford, 2004.

———. *Werke und Briefe*. Edited by Wilfried Barner. 12 vols. Frankfurt: Deutscher Klassiker Verlag, 1989.

Levenson, Alan. "Thoman Mann's *Wälsungenblut* in the Context of the Intermarriage Debate and the 'Jewish Question.'" In *Insiders and Outsiders: Jewish and Gentile Culture in Germany and Austria*, edited by Dagmar Lorenz and Gabriele Weinberger, 135–43. Detroit: Wayne State University Press, 1994.

Leventhal, Robert S. "The Parable as Performance: Interpretation, Cultural Transmission and Political Strategy in Lessing's *Nathan der Weise*." *German Quarterly* 61, no. 4 (1988): 502–27.

Levesque, Paul. "The Double-Edged Sword: Anti-Semitism and Anti-Wagnerianism in Thomas Mann's *Wälsungenblut*." *German Studies Review* 20, no. 1 (1997): 9–21.

Lévi-Strauss, Claude. *The Elementary Structures of Kinship*. Edited by Rodney Needham. Translated by James Harle Bell, John Richard von Sturmer, and Rodney Needham. Boston: Beacon, 1969.

———. *Structural Anthropology*. Translated by Claire Jacobson and Brooke Grundfest Schoepf. New York: Basic Books, 1963.

Lewes, George Henry. "Ages of Fetichism and Polytheism." In *Comte's Philosophy of the Sciences*, 273–87. London: Henry G. Bohn, 1853.

———. "Studies in Animal Life." *Cornhill Magazine* 1, no. 4 (1860): 438–47.

Lieberman, Debra, John Tooby, and Leda Cosmides. "The Architecture of Human Kin Detection." *Nature* 445 (February 15, 2007): 727–31.

———. "Does Morality Have a Biological Basis? An Empirical Test of the Factors Governing Moral Sentiments Relating to Incest." *Proceedings of the Royal Society London* 270 (2003): 819–26.

Locke, John. *An Essay Concerning Human Understanding*. Edited by Peter H. Nidditch. Oxford: Clarendon, 1975.

———.. *Two Treatises of Government*. Edited by Peter Laslett. Cambridge: Cambridge University Press, 1988.

Logan, Peter Melville. "George Eliot and the Fetish of Realism." *Studies in the Literary Imagination* 35, no. 2 (2002): 27–51.

Loraux, Nicole. *Born of the Earth: Myth and Politics in Athens*. Translated by Selina Stewart. Ithaca: Cornell University Press, 2000.

Lottmann, André. *Arbeitsverhältnisse. Der arbeitende Mensch in Goethes Wilhelm Meister-Romanen und in der Geschichte der Politischen Ökonomie*. Würzburg: Königshausen and Neumann, 2011.

Luhmann, Niklas. *Love as Passion: The Codification of Intimacy*. Translated by Jeremy Gaines and Doris L. Jones. Cambridge: Polity, 1986.

Lukács, Georg. *Goethe and His Age*. Translated by Robert Anchor. London: Merlin, 1968.

Lynch, Michael, and Bruce Walsh. *Genetics and Analysis of Quantitative Traits*. Sunderland, Mass.: Sinauer, 1998.

MacCannell, Juliet Flower. *The Regime of the Brother: After the Patriarchy*. Routledge: London, 1991.

MacLeod, Catriona. *Embodying Ambiguity: Androgyny and Aesthetics from Winckelmann to Keller*. Detroit: Wayne State University Press, 1998.

Mahl, Bernd. *Goethes ökonomisches Wissen. Grundlagen zum Verständnis der ökonomischen Passagen im dichterischen Gesamtwerk und in den "Amtlichen Schriften."* Frankfurt: Peter Lang, 1982.

Maierhofer, Waltraud. "Angelica Kauffmann Reads Goethe: Illustrations in the Goeschen Edition." *Sophie Journal* 2, no. 1 (2012). http://digitalcommons.mcmaster.ca/sophiejournal/vol2/iss1/1.

Makdisi, Saree. *Romantic Imperialism: Universal Empire and the Culture of Modernity*. Cambridge: Cambridge University Press, 1998.

Malt, Johanna. *Obscure Objects of Desire: Surrealism, Fetishism and Politics*. Oxford: Oxford University Press, 2004.

Mann, Thomas. "The Blood of the Walsungs." In *Death in Venice and Other Tales*, translated by Joachim Neugroschel, 253–84. New York: Penguin, 1998.

———. "Der Entwicklungsroman." In vol. 2 of *Aufsätze. Reden. Essays*, edited by Harry Matter, 115–18. Berlin: Aufbau-Verlag, 1983.

———. "Die Lösung der Judenfrage." In vol. 1 of *Aufsätze, Reden, Essays*, edited by Harry Matter, 128–32. Berlin: Aufbau-Verlag, 1986.

———. "Versuch über das Theater." In vol. 1 of *Aufsätze, Reden, Essays*, edited by Harry Matter. 83–124. Berlin: Aufbau-Verlag, 1986.

———. "Wälsungenblut." In *Sämtliche Erzählungen*, 301–25. Frankfurt: S. Fischer, 1963.

———. "Zur jüdischen Frage." In vol. 1 of *Aufsätze, Reden, Essays*. Edited by Harry Matter, 163–73. Berlin: Aufbau-Verlag, 1986.

Marchand, Suzanne. *German Orientalism in the Age of Empire: Religion, Race, and Scholarship*. Washington. D.C.: German Historical Institute; New York: Cambridge University Press, 2009.

Marcus, Sharon. *Between Women: Friendship, Desire, and Marriage in Victorian England*. Princeton: Princeton University Press, 2007.

Margolin, Sam. "'And Freedom to the Slave': Antislavery Ceramics, 1787–1865." *Ceramics in America* (2002): 81–109.

Marshall, David. *The Figure of the Theater: Shaftesbury, Defoe, Adam Smith, and George Eliot*. New York: Columbia University Press, 1986.

Martin, Raymond, and John Barresi. *Naturalization of the Soul: Self and Personal Identity in the Eighteenth Century*. London: Routledge, 2000.

———. *The Rise and Fall of Soul and Self: An Intellectual History of Personal Identity*. New York: Columbia University Press, 2006.

Marx, Karl. *Capital: A Critique of Political Economy*. In *Karl Marx, Frederick Engels: Collected Works*. New York: International, 1996.

———. *Capital: A Critique of Political Economy*. Translated by Ben Fowkes. New York: Vintage, 1977.

———. *Das Kapital: Kritik der politischen Ökonomie. Vol 1*. Vol. 23 of *Werke*, by Karl Marx und Friedrich Engels. Berlin: Dietz, 1970.

Marx Aveling, Edward, and Eleanor Marx. "Shelley and Socialism." *Marx To-day: Monthly Magazine of Scientific Socialism* 53 (April 1888): 103–16.

Masuzawa, Tomoko. *The Invention of World Religions, or, How European Universalism Was Preserved in the Language of Pluralism*. Chicago: University of Chicago Press, 2005.

Max Müller, Friedrich. *Address Delivered at the Opening of the Ninth International Congress of Orientalists*. Oxford: Oxford University Press, 1892.

———. *Introduction to the Science of Religion: Four Lectures Delivered at the Royal Institute in February and May, 1870*. London: Longmans, Green, 1882.

———. *Lectures on the Science of Language*. London: Longmans, Green, 1866.

———. "Max Muller on Darwin's Philosophy of Language." *Nature*, December 26, 1872, 145. http://digital.library.wisc.edu/1711.dl/HistSciTech.Nature18721226.

———. "On the Relation of the Bengali to the Arian and Aboriginal Languages of India." *Report of the Meeting of the British Association for the Advancement of Science* 7 (1847): 319–50.

———. *Suggestions for the Assistance of Officers in Learning the Languages of the Seat of War in the East*. London: Longman, Green, and Longmans, 1854.

May, Leila Silvana. *Disorderly Sisters: Sibling Relations and Sororal Resistance in Nineteenth-Century British Literature*. Lewisburg, Pa.: Bucknell University Press, 2001.

Mayer, Mathias. "Kraft der Sprache: Goethes 'Lebenslied' im Kontext monadischen Denkens." In *Monadisches Denken un Geschichte und Gegenwart*, edited by Sigmund Bonk, 113–31. Würzburg: Königshausen and Neumann, 2003.

Mayr, Ernst. "Speciation Phenomena in Birds." *American Naturalist* 74, no. 752 (1940): 249–78.

McClintock, Anne. *Imperial Leather: Race, Gender, and Sexuality in the Colonial Contest.* London: Routledge, 1995.
McInerney, James O., Davide Pisani, Eric Bapteste, and Mary J. O'Connell. "The Public Goods Hypothesis for the Evolution of Life on Earth." *Biology Direct* 6, no. 4 (2011). http://www.biology-direct.com/content/6/1/41.
McLaverty, James. "Comtean Fetishism in Silas Marner." *Nineteenth-Century Fiction* 36, no. 3 (December 1981): 318–36.
McLennan, John F. *Primitive Marriage: An Inquiry Into the Origin of the Form of Capture in Marriage Ceremonies.* Edited by Peter Rivière. Chicago: University of Chicago Press, 1970.
Meltzer, Françoise. "Theories of Desire: Antigone Again." *Critical Inquiry* 37, no. 2 (2011): 169–86.
Mendelssohn, Moses. *Jerusalem, or, on Religious Power and Judaism.* Translated by Allan Arkush. Hanover, N.H.: Brandeis University Press, 1983.
Metcalf, George J. "The Indo-European Hypothesis in the Sixteenth and Seventeenth Centuries." In *Studies in the History of Linguistics: Traditions and Paradigms*, edited by Dell Hymes, 233–57. Bloomington: Indiana University Press, 1974.
Miller, Paul Allen. "The Classical Roots of Poststructuralism: Lacan, Derrida, and Foucault." *International Journal of the Classical Tradition* 5, no. 2 (1998): 204–26.
Minden, Michael. *The German* Bildungsroman*: Incest and Inheritance.* Cambridge: Cambridge University Press, 1997.
Minter, Catherine J. *The Mind-Body Problem in German Literature, 1770–1830: Wezel, Moritz, and Jean Paul.* Oxford: Clarendon, 2002.
Mitchell, Juliet. *Siblings: Sex and Violence.* Cambridge: Polity, 2003.
Mitchell, W.J.T. *What do Pictures Want? The Lives and Loves of Images.* Chicago: University of Chicago Press, 2005.
Molendijk, Arie L. *The Emergence of the Science of Religion in the Netherlands.* Leiden: Brill, 2005.
Molstad, David. "'The Mill on the Floss' and 'Antigone.'" *PMLA* 85, no. 3 (May, 1970): 527–31.
Moretti, Franco. *The Way of the World: The* Bildungsroman *in European Culture.* London: Verso, 1987.
Morgan, Lewis Henry. *Ancient Society, or, Researches in the Lines of Human Progress from Savagery Through Barbarism to Civilization.* Chicago: Charles H. Kerr, 1877.
———. *Systems of Consanguinity & Affinity of the Human Family.* Lincoln: University of Nebraska Press, 1997.
Morpurgo Davies, Anna. *Nineteenth-Century Linguistics.* History of Linguistics IV. Edited by Giulio Lepschy. London: Longman, 1992.
Mosse, George L. *Towards the Final Solution: A History of European Racism.* Madison: University of Wisconsin Press, 1985.
Moxnes, Halvor. "Jesus the Jew: Dilemmas of Interpretation." In *Fair Play: Diversity and Conflicts in Early Christianity*, edited by Ismo Dunderberg, Christopher Tuckett, and Kari Syreeni, 83–103. Leiden: Brill, 2001.
Mühlhäusler, Peter. *Pidgin and Creole Languages.* London: University of Westminster Press, 1997.

Muller, Jean-Claude. "Early Stages of Language Comparison." *Kratylos* 31 (1956): 1–31.
Nersessian, Anahid. "Radical Love and Political Romance: Shelley After the Jacobin Novel." *Journal of English Literary History* 79, no. 1 (2012): 111–34.
Niekerk, Carl. "Der Anthropologische Diskurs in Lessings *Nathan der Weise*." *Neophilologus* 88 (2004): 227–42.
Nietzsche, Friedrich. *Nietzsches Werke. Kritische Gesamtausgabe*. Edited by Giorgio Colli and Mazzino Montinari. Berlin: Walter der Gruyter, 1967.
——. "On Truth and Lie in an Extra-Moral Sense." In *The Portable Nietzsche*, edited and translated by Walter Kaufmann, 42–46. New York: Penguin, 1976.
Nietzsche, Friedrich. *On the Genealogy of Morality*. Edited by Keith Ansell-Pearson. Translated by Carol Diethe. Cambridge: Cambridge University Press, 2007.
Noddings, Nel. *Caring: A Feminine Approach to Ethics and Moral Education*. Berkeley: University of California Press, 1984.
Nowitzki, Hans-Peter. *Der wohltemperte Mensch: Aufklärungsanthropologien im Widerstreit*. Berlin: Walter de Gruyter, 2003.
Nussbaum, Felicity A. *The Autobiographical Subject: Gender and Ideology in Eighteenth-Century England*. Baltimore: John Hopkins University Press, 1989.
Nussbaum, Martha. *From Disgust to Humanity: Sexual Orientation & Constitutional Law*. Oxford: Oxford University Press, 2010.
——. *The Fragility of Goodness: Luck and Ethics in Greek Tragedy and Philosophy*. Cambridge: Cambridge University Press, 1986.
O'Malley, William Martin, and John Dupré. "The Tree of Life: Introduction to an Evolutionary Debate." *Biology and Philosophy* 25 (2010): 441–53.
Oesterle, Günter. "Friedrich Schiller: *Die Braut von Messina*. Radikale Formrückgriff angesichts eines modernen kulturellen Synkretismus oder fatale Folgen kleiner Geheimnisse." In *Schiller und die Antike*, edited by Paolo Chiarini and Walter Hinderer, 167–75. Würzburg: Königshausen and Neumann, 2008.
Olender, Maurice. *The Languages of Paradise: Race, Religion, and Philology in the Nineteenth Century*. Translated by Arthur Goldhammer. Cambridge: Harvard University Press, 1992.
Oliver, Susan. *Scott, Byron and the Poetics of Cultural Encounter*. Basingstoke: Palgrave Macmillan, 2005.
Otis, Laura. *Membranes: Metaphors of Invasion in Nineteenth-Century Literature, Science, and Politics*. Baltimore: Johns Hopkins University Press, 1999.
——. *Organic Memory: History and the Body in the Late Nineteenth & Early Twentieth Centuries*. Lincoln: University of Nebraska Press.
Ovid. *Times and Reasons*. Translated by Anne and Peter Wiseman. Oxford: Oxford University Press, 2011.
Ozouf, Mona. "Liberty, Equality, Fraternity." In vol. 3 of *Realms of Memory: The Construction of the French Past*, edited by Pierre Nora and Lawrence Kritzman, translated by Arthur Goldhammer, 77–116. New York: Columbia University Press, 1992.
Paine, Thomas. *Common Sense, The Rights of Man, and Other Essential Writings*. New York: New American Library, 1969.
Paley, William. *Principles of Moral and Political Philosophy*. New York: Harper, 1860.

Parnes, Ohad. "Generationswechsel—eine Figur zwischen Literatur und Mikroskopie." In *Fülle der Combination: Literaturforschung und Wissenschaftsgeschichte*, edited by Bernhard J. Dotzler and Sigrid Weigel, 127–42. Munich: Wilhelm Fink, 2005.

Pateman, Carole. *The Disorder of Women: Democracy, Feminism, and Political Theory*. Stanford: Stanford University Press, 1989.

———. *The Sexual Contract*. Stanford: Stanford University Press, 1988.

Paxton, Nancy L. *George Eliot and Herbert Spencer: Feminism, Evolutionism, and the Reconstruction of Gender*. Princeton: Princeton University Press, 1991.

Perry, Ruth. *Novel Relations: The Transformation of Kinship in English Literature and Culture, 1748–1818*. Cambridge: Cambridge University Press, 2004.

Pfau, Thomas. "*Bildungsspiele*: Vicissitudes of Socialization in *Wilhelm Meister's Apprenticeship*." *European Romantic Review* 21, no. 5 (2010): 567–87.

Phelan, Peggy. *Mourning Sex: Performing Public Memories*. London: Routledge, 1997.

Pietsch, Theodore W. *Trees of Life: A Visual History of Evolution*. Baltimore: Johns Hopkins University Press, 2012.

Pietz, William. "Fetishism and Materialism: The Limits of Theory in Marx." In *Fetishism as Cultural Discourse*, edited by Emily Apter and William Pietz. Ithaca: Cornell University Press, 1993.

———. "The Problem of the Fetish, II: The Origin of the Fetish." *RES: Anthropology and Aesthetics*, no. 13 (Spring 1987): 23–45.

Pinkard, Terry. *Hegel: A Biography*. Cambridge: Cambridge University Press, 2000.

Pinto-Correia, Clara. *The Ovary of Eve: Egg and Sperm and Preformationism*. Chicago: University of Chicago Press, 1997.

Plato. *The Symposium*. Translated by Alexander Nehamas and Paul Woodruff. In *Complete Works*, edited by John M. Cooper, 457–505. Indianapolis: Hackett.

Poliakov, Léon. *The Aryan Myth: A Hisotry of Racist and Nationalist Ideas in Europe*. Translated by Edmund Howard. London: Chatto Heinemann for Sussex University Press, 1971.

Pollak, Ellen. *Incest and the English Novel, 1684–1814*. Baltimore: Johns Hopkins University Press, 2003.

Pollock, Griselda. "Beyond Oedipus: Feminist Thought, Psychoanalysis, and Mythical Figuration of the Feminine." In *Laughing with Medusa: Classical Myth and Feminist Thought*, edited by Vanda Zajko and Miriam Leonard, 67–117. Oxford: Oxford University Press, 2006.

Pollock, Sheldon, Benjamin Elman, and Ku-ming Kevin Chang, eds., *World Philology*. Cambridge: Harvard University Press, 2015.

Poovey, Mary. "Aesthetics and Political Economy in the Eighteenth Century: The Place of Gender in the Social Constitution of Knowledge." In *Aesthetics and Ideology*, edited by George Levine. New Brunswick, N.J.: Rutgers University Press, 1994.

———. "Writing About Finance in Victorian England: Disclosure and Secrecy in the Culture of Investment." In *Victorian Investments: New Perspectives on Finance and Culture*, edited by Nancy Henry and Cannon Smith, 39–57. Bloomington: Indiana University Press, 2009.

Popkin, Richard. *The High Road to Pyrrhonism*. Indianapolis: Hackett, 1980.

Porter, James I. *Nietzsche and the Philology of the Future*. Stanford: Stanford University Press, 2000.

Prater, Florian. *Schiller und Sophokles*. Zurich: Atlantis, 1954.
Prichard, James Cowles. *The Eastern Origin of the Celtic Nations Proved by a Comparison of Their Dialects with the Sanskrit, Greek, Latin, and Teutonic Languages: Forming a Supplement to Researches Into the Physical History of Mankind*. London: Houlston and Wright, 1857.
Priestly, T.M.S. "Schleicher, Čelakovský, and the Family-Tree Diagram." *Historigraphia Linguistica* 2, no. 3 (1975): 299–333.
de Quincey, Thomas. "The Antigone of Sophocles as Represented on the Edinburgh Stage." In vol. 14 of *The Collected Writings of Thomas de Quincey*. 14 vols. Edited by David Masson, 360–88. Edinburgh: Adam and Charles Black, 1890.
Rabinowitz, Nancy Sorkin, and Lisa Auanger, eds. *Among Women: From the Homosocial to the Homoerotic in the Ancient World*. Austin: University of Texas Press, 2002.
Ragan, Mark A. "Trees and Networks Before and After Darwin." *Biology Direct* 4, no. 43 (November 2009). http://www.biology-direct.com/content/4/1/43.
Rancière, Jacques. *The Politics of Aesthetics: The Distribution of the Sensible*. Translated by Gabriel Rockhill. London: Continuum, 2012.
Rank, Otto. *Das Inzest-Motiv in Dichtung und Sage. Grundzüge einer Psychologie des dichterischen Schaffens*. Leipzig: F. Deuticke, 1926.
Rantala, Markus J., and Urszula M. Marcinkowska. "The Role of Sexual Imprinting and the Westermarck Effect in Mate Choice in Humans." *Behavioral Ecology and Sociobiology* 65 (2011): 859–73.
Redfield, Marc. *Phantom Formations: Aesthetic Ideology and the Bildungsroman*. Ithaca: Cornell University Press, 1996.
———. *The Politics of Aesthetics: Nationalism, Gender, Romanticism*. Stanford: Stanford University Press, 2003.
Renan, Ernest. "History of the People of Israel." In *Studies in Religious History*, translated by William M. Thomson, 53–95. London: Mathieson, 1895.
———. *The Life of Jesus*. New York: Modern Library, 1955.
———. "Religions of Antiquity." In *Studies in Religious History*, translated by William M. Thomson, 1–52. London: Mathieson, 1895.
———. "What Is a Nation?" Translated by Martin Thom. In *Nation and Narration*, edited by Homi Bhabha, 8–22. London: Routledge, 1990.
Richardson, Alan. "The Dangers of Sympathy: Sibling Incest in English Romantic Poetry." *Studies in English Literature* 25, no. 4 (1985): 737–54.
———. "Rethinking Romantic Incest: Human Universals, Literary Representation, and the Biology of Mind." *New Literary History* 31, no. 3 (2000): 553–72.
Richardson, John. *Nietzsche's New Darwinism*. Oxford: Oxford University Press, 2004.
Riedel, Manfred. *Zwischen Tradition und Revolution. Studien zu Hegels Rechtsphilosophie*. Stuttgart: Klett-Cotta, 1982.
Ritschl, Friedrich. *De emendandis Antiquitatum libris Dionysii Halicarnassensis commentation duplex*. Opuscula Philologica. Vol. 1:471–515. Leipzig: Aedebus B. G. Teubneri, 1866.
———. *Thomae Magistri sive Theoduli Monachi ecloga Vocum Atticarum*. Halle: Libraria Orphanotrophei, 1832.
Ritter, Joachim. *Hegel und die französische Revolution*. Cologne: Westdeutscher Verlag, 1957.

Roberts, Hugh. *Shelley and the Chaos of History: A New Politics of Poetry*. University Park: Pennsylvania State University Press, 1997.
Robins, Robert H. "Leibniz and Wilhelm von Humboldt and the History of Comparative Linguistics." In *Leibniz, Humboldt, and the Origins of Comparativism*, edited by Tullio de Mauro and Lia Formigari, 85–102. Amsterdam: John Benjamins, 1990.
Roe, Shirley. *Matter, Life, and Generation: Eighteenth-Century Embryology and the Haller-Wolff Debate*. Cambridge: Cambridge University Press, 1981.
Romaine, Suzanne. *Pidgin & Creole Languages*. London: Longman, 1988.
Römer, Ruth. *Sprachwissenschaft und Rassenideologie in Deutschland*. Munich: Wilhelm Fink, 1985.
Rose, Jacquelin. *Sexuality in the Field of Vision*. London: Verso, 1986.
Rose, Paul Lawrence. *Wagner: Race and Revolution*. London: Faber and Faber, 1992.
Rosenfield, Kathrin. "Getting Inside Sophocles' Mind Through Hölderlin's Antigone." *New Literary History* 30, no. 1 (1999): 107–27.
Rousseau, Jean-Jacques. "Discourse on Political Economy." In *The Basic Political Writings*, translated by Donald Cress, 111–38. Indianapolis: Hackett, 1987.
——. *Emile or On Education*. Translated by Allan Bloom. New York: Basic Books, 1979.
——. *The First and Second Discourses and Essay on the Origin of Languages*. Edited and translated by Victor Gourevitch. New York: Harper and Row, 1986.
——. *Julie, or The New Heloise*. Translated by Philip Stewart and Jean Vaché. Vol. 6 of *The Collected Writings of Rousseau*, edited by Roger D. Masters and Christopher Kelly. Hanover, N.H.: University Press of New England, 1997.
——. "On the Social Contract." In *The Basic Political Writings*, translated by Donald Cress, 141–227. Indianapolis: Hackett, 1987.
——. *Politics and the Arts: Letter to M. D'Alembert on the Theatre*. Translated by Allan Bloom. Ithaca: Cornell University Press, 1960.
Row, T. Letter. *Gentleman's Magazine* 56, no. 2 (1786): 772.
Sabean, David Warren. "Kinship and Class Dynamics in Nineteenth-Century Europe." In *Kinship in Europe: Approaches to Long-Term Development (1300–1900)*, ed. David Warren Sabean, Simon Teuscher, and Jon Mathieu, 301–13. New York: Berghahn, 2007.
——. *Kinship in Neckarhausen, 1700–1870*. Cambridge: Cambridge University Press, 1998.
Sabean, David Warren, and Christopher Johnson. *Sibling Relations and the Transformation of European Kinship, 1300–1900*. New York: Berghan, 2011.
Sabean, David Warren, and Simon Teuscher, "Kinship in Europe: A New Approach to Long-Term Development." In *Kinship in Europe: Approaches to Long-Term Development (1300–1900)*, edited by David Warren Sabean, Simon Teuscher, and Jon Mathieu, 1–32. New York: Berghahn, 2007.
Sabean, David Warren, Simon Teuscher, and Jon Mathieu, eds. *Kinship in Europe: Approaches to Long-Term Development (1300–1900)*. New York: Berghahn, 2007.
Sade, Marquis de. *Philosophy in the Bedroom*. In *Justine, Philosophy in the Bedroom, and Other Writings*, edited and translated by Richard Seaver and Austryn Wainhouse, 177–367. New York: Grove, 1965.

Saine, Thomas. "Was *Wilhelm Meisters Lehrjahre* Really Supposed to Be a Bildungsroman?" In *Reflection and Action: Essays on the* Bildungsroman, edited by James N. Hardin, 118–41. Columbia: University of South Carolina Press, 1991.

Sammons, Jeffrey. "Heuristic Definition and the Constraints of Literary History: Some Recent Discourse on the Bildungsroman in English and German." In *Dazwischen: Zum transitorischen Denken in Literatur und Kulturwissenschaft*, edited by Andreas Härter, Edith Anna Kunz, and Heiner Weidmann. Göttingen: Vandenhoeck and Ruprecht, 2003.

———. "The Mystery of the Missing *Bildungsroman*, or: What Happened to Wilhelm Meister's Legacy?" *Genre* 14, no. 1 (1981): 229–46.

Sanders, Valerie. *The Brother-Sister Culture in Nineteenth-Century Literature*. Basingstoke: Palgrave, 2002.

Sapp, Jan. *Genesis: The Evolution of Biology*. Oxford: Oxford University Press, 2003.

Schadewaldt, Wolfgang. "Antikes und Modernes in Schillers *Braut von Messina*." *Jahrbuch der deutschen Schillergesellschaft* 13 (1989): 286–307.

———. "Hölderlin's Translations." In *Sophocles: The Classical Heritage*, edited by Roger David Dawe, 101–10. New York: Garland, 1996.

Schiebinger, Londa. *The Mind Has No Sex? Women in the Origins of Modern Science*. Cambridge: Harvard University Press, 1989.

Schiller, Friedrich. "An die Freude." In *Gedichte*, edited by Georg Kurscheidt. Vol. 1 of *Werke und Briefe*, 248–251. Frankfurt: Deutscher Klassiker Verlag, 1992.

———. "Concerning the Sublime." Translated by Daniel O. Dahlstrom. In *Essays*, edited by Walter Hinderer and Daniel O. Dahlstrom, 70–85. New York: Continuum, 1993.

———. *Die Braut von Messina*. In *Dramen IV*, edited by Matthias Luserke. Vol. 5 of *Werke und Briefe*, 279–384. Frankfurt: Deutscher Klassiker Verlag, 1996.

———. *On the Aesthetic Education of Man in a Series of Letters*. Edited and translated by Elizabeth Wilkinson and L. A. Willoughby. Oxford: Clarendon, 1982.

———. *Schillers Werke. Nationalausgabe*. 43 vols. Edited by Norbert Oellers and Siegfried Seidel. Weimar: Hermann Böhlaus Nachfolger.

Schilson, Arno. "Dichtung und (religiöse) Wahrheit: Überlegungen zu Art und Aussage von Lessings Drama *Nathan der Weise*." *Lessing Yearbook* 27 (1995): 1–18.

Schlaffer, Hannelore. *Wilhelm Meister: Das Ende der Kunst und die Wiederkehr des Mythos*. Stuttgart: J. B. Metzlersche Verlagsbuchhandlung, 1980.

Schlegel, August Wilhelm. "Life and Political Character of Sophocles—Character of His Different Tragedies." Translated by John Black. In *Sophocles: The Classical Heritage*, edited by Roger David Dawe, 159–70. New York: Garland, 1996.

Schlegel, Friedrich. *Lucinde and the Fragments*. Edited and translated by Peter Firchow. Minneapolis: University of Minnesota Press, 1971.

———. *Über J. G. Rhode: "Über den Anfang unserer Geschichte und die letzte Revolution der Erde*. Munich: Ferdinand Schöningh, 1819. Vol. 8 of *Kritische Friedrich-Schlegel-Ausgabe*, edited by Ernst Behler, 474–528. Zurich: Thomas-Verlag, 1975.

———. *Über die Sprache und die Weisheit der Indier: Ein Beitrag zur Begründung der Altertumskunde*. Amsterdam: John Benjamins, 1977.

Schleicher, August. "The Darwinian Theory and the Science of Language." In *Linguistics and Evolutionary Theory: Three Essays by August Schleicher, Ernst Haeckel, and Wilhelm Bleck*, edited by Konrad Koerner, translated by Alexander Bikkers, 1–70. Amsterdam: John Benjamins, 1983.

———. *Die deutsche Sprache*. Stuttgart: J. G. Cotta'scher Verlad, 1860.

———. *Die Sprachen Europas in systematischer Übersicht*. 1850. Edited by Konrad Koerner. Amsterdam: John Benjamins, 1983.

———. *Über die Bedeutung der Sprache für die Naturgeschichte des Menschen*. Weimar: Hermann Böhlau, 1865.

Schlipphacke, Heidi. "'Die Vaterschaft beruht nur überhaupt auf der Überzeugung': The Displaced Family in *Wilhelm Meisters Lehrjahre*." *Journal of English and Germanic Philology* 102 (2003): 390–412.

Schlözer, August Ludwig. "Von den Chaldäern." In vol. 8 of *Repertorium für biblische und morgenländische Literatur*, edited by Johann Gottfried Eichhorn, 113–176. Leipzig: Weidmann Erben und Reich, 1781.

———. *Vorstellung seiner Universal-Historie*. 2 vols. Göttingen: Dieterich, 1772.

Schmidt, Johannes. *Die Verwandtschaftsverhältnisse der Indogermanischen Sprachen*. Weimar: Hermann Böhlau, 1872.

Schmieder, Falko. "Zur Kritik der Rezeption des Marxschen Fetischbegriffs." *Marx-Engels-Jahrbuch* (2005): 106–27.

Schmitt, Axel. "'Die Wahrheit ruht unter mehr als einer Gestalt': Versuch einer Deutung der Ringparabel in Lessings 'Nathan der Weise' 'more rabbinico.'" In *Neues zu Lessing Forschung*, edited by Eva J. Engel and Claus Ritterhoff, 69–104. Tübingen: Max Niemeyer, 1998.

Schnapp, Alain. "Antiquarian Studies in Naples at the End of the Eighteenth Century: From Comparative Archaeology to Comparative Religion." In *Naples in the Eighteenth Century: The Birth and Death of a Nation State*, edited by Girolamo Imbroglia, 154–66. Cambridge: Cambridge University Press, 2000.

Schneider, David M. *A Critique of the Study of Kinship*. Ann Arbor: University of Michigan Press, 1984.

Schneider, Helmut J. "Der Zufall der Geburt: Lessings Nathan der Weise und der imaginäre Körper der Geschichtsphilosophie." In *Körper / Kultur: Kalifornische Studien zur deutschen Moderne*, edited by Thomas W. Kniesche, 100–124. Würzburg: Königshausen and Neumann, 1995.

———. *Genealogie und Menschheitsfamilie: Dramaturgie der Humaniät von Lessing bis Büchner*. Berlin: Berlin University Press, 2011.

Schor, Naomi. *Breaking the Chain: Women, Theory, and French Realist Fiction*. New York: Columbia University Press, 1985.

———. *Reading in Detail: Aesthetics and the Feminine*. New York: Methuen, 1987.

Schrift, Alan. "Genealogy and the Transvaluation of Philology." *International Studies in Philosophy* 20, no. 2 (1988): 85–95.

Schuchardt, Hugo. *The Ethnography of Variation: Selected Writings on Pidgins and Creoles*. Edited and translated by T. L. Markey. Ann Arbor, Mich.: Karoma, 1979.

———. Review of Max Grünbaum: *Mischsprachen und Sprachmischungen*. *Internationale Zeitschrift für allgemeine Sprachwissenschaft* 3 (1887): 291.

———. "Zu meiner Schrift, Slawo-deutsches und Slawo-italienisches.'" *Zeitschrift für die österreichischen Gymnasien* 37 (1886): 321–51.

Schwab, Raymond. *The Oriental Renaissance: Europe's Rediscovery of India and the East, 1660–1880.* Translated by Gene Patterson-Black and Victor Reinking. New York: Columbia University Press, 1984.

Schwartz, Marie Jenkins. *Ties That Bound: Founding First Ladies and Slaves.* Chicago: University of Chicago Press, 2017.

Schwarz, Hillel. *The Culture of the Copy: Striking Likenesses, Unreasonable Facsimiles.* New York: Zone, 1996.

Schwarzenbach, Sibyl. *On Civic Friendship: Including Women in the State.* New York: Columbia University Press, 2009.

Scott, James F. "George Eliot, Positivism, and the Social Vision of 'Middlemarch.'" *Victorian Studies* 16, no. 1 (1972): 59–76.

Scott, Michael. *Delphi: A History of the Center of the Ancient World.* Princeton: Princeton University Press, 2014.

Scriblerus Club (Arbuthnot, John, Alexander Pope, Jonathan Swift, John Gay, Thomas Parnell, and Robert Harley). *Memoirs of the Extraordinary Life, Works, and Discoveries of Martinus Scriblerus.* Edited by Charles Kerby-Miller. New York: Oxford University Press, 1988.

Sedgwick, Eve Kosofsky. "Tales of the Avunculate." In *Tendencies*, 52–72. Durham: Duke University Press, 1993.

Seidlin, Oskar. "Goethe's *Iphigenia* and the Humane Ideal." In *Goethe: A Collection of Critical Essays*, edited by Victor Lange, 50–64. Englewood Cliffs, N.J.: Prentice-Hall, 1968.

Sha, Richard. *Perverse Romanticism: Aesthetic and Sexuality in Britain, 1750–1832.* Baltimore: Johns Hopkins University Press, 2009.

Sharafuddin, Mohammed. *Islam and Romantic Orientalism: Literary Encounters with the Orient.* London: I. B. Tauris, 1994.

Sharpe, Eric J. *Comparative Religion: A History.* New York: Charles Scribner's Sons, 1975.

Shell, Marc. *Children of the Earth: Literature, Politics, and Nationhood.* New York: Oxford University Press, 1993.

———. *The End of Kinship: Measure for Measure, Incest, and the Idea of Universal Siblinghood.* Stanford: Stanford University Press, 1988.

Shelley, Percy Bysshe. *Laon and Cythna.* Vol. 2 of *The Poems of Shelley*, edited by Kelvin Everest and Geoffrey Matthew, 10–265. New York: Longman, 2000.

———. *The Letters of Percy Bysshe Shelley.* 2 vols. Edited by Frederick L. Jones. Oxford: Clarendon, 1964.

———. *Shelley's Poetry and Prose.* Edited by Donald Reiman and Sharon Powers. New York: Norton, 1977.

Shepher, Joseph. *Incest: A Biosocial View.* New York: Academic, 1983.

Shor, Eran, and Dalit Simchai. "Incest Avoidance, the Incest Taboo, and Social Cohesion: Revisiting Westermarck and the Case of the Israeli Kibbutzim." *American Journal of Sociology* 114, no. 6 (2009): 1803–42.

Simpson, David. *Fetishism and Imagination: Dickens, Melville, Conrad*. Baltimore: Johns Hopkins University Press, 1982.

Sjöholm, Cecilia. *The Antigone Complex: Ethics and the Invention of Feminine Desire*. Stanford: Stanford University Press, 2004.

Slote, Michael. *The Ethics of Care and Empathy*. London: Routledge, 2007.

Smith, Adam. *An Inquiry into the Nature and Causes of the Wealth of Nations*. Edited by R. H. Campbell and A. S. Skinner. Vol. 2 of *Glasgow Edition of the Works and Correspondence of Adam Smith*. Oxford: Clarendon, 1976.

———. *The Theory of Moral Sentiments*. Edited by D. D. Raphael and A. L. Macfie. Vol. 1 of *Glasgow Edition of the Works and Correspondence of Adam Smith*. Oxford: Clarendon, 1976.

Smith, Maynard. "Letters: Haldane." In *New Scientist 7*, no. 101 (July 29, 1976): 247.

Snow, C. P. *The Two Cultures*. London: Cambridge University Press, 1993.

Sophocles. *Antigone* (Greek). Edited by Mark Griffith. Cambridge Greek and Latin Classics, edited by P. E. Easterling, Philip Hardie, Richard Hunter, and E. J. Kenney. Cambridge: Cambridge University Press, 1999.

———. *Antigone*. In *Sophocles I: Oedipus the King. Oedipus at Colonus. Antigone*. Translated and introduced by David Grene, 159–212. The Complete Greek Tragedies, edited by David Grene and Richard Lattimore. Chicago: University of Chicago Press, 1991.

———. *Oedipus at Colonus* (Greek). In *Sophocles Fabulae*. Edited by Hugh Lloyd-Jones, 409–599. Cambridge: Harvard University Press, 1994.

———. *Oedipus at Colonus*. In *Sophocles I: Oedipus the King. Oedipus at Colonus. Antigone*. Translated and introduced by David Grene, 77–157. The Complete Greek Tragedies, edited by David Grene and Richard Lattimore. Chicago: University of Chicago Press, 1991.

Sprengel, Christian Konrad. *Das entdeckte Geheimnis der Natur im Bau und in der Befruchtung der Blumen*. Berlin: Friedrich Vieweg dem aeltern, 1793.

Stafford, Barbara Maria. *Visual Analogy: Consciousness as the Art of Connecting*. Cambridge: MIT Press, 2001.

Staum, Martin. *Labeling People: French Scholars on Society, Race and Empire, 1815–1848*. Montreal: McGill-Queen's University Press, 2003.

Steiner, George. *Antigones*. New York: Oxford University Press, 1984.

Stepan, Nancy. *The Idea of Race in Science: Great Britain 1800–1960*. Basingstoke: Macmillan, 1982.

Stoler, Ann Laura. *Race and the Education of Desire: Foucault's* History of Sexuality *and the Colonial Order of Things*. Durham: Duke University Press, 1995.

Stone, Lawrence. *The Family, Sex and Marriage in England 1500–1800*. New York: Harper and Row, 1977.

Strathern, Marilyn. *Kinship, Law, and the Unexpected: Relatives Are Always A Surprise*. New York: Cambridge University Press, 2005.

Stratton, Jon. *The Desirable Body: Cultural Fetishism and the Erotics of Consumption*. Manchester: Manchester University Press, 1996.

Strauss, Jonathan. *Private Lives, Public Deaths: Antigone and the Invention of Individuality*. New York: Fordham University Press, 2013.

Stroumsa, Guy G. *A New Science: The Discovery of Religion in the Age of Reason.* Cambridge: Harvard University Press, 2010.
Szombathy, Zoltán. "Genealogy in Medieval Muslim Societies." *Studia Islamica* 95 (2002): 5–35.
Talbert, Charles H. *Introduction to Fragments by Hermann Samuel Reimarus.* Translated by Ralph S. Fraser. Philadelphia: Fortress, 1970.
Taxidou, Olga. *Tragedy, Modernity and Mourning.* Edinburgh: Edinburgh University Press, 2004.
Taylor, Charles. *Sources of the Self: The Making of the Modern Identity.* Cambridge: Harvard University Press, 1989.
Thomason, Sarah Grey, and Terrence Kaufman. *Language Contact, Creolization, and Genetic Linguistics.* Berkeley: University of California Press, 1988.
Timm, Annette, and Joshua Sanborn. *Gender, Sex and the Shaping of Modern Europe: A History from the French Revolution to the Present Day.* Oxford: Berg, 2007.
Timpanaro, Sebastiano. *The Genesis of Lachmann's Method.* Edited and translated by Glenn W. Most. Chicago: University of Chicago Press, 2005.
Titzmann, Michael. "Literarische Strukturen und kulturelles Wissen: Das Beispiel inzestuöser Situationen in der Erzählliteratur der Goethezeit und ihrer Funktionen im Denksystem der Epoche." In *Erzählte Kriminalität. Zur Typologie und Funktion von narrative Darstellungen in Strafrechtspflege, Publizistik und Literatur zwischen 1770 und 1920,* edited by Jörg Schönert. Tübingen: Max Niemeyer, 1991.
Tobin, Robert. *Warm Brothers: Queer Theory and the Age of Goethe.* Philadelphia: University of Pennsylvania Press, 2000.
Toepfer, Georg. "Terminologische Entdifferenzierung in zwei gegenläufigen Übertragungsvorgängen: 'Geschichte' und 'Evolution' der Kultur und Natur." *Forum Interdisziplinäre Begriffsgeschichte* 3 (2014): 28–46.
Trautmann, Thomas. *Aryans and British India.* Berkeley: University of California Press, 1997.
———. *Lewis Henry Morgan and the Invention of Kinship.* Berkeley: University of California Press, 1987.
Tronto, Joan. *Moral Boundaries: A Political Argument for an Ethics of Care.* New York: Routledge, 1993.
Turner, James. *Philology: The Forgotten Origins of the Modern Humanities.* Princeton: Princeton University Press, 2015.
Vaget, Hans Rudolf. "Sang réservé in Deutschland: Zur Rezeption von Thomas Manns Wälsungenblut." *German Quarterly* 57, no. 3 (1984): 367–76.
van Wyhe, John. "The Descent of Words: Evolutionary Thinking 1780–1880." *Endeavour* 29, no. 3 (September 2005). 94–100.
Vekemans, Lot. *Schwester von.* Translated by Eva Pieper. Berlin: Kiepenheuer-Medien, 2014.
Vermeulen, Han F. "The German Invention of Völkerkunde: Ethnological Discourse in Europe and Asia, 1740–1798." In *The German Invention of Race,* edited by Sara Eigen and Mark Larrimore, 123–45. Albany: State University of New York Press, 2006.

———. "Origins and Institutionalization of Ethnography and Ethnology in Europe and the USA, 1771–1845." In *Fieldwork and Footnotes: Studies in the History of European Anthropology*, edited by Han Vermeulen and Arturo Alvarez Roldán. London: Routledge, 1995.
Vogl, Joseph. *Kalkül und Leidenschaft: Poetik des ökonomischen Menschen*. Zurich: Diaphanes, 2004.
Voss, Julia. *Darwins Bilder. Ansichten der Evolutionstheorie 1837–1874*. Frankfurt: Fischer Taschenbuch, 2007.
Wagner, Cosima. *Diaries*. Edited by Martin Gregor-Dellin and Dietrich Mack. 2 vols. London: Collins, 1980.
Wagner, Richard. "Judaism in Music." In *Stories and Essays*, edited and translated by Charles Osborne, 23–39. London: Peter Owen, 1973.
———. *Werke, Schriften und Briefe*. Edited by Sven Friedrich. Berlin: Directmedia, 2004. CD-ROM.
Wahrman, Dror. *The Making of the Modern Self: Identity and Culture in Eighteenth-Century England*. New Haven: Yale University Press, 2004.
Wallace, Alfred Russel. "Attempts at a Natural Arrangement of Birds." *Annals and Magazine of Natural History* 18, Second Series (1856): 193–214. http://people.wku.edu/charles.smith/wallace/S028.htm.
Wallace, Alfred Russel. "On the Law Which Has Regulated the Introduction of New Species." *Annals and Magazine of Natural History* 16, Second Series (1855):184–196.
Watt, Ian. *The Rise of the Novel: Studies in Defoe, Richardson and Fielding*. Berkeley: University of California Press, 1957.
Webster, Noah. *A Collection of Essays and Fugitiv Writings: On Moral, Historical, Political and Literary Subjects*. Boston: I. Thomas and E. T. Andrews, 1790.
Wegmann, Thomas. *Tauschverhältnisse. Zur Ökonomie des Literarischen und zum Ökonomischen in der Literatur von Gellert bis Goethe*. Würzburg: Königshausen and Neumann, 2002.
Weigel, Sigrid. *Genea-Logik. Generation, Tradition und Evolution zwischen Kultur- und Naturwissenschaften*. Munich: Wilhelm Fink, 2006.
Weinbaum, Alys Eve. *Wayward Reproductions: Genealogies of Race and Nation in Transatlantic Modern Thought*. Durham: Duke University Press, 2004.
Weineck, Silke-Maria. *The Tragedy of Fatherhood: King Laius and the Politics of Paternity in the West*. New York: Bloomsbury, 2014.
Weiner, Annette B. *Inalienable Possessions: The Paradox of Keeping-While-Giving*. Berkeley: University of California Press, 1992.
Weiner, Marc A. *Richard Wagner and the Anti-Semitic Imagination*. Lincoln: University of Nebraska Press, 1995.
Wellbery, David E. *The Specular Moment: Goethe's Early Lyric and the Beginnings of Romanticism*. Stanford: Stanford University Press, 1996.
Westermarck, Edvard. *The History of Human Marriage*. London: Macmillan, 1891.
———. *The History of Human Marriage*. Fifth edition. New York: Allerton, 1922.
Whitney, William Dwight. *Language and the Study of Language: Twelve Lectures on the Principles of Linguistic Science*. 1867. Hildesheim: Georg Olms, 1973.

———. "Strictures on the Views of August Schleicher Respecting the Nature of Language and Kindred Subjects." *Transactions of the American Philological Association* 2 (1871): 35–64.
Whitton, John. "Thomas Mann's *Wälsungenblut*: Implications of the Revised Ending." *Seminar* 25, no. 1 (1989): 37–48.
Wier, Allison. *Sacrificial Logics: Feminist Theory and the Critique of Identity*. New York: Routledge, 1996.
Willer, Stefan. "'Epigenesis' in Epigenetics: Scientific Knowledge, Concepts, and Words." In *The Hereditary Hourglass. Genetics and Epigenetics, 1868–2000*, edited by Ana Barahona, Edna Suarez-Díaz, and Hans-Jörg Rheinberger. Berlin: Max-Planck-Institut für Wissenschaftsgeschichte Preprint, 2010. https://www.mpiwg-berlin.mpg.de/Preprints/P392.PDF.
Wilpert, Gero von, ed. *Goethe-Lexikon*. Stuttgart: Alfred Kröner, 1998.
Wilson, Edward O. *Consilience: The Unity of Knowledge*. New York: Knopf, 1998.
Wilson, W. Daniel. *Humanität und Kreuzzugsideologie um 1780. Die "Türkenoper" im 18. Jahrhundert und das Rettungsmotiv in Wielands 'Oberon', Lessings 'Nathan' und Goethes 'Iphigenia.'* New York: Peter Lang, 1984.
———. "Science, Natural Law, and Unwitting Sibling Incest in Eighteenth-Century Literature." *Studies in Eighteenth-Century Culture* 13 (1984): 249–70.
Wingrove, Elizabeth. "Republican Romance." In *Feminist Interpretations of Jean-Jacques Rousseau*, edited by Lynda Lange, 315–45. University Park: Pennsylvania State University Press, 2002.
Wolf, Arthur P., and Chieh-shan Huang. *Marriage and Adoption in China, 1845–1945*. Stanford: Stanford University Press, 1980.
Wolfe, Carey. *What Is Posthumanism?* Minneapolis: University of Minnesota Press, 2010.
Woolf, Virginia. *A Room of One's Own*. San Diego: Harcourt, 1981.
Wright, T. R. "George Eliot and Positivism: A Reassessment." *Modern Language Review* 76, no. 2 (1981): 257–72.
Yasukata, Toshimasa. *Lessing's Philosophy of Religion and the German Enlightenment: Lessing on Christianity and Reason*. New York: Oxford University Press, 2002.
Young, Robert. *Colonial Desire: Hybridity in Theory, Culture and Race*. London: Routledge: 1995.
Zajko, Vanda, and Miriam Leonard, eds. *Laughing with Medusa: Classical Myth and Feminist Thought*. Oxford: Oxford University Press, 2006.
Zammito, John H. "Policing Polygeneticism in Germany 1775: (Kames,) Kant, and Blumenbach." In *The German Invention of Race*, edited by Sara Eigen and Mark Larrimore, 35–54. Albany: State University of New York Press, 2006.
Zedler, Johann Heinrich. *Grosses vollständiges Universallexicon aller Wissenschaften und Künste*. 1731–1754. http://www.zedler-lexikon.de/index.html.
Zeitlin, Froma. "Thebes: Theater of Self and Society in Athenian Drama." In *Nothing to Do with Dionysus? Athenian Drama in Social Context*, edited by John Winkler and Froma Zeitlin. Princeton: Princeton University Press, 1990.
Zerilli, Linda. *Signifying Women: Culture & Chaos in Rousseau, Burke, and Mill*. Ithaca: Cornell University Press, 1994.
Žižek, Slavoj. *The Sublime Object of Ideology*. London: Verso, 1989.

INDEX

Abduction from the Seraglio (Mozart), 196–97
abolitionists, 19, 125, 180–81, *181*, 291*nn*22, 23
accommodation, 5, 87, 89–90, 119, 168
action, 1, 166–67, 182, 238; in *Antigone*, 42–45, 48, 50–51, 56–57; in *Iphigenia in Tauris*, 137, 141–42; in *Laon and Cythna*, 84–86; in Lessing's works, 194–95, 215–16; structure of, 25–27; sympathy as motive for, 122
activity, affective, 80–81, 84–85, 94–95
adaptation, 22, 93, 150, 179
Adelung, Johann Christoph, 17, 131, 279*n*24, 291*n*27
Adorno, Theodor, 256*n*22
aesthetics, 21, 244*n*46, 257*nn*29, 30, 275–76*n*98; beauty, 38–39, 64, 75, 257*n*29; education in, 64, 78, 87; exclusion of erotic from, 64–65, 71; labor system and, 121–23; politics and, 28–29, 70–71, 88
Aesthetics (Hegel), 48
affect, 1, 7–8, 91, 188, 219, 238, 260*n*58; collectivities and, 8, 254*n*4; economy and, 64, 67, 76–77, 83, 270*n*56; education in, 95, 108–9; equality of, 73–74;

fraternity and, 4–5; instinctive, 231–32; language acquisition and, 100, 137; liberty and, 80–81; politics and, 28–29; religious genealogy and, 185
Agamemnon (*Iphigenia in Tauris*), 137–38
agency, 4, 28–29, 87–88; fetish and, 11, 110–12; joint, 31, 50, 57, 87–88, 118–19, 251–52*n*51; language and, 137, 141–42; of objects, 111–14, 118–19, 222
agglutination, 184, 211
Ahlzweig, Claus, 278*n*17
Alcibiades (*Symposium*), 77
alliances of siblings and spouses, 5, 14, 29, 89–90, 95, 106–8, 108–9, 143–46, *145*; modern economy and, 95–106
Alter, Stephen, 128, 285*n*73
"Am I Not a Man and a Brother?" slogan and seal, 19, 125, 181, *181*, 291*nn*22, 23
Ancient Society (Morgan), 230–31
Anderson, Marc, 216
Anthropological Society of London, 182
anthropology, 11, 174, 229; climatological, 218, 293*n*41, 294*n*48; cultural, 14, 20, 230–31, 234–35, 237; distancing of researcher from subject, 17; physical, 6,

anthropology (continued)
  174, 176–83, 211; sibling marriage in,
  91–94, 228–29, 231–33, 236–37; structural,
  31, 232, 235. *See also* kinship studies; race
  theories
Antigone (character), 63, 201, 247*nn*10, 11,
  249*n*33, 273*n*79; agency of, 38, 50, 57, 114;
  British veneration, 246*n*4; civic sphere
  enabled by, 223–24; self-knowledge,
  47–49
Antigone (Sophocles), 23–24, 33, 247–48*n*18,
  247*n*17; chorus, plural subjectivity, 37,
  40; dual grammatical form, 44, 50;
  elision of the sibling, 38–42; Grene's
  translation, 49, 249*n*33; Hegel's
  interpretation, 52–53, 252–53*n*58, 252*n*56;
  Heidegger's reading, 55–56; Hölderlin's
  translation, 48–49; "Hymn/Ode to
  Man," 54–55, 72; intersubjectivity in,
  37–38; journeying and dwelling in,
  54–56; kinship, the foreign, and the
  collective, 51–56; *Mill on the Floss*
  comparisons, 114–16; nineteenth-century
  obsession with, 35; political and
  historical concerns, 54–55; polyptoton,
  use of, 42, 46; reduction of, 36–37;
  synecdoche in, 41, 51, 118–19, 140,
  260*n*50, 281*n*41; transsubjectivity in, 28,
  37, 39, 41–42, 51; women as substitutes for
  men, 44
Antigone Complex, 37
Antigone's Claim (Butler), 36, 43
anti-Semitism. *See* race theories
Apollo, 135–136, 140, 200, 201
Aquinas, Thomas, 226
Arabs, 176–77
Aristotle, 26, 42, 133
Armstrong, Nancy, 10
arts, 70–71, 88, 214–18
Aryan concept, 30, 184, 204–14
Aryan languages (Iranian-Indian
  languages), 30, 142, 166
Athens, 54, 77

Auerbach, Nina, 117, 274*n*85
Aurnhammer, Achim, 266*n*38
authors: sibling relationships, 21, 24,
  286–87*n*87
autochthony, 51, 54, 57, 112, 113, 201
autonomy, 7, 11, 41, 249*n*33, 257*n*30, 267*n*39;
  fetish and, 111–13
Aveling, Edward, 93, 94
avuncular theory, 27

Bachofen, Johann Jakob, 14, 230, 231, 234,
  305*n*13
Balibar, Étienne, 298*n*85
barbarians, *134*, 135
Barresi, John, 11–12
Baudrillard, Jean, 275*n*95
Beatrice (*The Bride of Messina*), 73–75,
  258–59*n*38
beauty, 38–39, 64, 75, 257*n*29
Beer, Gillian, 116, 274*n*87
Beethoven's Ninth Symphony, 28, 61
Bennett, Benjamin, 249–50*n*50
Bentham, Jeremy, 227–28
Bhabha, Homi, 215
Biblical genealogies, 17–18, 142, 176–77, 184,
  208, 243*n*36, 288*n*4, 289*n*7, 289*n*11
Bild, 139–40, 281*n*37
Bildlichkeit, 136, 137
Bildungsroman, 96, 105, 263–64*n*18,
  264*n*23
biology, field of, 226
biopolitics, 95, 104–5, 121–22, 269*n*50,
  290*n*17
Bittles, Alan, 306*n*21
Blake, Kathleen, 274*n*84
bloodline, 8, 192, 195, 249*n*50, 285*n*72,
  298–99*n*85
"Blood of the Walsungs" (Mann), 216–23
Blumenbach, Johann Friedrich, 18, 178, 182,
  289*n*7, 290*n*15
Blundell, Mary Whitlock, 42, 249*n*31
Blutschande (blood shame), 206, 226,
  303*n*1

Böckh, August, 115
Böhme, Hartmut, 281*n*40
Bosphorus, 198
boundaries, 31, 52–53, 88, 277*n*6; community and, 53, 56; permeable, 2, 3, 8–9, 11–13, 20, 185; species, 21–22, 179. *See also* natural kinds; public/private divide; synecdoche (part-whole relationship)
boundary object, sibling as, 1, 30–31, 47–48, 52–54, 64–65, 70, 123–24, 127–28, 198–99
bourgeoisie, 5, 14–15, 29, 95–96, 98, 242*n*29
branching, 7, 22–23, 142–43, 159, 283*n*55, 287*n*73; coral, 152; epistemological, 130. *See also* tree model
Braun, Christina von, 206
Bredekamp, Horst, 152
The Bride of Abydos (Byron), 197–99, 201–4
The Bride of Messina (Schiller), 59, 64, 73–76, 135–36, 186, 199, 258–59*n*38
Brosses, Charles de, 139
brother-brother ties, 4–5, 12, 16, 24, 59, 89–90
brotherhood. *See* fraternity
"brothers and sisters," as term, 17
brothers-in-law, 16, 62–63
brother-sister ties. *See* incest; public/private divide; sibling; sibling action; *specific works*
Brown, Jane, 268*n*44, 269*n*50
Brown, Ricardo, 289*n*14
Brüderordnung, 72
Buber, Martin, 208, 295*n*54
Buddhism, 206, 209–10
Buffon, Comte de, 179, 244*n*47, 290*n*15
Butler, Judith, 13, 36, 37, 38, 42–43, 44, 252*n*56; inner and outer relationality of psyche, 47–48; omission of Ismene, 46–47
Butler, Marilyn, 298*n*81
Byrne, Peter, 292*n*32

Byron, Lord, 197–99, 297*n*68, 297*n*71; *The Bride of Abydos*, 197–99; "Written After Swimming from Sestos to Abydos," 198

Cadmus, 51, 56–57, 200–1
Camper, Pieter, 180, 291*n*20
cannibalism, 85, 261*n*63
capitalism, 4–5, 87, 120; anthropology and, 29, 90–92; appropriate desire as product, 94; bourgeoisie, rise of, 5, 14–15, 29, 94–96, 98, 107; marriage and, 92, 107–8; sibling accommodation as model, 5, 89–90
capitalist family relations, 92–95
Carter, Angela, 256*n*25
Cascardi, Anthony, 10
Cassirer, Ernst, 141–42
Castoriadis, Cornelius, 55
castration logic, 39, 41, 117, 234
Caygill, Howard, 122
Čelakovský, František, 147, 148, 283*n*56
Chamberlain, Houston Stewart, 208, 213, 214
Chateaubriand, Vicomte, 25
childhood, 13, 239*n*3; nursery, 5, 15, 109
Christianity, 30, 295*n*54; "Aryan" genealogy, 30, 184, 197; Christian-Islamic relations, 176, 197–204; Christian-Jewish relations, 204–14; grafting image, 188–89, 211; Islam, relation to, 189, 196, 260*nn*54, 55, 261*n*61
civic society, 1, 4–5, 53, 87, 254*n*4; beginnings of, 96; biblical and contractual arguments, 65; Creon (*Antigone*) and, 115–16, 252*n*56; exclusion of erotic from, 62, 64–65; female passion as threat to, 75–76; sister as bridge to, 52–53, 68–70, 101–2; women's reason undermined, 67–68. *See also* public/private divide
Civilization and Its Discontents (Freud), 62
clans, 107, 269*n*52, 291*n*23. *See also* kin-grids; kinship, lattice of
Clarkson, Thomas, 180–81

classification, 1–2, 8–9, 31, 129–30, 143, 161–64, 177, 180, 208–11, 277n7; action and, 25–27; contingency of, 21–22, 26, 128, 165, 197. *See also* epistemological systems; natural kinds
class structures, rise of, 5, 14–15
climatological anthropology, 218, 293n41, 294n48
Cohen-Vrignaud, Gerard, 297n79
Coleridge, Samuel Taylor, 228, 232, 304n6
collective identity, 8, 85–86, 212–13, 216–17, 254n4
collective networks, 35, 273n78
colonialism, 25, 37, 160, 175, 215, 236; fraternity as cover for, 134, 140–41, 182; Muslim/Christian borderlands, 176, 198
Committee for the Abolition of the Slave Trade, 180–81
commodity: four properties, 110–11; in *Mill on the Floss*, 112–13; sibling as, 88; sister as, 91, 109–10
commodity fetishism, 110, 120, 271n63. *See also* fetish
common ancestor, 1, 7, 19, 178; evolutionary theory, 154–55, 244n48; linguistics, 129, 142, 170–71, 283n59
communal marriage, 29, 92
community, 53–55, 252–53n58; *Gemeinwesen*, 53
comparative anatomy, 19, 129, 225
comparative method, 19–20, 171, 175, 240n6, 277n7, 283n55
comparative philology, 6, 19, 20–21, 29–30, 127, 159, 239n4, 287n88; "contamination," 146; race and religion languages, 30; *stemma*, 146, 146–47, 147. *See also* linguistics; philology
comparative religion, 6, 30, 111, 127, 183–87, 244n45
Comte, Auguste, 272nn70, 71
Condillac, Étienne Bonnot de, 129
Confessions (Rousseau), 78

conjugal family, 7, 14, 66, 228–29, 269n56
consanguineal family, 60, 228, 231, 269–70n56, 305n14
consciousness, 10–11
consent, 28, 64–70, 75, 101; Locke's view, 65–66; tyranny and, 83–84
consilience, 233
contact languages, 21, 156–57, 283n62
contract theory, 53, 65–67, 256n19
Corbett, Mary Jean, 25
creation theories, 17–18
creoles and creolization, 21, 156–57, 283–84n62
Creon (*Antigone*), 37, 44, 46, 247n17, 250n36; civic sphere and, 115–16, 252n56; refers to women as fields to plow, 46, 65–66
Crimea, 135, 186
cultural anthropology, 14, 20, 230–31, 234–35, 237
cultural history, 129, 279n24
cultural kinship, 231
cultural-symbolic approach, 267n40, 292n32
culture, 279n24; inauguration of in incest taboo, 90–92, 233–35; stages of, 120

Darwin, Charles, 9, 19, 244n47, 286n82; contingency of classification, 21–22, 26; *The Descent of Man*, 180; diversification theory, 150–56, 152, 154, 155; gender-neutral language, 164–65; "I think" sketch, 150, 152; linguistics, awareness of, 128–29; species, nineteenth-century anxiety about, 164, 167, 171; on species and varieties, 286n79. *See also* natural kinds; *On the Origin of Species* (Darwin)
Darwin-Wedgwood clan, 269n52, 291n23
Davidoff, Leonore, 5, 14, 29, 98, 106–7, 239n3, 242n29, 266n33
death drive, 39, 43, 71–72
definitions, as relational, 2–3, 127–28, 156
Deleuze, Gilles, 13, 69, 94, 119, 256n24
Delphi, oracle at, 200, 297n75
democracy, 54, 62, 69, 100, 238, 258n37

Derrida, Jacques, 5, 36, 63
Descartes, René, 10
descent: community of, 163; Greek male line, 56; historical, 129–30; of language, 132–33; managing, 175; not only form of evolutionary relatedness, 22
The Descent of Man (Darwin), 180
desire: education of, 29, 88, 93–94; ethical commitment and, 43; generalizing, 76–81; law of, 38–39; particularity of, 43–47, 50–51, 76–77; renunciation and, 274n86, 275n91; will and, 81
detail, 41
development, personal, 9–10, 263–64n18, 264n23
Dick, Anneliese, 106
differential difference, 85–86
differentiation: degrees of sameness, 8, 38; of languages, 132–33; naturalization of, 78–79; species, 150, 154, 165
disciplines, differentiation of, 2, 8, 26, 31, 184–85, 226–38, 240n6, 244n44; linguistics compared with evolutionary theory, 128–29, 132–33, 154, 156–62, 170; morality, 172–73; naturalization of, 78–79. *See also* evolutionary theory; genealogical systems; humanities; linguistics
double-consciousness, 220
Du Bois, W. E. B., 220
Du culte des dieux fétiches (de Brosses), 139

economics, 29–30, 273n78, 274n84; aesthetics and, 120–24, 275–76n98; affect and, 64, 67, 76–77, 83, 270n56; education in, 64, 86–87, 94, 108–9; invisible hand, 104; modern, sibling networks and, 95–106, 273n78
education, 256n26, 262n2, 268n44; aesthetic, 64, 78, 87; affective, 95, 108–9; of desire, 29, 88, 93–94; economic, 64, 86–87, 94, 108–9; maternal, 97, 296n58, 296n60; paternal, 99–100, 193–94, 296n60; religious, 189

egalitarian principles, 28, 63–64, 67, 70, 74–76, 79, 109
Egypt, 133, 134, 186–87
Eichhorn, Johann Gottfried, 280n29
Eisenstein, Zillah, 253n3
Elden, Stuart, 53
The Elementary Structures of Kinship (Morgan), 91
Eliot, George, 24, 30, 222, 271n67, 272nn70, 71, 272n73, 276n102; *Antigone*, reading of, 115–16; "Brother and Sister," 125, 130, 167–68; Darwin, knowledge of, 286n85; fetish, interest in, 112; *Middlemarch*, 116–17; "Notes on Form in Art," 118; *Wilhelm Meister*, review of, 123. *See also The Mill on the Floss* (Eliot)
Elshtain, Jean Bethke, 36
Emile (Rousseau), 67–68, 75, 77–78, 268n44
Empire (Hardt and Negri), 95
endogamy, 29, 182–83, 214, 218, 231, 232, 307n25
Engels, Friedrich, 5, 29, 91–94, 262n9
England, 13–15, 80, 122, 160–61. *See also* Great Britain
Enlightenment, 177, 185, 187, 256n22
epigenesis, 18, 178–79, 256n25
epigenetics, 237, 243n38
epistemological systems (knowledge-systems), 1–2, 23, 26–28, 31, 127–30, 164, 170–73, 225–26; ontogenetic and phylogenetic overlap, 7, 29–30, 131–33, 135, 167–68, 170, 234. *See also* evolutionary theory; genealogical systems; linguistics; sibling logic
equality, 4–5, 62, 73–74
erotic, the, 29, 64, 68–69, 71, 75–80, 196, 259n43
Errington, Joseph, 160, 163–64, 285n77
Esty, Joshua, 113, 273n82, 274n84
Eteocles (*Antigone*), 37, 44
ethical consciousness, 43
The Ethics of Psychoanalysis (Lacan), 38–39, 42
ethnical periods, 230–31

ethnography, as term, 183
Ethnological Society of London, 182
ethnology, 174–75, 183
Ettinger, Bracha, 37, 39–40, 41–42
eugenics, 93, 214, 232, 235, 236
European Union anthem, 28, 61
Evans, Isaac, 167, 286n86
evolution, as term, 284n64
evolutionary biology, 143
evolutionary psychology, 236–37
evolutionary theory, 19, 124, 127, 162–65; common ancestor, 154–55; diversity, 129; genealogical form, 21–22; lateral gene transfer, 22, 157; linguistics and, 29, 128–30, 162–65, 285n73; Marxism and, 93
evolutionary tree, 21–23, 130, 143, 150–54; emergence of, 143; hybridization, 21–22; phylogenetic map vs. genetic map, 22
exchange, 86, 88, 105, 235; inaugurates culture, 90–92; keeping-while-giving, 109, 140, 275n91; refusal of, 114–15, 141; of sister, 86, 90–92, 109–10, 235
exogamy, 21, 182–83, 231–233, 307n25

facial angle, 180
factishism, 111–12, 118, 140, 157, 165
Familie, as term, 98
family: capitalist relations, 92–95; conjugal, 7, 14, 66, 228–29, 269n56; consanguineal, 60, 228, 231, 269–70n56, 305n14; as inescapable, 104–5; extended, 14–16; 97–99, 107–9; as model for state, 256–57n26, 267–68n42, 268n47; nineteenth century, 13–17; nuclear, 15, 95, 97–98, 103, 108, 265n25, 266n32; resemblance, 18, 307n25; as term, 98; triangle, 27, 28, 38, 94, 97–98, 173; women's: financial power within, 107–8. *See also* kinship
family business, 94–95, 98, 103, 107–8
The Family, Sex, and Marriage in England, 1500–1800 (Stone), 13–14, 16, 27, 97

family tree, 6; aristocracy, 144–46, *145–46*, 162–64; fifteenth-century, 143–44. *See also* genealogical tree; linguistic tree
father, 4, 18, 40–41, 44, 69, 79, 94, 97–101, 103, 116, 119, 133, 190–95, 230, 231, 272n69; ruler as, 64–66. *See also* education, paternal; fraternal, transition from patriarchy to fratriarchy; Law of the Father; oedipal complex; paternal authority; paternity
Feldt, Jakob, 296n62
female specificity, 39–40
Ferguson, Harvey, 11
fetish, 11, 110–19, 222, 271nn63, 64, 271n67, 272nn69, 272n71, 275n95; agency of object, 111–14, 118–19, 222; autonomy and, 111–12; commodity fetishism, 110, 120, 271n63; four properties, 110–11; Goethe's use of term, 281n40; language for, 139–40; in *The Mill on the Floss*, 111–13, 117; mystical, 110, 120; tree structure as, 165. *See also* object
Fichte, Johann Gottlieb, 53, 96, 298–99n85
Filmer, Robert, 65, 81, 229, 255n12
financial partnership, 5, 14, 29, 89–90, 95, 106–8; women's power within families, 107–8
first families, 90, 91, 94. *See also* nuclear family
fission questions, 11–12
Flannery, Denis, 79–80
Foley, Richard, 259n43
foreignness, 28, 37, 39–41, 47, 52, 55, 56, 73, 75, 161–62, 214–15, 218, 275n94
Forster, Georg, 182, 290n18
Forster, Michael, 132
Foucault, Michel, 3, 6, 13, 26, 130, 239n1, 268n47; Birth of Biopolitics lectures, 95; *The History of Sexuality*, 95; neoliberalism vs. liberalism in, 104; on Nietzsche, 170–71
Foundations of the Nineteenth Century (Chamberlain), 208, 213, 214

fraternity, 6, 12, 254n4; affect and, 4–5; brothers-in-law, 62–63; as cover for imperialism, 134, 140–41, 182; gendered and exclusive, 61–64; group-oriented, 196; nation and, 69–70, 86, 98; race theory and, 19, 125, 181, 291nn22, 23; as structural bond, 43–44, 100–1; substitute for paternity, 100, 102–3; as threat, 4, 12, 16, 101; transition from patriarchy to fratriarchy, 63–64, 95, 187–90. *See also* universal siblinghood

fratriarchy, 29, 63–64, 95, 187–90

free market, 29, 92, 104

French Revolution, 4, 25, 61, 76; aftermath, 87–88; authority, disavowal of, 141; Marx's view, 112; Shelley's view, 80; Schiller's view, 259n39; *Wilhelm Meister* and, 96–97, 106

Freud, Sigmund, 13, 36, 233–35, 306n20; castration logic, 117; *Civilization and Its Discontents*, 62; family triangle, 27, 28, 38, 94; oedipal complex, 36; subject- and object-identification, 85; *Totem and Taboo*, 25. *See also* oedipal complex

Freytag, Gustav, 122, 275n94

Frosch, Thomas, 260n56

fusion, 11–12, 240–41n17

futurity, 6, 13, 18, 26–27; allegiance to first family precludes, 38–40, 101, 116

Garloff, Katja, 296n59

Geiger, Abraham, 207

Gemeinwesen (community), 53

genealogical sciences, 17–23

genealogical systems, 1–2, 6, 124, 127–28, 130, 131, 274n87; affect and, 7–8; diffusion and diversification, 19, 21, 22, 142–43, 159, 175, 177; sibling function, 2–3. *See also* disciplines, differentiation of; epistemological systems; evolutionary theory; linguistics

genealogical tree, 8, 130; emergence of, 143; Indogerman tree, 147, 149; religion and, 209–10; as temporal and causal, 159. *See also* evolutionary tree; family tree; linguistic tree

genealogical method of current book, 6, 225

generation, as term, 98

genetic, as term, 129

genetics, 18, 22, 98, 230, 235–36

Germanic languages, 166; Indo-European (Indogermanic) languages, 30, 142, 147, 149, 183–84, 205. *See also* Aryan concept

Germany, 187; race theory, 30–31, 176, 205–6; transition to Romantic period, 131–32. *See also specific authors*

Geschwister, 16–17, 98, 242n30

Gilman, Sander, 216

Gobineau, Arthur de, 180, 213–14, 217–18, 221, 290n18

Goethe, Johann Wolfgang, 30, 33, 117, 250n42, 266n38, 269n50; intersubjectivity in, 141–42; metamorphosis concept, 26; population groups, differentiation, 142–43; Prometheus fragment, 280n34. *See also Wilhelm Meister's Apprenticeship* (Goethe)

Goetschel, Willi, 188, 189

Goldhill, Simon, 37, 50

Gourgouris, Stathis, 55, 57

grammar, 20–21, 129, 130158–61, 184, 220–21

Great Britain: Islam and, 80, 186–87; race theory, 30, 176. *See also* England

Greece, linguistic theory, 133, *134*, 149

Greek, Latin, and Sanskrit, 156

Greek-Italo-Celtic split, 166

Greiner, Rae, 276n102

Grene, David, 49, 249n33

Griffith, Mark, 42, 49, 249n33

Griffiths, Devin, 240n6, 275n92, 286n80

Grimm, Jakob, 23, 159

Grimm, Wilhelm, 23

Grosz, Elizabeth, 26, 164, 246n63

group psychology, 38, 52, 249n28

Gruber, Johann Gottfried, 182

Grünbaum, Max, 284n63

Guattari, Félix, 13, 94, 119
gynecocracy, 231

Haeckel, Ernst, 128
Haldane, J. B. S., 307n26
Haraway, Donna, 8–9
Hardt, Michael, 95
Harley, Alexis, 240n5
Heath, Peter, 159
Hebrew, 204
Hegel, G. W. F., 10, 33, 76, 252n56; brother as pure being, 43; dialectic of recognition, 37; nationality, view of, 254n61; Oedipus, view of, 48; sister as bridge to civic sphere, 52–53, 68–70, 101–2
Heidegger, Martin, 36, 55–56
Hellespont, 198
Hemings, Sally, 183
Herder, Johann Gottfried, 26, 230, 278n12, 279nn23, 24, 292n29; fraternity as cover for imperialism, 134, 140–41, 182; Goethe, influence on, 135; "On the Origin of Language," 129, 131–33; "This Too a Philosophy of History for the Formation of Humanity," 133–34, *134*
Hertz, Neil, 115, 116
Heschel, Susannah, 207
Hess, Jonathan, 257n30
heteronormativity, 47
Hinduism, 206
historical descent, 129–30
historical research, 6, 240n6
historical disciplines, 157–58, 171–72, 225, 235, 284n64. See also humanities
historicism, 10–11, 25–27. See also action
The History of Sexuality (Foucault), 95
Hoenigswald, Henry, 20, 277n7
Hogle, Jerrold, 260n56
Hohendahl, Peter Uwe, 72, 101
Hölderlin, Friedrich, 36, 48–49, 251n50
Holocaust, 223, 236
Homans, Margaret, 272–73n76, 286–87n87
Honig, Bonnie, 249–50n36, 252n52

horizontal kinship models, 35, 102–4, 130, 234–35
Horkheimer, Max, 256n22
human diversity, 6, 17–19, 28, 176–78, 180–81
human essence, 54–55
human genome, 237
humanities, 29, 157, 196, 225, 237–38, 284n64; and sciences, 157–62, 169–72, 196, 226–38. See also disciplines, differentiation of; historical disciplines
humanity, as linguistic, 132–33
human sciences, 3, 7–8, 17–18, 127. See also anthropology; linguistics; race theories
Humboldt, Wilhelm von, 24, 159–60, 184, 285n77
Hume, David, 185, 289n11
Hunt, James, 182
Hunt, Lynn, 25, 64–65, 101
hybridity, 52, 128, 244n47, 286n82; comparative religion and, 244n45; evolutionary theory, 21–23, 163–64; language as immune to, 128, 157–58, 160–62; languages, 156–57, 166–67; linguistics and, 20–21; race theories, 179–80, 214

identity, 25–26; collective, 8, 10, 85–86, 212–13, 216–17, 254n4; insecurity of, 3, 8; material component, 188; personal, 9–12, 241n19
identity politics, 1–2, 8, 248n23
idol, 112, 120, 138, 271n67, 272n69
imagination, 12–13, 121, 123
inbreeding, 213, 217, 236, 304n5, 306n21
incest: *Blutschande* (blood shame), 206, 226, 303n1; double role of sisters, 16, 63, 71; inauguration of culture and, 29, 90–92, 233–35; intergenerational, 39, 72, 73, 101, 102–3, 234–35; Islam as site of, 186, 292–93n35, 292n34; Judaism as site of, 205–6, 213–14, 261n66; in literature, generally, 16, 23–25, 245n57; as model for just society, 80–86; sibling marriage in anthropology, 91–94; mother-son, 39,

48–50, 56, 72, 101, 201, 234. *See also* oedipal complex; specific works of literature
incest aversion, 16, 31, 226–29, 232–34, 236–37, 243*n*34, 307*n*25; codifications, 227–28, 237
incest bans, 15–16, 107, 242*n*29, 304*n*10
incest taboo, 31, 95, 231; inaugurates culture, 90–92, 233–35
The Incest Theme in Literature and Legend (Rank), 21
individuality, 20, 93–94, 105, 109, 140, 142, 190, 204, 273*n*78; in *Antigone*, 4, 37, 51, 56, 62, 251*n*43; capitalism and, 88–89, 262*n*2, 262*n*5, 274*n*86, 275*n*94; "French bourgeois revolution" and, 95–96; passion and, 5, 63, 76–79, rise of, 4, 6–7, 10, 12–14, 62, 86, 88–89, 91, 96, 108; socialism and, 93–94, 110–12
Indo-European (Indogermanic) languages, 30, 142, 147, 149, 183–84, 205
Inequality of Human Races (Gobineau), 213
inheritance, 4, 16, 18, 31, 189, 305*n*13
in-laws, 14, 16, 103, 107, 119, 175, 266*n*32, 270*n*56
innate determinism, 237
interdependence, 90, 105, 107, 276*n*102
intergenerational incest, 39, 72, 73, 101, 102–3, 234–35
intersubjectivity, 37–38, 47–48, 141–42
interventionism, 104
Introduction to the Science of Religion (Max Müller), 208–10, 209
Iphigenia (character), 135–42, 281*n*35, 281*n*41; civic sphere enabled by, 223–24
Iphigenia in Tauris (Goethe), 125, 130, 135–42, 165; prehistory of, 137–38; setting, 186
Iphigenie, Orest und Pylades (Kauffman), 137, 138
Iranian-Indian languages (Aryan), 30, 142, 166
Irigaray, Luce, 13, 36, 41, 46, 248*n*21

Islam, 207, 297*n*78; Christian-Islamic relations, 176, 197–204; as cover for critique of religion, 260*n*54, 261*n*61; geographic and cultural borders, 176, 197–204; Jewish scholarship on, 207–8; in *Nathan the Wise*, 186, 187, 196–97; as site of sibling incest, 186, 292–93*n*35, 292*n*34; as submission, 80
Ismene (*Antigone*), 28, 33, 37, 43–44, 49–50, 57, 114, 249–50*n*36, 250*n*38, 250*nn*41, 42, 252*n*52; omission of, 44–47

jackdaw, Jew as, 223–24
Jefferson, Thomas, 183
Jesus, Aryanization of, 207–8, 300*nn*100, 102
"Jewishness in Music" (Wagner), 214–15
Jews, 126, 300–1*n*111; alienation, 110, 211; conjugal metaphor, 86; jackdaw image, 223–24; Jesus, Aryanization of, 207–8, 300*nn*100, 102; mimesis and, 195, 215–16, 222; Noahdic genealogies and, 176–77; proscription on intermarriage, 205–6, 213–14, 261*n*66; psychoanalytic theory, association with, 306*n*20; as site of incest, 205–6, 213–14, 261*n*66. *See also* race theories
"Jews and Indogermans" (Lagarde), 223
jointness, 12, 39–42, 51, 82–83, 118–19. *See also* subjectivity
Jones, William (Oriental Jones), 18, 19, 135, 157–58, 161, 280*n*27; population projection, 143; "Third Discourse before the Asiatic Society," 142
joy, 99–100
Judaism, 30, 295*n*54, 296*n*62, 296*n*64; Christian-Jewish relations, 204–14; Eastern Jew as racial intruder, 30–31; Islam, relationship to, 207
Julie (Rousseau), 77–78, 93–94
justice, 75, 79–80, 115, 122, 226–27, 261*n*60

Kant, Immanuel, 10, 244*n*46; beauty, exclusion of erotic from, 64, 75; "On the

Kant (*continued*)
  Use of Teleological Principles," 226; race theory, 18, 178–80, 227, 289*n*7, 290*n*15, 304*n*4
Kauffmann, Angelica, 137
Kaufman, Terrence, 283*n*61
Kawi language, 159–60, 161
keeping-while-giving, 109, 140, 275*n*91
kibbutz children, 306*n*24
kin, as term, 230
kin-grids, 98
kin recognition, 237
kinsfolk, 230, 233
kinship: anti-Semitic policing, 206–8, 215, 223–24; cultural, 231; deconstruction of, 8–9; formation of class structures, 14–15; horizontal models, 35, 102–4, 130, 234–35; as juridical, 305*n*13; large-scale, 127–28, 245*n*58; lattice of, 101, 107, 239*n*3, 242*n*29, 266*n*32; at level of race and religion, 175–76; polis and, 54; social vs. natural, 230; as term, 17, 230, 242*n*26; vertical models, 36, 37–38, 130, 234–35, 239*n*1
kinship studies, 14, 17, 29, 229–32
Kittler, Friedrich, 96–97, 103, 265*n*25, 278–79*n*19
knowledge-systems. *See* epistemological systems (knowledge-systems)
Koschorke, Albrecht, 266*n*32
Krimmer, Elisabeth, 106
Kristeva, Julia, 13, 253*n*3
Kucich, John, 113, 272*n*76
Kuper, Adam, 107

labor: aesthetics of system, 120–24; affective labor, 95; division of, 5, 88–89, 262*n*5, 272*n*74; immaterial labor, 95; sanitization of, 120–21
labor value, 90, 110, 120
Lacan, Jacques, 33, 36, 37, 42, 43, 234, 248*n*21; *The Ethics of Psychoanalysis*, 38–39
Lagarde, Paul de, 126, 205, 213, 223, 300–1*n*111
Lamarck, Jean-Baptiste de, 150, *151*

language: contact languages, 21, 156–57, 283–84*n*62; daughter language, 19, 131; dialects, 131, 163, 166–67; diversification, 132–34, *134*, 140; double-genealogy, 29–30, 131–33, 135, 167–69; European heritage and, 17–18, 135, 142, 166–67, 175–77, 184, 204–5, 208–13, 215, 280–81*n*27; Greek, Latin, and Sanskrit as related, 18, 135, 142; historical vs. ahistorical languages, 205; learned through sibling, 29–30, 136–37, 140–42, 167–69; *lingua maternal*, 130; mother tongue, 18–19, 29–30, 130–34, 278*n*17, 278–79*n*19, 285*n*73; as organism, 160–61; sister languages, 19, 128, 130, 156. *See also* linguistics
language communities, 298*n*85
language families, 6, 18, 130–31, 284*n*69; parthenogenesis of, 9, 20–21, 146, 161, 164; religion, divergence from, 208–10, *209*. *See also* languages; linguistics; mother tongue; sister languages
Lanzinger, Margareth, 242*n*32
Laocoön: An Essay on the Limits of Painting and Poetry (Lessing), 123, 194–95
Laon and Cythna (Shelley), 29, 59, 79–86, 93, 167, 204, 259*n*47, 260–61*n*59, 260*n*54, 260*n*56, 260*n*58, 261*n*63; as *The Revolt of Islam*, 80, 186, 203–4, 260*n*54; revolutionary tendencies, 93
lateral gene transfer, 22, 157
Latin, 18, 125, 130–31, 135, 142, 156, 169
Latour, Bruno, 111–12, 118, 165
lattice of kinship, 101, 107, 239*n*3, 242*n*29, 266*n*32
Law of the Father, 100, 101, 104, 234, 280*n*34
Lazarus, Moritz, 212–13
Leask, Nigel, 203
Leavitt, Gregory C., 306*n*21
Lectures on a Science of Religion (Max Müller), 19
Lectures on the Science of Language (Max Müller), 160
Leibniz, Gottfried Wilhelm, 279–80*n*27

Leonard, Miriam, 52
Lessing, Gotthold Ephraim, 24, 75, 123, 185, 258n35, 292n32, 293n37, 293n41, 293–94n45; *Fragmentenstreit*, 187; truth as a process, 26, 191–92; visual-auditory split, logic of, 193–95, 215;
—Works: "The Education of the Human Race," 188–89, 196; *Laocoön: An Essay on the Limits of Painting and Poetry*, 194. *See also Nathan the Wise* (Lessing)
letter correspondence, 95
Letters on Aesthetic Education of Man (Schiller), 70–71
Levenson, Alan, 216
Levesque, Paul, 216, 218
Lévi-Strauss, Claude, 5, 29, 94, 233–35; exchange of sisters concept, 86, 90–91, 109
Lewes, George Henry, 168, 272n70, 286n86, 287n88
liberalism, 94
Liberté, Egalité, Fraternité motto, 61–62
Life of Jesus (Renan), 24, 207–8
lineage, 6, 7; sex and, 9; speculative nature of, 100
linear models, 6, 7, 9, 133, 196, 197, 270n56
linguistics, 284n69, 286n77, 294n48; agglutination, 184, 211; bloodline rhetoric, 285n72, 298–99n85; common ancestor theory, 129, 132–33, 142, 170–71, 283n59; diversifying structure, 20, 154–56, 157–62, 285n73, 287n88; evolutionary theory and, 29, 128–30, 162–65, 285n73; genetic as term in, 129, 158; grammar, 20–21, 129, 158–61, 184, 220–21; hybridity as threat, 20–21, 156–58, 160–62; institutionalization of, 161–62; inflection, 184, 212; ontogenetic and phylogenetic overlap, 29–30, 131–33, 135, 167–69; organisms, words as, 285–86n77; Origin of Language essays, 128–29, 132; parthenogenesis, 9, 20–21, 146, 161, 164; performative theory and praxis, 42–43, 130–31, 135, 228, 232;

primordial orality, 280n34; race theories and, 30, 159–63, 174, 176–77, 183–84, 205, 210–12, 285n72; ripple/wave theory of influence, 157, 166–69; sibling logic of, 6, 21, 30, 130, 166–67. *See also* comparative philology; languages; philology
Linguistic Society of Paris, 128, 170
linguistic tree, 22, 147, *148*
Locke, John, 10, 11–12, 53, 65, 241n20, 255n12
Logan, Peter Melville, 118
Long, Edward, 289n11
Loraux, Nicole, 54
Lottmann, Andre, 268n43
love: as code, 108; consent and, 84; generalizing, 76–81; marriage based on, 94, 108; outward movement, 83–84; particularity of, 43–47, 50–51, 76–77; race theory and, 178. *See also* desire
Luhmann, Niklas, 14, 108
Lukács, Georg, 96

MacCannell, Juliet Flower, 4, 91, 262n8
Maggie (*The Mill on the Floss*): Antigone comparison, 114–15; loyalty to family, 116; Maggie's Fetish, 112; objects and, 113–15, 118–19; obligation, sense of, 114–15
Maine, Henry, 305n13
Makdisi, Saree, 203–4
Malay island, 159–60
Man, Paul de, 71
Mann, Thomas, 216–23, 296n64, 301nn124, 125; "Blood of the Walsungs," 216–23; "On the Jewish Question," 218–19; "Solution to the Jewish Question," 221; "Tackling the Theater," 218
manuscript studies, *146*, 146–47
Marchand, Suzanne, 207
Marcus, Sharon, 94
Margolin, Sam, 181
marriage: based on preference, 14, 43, 63, 92–93; communal, 29, 92; contractual form of consent, 67–68; cousin, 15–16, 29, 107, 242n29, 242n32, 269n52;

marriage (*continued*)
    dispensations, Catholic, 15, 242*n*32, 269*n*52; double-sibling, 29, 107; endogamy, 29, 182–83, 214, 218, 231, 232, 307*n*25; exogamy, 21,182–83, 231–33, 307*n*25; group, 92, 93; Jewish proscription on intermarriage, 205–6, 213–14, 261*n*66; sibling, as communist solution, 91–94; sibling bonds deepened, 15
Martin, Raymond, 11–12
Marx, Eleanor, 93, 94
Marx, Karl, 106, 112, 120, 262*n*9
materiality, 135, 190–91, 195
matriarchy, 14, 231
matrixial, 39–40, 41
Mauss, Marcel, 273*n*78
Max Müller, Friedrich, 19, 30, 162, 164, 169, 170, 184, 214, 285*n*70, 285*nn*72, 73, 300*n*105; *Introduction to the Science of Religion*, 208–10, 209; *Lectures on the Science of Language*, 160–61
May, Leila Silvana, 25, 109, 117, 239*n*3
Mayr, Ernst, 22, 125, 165
McClintock, Anne, 222
McLennan, John Ferguson, 230–32, 305*nn*13, 14, 15
Meltzer, Françoise, 47
Memoirs of Martinus Scriblerus (Scriblerus Club), 241*n*19
memory, 11, 113, 116–17, 119
Mendel, Gregor, 18
Mendelssohn, Moses, 86, 213
mergers, 6, 9, 20–21, 88, 157, 179; dual grammatical form, 44; of systems, 166–69
Merrill, Bruce, 78
metamorphosis, 26, 137
Metcalf, George, 131
Michaelis, Johann David, 188
Middlemarch (Eliot), 116–17
Miller, A. V., 53
Miller, Paul Allen, 36

The Mill on the Floss (Eliot), 109, 272*n*72, 272–73*n*76, 273*nn*78, 79, 273*nn*82, 83, 274*n*84; Antigone comparison, 114–16; desire and renunciation in, 274*n*86, 275*n*91; fetish in, 111–13, 117; as fetish object, 118; internal principles and external norms, 115–16; labor relations in, 122; memory in, 113, 116–17; narration, 119, 275*n*91; Say's Law, 274*n*86; structure of, 114
mimesis, 195, 215–16, 222
mirroring, 41–42, 52, 217
miscegenation, 21, 175, 178, 206, 303*n*1
Mitchell, Juliet, 38, 52, 257*n*32
Mitchell, W. J. T., 111; 271*n*67, 272*n*69
modernity, 64, 88, 102, 106, 131, 226, 229–30; bourgeoisie, rise of, 15, 98; capitalism, rise of, 4, 16; consent, significance of, 28, 64–70; fraternal state, 61–64, 86, 95; genealogical organization of knowledge, 143, 170, 225–26; kin grids emerge, 14–15, 98, 108; novel, rise of, 10; orthodoxies regarding, rise of, 6–7; subject, rise of, 6–7, 9–13, 95–96, 105, 108, 234; three relations of, 11. *See also* capitalism; epistemological systems; linguistics; race theories
monarchy, 65
monogenesis, 18–19, 170–71, 179–80, 182, 283*n*59, 289*n*7
Montesquieu, Baron de, 25, 292*n*34
moral fictions, 123
morality, history of, 171–72
morals: innate moral sentiment, 237; nature and, 227–28
Morgan, Lewis Henry, 29, 91–92, 241*n*25, 262*n*9, 305*n*13; *Ancient Society*, 230–31; on consanguineal family, 60, 305*n*14; *The Elementary Structures of Kinship*, 91; *Systems of Consanguinity & Affinity*, 14, 230, 231
morphological similarities, 26, 130, 143
mother/maternity, 18, 28, 38, 40–41, 70, 72, 81–82, 103–104, 136–37, 143, 167, 178,

223–24, 231, 236, abjection of, 235, 237, 253n3; as cultural-symbolic, 267n40; equal love for offspring, 73; love of, 73–74; nation as mother, 70, 257n26; nature as mother, 81–82; maternal authority, 65–66; mother-child dyad, 28, 38–40, 118; race and, 178, 183, 206; Sade's rejection of, 69–70; sister substituted, 82, 125, 156; universal, 82
Mother Right (*Das Mutterrecht*) (Bachofen), 14, 230
Mothers of the Disappeared (Argentina), 36
mother tongue, 18–19, 29–30, 278n17, 278–279n19, 285n73, 130–34, 169; as protolanguage, 29–30, 131, 132; Scythian as, 135
Moxnes, Halvor, 208
Mozart, Wolfgang Amadeus, 196–97
Muslim-Christian relations, 176, 186, 198, 292–93n34
Muttersprache, 130–31. *See also* languages, mother tongue
mythology, comparative, 210–11

naming, 132, 137
Napoleon, 53, 186
narcissism, 41, 83, 215, 217
Narcissus, 41, 217
Nathan the Wise (Lessing), 75, 125, 141, 249–50n50, 258n35, 292n32, 294nn48, 49, 295n57; classification in, 188; comparative religion, foundation of, 187–88, 190, 197; history, significance of, 192–94; inherited difference in, 188, 190–96; Islam in, 186, 187, 196–97; monotheistic religions, focus on, 185–97; reason in, 187–88; religion and, 187–97; representation in, 190–91; ring parable, 189–91; transition from patriarchy to fratriarchy, 61–64, 86, 95, 187–90; truth as process, 191–92; visual-auditory split, logic of, 193–95

nationality, 9, 37, 86, 162, 198; race as, 208–9, 212, 253n61
natural kinds, 6, 22, 128, 164; race theories, 178–80
natural law, 18, 65, 225, 227–28
natural right, 226–27
nature, 52–53, 71–72, 75, 82, 89, 113, 164, 174, 194, 208, 211–12, 225–28
Nazis, 56, 206, 208
Negri, Antonio, 95
neoliberalism, 104
network model, 23, 244n52
Nietzsche, Friedrich, 6, 13, 24, 169–73, 191, 240n4, 287n89, 287–88n92, 288n95; "Homer and Classical Philology," 170; *On the Genealogy of Morality*, 171–173 "Untimely Meditation," 170; *We Philologists*, 170
Noahdic genealogy, 17–18, 142, 176–77, 184, 208, 243n36, 288n4; Semitic language, as term, 183
novel, 10; financial plots, 273n78; interiority, 96; narration, 275n91. *See also Bildungsroman*
nuclear family, 15, 95, 103, 108, 265n25, 266n32; family triangle, 38, 94, 97–98; *Wilhelm Meister* and, 97–98, 103
nursery, 5, 15, 109
Nussbaum, Felicity, 10

object: agency of, 111–14, 118–19, 222; fluidity in relations, 139–40; metamorphosis, 26, 135; of representation, 190–91. *See also* fetish
"Ode to Joy" (Schiller), 28, 61–62, 99; exclusion of women, 61–62
"Ode to Man" (*Antigone*), 54–55, 72
oedipal complex, 21, 27, 36, 39, 47–48, 235, 247n10, 250n38, 305n20
Oedipus at Colonus (Sophocles), 44, 45, 247n17
Oedipus Rex (Sophocles), 36, 45, 48, 72
Olender, Maurice, 205

"On Love" (Shelley), 83
On the Aesthetic Education of Man (Schiller), 64, 76
On the Genealogy of Morality (Nietzsche), 171–73
On the Language and Wisdom of the Indians (Schlegel), 129, 158, 183
"On the Origin of Language" (Herder), 129, 132–33
On the Origin of Species (Darwin), 19, 21, 128, 150, 171; analogies, 162–63; comparative religion and, 184–85; title, 128–29; Tree of Life, 143, 150–54, *154*
ontogenetic and phylogenetic overlap, 7, 29–30, 131–33, 135, 167–68, 170, 234
operas, Turkish, 196–97
The Order of Things (Foucault), 26, 239*n*1
Oresteia (Aeschylus), 40
Orestes (*Iphigenia in Tauris*), 135–42
organic memory, 232
Orientalism, 302*n*124, 303*n*136
Oriental Renaissance, 135, 176
The Origin of the Family, Private Property and the State (Engels), 92–93
Otis, Laura, 232
Ottoman Empire, 186–87, 198; foreshadows French Revolution, 203–4

Paine, Thomas, 73, 75
Paley, William, 304*n*10
parthenogenesis, 9, 20–21, 146, 161, 164
partial others, 28, 38, 86, 88, 238, 260*n*50. *See also* subjectivity
particularity, 295*n*53; of fetish, 118; of love, 5, 43–47, 50–51, 63, 76–79. *See also* universality
part-whole relationship. *See* synecdoche (part-whole relationship)
passion, 259*n*47; civic sphere, exclusion from, 62; female as threat, 75–76; government grounded on, 79; politics and, 28; as slavery, 67–69, 75, 81, 83–86

Pateman, Carole, 4, 66–67, 108, 255*n*12
paternal authority, 4, 25, 64–66, 79, 97, 99, 102, 104, 235
paternal ideology, 99. *See also* education, paternal; father
paternity 40, 44, 81, 98, 178, 232, 256*n*25; and race, 178; uncertain, 25, 69, 93, 97, 100, 102–3, 223, 231, 255*n*18
paternity, uncertainty of, 25, 69, 93, 222–23, 231, 255*n*18
Patriarcha (Filmer), 65
Perry, Ruth, 269–70*n*56
Persian, 204, 207
Persian Letters (Montesquieu), 25, 292*n*34
personal identity, 9–12, 241*n*19. *See also* subjectivity
phallic logic, 41, 43, 103
Phelan, Peggy, 250*n*38
phenomenological method, 292*n*32
Phenomenology of Spirit (Hegel), 33, 43–44, 48, 52–54, 76, 101–10
philia, 42, 53
philology: classical, *146*, 146–47, 157–58, 169–70; Nietzschean genealogy and, 169–73. *See also* comparative philology; linguistics
Philosophie Zoologique (Lamarck), 150, *151*
philosophy: of language, 131–33, 135–42, 159–60, 184; as term, 158, 159. *See also* linguistics, performative theory and praxis
Philosophy in the Bedroom (Sade), 29, 64, 69
Philosophy of Right (Hegel), 53
Phoenicia, 133, *134*
physical anthropology, 6, 174, 176–83, 211. *See also* race theories
Pietz, William, 110–11, 120
play, 99–100
Plutarch, 199
police state, 71, 121–22
polis, 37, 40, 51–54

politics: affect and, 28–29; art as, 70–71; epistemological issues, 30; kinship and, 35; prioritized over erotic, 68–69, 75
The Politics of Friendship (Derrida), 5, 63
Pollak, Ellen, 25
polygenesis, 18–19, 170–71, 175, 179–80, 182, 205, 206, 213, 283n59, 289n11, 290n14
Polyneices (*Antigone*), 28, 37, 39, 43–47, 57
polyptoton, 42, 46
Poovey, Mary, 90, 273n78, 275–76n98
posthuman, 9
poststructuralism, 36
preformationism, 18, 178–79, 243n38, 256n25
Prichard, James Cowles, 174
primitive, 120–21, 133–34
Primitive Marriage (McLennan), 14, 230–32
primogeniture, 4, 16, 70–76; distributive justice incompatible with, 75
private property, 93, 100, 103, 112–13, women as, 92–93
progressive history, 92, 132–34, *134*, 188–89, 196, 230–32
prokaryotes, 22
protolanguage, 29–30, 131
psychoanalytic theory, 24–25, 101, 234, 246n2, 279n19, 280–81n34; Jews associated with, 306n20; dualism of, 37–38; move from text to author, 21; oral stage, 85; parental pair, 37–38; primary relationality, 37–38; family triangle, 27, 28, 38, 94, 97–98, 173; vertical kinship models of, 36, 37–38, 239n1. *See also* Butler, Judith; Deleuze, Gilles; Freud, Sigmund; Irigaray, Luce; Lacan, Jacques; oedipal complex
public/private divide, 14, 25, 64–70, 253n3; brother-sister relationship as boundary, 52–54, 64–65, 70; illusory nature of, 81; interpenetration of, 79; Jewish community and, 86
purity, 21, 31, 39, 161–62, 195, 203, 206, 215; racial, 56, 162, 213–15, 223, 303n140; of siblinghood, 33, 39, 43–44, 71, 76, 109, 223–24, 303n140
Pylades (*Iphigenia in Tauris*), 135–41

queerness, 27, 47, 72, 78–80, 248n23, 250n38, 305n12

race, 6, 9, 174; fraternity and, 63; linguistics and, 174–75; miscegenation fears, 21, 175, 206, 303n1
race theories, 11, 30, 176, 283n59, 289n7, 289n14; aesthetic element, 21, 180; "Am I Not a Man and a Brother?" slogan, 19, 125, 181, 291nn22, 23; anti-Semitism, 300n100, 300n102, 300–1n111; attraction-repulsion dynamic, 21, 180, 213, 232, 290n16, 290n18; Eastern Jew as racial intruder, 30–31; epigenesis and, 18, 178–79; fraternity and, 19, 125, 181, 291nn22, 23; Jewish participation in debate, 212; linguistics and, 30, 159–63, 174, 176–77, 183–84, 205, 210–12, 285n72; monogenesis, 18–19, 179–80, 182; nation and, 208–9, 212, 253n61; natural kinds, 178, 179–80; Noahdic genealogies, 17–18, 176–77, 184; physical anthropology, 6, 174, 176–83, 211; polygenesis, 18–19, 170–71, 179–80, 182, 205, 206, 213, 283n59, 289n11, 290n14; preformationism and, 18, 178, 243n38, 256n25; republicanism and, 182; as sexuality theory, 290n17; slavery rationalizations, 177, 289n11; visual aspect, 180, 215–16. *See also* Jews
Rancière, Jacques, 70–71
Rank, Otto, 21
rape, 68, 69, 79, 225n18
reason, 67–68
recognition, dialectic of, 37
Redfield, Marc, 70–71, 122, 264n18, 269n50, 276n100
regime of the sibling, 91, 95
Reimarus, Hermann Samuel, 185, 187, 189, 191, 207, 293–94n45

religion, 30, 174, 183; as inheritance, 189; church titles, 195; comparative, 6, 30, 111, 127, 183–87, 244n45; comparative mythology, 210–11; conversion, 175; cultural-geographical approach, 187; early modern division, 190; genealogical trees, 209–10; identity and, 191–92; Jesus, Aryanization of, 207–8, 300n100, 300n102; language families, divergence from, 208–10, *209*; linguistics and, 175; monotheistic, 185–97; progression narrative, 196; as relational, 191–93; relation of Islam and Christianity, 185–87, 189–90, 196–204; relation of Judaism and Christianity, 204–14; value-laden analysis, 185, 191–92. See also Christianity; Islam; Judaism

Renan, Ernest, 24, 30, 175, 207–8, 210–12, 300n100; comparative mythology, 210–11

René (Chateaubriand), 25

representation, 112, 119–20, 133, 136–42, 195, 215–16; directness, 216; objects of, 139, 190–91. *See also Bildlichkeit*; philosophy; signification

reproduction, theories of, 18, 243n38, 256n25

republicanism, 82, 86, 182; failure of, 99–100

resemblance, 40, 73, 141, 193–94; comparative methods, 19; epigenesis and, 18, 178; family, 18, 307n25; preformationism and, 18, 178

The Revolt of Islam (Shelley), 80, 186, 203–4, 260nn54, 55

Richardson, Alan, 25

Richardson, John, 288n95

Ritschl, Friedrich, *146*, 146–47, *147*, 154, 170, 283n55, 287n92

Roberts, Hugh, 261n60, 261n63

Rosenfield, Kathrin, 49, 51

Rousseau, Jean-Jacques, 64, 75, 76, 255nn17, 18, 256–57n26, 268n44; abstracting attitude towards love, 77–79; consent, view of, 67; democracy, failure of, 93–94; on languages, 129; rape, 68, 69; —Works: *Confessions*, 78; *Emile*, 67–68, 75, 77–78, 268n44; *Julie*, 77–78, 93–94

Row, T., 12, 241n20

Sabean, David Warren, 5, 14, 29, 98, 108

Sade, Marquis de, 29, 60, 64, 79, 93, 256n22, 256nn24, 25, 26; on rape, 69; republican views, 69–70

Said, Edward, 176

sameness, 4–5, 87; degrees of, 52; differential degrees, 8, 38; equality and, 62; love and, 79–80, 83–85, 217

Sammons, Jeffrey, 264n18

Sanborn, Joshua, 4, 63

Sanskrit, 159–60, 204, 207

Saussure, Ferdinand de, 2, 161

Say's Law, 274n86

Schemann, Ludwig, 214

Schiller, Friedrich, 88, 121–22, 123, 258n34 —Works: "Concerning the Sublime," 71–72, 75; *Letters on the Aesthetic Education of Man*, 64, 70–71, 76, 88; "Ode to Joy," 28, 61–62, 64. *See also The Bride of Messina* (Schiller)

Schlegel, August Wilhelm von, 24, 48

Schlegel, Friedrich von, 24, 161, 184, 287n89; *Athenaeum Fragments*, 96; *On the Language and Wisdom of the Indians*, 129, 158, 183–84

Schleicher, August, 128, 156, 163, 170, 283nn55, 56, 285–86n77, 287–88n82; language trees, 147, *148*, *149*; on speech capability, 205; *Sprachsippe* (*Sprachstamm*), 149

Schlözer, August Ludwig, 129, 183

Schlyter, Carl Johan, 146

Schmidt, Johannes, 125, 156, 157, 166–69

Schnapp, Alain, 190

Schneider, David, 230

Schneider, Helmut, 188, 196, 295n53, 296n60

Schor, Naomi, 41
Schuchardt, Hugo, 156–57, 284*n*63
Schwab, Raymond, 135
Schwarz, Hillel, 12
science, 1, 20, 29–30, 124, 135, 174, 182, 184–85; and humanities, 157–162, 169–172, 196, 226–238; differentiation as precondition, 160; as term, 158, 159
science of culture, 277*n*3, 291*n*27
science of religion, 184–185, 187–190, 192, 197, 208, 210–11
Scythian theory, 135, 140, 280*n*27
second families, 90
Sedgwick, Eve Kosofsky, 27, 38
Seidlin, Oskar, 281*n*41
self-knowledge, 47–49, 52
self-love, 41–42. *See also* narcissism
Semitic, 30, 175, 183–84, 204–14, 292*n*29. *See also* Judaism
sexual selection, 180, 290*n*16, 290*n*18
Sharafuddin, Mohammed, 297*n*72
Sharp, Granville, 180–81
Sharpe, Eric, 184–85
Shell, Marc, 64, 245*n*58, 254*n*7
Shelley, Mary Wollstonecraft Godwin, 80, 81
Shelley, Percy, 79, 93, 213, 229, 259*n*47, 260*n*51; "On Love," 83; *The Revolt of Islam*, 80, 186, 203–4, 260*nn*54, 55. *See also Laon and Cythna* (Shelley)
Shepher, Joseph, 237
sib, as term, 165
sib group, 98
sibling: as boundary object, 1, 30–31, 52–54, 64–65, 70, 123–24, 127–28, 198–99; brother-sister pair, 15–16, 48, 109; as commodity, 88, 91, 109–10; defies autonomy and integrity, 12–13, 38–42, 51, 89–90, 119, 139–40, 168–69, 183, 217, 223; elision of, 1, 36, 38–42; emerging modern significance of, 4–8, 13, 15–17, 97–99; as figure of democracy, 73–76, 81–82, 99–100, 106–9; in historical systems of development, 1–2, 127–128, 130, 156, 164–65, 167, 177–78, 180–81; in literature, 13, 23–24, 23–25; matter/meaning constellation, 193–95; monotheistic religions as siblings, 187–97, 208; as partial other, 28, 38, 88, 238, 257*n*32, 260*n*50; purity of relationship with, 33, 43–44, 109; as sign of alternate histories, 27, 172–73; as term, 17, 30, 165, 243*n*35, 291*n*22; as threat, 4, 115, 141. *See also* incest; public-private divide; *specific titles and authors*
sibling action, 1, 27, 86, 137, 141–42, 166–67, 182, 194–95, 238; in *Antigone*, 42–45, 48, 50–51, 56–57
sibling complex, 21, 24, 257*n*32
sibling logic, 6, 8, 22, 28, 106, 133; as epistemological tool, 127–28; inverse, 31, 237; jointness, 82–83. See also subjectivity
sibling networks, 5, 14, 291*n*23
sibling species, 22, 128, 165, 244*n*48
Sicily, 186
signification, 15, 112, 164, 275*n*95; philosophy of language, 130, 133, 135, 137, 141. *See also* philosophy; representation
sim pua (minor marriages in Taiwan), 238
sippe, 98
sister: blessing of, 73, 136–37; as bridge to civic sphere, 52–53, 68–70, 101–2; disenfranchisement of, 4–5; egalitarian form of affect, 28, 63; exchange of, 86, 90–92, 109–10, 235; as facilitator of relationships, 16, 95; purity of relationship with brother, 33, 39, 43–44, 71, 76, 109, 223–24, 303*n*140; self-overcoming, 75, 77; Thebes as, 51–52
sister-brother ties, *See* incest; public/private divide; sibling; sibling action; *specific works*
sister-in-law: as potential marriage partner, 15–16
sister languages, 19, 128, 130, 156, 204
sister-sister ties, 16, 24, 33, 95, 231; Antigone and Ismene, 44–47, 49–51, 56–57
sister species, 286*n*82

Sjöholm, Cecilia, 247n10
slavery, 18–19, 21, 93, 175, 177, 180–83, 256n24, 289n11, 290n14, 292–93n35; abolitionists, 19, 125, 180–81, *181*, 291nn22, 23; passion as, 67–69, 75, 81, 83–86
Slavic languages, 166
Smith, Adam, 5, 12–13, 29, 91, 94, 203, 262n2, 268n43; accommodation, 5, 89–90; commodity, view of, 90, 120; first and second families, 90, 94; invisible hand, 104; labor, division of, 5, 88–89, 121–23, 262n5; sympathy, view of, 59, 89, 121–23, 169; systems, view of, 120–22; *The Theory of Moral Sentiments*, 12, 89, 121–22; *The Wealth of Nations*, 88, 89–90, 122, 262n2, 276n98
Snow, C. P., 229
socialism, 91–94
social sciences, 98, 161, 232
social standing, 107–8
sociobiology, 229, 232, 236
solipsism, 78, 80
Sophocles. See *Antigone* (Sophocles); *Oedipus at Colonus* (Sophocles); *Oedipus Rex* (Sophocles)
Sources of the Self (Taylor), 10
Spartoi, 51, 57, 201
species, 287n88; boundaries, 21–22, 124, 125, 128, 164–65, 168, 179; common ancestor, 244n48; Darwin's "I think" sketch, 150, *152*; hybridization, 21–22; language comparison, 124, 128–29, 166–67, 285n73, 287n88; natural kinds rejected, 164; nineteenth-century anxiety about, 164, 167, 171; sibling species, 22, 128, 165, 244n48, 286n82; as term, 165; as unit of care, 9
spermaticism, 256n25
split personalities, 12, 240–41n17
spontaneous generation, 150
Stafford, Barbara, 38
state, 1, 5, 16, 28, 37, 52–53, 67–68, 88, 223, 252–53n58; aesthetics, 78, 121–22; family as model for, 65–66, 70–71, 256–57n26, 267–68n42, 268n47
Steiner, George, 36, 37
Steinthal, Heymann, 212
stemmata, 146–47, *147*, 170
Stevenson, Robert Louis, 11
Stone, Lawrence, 13–14, 16, 27, 97
The Strange Case of Dr. Jekyll and Mr. Hyde (Stevenson), 11
Strauss, David Friedrich, 207, 272n73
Strauss, Jonathan, 251n43
Stroumsa, Guy, 185
structural anthropology, 31, 232, 235
structuralism, 161–62
subject: joint agency with object, 118–19; novel and formation of, 96; object separated from, 11, 139; self differentiated from other, 11, 38; variants, 27; women as, 13. See also fetish; identity
subjectivity, 1, 4, 35; formation through others, 140; increasing self-sufficiency, 7; intersubjectivity, 37–38, 47–48, 141–42; joint, 39–42, 47–48, 51, 53–56, 82, 88, 114–15, 118–119, 136, 140, 204, 252n51; language praxis as basis of, 130, 141–42; modern economic subject, 88; origins, 6–7; personal development, 9–10, 263–64n18, 264n23; transsubjectivity, 28, 37, 39, 41–42, 51, 105
sublime, 71–72, 75
substitutive logic, 4, 41, 44, 46, 102–4, 117, 137–38
surveillance, 103, 108, 267–68n42
symbiotic associations, 22
symbolic order, 39–40, 75, 106
sympathy, 82–84, 89–95, 169; aesthetics and, 122–23; harmony and, 90–91; imaginative, 121, 123; personal interaction required, 59, 89, 121. See also accommodation; Smith, Adam
Symposium (Plato), 76–77

synecdoche (part-whole relationship), 41, 140, 259–60n50; in *Antigone*, 51, 281n41; in *The Mill on the Floss*, 117–19
Systems of Consanguinity & Affinity (Morgan), 14, 230, 231

taste, 71, 180
Tauris, 135
Taylor, Charles, 10
Teuscher, Simon, 108
textile: as symbol of commerce, 90, 120, 122, 275n94
Thebes, 51–52, 56–57, 198–201; role for Athenians, 54–56
The Theory of Moral Sentiments (Smith), 12, 89–90
Thomason, Grey, 283n61
Timm, Annette, 4, 63
Timpanaro, Sebastiano, 146–47
totem, 111, 271n67, 272n69
Totem and Taboo (Freud), 25
trade, 89–95. See also free trade
transsubjectivity, 28, 37, 39–42, 51
trauma, inheritance of, 38, 228, 248n20
Trautmann, Thomas, 210, 282n47, 300n105
tree model, 6, 29, 244n52, 274n87, 282n47; evolutionary tree, 21–22; grafting image, 188–89, 211; legal systems, 305n13; linguistic tree, 21–22; religious systems, 208–10, *209*; roots and branches, 22, 117, 119; trunk (*Stamm*), 133–34, *134*, 188–89, 211, 214, 293n42. See also branching
truth, 26, 185, 189–92
Turanians, *209*, 209–10
Turkish, 204–5
twins, 41, 235–36; conjoined, 12, 241n19; identical, 12, 79, 241n20; in "Blood of the Walsungs," 217–18, 222–23; in *The Valkyrie*, 218–19
The Two Cultures (Snow), 229
tyranny, 67, 73, 79, 81, 83–84, 191

unconscious, 241n20
universality, 46, 55,100, 230, 233, 235–36, 262n9, 276n100; eroticism and, 76–80, 196, 259n43; equivalencies, 105–6; European Union web text, 61; of incest prohibitions, 229–30; desire for systematicity, 121–22; reason and, 28; of religion, 189–90, 294n50, 296n62; sameness and, 53, 84, 86; sex roles, 50–51, 68, 76, 204
Universallexicon (Zedler), 226
universal siblinghood, 64, 71, 103, 141, 190, 196, 245n58, 254n7; paradox of, 61–63, 70, 86, 100, 260n58

The Valkyrie (Wagner), 216, 218–19
value systems, 170–73, 190–91
vertical kinship models, 36, 37–38, 197, 130, 234–35, 239n1
visual-auditory split, logic of, 193–95, 215–16
Vogl, Joseph, 268n43
Volk, 162, 205–6; Jewish views, 212
Völkerkunde (ethnology), 174, 183
Völkerpsychologie, 212
Voltaire, 289n11
Vorstellung seiner Universal-Historie (Schlözer), 129

Wagner, Cosima, 214, 301n121
Wagner, Richard, 208, 214–17, 301n119, 301n121; "Jewishness in Music," 214–15, 221; opera theory and race, 215–21; *The Valkyrie*, 216, 218–19
Wahrman, Dror, 10, 12, 241n20
Wallace, Alfred Russel, 150, 151, *153*
Washington, Martha, 183
Watt, Ian, 10
The Wealth of Nations (Smith), 88, 90, 122, 262n2
Webster, Noah, 228, 232
Wedgwood, Josiah, 19, 181, 291n23
Weinbaum, Alys Eve, 9, 93

Weiner, Annette, 109, 140
Wellbery, David, 280–81n34
Westermarck, Edvard, 31, 232–34, 236
"What Is a Nation?" (Lazarus), 212–13
"What Is a Nation?" (Renan), 212
Whitney, Dwight, 161–62
Wilhelm Meister's Apprenticeship (Goethe), 23–24, 29, 59, 115, 167, 260n57, 267n39, 267–68n42, 268nn43, 44, 276n100; *Athenaeum Fragments*, 96; *Bildungsroman* genre and, 105; economics in, 105–6; family, society, and subject, constellation of, 98–99; fetish in, 120; French Revolution and, 96–97, 99–100, 103, 106; Islamic setting, 186; Mignon as child of incest, 199–204, 266–67n38, 292n35; Mignon's song, 199–202; multiple siblings in, 97–98, 100; play vs. useful in, 99–100; republicanism in, 99–100; shift in familial norms in, 97–98, 103, 141; Tower Society, 98–99, 106–7, 115

Wilson, Daniel, 196–97, 266–67n38
Wilson, E. O., 233
Wingrove, Elizabeth, 255n17
Wissenschaftslehre (Fichte), 96
Wolf, Arthur, 237
Wollstonecraft, Mary, 69
womb as shared between siblings, 39–40
women, affective labor performed by, 95; disenfranchisement of sisters, 4–5; financial power within families, 107–8; as private property, 92–93; as speaking sign, 110; stereotypes of femininity, 46, 49; as subject, 13. *See also* sister
woolen coat figure, 90, 120

Yiddish, 157, 220

Zammito, John, 289n7
Zedler, Johann Heinrich, 17, 131, 226, 228, 237, 243n34
Zeitlin, Froma, 54
Zumpt, Carl Gottlob, 146

GPSR Authorized Representative: Easy Access System Europe, Mustamäe tee
50, 10621 Tallinn, Estonia, gpsr.requests@easproject.com

www.ingramcontent.com/pod-product-compliance
Lightning Source LLC
Chambersburg PA
CBHW021930290426
44108CB00012B/793